Getting Connected

The Internet at 56K and Up

Getting Connected
The Internet at 56K and Up

Kevin Dowd

O'Reilly & Associates, Inc.

Cambridge · Köln · Paris · Sebastopol · Tokyo

Getting Connected: The Internet at 56K and Up
by Kevin Dowd

Published by O'Reilly & Associates, Inc., 101 Morris Street, Sebastopol, CA 95472.

Editor: Mike Loukides

Production Editor: Jane Ellin

Printing History:

June 1996:   First Edition

Nutshell Handbook and the Nutshell Handbook logo are registered trademarks of O'Reilly & Associates, Inc.

Many of the designations used by manufacturers and sellers to distinguish their products are claimed as trademarks. Where those designations appear in this book, and O'Reilly & Associates, Inc. was aware of a trademark claim, the designations have been printed in caps or initial caps.

While every precaution has been taken in the preparation of this book, the publisher assumes no responsibility for errors or omissions, or for damages resulting from the use of the information contained herein.

This book is printed on acid-free paper with 85% recycled content, 15% post-consumer waste. O'Reilly & Associates is committed to using paper with the highest recycled content available consistent with high quality.

ISBN: 1-56592-154-2 (domestic)
       1-56592-203-4 (international)

[12/96]

Table of Contents

Preface

I have had the privilege of witnessing many people's first Internet experiences. It is as if they're trapped in a darkened basement, clinging to a candle. There are cobwebs in the rafters, and plumbing going every which way. And all the while their guide is gushing, "Isn't this the greatest thing you've ever seen?!"

Often, the guide is a book. Whole shelves are dedicated to exploration, browsers, and do's and don'ts; they talk about the Internet as a playground. This book is different—it's about the plumbing. We'll cover the gory details—how the network works, how to maintain a full-time connection, Internet security, even wide area networking protocols.

If you're the person who will be bringing Internet connectivity to a business, school, or club, then you have probably already realized that it is going to be a multidisciplinary challenge. You will have to be part businessperson, part electrician, and you will have to crawl over networking software like a spider eating its mate. Then, if your Internet connection gets breached by crackers, there's a chance that your company will lop your head off. And lastly, there's the dreaded end-user problem; you will be answering silly questions forever. In the short term, you are going to have to figure out how to shop for a connection, prepare a server, and secure your site. Longer term, you will need to set up information services, glue your electronic mail systems together, and extend Internet connectivity to the desktop.

Still, it's great fun. One rarely gets to undertake projects where the success rate is high, the visibility is high, and the rewards are good. If you have been nominated for the job, then good for you. If not, you might consider championing Internet connectivity. Your company is going to be connected sooner or later. You may as well be the person who gets the credit.

Be forewarned, however: there are prerequisites. It will take perseverance and talent to get the job done. I'm not so interested in your Internet experience; Internet connectivity may be completely new to you. However, I *am* going to assume that you have a natural affinity for things technical, even though your strengths may be in areas other than Internet connectivity—PC LANs or software development, for instance.

Most technical Internet books build from the bits upwards. They start with a general discussion of packet switching, then carefully build up through IP addressing, gateways, DNS, and specific Internet services. Several excellent books that take this approach are available from O'Reilly & Associates, including *TCP/IP Network Administration*, by Craig Hunt, *DNS and Bind*, by Paul Albitz and Cricket Liu, and *Managing Internet Information Services*, by Liu, Jerry Peek, and friends. We're going to do something different, however. We are going to start with function, and work both sideways and downward.

You will find that the book has several personalities. Some sections—particularly near the front of the book—are lighter reading, approachable by all audiences. Depending on your background, the material may already be familiar to you. On the other hand, you may find welcome insight into aspects of the Internet that you assumed you understood thoroughly. Later chapters are fairly technical. In a few spots, we pursue related topics just because they are interesting.

I know that priorities change: what's really important to you today may not be so important tomorrow. Accordingly, I have tried to keep all chapters modular.

Chapter 1 provides a framework for bringing in an Internet connection, and answers some common questions about the Internet's funding, maintenance, and structure. In Chapter 2, we explore service options and attempt to understand how "big" a connection you will need.

Chapter 3 helps you critically analyze and compare Internet Service Providers (ISPs), and helps you understand contract options and fees. In Chapter 4, we investigate circuit and equipment needs.

Chapter 5 discusses the task of programming a router and provides a few examples. Chapter 6 provides some explanations of ISO and IP networking as background information for programming the router's serial interface.

Chapters 7 through 12 provide technical background and practical configuration advice for a variety of physical and link layer network technologies. These chapters are important because your Internet service will be provided using a combination of these technologies—Frame Relay, ATM, SMDS, X.25, PPP, SLIP, or HDLC. Chapter 13 briefly discusses routing. Chapter 14 explains physical network technologies—DDS (56K), ISDN, T1, and more. Chapter 15 talks about circuit turn-up and debugging.

Chapter 16 addresses security, system audits, and Internet firewalls in detail. Everyone connecting to the Internet will want to become familiar with this material. For those who are comfortable with UNIX and C, the chapter goes on to discuss in-house firewall construction.

Chapters 17 and 18 cover key infrastructure pieces: domain name service and electronic mail. We will look at baseline configurations, plus configurations for operation behind a firewall. We will also talk about marrying Internet services to in-house mail systems, such as Lotus cc:mail and Microsoft Mail.

Chapter 19 discusses IP connectivity for Macs and PCs. We will learn how to configure IP stacks for a variety of configurations, and explore dynamic address assignment.

My deepest hope is that you will say: "Ah! This is the book I have been looking for." It's the result of years of work, and years spent connecting organizations to the Internet. It's also the book that *I* was always looking for. I feel lucky to be the person who got to write it.

Conventions

Italics	used for emphasis, as well as to denote file, directory, domain, and command names. Also used for *ftp* and Web sites.
Bold	used in code examples and in discussion to show user-typed input.
`Constant Width`	used to set off indented examples of computer output, code, or, in discussion, to refer back to code. Character strings such as "a" are set in quotation marks.

Acknowledgments

Unbounded thanks to my wife, Paula, for putting up with the lost weekends and non-vacations that went into this book. And congratulations to her for bearing a son, Ian, during the time the book was being written. Of course, Ian too, *in utero*, missed a few weekends and a vacation ... Also thanks to my parents, family, and in-laws.

Great thanks to Mike Loukides for his extraordinary abilities as an editor. Thanks too to Tim O'Reilly for his faith and patience. I'd also like to thank my co-worker Eric (Rick) Romkey for reviewing the material as it was extruded. My thanks to reviewers, including Bob Tinkelman, Eric Raymond, Howard Burke, Ed Dorso, John Curran, and Eric Pearce, plus other facilitators, including John Crouse and

Darryl Pope. And of course, thanks to the crew at O'Reilly & Associates, including Chris Reilley, who did some incredible illustrations (again), Edie Freedman for the cover, Jane Ellin for the production work, Lenny Muellner for Tools support, Clairemarie Fisher O'Leary for doing quality control, organizing freelancers, and helping with Appendix G, Nancy Priest and Eden Reiner for their work on the design, Kismet McDonough-Chan for quality control, David Futato, Michael Deutsch, and Barbara Coughlin for their work on Appendix G, Nicole Gipson Arigo for stepping in at the last minute to help finish the production work, and Sheryl Avruch for making sure everything ran smoothly.

1

Getting Connected to the Internet

Say that over lunch I shake my tuna sandwich at you and remark, "Fred, our companies work together often. We should join networks so that we can share information." That afternoon you lean out the window and toss the tail end of your network backbone across to me, I pull it through the bathroom window, and join it to our network through a device called a *router* (or, alternatively, a *gateway*). Traffic from one building, bound for the other, passes through the router. The rest remains on its respective sides. By joining our networks in this way, we have formed a small *internet*.

Other organizations could connect up too, adding routers at convenient spots. Say, for instance, that Joe in the building across the way also "gateways" to you—this time through the cafeteria window. Now, in order for me to reach Joe's network, I will have to transit your network (passing first through my bathroom, and then through your kitchen). There may even be several paths between my network and Joe's, some of which don't involve you at all. It depends on how the networks join together.

Like the wires dangling from the story above, the *Internet* is a network of networks—just a whole lot bigger. It spans the globe, reaching hundreds of thousands of individual networks, and several million computers. All of them speak *Internet Protocol* (IP), developed for DARPA (Defense Advanced Research Projects Administration) in the late 1970s. IP is very flexible; the internetwork topology can be anything you like—a straight line, a tree, a god-awful tangle. IP routing protocols help networks "discover" one another, without help from humans. The same qualities also make IP networks robust; if a backhoe cuts through one portion, the rest of the network automatically updates its routing tables to avoid the dead sections.

Ownership and management of the Internet—like the Internet itself—is noncentralized; no single organization is in charge. Observers and participants sometimes like to tease themselves that there's a recreational chaos to the whole thing, but there really isn't. The Internet runs pretty well, especially considering its size and complexity. It works because there is agreement about how it should work, because there are organizations that watch out for its well-being, and because there is money pouring into it all the time.

An Internet Connection

I guess I don't hear the question quite as often these days, but people used to ask: "Isn't the Internet free?" The misconception came from the fact that governments around the world have historically funded large tracts of the network with tax dollars; for some people, access *was* (or is) free because they were shielded from the costs. Furthermore, there is a tremendous amount of information available for the taking—again, free. However, the Internet is not free; it is largely a commercial operation. *Somebody* pays for it. Typically, it is you, the person who orders Internet service.

Who do you pay? Your provider might be a national or international *Internet Service Provider* (ISP), such as PSI, UUNET, BBN, Sprint, MCI, etc. * Each of these companies operates a wide area network, of which you become a part when you sign up for service. You can reach everyone else on the Internet because these companies trade traffic with their competition via routers, or high speed networks, tucked into wiring closets and sprinkled about the Internet.

You might, on the other hand, connect through a local Internet service provider. Like the national firms, a local provider maintains a wide area network, which grows to include you when you sign up for service. Technically, local providers are once removed from the "centers" of the Internet; they purchase bandwidth from one of the national providers, and resell it. On the surface, this would appear to put them at a disadvantage because their bandwidth is twice warmed-over. However, good service is a function of more than the speed of an ISP's backbone. Network loading, the quality of the company, and network operations support all play a part.

In addition to an ISP, you will also need to hire an exchange carrier—a telephone company. They will operate the physical (and possibly virtual) network that brings routed Internet service to your organization. If your exchange carrier is an ordinary local phone company, then your physical network will most likely be an ordinary leased line of 56 Kbit/S or higher capacity. It may also be something

---

* See Appendix B, *Calculating Your Bandwidth Requirements.*

Internetworking the Commercial Internet

Some of the main trunks of the Internet—both in the United States and abroad—are funded by national governments in support of specific kinds of activities, such as research and education. These networks (MILNET, NSI, ESnet, and NORDUnet, to name a few) operate under "acceptable use policies," which restrict commercial activities. Other portions of the Internet bear no commercial restrictions. These networks are private ventures, paid for by their subscribers, often for the express purpose of conducting business. Both sections—publicly funded and privately funded—are interconnected. The trick has been to try to keep commercial traffic off the public sections of the Internet.

In 1991, a handful of network carriers joined together to form the Commercial Internet Exchange Association (CIX), a nonprofit corporation devoted to commercial Internet cooperation. At the time, the National Science Foundation (NSF) backbone was the main Internet trunk. The idea was that by expressly routing commercial traffic through the CIX exchange point(s) (there are two at present, in Santa Clara, CA, and in Washington, D.C.), commercial organizations could have visibility in publicly funded networks without passing an undue amount of commercial traffic through them. CIX now includes 177 member networks.

Other North American (non-CIX) exchange points exist as well, including MAE-West (San Jose), MAE-East (Washington, D.C.), and some upcoming MAE locations—all operated by MFS Datanet. Additionally, there is an exchange point called SWAB, operated by Bell Atlantic (Washington, D.C.), and Federal Exchange Points (FIX-West and FIX-East), located at NASA Ames, and College Park, Maryland, respectively.

The NSF backbone is being reworked as well. In 1994, MCI received a National Science Foundation contract to operate an OC-3 (155 Mbit/S) backbone, connecting supercomputer centers and four regional *Network Access Points* (NAPs), located in New York, Chicago, San Francisco, and Washington, D.C. The NAPs are managed by Sprint, Ameritech and Bellcore, Pacific Bell and Bellcore, and MFS Datanet, respectively.

European regional network exchange points include Ebone (continent), LINX (UK), and several *Distributed Global Information Exchanges* (D-GIXes), located in Stockholm and Paris. NSF, Sprint, and NORDUnet have sponsored transatlantic traffic, tying regional European networks and exchange points together with North America.

more exotic—ISDN, or perhaps optical fiber. In many cases, you won't hire the exchange carrier directly; Internet service providers often pass the charges through on your bill. Sometimes (as in the case of Sprint or MCI, for instance), the ISP and exchange carrier are the same company.

Responsibility for the rest of the pieces—equipment, day-to-day support, security, Internet applications—can fall on either side of the fence; they can be your problems, or they can belong to the provider. Depending on who you ultimately decide to go with, you may be able to pick from an assortment of options, ranging from complete outsourcing of installation, security, and maintenance, to a roll-your-own kind of connection. Usually, it comes down to a question of which parts you want to pay for, which parts you are willing to manage on your own, and how much you are willing to pay.

Timeline

There's a lot to do, but as with any large project, a little bit of planning will make an overwhelming list of tasks feel manageable. I can't tell you *exactly* how much time will pass from the moment when you decide to go ahead with an Internet connection to the moment when you puff a fat cigar and pull up the first Web page. But I am going to guess it will be eight weeks, maybe less.

Week 0

At the outset, you need to identify the Internet applications people will use, estimate bandwidth requirements, understand the equipment needed, evaluate Internet service providers, and pick service options. Of course, you will want to choose a domain name too (e.g., *atlantic.com*).

It will also be a good idea to think about your security needs before proceeding; uncertainty about Internet security has torpedoed more than a few otherwise enthusiastic Internet connectivity plans. Will you need a firewall? If so, will you construct it, buy it, or hire somebody to secure your site for you? Most organizations can't proceed until these questions are answered.

Week 2

Once you have your plans, you will need to make a contract with an Internet service provider, and possibly hire an exchange carrier for the physical connection. If you are in charge of purchasing your own data communications equipment, you should get that under way too; some brands of routers have long manufacturer delivery times.

It will take a while for the circuit to come in—probably from four to six weeks. In the meantime, you should probably get started on your security plans, prepare a server (or servers) (for DNS, SMTP mail, the Web, FTP, and so on), and plan for desktop access to the Internet (provided you haven't outsourced these pieces). This is also a good time to think about electronic mail integration; how will you glue Internet mail into your current email system?

Week 6

Tempus fugit. By the sixth week, you should be sitting on your hands and swinging your feet, bored. At long last, you will be visited by the phone company, come to install the physical circuit. They will pull a line into your wiring closet, screw a network termination unit into the wall, and disappear. At this point, you may wish to connect the data communications equipment, and give your Internet service provider a call. Once the physical circuit is in, the service provider should be able to give you a definite date for circuit "turn-up," probably within a few days.

Week 7

During the seventh week, you and the Internet service provider will rendezvous on the telephone, to bring up the Internet connection. Your data communications equipment should be powered up and functional. Your router should be set to go: addresses, routing, and endpoint identifiers programmed in advance. Likewise, your server hosting DNS, SMTP mail, etc., should be configured and ready for all comers.

Once the connection is "up," the clock starts ticking; your Internet service provider will begin charging for the service.

Week 8

A few details usually linger another week or so. If you are getting a news feed, for instance, it may be several days before activation. This, too, may require a phone call with the service provider. Likewise, DNS usually needs some tweaking after circuit turn-up. Particularly, you may need to register reverse (address-to-name translation) zones for your network, or you may need to migrate responsibility for the primary nameserver for your domain away from your ISP, and over to a machine on your network.

How Much Is This Going to Cost Me?

In the chapters that follow, we will expand considerably on the scenarios you might want to investigate—do-it-yourself connectivity, long distance connections, connectivity with the right to redistribute bandwidth, firewalls. In the meantime, I am going to assume that you are interested in a simple full-time connection with nearby access, a secured router, and a modest server. I'll also assume that you plan to bring the connection up yourself (hence, this book). I'm putting my head in the sand a little; there are true costs to labor, of course. As a benchmark, let me say that if you hired me, I would probably charge you between $6,000 and $10,000 for the labor covered in this book. Your time has similar value.

There are some one-time and some recurring components associated with your connection. The one-time components include hardware: a CSU/DSU or multiplexor, a router, and a server. There will also be one-time connection set-up costs, charged by both your Internet service provider and your exchange carrier. The breakdowns can be a little confusing; some service providers charge you individually for every little portion of the connection—the cost of the circuit, rental of a port on their router (called a port charge), cost for the routed Internet traffic, a PVC charge (for a virtual circuit). I'll try to assemble these into the big picture.

Representative Costs

Let's assume that you will connect to an access provider with a *Point of Presence* (POP) nearby. Accordingly, the physical circuit will involve your local telephone company alone. Long-haul connections, by comparison, can involve both your local phone company and an interexchange carrier; there can be several additional components added to the bill (we discuss circuit types and charges in more detail in Chapter 4, *The Circuit*).

Table 1-1: Representative Connection Costs

	56 Kbit/S FR	T1 Dedicated	10 Mbit/S SMDS	T3 ATM NAP
CSU/DSU or Mux	$ 250	$ 1,000	$ 3,000	$ 5,000
Router	$ 1,800	$ 1,800	$ 2,500	$ 6,000
Server	$ 2,500	$ 2,500	$ 3,500	$ 10,000
Transport One-time	$ 800	$ 1,200	$ 3,000	$ 5,000
Transport Recurring (annual)	$ 1,500	$ 4,800	$ 36,000	$ 25,000
Internet Service One-time	$ 1,200	$ 2,500	$ 3,500	$ 5,000
Internet Recurring (annual)	$ 4,800	$ 18,000	$ 30,000	$ 60,000
Year One	$12,850	$31,800	$81,500	$116,000

Table 1-1 suggests some possible first-year costs for a variety of connection types.* The 56 Kbit/S Frame Relay charges, shown in the first column, are typically fixed, without regard to distance. T1 (1.54 Mbit/S) dedicated access (column 2), on the other hand, is usually mileage-sensitive; the farther away you are from the POP, the more it will cost. T1-speed connectivity may be available to you in Frame Relay too, though T1 Frame Relay circuits can cost more than dedicated connections for nearby destinations.

The last two columns represent connections that aren't terribly common, though you *can* buy them now, and you will probably see more of them in the next few years. SMDS, shown in the third column, is a high-speed, metropolitan area network technology. As with Frame Relay, the pricing assumes that you are within a geographical area served by the network, and will pay a flat-rate tariff. I show a 10 Mbit/S price estimate; however, speeds for SMDS networking can go as high as 45 Mbit/S and beyond. The connection we are talking about here is pretty fast; compare with a vanilla Ethernet network—also rated at 10 Mbit/S.

DS3 (T3) connectivity is shown in the last column. Surprisingly, a dedicated T3 (45 Mbit/S) or OC-1 circuit doesn't cost proportionally more than a dedicated T1, given the great difference in performance. The estimate shown for T3 Internet service presumes service through an NSF NAP. Other varieties of T3 access are available too, particularly through a few of the national ISPs.

You will note that I included the cost of an Internet server in the table. This would be a machine that could act as a mail hub, news server, DNS server, or even a firewall. Naturally, the server horsepower should match the kind of traffic you expect. You might find it surprising, however, that for everything through T1 connectivity, a high-end PC running UNIX makes a fully capable server.† You will also note that I bumped up the server cost estimates for both the SMDS and ATM scenarios. This is because I imagine that you will want more capable hardware servicing the end of a very high-speed connection. In fact, the notion of a single server is fairly ludicrous; if you are buying a DS3 circuit, you probably have some grand plans for the bandwidth—perhaps involving a whole computer center.

There can be fees beyond those in the table, including charges for domain name service or a news feed, for instance. Likewise, there may be fees for managing data communications equipment, or providing site administration. Other costs involve the desktop environment and a dial-up strategy for members of your organization when they are out on the road. You will also want to choose a set of

---

* Note: these are 1996 guesstimates. Over time, they can be expected to drop, with hardware costs receding most quickly, and service/support costs lagging behind.

† Consider a high-end PC running *Linux*. Linux is a very capable UNIX rewrite, available at no charge. Everything you might need in a server has already been ported and tested under Linux. We use it all the time.

software clients for the many Internet services, and make them available to the rest of the company. Many are free, but some require licenses. A little bit of in-house training may be in order too. Long term, you should budget from four to twenty man-days per month for server maintenance and modifications, depending on your applications.

Where Do We Go From Here?

If you haven't had a chance yet, it might be a good idea to skim through the book. Consider that I have to approach the process serially—from service selection to desktop integration—lest the book be a jumble. You, on the other hand, have the option of starting several fires at once. In my serial version, we will begin by weighing your options for ISPs and data circuits. From there, we will build a server and implement a security strategy. In your parallel version, you can start thinking about all of these things at once.

2

Service Options

Too many times I have gone into the car dealer looking for a car that fits a lifestyle I *might* have—if I bought the car. I'm older now; I just buy station wagons, load them with random stuff, and drive the paved roads around town. No more day-dreams of cruising down moonlit beaches, of wind-blown hair and open high-ways, of tossing the keys to envious valets. I have owned one sort of interesting car, but frankly I just ended up loading it with random stuff and driving around town.

Anyway, having set the mood, let me ask: What do you plan to do with your Internet connection? The question is very important because the answer will help you determine what kind of connection to pursue. Do you need a dedicated link, intermittent (dial-up) access, no access at all? For many folks, a high-speed Inter-net connection is unnecessary—particularly for those with plans that revolve around a Web server. Good service can be rented cheaply from others. In fact, you can often buy Web or FTP space behind a fast (say, T1) connection on a profes-sional provider's site for far less than it would cost you to bring a slower 56 Kbit/S connection into your organization.

On the other hand, if you want to bring full Internet service to the users of your organization, you will clearly need a connection of your own. But how fast should it be? We looked at some representative connection costs in the previous chapter; perhaps the dollars will ultimately decide the speed of the circuit. However, it is as important to understand whether you will have the bandwidth you need as whether you can afford it; we need to quantify your site.

You also have to decide how much help you will need. *I* might be comfortable buying a raw Internet pipe from a short-tempered, overworked service provider, but this may not suit *you*. Accordingly, your evaluation of ISPs (Internet Service

Providers) will be focused not just on bandwidth and price, but on service options as well.

Perhaps most important is the ISP's talent level and organization. You will find that ISPs run the gamut from wannabes to companies that are too important to speak with you; it really is a jungle. But we'll get to that later. For now, let's talk about you.

What Support and Services Do You Need?

The most basic Internet connections come with no technical support at all. The ISP will be responsible for the network and for routed IP, but it will be your job to handle things like domain name service, SMTP mail backup, and router configuration. If you do have a problem, you *can* hire the service provider, generally at a steep rate like $175/hour. On the other hand, you might be perfectly happy to let somebody else do the grieving; some providers will turnkey everything, from firewall maintenance to end user technical support. My guess is that you are planning to manage many of the details yourself (after all, you *are* reading this book . . .).

Internet connectivity entails a lot of subtasks—everything from operating the wide area network that brings the Internet into your site to paying the bills. Of course, you can't expect your ISP to pay your bills, nor do they want you anywhere near their WAN. However, there is some intervening ground that could belong to either of you:

Domain Registration	IP Network Registration/Routing
In-addr.arpa Registration	Nameservers
Data Communications Equipment	A USENET News Feed
Network Monitoring	Trouble-Ticket Generation
Router Maintenance	Security Maintenance
Network Usage Reporting	End-User Technical Support

The question that needs to be settled is: "Who does what?" In the next sections, we will briefly visit each topic, to understand what is entailed. This should help you decide whether to handle them yourself or pass them to your ISP or a third party. In some cases, you may wish to exclude ISPs if they cannot provide a particular service. You will find that many of these topics are expanded later in the book.

Start-up Issues

Start-up issues sometimes push organizations toward more expensive support plans. After a bit of time goes by, the network administrator may say to herself: "Ah! I could have handled that, if only I had understood it when we bought the connection." Let's look at start-up issues now, and see if we can cut the learning curve.

Domain Registration

One of the first things you will choose is a domain name (such as *atlantic.com*). In most cases—not all—the Internet access provider will register the domain on your behalf when the connection is ordered, and that will take care of it.

In some cases, however, you might want to register in advance. Perhaps you want to make sure the domain name is reserved, while you go about selecting a provider. Or perhaps you would like to save yourself a few dollars—domain registration can be an extra cost item. With a few ISPs, you will even have the option of purchasing cheaper service all around if you handle the domain details yourself. There's just this little chicken-and-egg problem: you have to be on the Internet already—have to have two DNS servers (*nameservers*)—in order to host your own domain. * Fortunately, you can start the domain registration process off-site, in advance; any two Internet sites can host your primary and secondary nameservers. You might hire a local ISP, for instance, to provide the initial nameservers for your domain. Once the connection is turned up, the primary nameserver can be migrated over to your network, where you will have control over the data kept within it. The secondary can stay where it is, or migrate to the ISP you ultimately select for Internet access.

Technically, you could bring up your Internet connection first, and apply for a domain name later. However, the turnaround time for some domains (e.g., .org or .net) has stretched out to nearly a month; you'd be without a domain for a long time. Furthermore, this would leave you essentially unable to receive mail or provide Web service; without a domain, people can only find you by your IP address.[†]

While we are on the subject, let me suggest that you should plan to run the primary nameserver on your hardware, regardless of how the domain gets registered. If you are on a bare-bones maintenance plan, this will generally be required. But

---

* Chapter 17, *Domain Name Service*, describes the domain registration process.

† Note that the InterNIC is charging for domain registration and maintenance as of late 1995. Domain registration used to be subsidized by the fees the NSF pays to NSI. However, under the services agreement between NSI and the NSF, the InterNIC can recover costs for domain handling. The rate is $50/year, collectible on the domain registration anniversary. New registrations are $100, good for 2 years.

with higher levels of support, you often have the choice of leaving the primary nameserver maintenance up to the ISP. Whenever you need a change, you send them a note, or give them a call, and they make the nameserver updates. The trouble is that it may take them days to get to it; carriers often update nameservers on a schedule. You, on the other hand, can feel the tingling sensation of immediate gratification if you keep the primary nameserver on your own hardware; updates can be propagated immediately.*

IP Network Registration/Routing

In order to exchange information with the Internet, your organization must have at least one registered (people often say *legal*) network on the other side of the data communications equipment. When it comes time to order an Internet connection, the access provider will ask if you already have a registered network or networks. If you don't, they will probably offer you one. If you do, they may charge a certain annual or monthly fee for the privilege of using that network as part of your connection. If you have several network numbers within your LAN, they may charge you even more.

You might ask yourself, "What difference does it make if you have one or several networks on your side of the Internet connection?" After all, they are charging you a flat rate for bandwidth. The reasoning is this: in order for your network or networks to be able to talk to the rest of the Internet, your carrier has to broadcast reachability (routing) information to the rest of the Internet. The fee is for the maintenance of additional entries in their routing tables.

Early in 1994, larger Internet service providers adopted what is known as *Classless Internet Domain Routing* or CIDR (pronounced "cider"), developed cooperatively by BARRNet, OARnet, cisco, and Merit. CIDR helps to tame two problems facing the Internet: address depletion, and an explosion in the size of routing tables.

For argument, say that you are connecting to the Internet, and that you want registered IP addresses for all of your in-house hosts. Your network may be larger than the 254 hosts that a class C network number can accommodate; you might prefer a class B network (16,382 hosts). However, the InterNIC has been reluctant to hand out class B (and A) addresses, due to short supply. Instead, your petition would probably be answered with a handful of class Cs, with a total address count more closely matching the number of hosts on your LAN.

One problem feeds another: assigning multiple class C networks in lieu of a single class B makes better use of the total address space, but it increases the number of networks that have to be routed. The Internet has been growing out of control

---

* The exception might be if you have a firewall. See Chapter 16, *Internet Security*.

The InterNIC

In 1992, the National Science Foundation released a solicitation for organizations to provide NIC (*Network Information Center*) services to the nonmilitary NSFNET community. Three companies got the job: General Atomics (GA) was contracted to provide information services, AT&T became responsible for maintaining directories and databases, and Network Solutions, Inc. (NSI) provided an Internet registry for networks and domain names. (NSI subsequently replaced GA in the information services provider role.) Taken collectively, they were known as the *InterNIC*. Technically, the work was in support of the NSFNET. But like the NSFNET itself, the three NIC components actually serve a much larger community; the InterNIC administers network and domain registration requests for the whole United States (.com, .edu, .gov, .org, .net), and it participates passively in registrations for the rest of the world.

Non-U.S. domains are (typically) served by local and regional registries; RIPE (Reseaux IP Europeens) oversees European regional registry; APNIC (Asia Pacific Network Information Center) handles the Asia Pacific region. The InterNIC delegates the rest. These regional NICs may further delegate authority by country or community. Accordingly, if you wish to register a domain name or request an IP network number, you will need to interact with the InterNIC, or with your closest regional NIC.

anyway—this was already a problem. However, with multiple class Cs being substituted where a class B might have been used, the problem only gets worse. The trick, then, is to be able to hand an organization a bundle of class C networks, say 16, without having to advertise 16 new routes. Better yet, it would be helpful to be able to hand out hundreds of class C networks, to hundreds of organizations, without adding *any* new routes.

CIDR reduces the routing table burden by bundling aggregates of networks together and advertising them as if they were one. Think about how this might work: if you have network 205.246.144, and someone else using the same ISP has 205.246.145, then the two networks could (theoretically) be advertised to the rest of the Internet as one. The distinction between you and your neighbor does not matter until the traffic gets routed back into your own provider's network.

To bundle groups of Class C networks (or other networks) together, we have to treat them less specifically than we might otherwise. The technique, called *supernetting*, applies a broad network mask to groups of networks. By shifting the netmask to the left, we tell routing equipment that some portion of the network field is insignificant, and that groups of networks should be routed together, as one. Supernetting is a key component of CIDR. Groups of (class C) networks with similar high-order address bits can be shuffled about as one network when crossing the main conducts of the Internet.

As of autumn 1995, you can no longer register a single, non-CIDR IP address. If you already have one, you can use it. However, new address assignments are being made in blocks of no fewer than 64 class C networks. Internet service providers will give you a price break if you agree to use *their* network numbers in lieu of ones you might already have registered. These substitute CIDR networks will be less burdensome for the provider to route and maintain. The downside is that the network number belongs to them; if you switch providers in a year, all of your in-house addresses will have to change. For my money, the risk is minimal, and you should take the price break. In fact, unless you already have a non-CIDR address, it is going to be very difficult to get hold of one—someone else will have to bequeath it to you. The network address details of your company are (hopefully) going to be hidden behind domain name service anyway. When it comes time to change addresses, only the nameservers should care.[†]

In-addr.arpa Registration

Domain name service provides a mapping between names that people are comfortable with—say, *foo.gznz.com*—and IP addresses, which are convenient for computers. Just as you will want to have a nameserver for "forward" queries (name-to-address), you will also want to serve the reverse, address-to-name mapping. This will allow remote computers to tell more about who is visiting their site. Consider that they have your IP address already; reverse look-ups provide a way to find your name. In a few instances, remote sites will even deny your connection requests if no reverse mapping is available.

---

* Associated with each logical network is a network mask (*netmask*, for short) that describes which portion of the address specifies the network, and which part describes the host. A class C network, for example, has a default netmask of 255.255.255.0, indicating that the first three octets (bytes) are dedicated to the network number, and the last eight bits describe the host. A network can be subdivided into smaller *subnets* by locally changing the netmask. For instance, a new netmask of 255.255.255.192 extends the network portion of the address field to the right by two bits. In Internet parlance, the network has been divided into four subnets.

† One possible complication: if you are hosting domains for other sites, the nameserver addresses you send to the InterNIC will be part of your ISP's CIDR block. When it comes time to move to another ISP, all of those domain registrations have to be amended too.

In order to serve the reverse mapping, you need to register the *in-addr.arpa* domain for your IP network(s).[*] Taking care not to get too bogged down in the syntax for the time being, say that your network number is 198.252.200.0. You would then register the reverse domain, *200.252.198.in-addr.arpa.* Each entry in the domain zone definition would list an IP address (written backwards) and its associated name. A reverse look-up for host number 1 (*1.200.252.198.in-addr.arpa*), for example, might return the name foo.gznz.com—the actual translations are up to you.

Often, sites don't pursue reverse (in-addr.arpa) registration until after they are already connected to the Internet. This avoids the register-and-migrate process that we discussed with forward domains a few moments ago. However, it is entirely possible to register an in-addr.arpa network in advance, if you wish to make reverse mappings available without delay.

Note that in the case of CIDR networks, the ISP may already have the in-addr.arpa domain registered. If so, the ISP may *delegate* responsibility for your portion of the CIDR block to you, on request. This makes setting up reverse mappings much quicker than it would be if you had to apply to the InterNIC for registration. Whatever the case, you should run the in-addr.arpa nameserver yourself if you can. Otherwise, make sure that your provider will host it on your behalf.

Nameservers

As I mentioned earlier, you need at least two nameservers—computers that respond to DNS queries—for each domain associated with your site. One nameserver acts as the *primary*, the authority for the domain information. The other acts as a *secondary*, a mirror. People sometimes stage primary/secondary pairs of nameservers on the same network, though technically they should be located on different networks, preferably networks operated by completely different ISPs. This way, if a network failure makes one of the nameservers unreachable, the other will be able to answer queries in its stead.

I've said it already, though maybe not so directly: you can hire your ISP to run your secondary and primary nameservers on your behalf. Having them maintain your secondaries will be a convenience. However, you will lose a measure of control over your domain if they maintain the primary nameserver; updates will require a phone call or a mail message, which means there's a delay. Unless you

---

[*] Chapter 17 tells how to set up the domain zone files. The form for registering is available from *ftp://rs.internic.net/.*

are terribly uncomfortable with managing DNS, I suggest that you run your own primary nameservers.*

Data Communications Equipment

Naturally, some digital communications equipment is part of every full-time Internet connection. Depending on the ISP, you may be required to purchase your own data communications hardware, or the provider may supply it to you. In some cases, they own and maintain the equipment themselves and you aren't even allowed access to the equipment on your premises. Of course, if the equipment belongs to the service provider, then you won't have to worry about compatibility or installation. At the same time, you lose some flexibility; whenever you want to make a change (to the access lists, for instance), you have to get in touch with the service provider and have them take care of it. That can take time.

What if the provider doesn't supply the data communications equipment? The best way to come up with a short list of equipment possibilities is to ask the ISP what brands they recommend, sell, or use. Not only will this assure you that the equipment you eventually buy will be fully compatible with the provider's, but you can also assume that the provider's staff knows something about configuring the equipment. This could ease the confusion, should you have a problem when it finally comes time to "turn up" the circuit.†

Router Configuration

Router configuration, or, more generally, data communications equipment configuration, is another start-up issue that can either belong to you or to your ISP. If you sign up for a basic level of service, and purchase a CSU/DSU and router yourself, then it is pretty certain that the job of configuring the equipment will fall on your shoulders. If, on the other hand, you buy the equipment from the ISP, it may ship preconfigured; this could save you time. Please, ask!

Unfortunately, router configuration can be one of the scariest parts of Internet connectivity the first time around. To begin with, the router programming environment is apt to be unlike anything else you have worked with. Second, the LAN or WAN technologies used for your particular connection may be completely new to you; there can be a new bucket of acronyms to swallow.

We discuss router configuration in various degrees of detail in the chapters ahead. You may save some time, however, if you can have the router configured in advance, either by the access provider or by the company that sells you the

---

* See Chapter 17.
† We cover data communications equipment in more detail in Chapters 4, *The Circuit*, and 14, *Physical Networks*.

equipment. Better yet, ask your prospective ISP for a copy of a similar configuration, representative of a customer's router. Using this as a starting point, you can modify the addresses and endpoint identifiers to match your own.

Note that no router configuration will be complete without implementing access lists—rules that restrict traffic into and out of your network. Again, this can be tricky the first time around. See Chapter 16 for an explanation of the procedure, and Appendix A for some sample access list sets.

A USENET Newsfeed

It was once much easier for one Internet site to casually extend the favor of feeding USENET news to another. I might have a friend at a university who was willing to feed our company, for example. Someone else might contact me looking for news, and I'd feed them. Often, sites fed multiple other sites. There wasn't a problem with volume; the community that read and posted news was smaller than it is today.

A couple of things have changed the politics of newsfeeds. For one, a feed can amount to many tens or hundreds of megabytes per site, per day (as much as 600 MB/day). Agreeing to feed just a few sites can place an annoying burden on your server and network, particularly if you have a low-speed connection.

More importantly, newsfeeds are now regularly extended by Internet service providers to their customers, sometimes for an additional charge. The carrier agrees to feed you whatever groups you please, and may even be willing to help you set up your end of the feed. However, provider-sponsored newsfeeds can also come with the added condition that, though you may feed news to whomever you like, you agree not to forward any of their postings back through your connection. This restriction makes it tricky (or in violation of a contract) to act as a feed for another site.

Though it may cost you as much as $100 a month for a newsfeed through your carrier, you might consider whether it isn't worth the extra money. For one thing, you should be able to expect a higher level of service when you are paying someone for news. If the newsfeed breaks, it is the carrier's job to put it right. If a cooperative feed goes down for several days, on the other hand, you will have no right to complain—your friends are doing you a favor feeding you news in the first place.

Second, the news may flow more steadily from the carrier's news hub; there should be less contention for network bandwidth if the feed comes over the carrier's own network than if you get a feed from elsewhere on the Internet. Likewise, a feed from within your provider's mid-level or campus network is more

Internet-friendly than if you drag postings halfway across the universe. Fewer networks will be involved in the feed.

Also, you might step back and consider whether you actually want a newsfeed at all. For starters, news chews up bandwidth, disk space, CPU horsepower, evenings, and weekends; it can be a pain to maintain. The community of news junkies should probably number in the teens before you agree to erect an in-house server. Furthermore, for many connections, the news you might want is more than you can fit down the pipe; a 56 Kbit/S connection is *too* slow for a full newsfeed, for instance. And even a partial feed can interfere with useful work. Passing up a newsfeed doesn't mean that you have to forgo news, however. You may be able to read news remotely.

Remote News Hubs

Your service provider may also offer a remote news hub as an alternative to a regular newsfeed. A little background will help explain: USENET newsreading is a client/server application, based on a protocol called NNTP (*Network News Transfer Protocol*). NNTP serves two functions: it is the vehicle for client/server newsreader applications, and the protocol by which sites *feed* one another.

Typically, the server is your own news hub—a computer kept on your local area network (it might be the same computer that is acting as nameserver, SMTP host, etc.). A personal computer user in your organization might "aim" her newsreader at your news hub, for instance, and browse news across the LAN. This is not the only possibility, however. Though performance will be best if the newsreader NNTP conversation is conducted across the local Ethernet, it is also possible for the news hub to be located elsewhere on the Internet.

In addition to supplying newsfeeds, your prospective provider may also offer the option of reading remotely from their server, perhaps at a reduced charge, or at no cost. If yours is a small site, my advice is to take the remote newsfeed option, if it is free, and try it. If you find you can't stand the performance, you can always upgrade to a real feed later. Otherwise, I'll warn you in advance that remote news-reading can be a lot less interactive than reading from a news hub that is maintained locally. On the positive side, a remote news hub requires no maintenance or disk space on your part, and doesn't chew into your own bandwidth allocation when you are not using it.

Ongoing Maintenance Issues

As with start-up issues, ongoing maintenance of the connection and the network infrastructure can belong to you or to your ISP. Some of the tasks, such as external network monitoring, are natural follow-ons to the services ISPs provide anyway. Others, such as end user technical support or firewall maintenance, are beyond the basic suite of services, and will definitely cost extra—if your ISP offers these services at all.

Network Monitoring

Typically, larger ISPs continuously monitor their own networks, all the way down to their customers' routers. Usually, the service is provided as part of the basic connectivity package, and won't cost extra. Smaller, hometown ISPs, on the other hand, may or may not monitor their networks; it may be up to the subscriber to identify network trouble, and report it back to the ISP. Naturally, you will want the ISP to monitor your network, if possible. Be sure to ask.

Network monitoring technique varies with the ISP. Many use SNMP (*Simple Network Management Protocol*). When programming your router, you indicate that you will be part of an SNMP *community*, and that status regarding your circuit may be collected along with that of others within the community. Other ISPs use automated pinging (ICMP echo/response), simply to indicate if a customer's circuit has gone down. If the remote router doesn't respond, the ISP may assume that the customer is off-line. Other techniques are possible too; at least one international ISP (PSI) uses RIP (routing) updates as a wellness check.

Trouble-Ticket Generation

Proactive troubleshooting goes hand in hand with proactive network monitoring. If your ISP is watching your network connection, they may also take it upon themselves to log and investigate lost connections. At the very least, you want them to give you a phone call. Consider that your site needs to be available to the world 24 hours a day, particularly if you are running a Web server. If the connection goes down—especially if you don't know about it—it could mean lost business.

Router Maintenance

As I mentioned earlier, with some ISPs you are responsible for providing your own router and CSU/DSU. In other cases, the ISP owns the router, and you aren't even allowed to log in and make changes. This cleanly cuts the community of Internet subscribers into two camps: those who depend on the ISP for router updates, and those who have to find another means. Being in the second group doesn't necessarily set you wandering foggy streets, crying out for a router programmer. You can often go back to the ISP and hire them to make router updates for you, either as an add-on to the monthly bill, or on an hourly basis. Smaller ISPs are often more flexible about this, by the way. Large ISPs may "offer" the service, yet be unsure who within the company is responsible for actually providing it.

A natural question to ask is: What kind of updates does a router require? Aside from the obvious need for an occasional software revision,[*] routers may need tweaks to access lists (security), a change in the SNMP community designation, or updates in response to network changes. One might also need to know one's way around the router for circuit troubleshooting.

Again, I believe that if you can handle router maintenance yourself, you should. This will give you instant turnaround when you need to make changes. But as I said earlier, router programming can be scary; you might want someone else to bootstrap your configuration, after which you can slide into the job at your leisure. As you become better acquainted with the router, you can take over its maintenance altogether.

Security Maintenance

Router access list programming, mentioned above, is a form of security maintenance. Typically, one would instruct the router to allow outbound Internet traffic to anywhere, but prohibit inbound traffic to all but a few destinations on the local LAN—typically an SMTP mail hub, Web server, or FTP server. Really, router security maintenance is just an extension of general router maintenance, though some ISPs charge for it separately. The decision about who should program router security is almost necessarily tied to the decision about router maintenance; if you are going to manage one, then you will probably manage the other.

Beyond the router, you will find that some ISPs will be willing to lease you a firewall, maintain it, and provide periodic reports. This would be a truly turnkey operation; the ISP delivers sanitized Internet access to your LAN, without the mess and fuss, usually in exchange for a substantial monthly fee. Sad to say, if you would like that level of support, then there is little in this book that will help you; a turnkey operation is typically "hands off."

In addition to firewalls, a few ISPs offer end-to-end encryption between specially designated Internet sites, both of which would be serviced by the same ISP. It works like this: traffic to random Internet sites would be unencoded (cleartext), just as with a vanilla Internet connection. Traffic to designated sites, on the other hand, would be ciphertext, based upon keys distributed to the two sites.[†] Typically, encryption is implemented at the router, or on the firewall. Of course, encryption can also be done on an application-to-application basis, from within your network. However, this form of security won't involve the ISP, and will pass transparently through even the most basic Internet connection.

---

[*] Software upgrade: trade your old bugs for new ones.

[†] Actually, only the data is ciphertext; the IP header remains intact.

Network Usage Reporting

An ISP that monitors their network with SNMP already has a vehicle for collecting traffic statistics. Sometimes, the ISP will provide these as part of the baseline network support package. In other cases, they bundle traffic reporting with higher levels of support.

Network statistics are terrifically useful. You can see the daily peak traffic demand and daily averages. In many cases, you can also tell which applications are used most, which users are responsible for generating the greatest portion of the traffic, and where the traffic is going. It may just be interesting at first. However, the data begins to matter when someone within the company needs to justify the cost of the connection, or needs to build a case for a larger pipe. *

If your ISP offers traffic reporting as part of the basic package, take it. Otherwise, you will need to weigh the cost of the higher level of support against the expected value of the statistics. By the way, firewalls generate traffic statistics too, including information about most-often-visited sites; you might be able to meet your tracking requirements that way.

End-User Technical Support

ISPs that sell complete turnkey Internet service may extend that service all the way back to the desktop. They would, for example, provide the PC configuration consulting, the browsers, and a helpline for end user support. Again, this would be a very "hands off" solution; your involvement would be limited to paying the substantial bills, supplied as part of the service.

Bandwidth

How big should a given organization's pipe to the Internet be? One school of thought says that you should get as much bandwidth as you can afford. Consequently, the answer often comes from a budget, rather than from traffic analysis. This is understandable; for many companies, Internet connectivity is viewed as a pilot project, or an experiment. Likewise, traffic assessment is empirical, à la: fill it with bricks until it sinks; count the bricks (N); declare the capacity to be N-1 bricks. The trouble is that the process of loading down an Internet connection until it collapses ignores any standards you might have set for service. Remember, people visiting a Web server on an N-1 bricks Internet connection are going to suffer intensely.

So, how much bandwidth do you really *need?* The estimate can be tricky. One's natural inclination is to think of bandwidth in terms of time spent drumming one's

---

* It's also good to have records of activity in case of litigation—particularly litigation with employees.

fingers on the desk, waiting for something to happen. Interactive response *is* one element in the picture. But there's another piece too: aggregate bandwidth or volume. This noninteractive or *batch* load could come from applications like electronic mail, USENET news, or automated file transfers. And it can be significant—don't assume it's not there. To truly estimate bandwidth requirements, you have to weigh both types of activities together, interactive and batched, and make some guesses about their relative importance. You might also need to balance the trade-off between snappy response for your own community of users versus snappy response for the rest of the world.

Making Bandwidth Estimates

Internet traffic peaks in the mid-afternoon (EST). This is the time when Western Europe, and all of North America are bashing away at each other's servers. Because each site (more or less) participates in the melee, we can make the wild assumption that your traffic, too, will demonstrate a similar curvy load—rising and falling smoothly, in correspondence with the rest of the Internet.

For planning purposes, say that batched traffic ebbs and flows with the time of day. By contrast, interactive transfers will be viewed as discrete events of a particular size (the number of bytes), with a particular width (the desired time it takes for a transfer) and height (the necessary bandwidth to meet the time requirement).

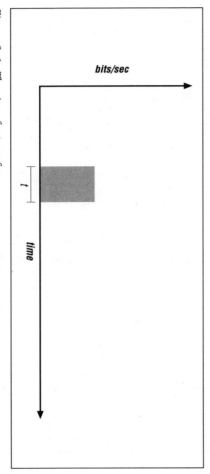

Figure 2–1: The size of a transfer

The block shown in Figure 2-1 depicts an interactive transfer—perhaps a Web page hit or an interactive FTP transfer. We can fool around with the block's geometry, adjusting the desired time, to make the rectangle taller and skinnier or shorter and fatter, until it matches your desired parameters. Approaching the exercise, however, we need to have some idea of how big an average transfer will be (e.g., how big one of your Web pages is), and of what we feel to be the minimum acceptable transfer rate. Then, we need to estimate how many of these transfers are likely to run concurrently. In more graphic terms, we need to estimate how many of these blocks are likely to stack up on one another at the peak hours of the day. These stacks of blocks will be superimposed upon the undulating back of the batch loading to give us a plausible estimate of your bandwidth requirements.

Well, now that I have you all greased up, it's time to let you down: we're done talking about bandwidth estimation for the time being. For some of you, that will be a relief, because the details can drag on. For those who would like to make a guesstimate of bandwidth requirements, Appendix B contains a worksheet (like a tax form) that you can use to profile your site. In the next chapter, we will estimate the spare capacity in your proposed ISP's network. You can take the two numbers—your requirements, and their headroom—and compare. For now, I am going to proceed under the assumption that you have your bandwidth requirements roughly in hand.

Choosing a Network Technology

As I suggested earlier, price may ultimately decide the speed of your Internet connection. This, in turn, will decide the circuit technology to use. A note of caution: the process of circuit selection will often involve comparing some incompatible technologies. You might, for instance, weigh a slower, 56 Kbit DDS connection against a faster, fractional T1 connection. The two networks are based on different encoding and data representation methods, which means that some of the data communications equipment you might buy for a DDS connection will be incompatible with a fractional "T." I won't belabor the differences here—we will talk about circuit technologies at length in Chapters 4 and 14. However, I want you to be aware that the circuit and a portion of the hardware you might buy for a slower connection might not be transferable to a faster connection. In short, consider your future bandwidth requirements in addition to your present requirements, to avoid re-engineering part of your connection.

Choosing a Provider

Okay. We have considered bandwidth, service options, and support. Even if this leaves you unsure about whether you will farm certain pieces out, at least we have had a look at the most common ISP service and support options. Of course, I explained the options as if they were fruit to be plucked from a bowl, with the prerogative of preferring one piece to another. However, you could use the service options another way: to disqualify ISPs. You might, for instance, have an unambiguous need for one of the higher levels of support, or for a cheap connection. This will streamline your decision process by effectively tossing out ISPs who don't meet the basic requirements. Whichever way you choose to go, you should at least develop an understanding of the service and support choices you will need to consider, before evaluating and implementing a connection to the Internet.

3

Choosing a
Service Provider

This chapter and the previous chapter go together; we are approaching the same questions, but from two different angles. It's as if we are mediating a settlement between two parties. We asked you, "What do you want?" Now we will ask the Internet service provider, "What can you offer?" In theory, we are past "what you want," which should have helped pare the list of potential ISPs; those left standing should match your paper criteria for services and support. The next step is to take a critical view of the "maids in waiting," to decide if they can really do what they say they can.

How can we predict a good marriage? We have to judge on other measures than price and options; the provider's network infrastructure and technical skill are very important. Accordingly, we will start by discussing how ISPs build their networks. This will give us some insight into issues of network loading, peak usage, and connectivity to the rest of the Internet. Then we will discuss the other parts of the ISP business—support, and redundancy in staff and equipment. By the end of the chapter, we will have (hopefully) skinnied the list of contenders further (perhaps there will be none left). Finally, we will discuss a few contract and payment details.

How ISPs Construct Their Networks

With only some oversimplification, we can cut the world of ISPs into four camps: *backbone*, *national*, *regional*, and *local* access providers.

The backbone providers are the big nationwide outfits that effectively control Internet routing and own significant pieces of the backbone (T3 and large pipes carrying huge volumes of long-haul traffic). They correspond to what used to be called "the core" back when the National Science Foundation ran the Internet on tax dollars. Currently, the backbone providers include UUnet, PSI, ANS, Sprint, MCI, and Agis/Net99—sometimes called "the Big Six."

A national provider is a nationwide Internet retailer that buys capacity and routing service from multiple backbone providers and runs points of presence (POPs) for dial-in access country-wide. At present, Netcom and the traditional national commercial BBS services like CompuServe, Delphi, and Prodigy fall in this category.

A regional provider is like a national provider that operates in one geographic region. Some of the regionals (like CERFNet) used to be midlevel academic sites back when the NSF ran things, and now run as nonprofits serving a particular class of site primarily with dedicated lines. Most are commercial outfits that will cheerfully serve anyone who can reach one of their POPs, and sell both dedicated and dial-in access. Well-known commercial regionals include SFNet (West Coast), NetAccess (East Coast, centered on Philadelphia), and Digital Express (East Coast, centered in Washington, D.C.).

A local provider is a "mom and pop" outfit that resells bandwidth from a single, regional (or, less often, national) provider, usually for both dial-in and dedicated connections. The line between locals and regionals is a bit fuzzy, but it is usually crossed when a local provider connects to more than one backbone.

It is likely that you will end up choosing from among one or two regional providers, several local providers, and one or two of the "Big Six." Broadly, and with exceptions, service from a regional or backbone provider tends to be more reliable and faster, but also more expensive, than service from a local. It's tempting to conclude that there's a straight trade-off; the farther "upstream" you go, the better but more expensive the service gets. However, the picture gets complicated by questions about loading of network legs and the percentage of end user access at each POP. A particular regional provider may have greater capacity in its backbone than any of your local providers, for instance, but have little or no bandwidth left by the time they get to your town. On the other hand, a small "mom and pop" outfit may not be offering a lot of maximum bandwidth to the regional, but be lightly enough loaded that your effective bandwidth is high.

Anyway, rather than digress every time the issue comes up, I thought we might take a few moments to understand how an ISP builds a network, and from there speculate where the bandwidth goes.

National/Regional Network Infrastructure

For argument's sake, say that we have a new company called DeadBeat that wants to create an IP network with three points of presence, as depicted in Figure 3-1: one in New York, one in Houston, and one in Washington, D.C. In order to start, they will need to locate one or more long-distance exchange carriers who will be willing to lease data lines. This will give DeadBeat a *physical* network over which they can provide services to the three target cities.

Alternatively, DeadBeat could lease a *virtual* network. Link layer technologies such as ATM and Frame Relay make it possible for an exchange carrier to "peel off" some guaranteed bandwidth and sell it to others. The customer can use this bandwidth to build their own private IP network. In service, traffic shares switches and wiring with other, unrelated, network activities, flowing across the carrier's physical network. At the nodes, traffic is broken out; only the private network traffic reaches DeadBeat's facilities. And, as you have probably guessed, an ISP's infrastructure doesn't have to be created from a single technology; networks can be a combination of physical and virtual networking.

To complete the picture, DeadBeat will need data communications equipment. Depending on DeadBeat's capabilities and budget, they might purchase and manage all of the equipment themselves, or, in other cases, they might pay the long-distance carrier to manage the physical network, leaving DeadBeat to worry about the routing. Once DeadBeat gets to the point where the three cities can trade packet traffic seamlessly, they will have completed their private network backbone.

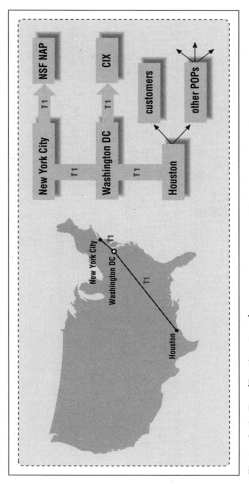

Figure 3–1: DeadBeat's network

To tie into the Internet, DeadBeat will need to tap one or more of the exchange points, scattered geographically across the country. A tie to the NSF backbone (through a NAP) would bring DeadBeat close connectivity with the academic, education, and research legs of the Internet. DeadBeat would also want to consider becoming a member of the Commercial Internet Exchange (CIX), or perhaps participating in one or more regional exchange points, such as MAE-EAST.

Of course, DeadBeat is going to need customers in a hurry; time is money. Where do the customers hook up? Anyplace DeadBeat has a spare router and capacity—a Point of Presence (POP). In our example, this would be New York; Washington, D.C.; and Houston to start. From the perspective of the rest of the Internet, Dead-Beat's customers' networks look like an extension of DeadBeat's private network. Whenever a new customer comes online, DeadBeat advertises reachability information to the rest of the Internet, and the customer becomes part of the Internet too.

Naturally, we skipped a lot of horrible details along the way. However, we should be able to describe some features of the network that DeadBeat has created, and be able to say what makes it "good," and what might be lacking.

Available Bandwidth

Each of the legs of DeadBeat's network has a fixed capacity. In the picture above, the links are shown at T1 (DS1) speeds (1.544 Mbit/S). On the day that DeadBeat opens for business, the utilization rate will be zero; there will be a full 1.536 Mbit/S available all the way from Houston to New York. As customers are added, the utilization changes. A new 56 Kbit/S customer connection in Houston might add a daily-averaged 3 Kbit/S load to the Houston-Washington leg, for instance. This, in turn, would burden the other legs just a bit, depending on where the traffic is ultimately bound.

Customers in other locations add to the utilization, too. Like the Houston site that purchased the 56-Kbit connection, they will make only partial use of the bandwidth they have contracted for. Consider, however, that every one of DeadBeat's customers imagines that DeadBeat will be able to supply full service on demand, should they ever need it. Here, then, is DeadBeat's dilemma: how much can they overbook their network? In the same way that a bank doesn't keep enough cash to cover a panic, DeadBeat doesn't expect every customer to demand all of the bandwidth they purchased, all at the same time. Likewise, they don't want to let resources go to waste. To make ends meet, DeadBeat is going to *have to* oversell their network, perhaps tens of times.

As one of DeadBeat's prospective customers, you should be concerned about their subscription commitments, peak bandwidth, and utilization rates. And you should care not just about utilization across their backbone, but also through the links that they have made into the rest of the Internet. It does you little good if DeadBeat's private network is 5 percent utilized, but their links with the exchange points are running at 70 percent. Likewise, you're in trouble if you sign up through an over-subscribed POP. Imagine sharing the Houston leg with 150 other active customers.

Anyway, the picture should be becoming clear. Internet service providers have a certain amount of bandwidth available in their internal backbone and external connections. They can never run at 100 percent—networks start to fail miserably at close to 70 percent. When considering an ISP, you will want to try to get some insight into their network structure, and understand the likely paths your traffic will follow. Are you near the center of the network, or on the periphery? If it looks as if you are going to be squeezed at times, you will have to place a value on the lost connectivity and consider whether it's worth buying a better grade of service.

One more thing to consider: How heavily is the provider involved in end user Internet access connections? Many carriers are selling off spare bandwidth as SLIP or PPP connections. The number of end-user sessions they can cram in is both essentially unbounded and self-limiting; users will get tired of the response time and go away for a while, but there will always be others dialing in. It can be a great way for the carrier to squeeze every drop from their network. For you, however, a network swamped with end-user activity may be a disaster. Later in this chapter, we will try to place your ISP's network on a spreadsheet, and see how well their capacity matches your requirements.

Local-Level Network Infrastructure

We have already looked at national and regional networks. By comparison, ISPs that resell bandwidth purchased *from* national-level service providers maintain what are called *local-level* networks. In NSF days these were often called *campus-level* networks, reflecting the Internet's roots in academia. The split is depicted in Figure 3-2.

As I mentioned earlier, there can be some risk that the available bandwidth through a local ISP will be twice warmed over; the upstream, national-level service provider may have already beaten their own network to death before feeding connectivity to the local-level ISP. However, it can go the other way too; a local ISP with a connection into the right regional or national provider may have more spare capacity than the local POP of the competing national ISP. It often depends on the number of customers each has collected in the area.

The ISP as an Organization

A good, zippy connection matters a lot. However, there are also other, qualitative factors that should weigh into your decision to go with a particular ISP. The size and capabilities of the ISP's staff, the length of time the provider has been in business, and the hours that they keep all count. Consider that your Internet connection is going to be part of your business presence. If the ISP has a problem with their network, it can affect the world's perception of you.

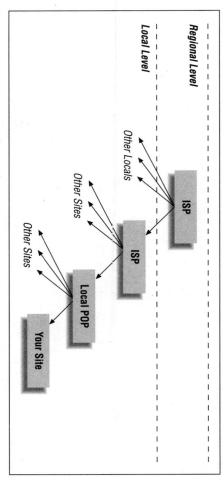

Figure 3-2: Connectivity hierarchy

Technical Support Staff

The larger ISPs typically divide technical support into presales and postsales categories. When scoping out the connection, or turning up the circuit, you will interact with a few folks who understand internetworking very well. Often, however, these people disappear once the connection is running; ongoing support questions are steered toward a postsales crew. The talent level of the postsales support crew is critical; their experience level reflects the depth of technical expertise of the ISP you are considering.

Of course, you could just ask the ISP, "How good are your people?" On the other hand, you might look for some telltale signs that predict the quality of the postsales support: first, does the ISP make a distinction between network operations support and technical support? Network operations should be concerned with behavior of the physical network, and the data link protocols. Technical support should be everything else—news, domain names, etc. If the ISP does not differentiate between the two, then you may one day find yourself in a queue behind confused, dial-up PPP users when you have a real network outage (frustrating).

Second, how does one contact the ISP to make maintenance changes in news feeds, domain information, or router access lists? Many providers maintain an assortment of email addresses, such as *hostmaster@deadbeat.net*, *news@deadbeat.net*, etc., for routine updates. This may not seem like the most expedient way to get service, but consider that by mailing to a maintenance address, you have already categorized your request; it is more likely to get to the right person the first time around. Furthermore, if others are mailing routine requests too, the phone is more apt to be free when a real problem occurs. (Naturally, this all presumes that the ISP watches its mail.)

A newsletter or monthly traffic report with some good technical meat is another tip-off about the caliber of the support organization. It shows that some of the ISP's good people have enough spare work time to write, and that the whole day isn't spent putting out fires.

Network Operations Center

Smaller organizations joining the Internet often don't have a dedicated technical staff, an operator watching over the computer room, or even a computer room, for that matter. In fact, the Internet connection may be a 24-hour, "lights-out" operation. The danger is that if the link fails, half a day may pass before anyone in the company notices. This can be bad for your image.

You will discover that larger ISPs operate *network operations centers*, or *NOCs*. NOC operators watch over their wide area network (via SNMP, by periodic pinging, or by monitoring routing broadcasts). They can watch your equipment too. In fact, a proactive NOC can call *you* to tell you that you have a problem, even before you are aware of it.* Furthermore, a larger ISP's NOC will be staffed with at least one person 24 hours a day. This can be important; though interactive traffic does tail off in the evening, there is still some activity in the wee hours of the morning. The Internet is global, after all; my night may be your day.

Redundancy

Redundancy is important, too. If a cola takes out a router, you want the ISP to be able to recover quickly—certainly in less time than it takes to "red label" another router from the manufacturer. This means that the ISP will have to maintain spares for all kinds of equipment—CSU/DSUs, routers, and servers.

Furthermore, you want redundancy in the staff. If the Number 9 bus mows down technical support specialist Fred Smith on his way to work, one morning, you don't want the ISP to fold up shop. Likewise, if Fred's long day is coming to a close just as your connection explodes, you want there to be somebody else to talk you through it.

Both of these needs—redundancy in staff and equipment—suggest that the ISP should be an organization with a certain amount of mass and longevity. They don't have to be huge. But you should think twice about trusting your organization's connectivity to a group that takes weekends off.

---

* I have a good-and-bad story to relate here. One summer afternoon we took a lightning hit. Among the victims was our main server, the LEC termination unit, and the DSU. While the room floated in the acrid and exclusively-priced smell of burned electronics, the phone rang: it was the NOC group of our carrier (PSI), calling to tell us that we were down. Of course, we knew we had a problem, but it was a pleasant surprise to learn we had a guardian angel.

Available ISP Bandwidth Estimates

Each provider's network infrastructure, capacity, and loading are different. From a buyer's point of view, the trick is to balance the cost of a connection against the expected level of service. No ISP can guarantee you full bandwidth to every location you might ever want to visit; networks are just too complicated. However, it would be nice to derive a number that suggests, in general terms, the performance we can expect.

Capturing an estimate of the true bandwidth availability between arbitrary Internet sites is pretty tricky. A number of variables come into play: connection speeds, topological distance (link speeds and numbers of hops), traffic through the local POP, traffic through the carrier's internal network, traffic through the exchange points, etc. And time of day changes the relative importance of each variable. A session between two random Internet sites is usually pretty zippy in the early morning hours. During the middle of the day, however, proximity becomes more important; for widely separated destinations, congestion of intervening networks limits performance without much regard for the speed of the end user's Internet hook-up. Two sites within the same ISP's infrastructure, on the other hand, are in closer proximity, and will cross a smaller number of congested networks. This will (should) give them a greater portion of their total bandwidth allocation.

Topology Questions

When considered in geographic terms, the Internet is a tangle. As many as a dozen providers may offer Internet service to your city or town. Each conducts traffic back through central facilities (and connections to other networks) in different cities. This means that if I have chosen access provider A, and you have chosen provider B, traffic between us may make many "hops," even though we might live across the street from one another.

In critical applications, or in situations where you have several steady Internet information partners, it may be worth a little bit of extra investigation to see how topologically distant you will be from one another. If you each sign up with the same provider, you will be able (hopefully) to remain within the carrier's private network, and skip the major Internet exchange points. This may provide you with a steadier supply of bandwidth, and lower latency.

Likewise, the extent to which competing traffic impinges on your bandwidth allocation depends on the total amount of bandwidth you have purchased. Consider that if you bought a 56 Kbit/S Internet connection, it might well pass through a previously oversubscribed link. If you had contracted for a T1 connection instead, might you again have been connected through the same link? The T1 connection is going to be able to push through a bigger chunk of traffic only because it can overload the network through the POP faster than some of the other customer connections! Here's the point: The slower the link, the more likely you are to get a significant fraction of the bandwidth you paid for. A 300 baud connection (if such a thing existed) would almost always be satisfied through the local POP. Full T1 bandwidth probably depends on nobody else using the POP at all, and may also depend on networks behind the POP being quiescent as well.

Anyway, let's keep sight of our goal. We are trying to make an estimate of your proposed ISP's ability to deliver Internet traffic to your site. In Appendix B we profiled your requirements (or you made a wild guess). We want to draw two curves—your requirements and the carrier's capabilities—and find a space between them. Unfortunately, real data about the connection you *might* buy is going to be difficult to collect. And even if we had a way to measure traffic and hops between your site and all the destinations you could possibly ever care about, it would still be a challenge to come up with a model that accurately captures the effect of all the variables. In short, we are going to have to guess.

Earlier in this chapter, we talked about the way access providers construct their networks. How well did your proposed provider fare? You may never know the whole of it, of course, but from what you can gather, let's rate their connectivity. From this, we will construct a simplistic model. I have chosen a few potential bandwidth attenuators, and scaled them unscientifically. Among my assumptions is that in the worst case you are able to squeeze out just 25 percent of the bandwidth you contracted for, particularly during the day's peak hour (you can choose another pessimistic figure if you like). We are also going to ignore the fact that a site with which you might want to trade traffic has the same constraints as you; they too could have a less-than-ideal connection to the Internet.

Available Carrier Bandwidth

1) Connection speed penalty   _____
2) Crowded POP penalty   _____
3) Carrier backbone speed penalty _____
4) Relative bandwidth penalty   _____
5) Carrier connectedness penalty   _____
6) End-user access penalty   _____
7) Penalty totals   +

8) Load factor   _____
9) Worst case scenario   _____
10) Multiplier   _____
11) Your connection bandwidth   _____

12) Available bandwidth (choose hour) _____

Line 1 — Your connection speed

How fast a connection are you considering? The faster the connection, the more, by proportion, a midday bandwidth crush will affect you. Choose the appropriate penalty from the left column of the table below, and enter it on line 1.

Penalty	Your connection speed will be . . .
0	Less than 56 Kbit/S
5	56 Kbit/S
10	128 Kbit/S
15	512 Kbit/S
20	1.54 Mbit/S (T1 Speed)

Line 2 — How crowded is the POP?

The carrier's POP may represent a choke point between your site and their backbone, particularly if there are a large number of customers sharing the POP with you. As before, choose the penalty in the left column and enter it on line 2.

Penalty	The carrier's local POP is . . .
0	Empty, you are the only customer on the POP
4	Not very crowded
8	Crowded
8	The provider won't reveal this information

Line 3 — How fast is the provider's backbone?

In some cases, it can be difficult to point at a particular portion of the network and say, "That is the backbone." However, you can identify the segments where there is connectivity to Internet exchange points, or where many cities' POPs are concentrated. Choose the most important looking segment(s) (from the ISP's network map if possible), call them the backbone, and make a choice of backbone speed from the list below.

Penalty	Carrier's backbone speed is . . .
0	45 Mbit/S (T3 Speed)
6	1.54 Mbit/S (T1 Speed)
21	56 Kbit/S

Line 4 — *How does your connection speed relate to backbone speed?*

This question asks whether your connection is going to be a drop in the bucket for the carrier's network backbone, or whether you are purchasing enough bandwidth to be one of their charter customers. In theory, the more headroom available, the less likely you are to be squeezed by other customers. Enter the penalty from the list below onto line 4.

Penalty	Your connection is . . .
0	Less than 5% of backbone speed
4	20% of backbone speed
8	50% of backbone speed
8	Unsure of the proportion
20	100% of backbone speed

Line 5 — *How well is your provider connected to the Internet?*

The number of exchange points is important because it means that traffic coming into and leaving your provider's network can follow less circuitous routes. This reduces contention; some of the exchange points (MAE, CIX, etc.) are fairly crowded. The fewer exchange points your traffic has to cross, the better your performance should be.

Penalty	The carrier is . . .
0	Very well connected
4	Fairly well connected (say two exchange points)
6	Not telling how well they are connected
10	Not well connected (one exchange point)

Line 6 — *End-user programs*

Just by their sheer numbers, end users can blot up spare bandwidth pretty voraciously. Technically, they shouldn't be evaluated on the same time-of-day loading curve as the other activities we have looked at; end users tend to use the Internet during other hours of the day. But we need to account for them—at least a bit. Choose your proposed carrier's end-user solution from the list below.

Penalty	End-user access: the carrier has . . .
0	No end-user access programs
3	A limited end-user base

Penalty	End-user access: the carrier has . . .
7	A large end-user base

Line 7 — Total penalties

Add the penalties recorded in lines 1 through 6 and record the result in line 7.

Line 8 — Load factor

Just as we used a table of factors to calculate your hourly traffic demand, we are going to have to scale the penalties just tallied to reflect time-of-day loading. Again, we will restrict the rest of the exercise to concentrate on a particular hour of the day (you pick the hour). To generate the complete available bandwidth curve, repeat this step and the ones following for each of the 24 hours of the day.

Table 3-1: Scale Factors by Hour (scale_factor(hour)) (EST)

Hour	Factor	Hour	Factor
00	.037	12	.050
01	.035	13	.051
02	.033	14	.051
03	.030	15	.052
04	.029	16	.051
05	.026	17	.051
06	.026	18	.052
07	.028	19	.050
08	.035	20	.047
09	.041	21	.045
10	.048	22	.043
11	.049	23	.040

Table 3-1 shows the traffic demand scale factors for each of the hours of the day. Figure 3-3 shows the hourly activity profile they represent ("prime-time" business hours are indicated by dark bars).* These are the same scale factors that we used when calculating your organization's traffic demand, earlier. Choose the entry for the hour of the day you are most interested in. Enter the scale factor on line 8.

Line 9 — Worst case scenario

Earlier, I suggested that with the worst case scenario, you might be lucky to cull 25 percent of the bandwidth you contracted from your Internet connection during the peak hours of the day. The number has some empirical basis; I have seen that kind of bandwidth from poorly equipped connections. If you can agree with my

* These figures were derived from traffic data through MAE-East.

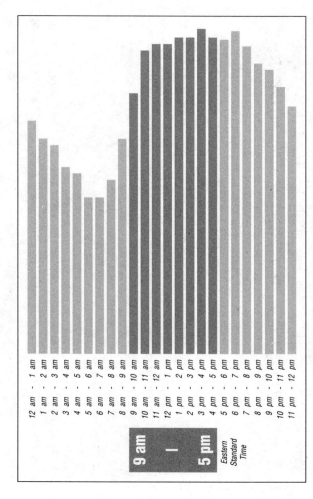

Figure 3-3: Internet loading by time of day (East Coast)

estimate, place .25 on line 9. Otherwise, choose your own number.

Line 10—Multiplier

Now, taking the value on line 9, the scale factor for the peak hour in Table 3-1 (.051), and the worst case penalty total (86), we will come up with a dimensionless multiplier for the penalties you tallied in line 7. Calculate the multiplier as follows:

```
multiplier = (1 - line_9) / (86 * .051)
```

Enter the multiplier on line 10. From this, we can make a simple linear projection of the available bandwidth for each hour of the day (this figure stays the same for all of the hourly calculations).

Line 11—Your connection bandwidth

Enter on line 11 the bandwidth you will be purchasing, e.g, 56 Kbit/S (56000).

Line 12—Available bandwidth

To estimate the available bandwidth for the hour in question, choose the appropriate scale factor from Table 3-1. Combine this with the bandwidth allocation and penalty factors according to the equation below:

```
available_bandwidth(hour) = line_11 - line_10 * scale_factor(hour) * line_7 * line_11
```

Record the result on line **12**. We now have a crude way to estimate the spare bandwidth available for each hour of the day. Most people will be interested in the peak (10:00 a.m.).

How well does the figure in line **12** compare with the result from Appendix B, your hourly total traffic demand? For those with Internet access providers who are well connected, the penalty won't be too unbearable (check the price, though). Others may find that they counted on far more bandwidth than the proposed connection can spare. I hate to admit it, but it wouldn't surprise me; many providers are squeezing their networks pretty hard. So if your budget is tight, I'll just point out that during the peak hours of the day, the Internet gets pretty sluggish. And since nobody expects stellar performance from the Internet at midday, you will be forgiven if access to your information is a little slow.

Contracting for an Internet Connection

Think of yourself as Mommy or Daddy, conducting a family trip to the carnival. You have to budget money for fried dough, watch out that the "carnies" don't turn the children into bearded women and elastic men, and pre-approve the outhouses. A lot of forethought and contingency planning takes place on the way. Eventually the station wagon lurches to rest in a rutted parking spot—the Internet connection comes up—and all of the wild-eyed kids spill out of your corporate network and into the world. They play with wild abandon, blissfully unaware of the time you spent grieving over the details.

Contract Basics

Here is the arrangement in a nutshell: The ISP provides you with Internet service, and you pay them money. The contract will probably say little in terms that you recognize; the language is typically devoted to requirements, terms, conditions, losses, and limitations of the service. It may furthermore enumerate a variety of one-time and monthly charges. I have seen more than one case where the Internet connection was delayed while lawyers waded through contract articles. In the next few sections, we will go over some of the most common clauses.

Term

Contracts for full-time Internet connectivity are usually drafted in increments of years, and usually offer discounts for multi-year commitments; the longer the commitment, the softer the rate. For example, a two-year contract may discount 10 percent annually from the cost of a one-year connection. The danger here, of course, is that Internet access rates are falling anyway; even with a 10 percent discount you may end up paying more next year than you would if you merely renewed at the end of a year. I'd cast a wary eye on multiyear commitments.

From the ISP's point of view, the monthly or quarterly fees you pay help to amortize a portion of the start-up costs. This may be particularly true if the ISP includes equipment in the deal; they expect your payments to retire the cost of equipment over the first year. For this reason, you probably won't find a clause that allows you to opt out after a month, or a quarter. From the ISP's point of view, you are liable for a full term of payments on the original schedule you agreed to. Don't sign if you aren't sure. Also, don't be surprised if the access provider requests credit details for your organization. Lots of small outfits are getting into the Internet business, or springing up specifically to be part of the Internet. Since fees are predicated on a term of service, access providers are looking for assurance that your company will be around for the duration.

In some cases, the first quarter's fees—or even the whole year's—are required up front. Other payments are made according to a schedule, and may include finance charges if late. Typically, the contract will contain a sixty-day cancellation clause. Consider that even if you have a beef with your ISP, and feel justified in withholding payment, they have to pay the exchange carrier for the circuit (probably); it costs money to have you connected, even if you aren't using the service.

Requirements and restrictions

In addition to terms, the contract will probably contain several paragraphs detailing requirements and guidelines that *you* are to follow. These might cover equipment selection, the environment in the wiring closet, payment schedules, and restrictions on certain types of network traffic, including use of the network for unlawful purposes.

Note that every network carries an *Acceptable Use Policy* (AUP), which describes the nature of the traffic allowed to cross the network. Some parts of the Internet fall under AUPs that restrict commercial activity. This is particularly true for those sections that are funded by governments, for research and education. Your connection through an ISP is unlikely to carry any such restrictions, though your exchanges with remote sites residing on restricted networks may be (technically) subject to policy. In general, you don't have to worry about commercial activities; your ISP will route over portions of the Internet with AUPs that allow commercial traffic.

Redistribution

One common restriction sometimes takes people by surprise: most contracts disallow bandwidth redistribution; you may not extend Internet service to any other organizations through your connection. This is a tough bit of news for somebody running a BBS with an idea that they would like to open up access to the rest of the world. An Internet connection is an expensive proposition anyway, but it gets even more costly when one wants to redistribute bandwidth—typically four to six times the cost of a private connection. Furthermore, most national ISPs don't offer redistribution privileges at any price—particularly at the low end of the bandwidth scale. Local, hometown ISPs may be more liberal on the issue; they often sell bandwidth without restrictions.

Where redistribution restrictions exist, people sometimes craft ways around them. The contract may clearly state that an Internet connection is being sold to a single organization. Members of the organization may use the connection; others may not. The word play comes in when one defines the "organization." The organizational lines of a business are clear-cut, for instance. But what if one is a member of a "club"? Can the club arbitrarily accept new members, and give them Internet access? How does the club differ from a BBS? The lines get pretty fuzzy here. The right thing to do is get a clarification from the service provider up front, before buying the connection.

Losses

Networks are complex beasts, with lots of interdependent functions. A seemingly innocent change in a routing table can break a reliable connection halfway across the planet. Understandably, Internet service providers are loath to guarantee your Internet access. Particularly, they won't be willing to warrant the service against the million-dollar business losses you might claim if the connection were to break at a critical instant. Contractually, losses are usually limited to the value of the service, and only apply to the connection between your site and the ISP's functional network. In other words, "if your connection is down for a day, we'll give an extra day, gratis." Of course, this is cold comfort if the Internet is a critical piece of your business plan. The best defense is to choose your provider wisely.

Charges

How much will all this cost? We already took a stab at representative costs in Chapter 1, *Getting Connected to the Internet*. But as we have been seeing ever since, you may choose options beyond the basic suite, and that will change the figures. Furthermore, we haven't taken the time to perform a breakdown of basic connectivity charges; some ISPs itemize multiple subfees. It's a little silly to worry about them in our case, perhaps; you are going to pay the bottom-line price whether there's a breakdown or not. However, the subfees start to make sense if you one day pursue something beyond a basic Internet connection—say, a company WAN of which Internet connectivity is just one component. In a few spots, we will talk about material we haven't covered yet; some of the physical circuit concepts are expanded in the next chapter.

In addition to circuit and basic Internet service fees, we will also account for the support and service options we discussed in the previous chapter. The goal is to develop a simple spreadsheet that you can use for quantitative comparison of ISPs.

Physical circuit

Circuit costs will be a combination of one-time fees and recurring charges. This includes the costs of data communications equipment, and any extra circuit installation charges. Fees for use of public-data-network-flavored data link protocols (e.g., Frame Relay) may ultimately either be paid to your exchange carrier or be buried within your ISP's rate schedule, depending on who operates the network. Additionally, public data network charges may include assessments for information rate commitments, independent of the physical circuit speed (see Chapter 4 for more details).

Table 3–2: Circuit Costs

Item	Unit Cost	Multiplier	Item Total
Network Termination Unit		(one-time)	
CSU/DSU or Mux		(one-time)	
Special Construction Fees		(one-time, if applicable)	
Circuit Installation		(one-time)	
Monthly Circuit Fees		**x 12**	
Public Data Network Install		(one-time, if applicable)	
Flat Monthly Public Network Fee		(if applicable) **x 12**	
Monthly CIR Fee		(if applicable) **x 12**	
Port Install Charge		(one-time, certain ISPs)	
Monthly Port Fee		(certain ISPs) **x 12**	
Internet Service Install		(one-time)	
Monthly Internet Service		**x 12**	
Subtotal			

Table 3-2 summarizes common circuit costs. Some items may not apply to you, either because they are covered by your ISP or because they are associated with a technology that you are not using.

The first line is reserved for network termination equipment. The nature of the equipment will vary, depending on the speed and technology of your Internet connection. DDS or T1 termination units, for example, regenerate an incoming electrical signal, before applying it to your CSU/DSU. SONET OC-3 (155 Mbit/S) network termination equipment, to take a completely different example, recovers an electrical (STS-3) signal from an optical carrier. Usually, network termination equipment belongs to the exchange carrier, and is covered in the circuit cost. An exception might be if you are connecting over a private circuit, and are required to provide your own network termination equipment.

The next line represents CSU/DSU or multiplexor costs. If you are leasing, these costs may either be exposed to you, or buried within your ISP's service fees; often the ISP rents the equipment for an unstated price. In other cases, you are responsible for purchasing your own CSU/DSU—a one-time charge.

Special construction fees, line 3, apply when you have asked the exchange carrier to bring a digital line into an area where service is not yet available or imminent. These fees can be substantial, and may even sink your plans for an Internet connection.

One-time and monthly circuit fees, lines 4 and 5, cover the cost of the physical connection between you and your ISP, or between you and a public data network. If your local exchange carrier (telephone company) operates the public data network, the circuit and network fees will typically be bundled together. In other cases—where the ISP is operating its own private network using public data network protocols—the two fees may appear separately. Additionally, in the case of public data networks, there will be a charge for a service rate commitment. Often, commitments can be purchased in increments of 8 Kbits/S.*

Port fees, lines 9 and 10, apply to dedicated, point-to-point circuits. The "port" is a serial router interface that the ISP provides for your Internet connection. Port fees don't (shouldn't) appear on quotes for connectivity through carrier-operated public data networks. With a public data network, the ISP needs just a single connection into the network in order to supply Internet traffic to multiple customers; you shouldn't be charged for a port that others are sharing.

Internet service and support

Internet "service" arrangements can vary from a simple, unadorned pipe to a secured, managed connection. We discussed the possibilities in the previous chapter. Service options appear in Table 3-3.

---

* Many carriers' Frame Relay networks are not (yet) heavily utilized, meaning that there is plenty of bandwidth available. Frame Relay allows users to burst beyond their committed information rates, to take advantage of any spare network capacity. Companies have been signing up to Frame Relay networks with committed information rates of 0 Kbit/S, since they "always" have some capacity to spare. It's cheaper and (provided the network *remains* underutilized) just as good as a more expensive connection.

Table 3-3: Service and Support Costs

Item	Unit Cost	Multiplier	Item Total
Internet Service Install		(one-time)	
Monthly Internet Service		x 12	
Domain Registration Fees		(one-time)	
Network Registration Fees		(one-time)	
Monthly Additional Routing Fees		x 12	
Monthly Nameserver Fees		x 12	
Router Configuration Fees		(one-time, if applicable)	
Monthly Newsfeed Charge		x 12	
Network Monitoring/Trouble Fee		x 12	
Security Maintenance		x 12	
Other Support Fees		(one-time)	
Other Monthly Support Fees		x 12	
Subtotal			

Internet service fees, shown on the first and second lines, are the amounts the ISP will charge for your Internet connection. There may be subservices bundled into the fee—such as nameserver maintenance or domain registration—that are impossible to break out separately. If that's the case, just count the bundled cost, and skip the associated line items below. Just be sure that whether you are comparing bundled or cafeteria-style proposals, you end up with the same general suite of services.

Lines 3 though 6 account for extra fees that some ISPs charge for network or domain registration, nameservice, and routing. Line 7 lists optional router configuration costs. Again, these may not be payable to your ISP; you may wish to hire a third party to configure your router. Newsfeed costs, monitoring, maintenance, and unaccounted for support fees appear near the bottom of the table.

In-house costs

In the previous chapter we talked about some other costs—a server, training, desktop software, your own time—that also need to be counted as part of the effort. Unlike the items in the sections above, which may vary with ISPs, the in-house costs should be the same, regardless whom you eventually go with.

Table 3–4: In-House Costs

Item	Unit Cost	Multiplier	Item Total
A Server	(one-time)		
In-House Installation Effort	(one-time)		
Training	(one-time)		
Desktop Integration, Software	(one-time)		
Server Maintenance		x 12	
Subtotal			

You will need to analyze your requirements, and assess your organization's familiarity with IP connectivity (and networking in general) in order to fill out Table 3–4. I can help with a few items. A server can usually be a PC or an orphaned UNIX machine; this should put the server cost in the $2,000 range. The time the in-house staff spends on installation should cost between $5,000 to $10,000, depending on aptitude and the complexity of the installation. Training can range from zero dollars to an astronomical amount; the size of the community makes all the difference. Likewise, desktop software can cost you nothing, or cost a small fortune, depending on whether you want freeware or commercialware. As with installation costs, server maintenance costs are partly a function of the complexity of the Internet applications you have planned.

Cost totals

The anticipated cost for the first year is the total of the three subtotals above—in-house costs, plus service and support costs, plus circuit costs. We collect them together in Table 3–5, below.

Table 3–5: First Year Estimated Costs

Item	Item Total
Circuit Costs	
Service and Support	
In-House Costs	
Total	

Of course, second-year costs will be considerably lower. You will have progressed along the learning curve; one-time fees will not recur. If you decide to switch ISPs, you can even migrate some of the one-time costs to the new connection. You won't have to pay for the server, the experience, the desktop environment, or perhaps even the data communications equipment, a second time.

4

The Circuit

Occasionally, I speak with someone who has either been pricing digital circuits from exchange carriers (phone companies), or already has a digital connection back to the phone company—often for voice communications. They ask: "I already have a digital circuit. What do I have to do to connect it to the Internet?" The question is a fair one; a circuit is certainly part of the picture. However, planning the digital connection apart from choosing a service provider is often a wasted effort. For one thing, you don't know where the other end of the connection has to go until after the provider is chosen. Furthermore, it may not be your job to requisition the circuit in the first place; Internet Service Providers (ISPs) often order local circuits on a customer's behalf, and pass the charges through as a line-item on the monthly bill.

There are exceptions, of course. For example, if your connection to the access provider is made through a public data network (frame relay or X.25), it may be up to you to link to the network, and from there connect through to the Internet service provider. And in the case of long-haul, high-speed lines, you will probably want to shop around.

Whether you're one of the exceptions or not, it helps to know how you are connected, and particularly what components go into your monthly bill. Once you have these things in hand, you can decide what options (if any) you might prefer.

LECs and IXCs

Who sells digital circuits? You might be surprised; your area may have a large number of competing exchange carriers. Naturally, the faster connections will cost more. However, rates also vary according to the nature of the circuit, the distance traveled, and, to some degree, the carrier chosen.

In the U.S., telephone companies have been explicitly permitted, prohibited, or required to provide certain services to end users, and to other carriers.

Furthermore, companies that provide local access have been forbidden from providing long-haul access, and vice versa (this is changing rapidly).* Ironically, this split will make understanding physical connectivity options a little bit easier for us. Because of the passing heavy regulation, we can more easily see where one service (say, long-haul) begins, and another (local) ends. When you look at other countries, the lines between services may be more or less apparent; the distinction between the equivalents of Interexchange Carriers (IXCs) and Local Exchange Carriers (LECs) may not exist, or be quite so obvious. However, many of the basic concepts we discuss here should be transferrable.

Why LECs and IXCs?

In 1984, the U.S. Federal government forced divestiture of AT&T, creating seven local Bell operating companies. Each was allowed to provide local telephone service but was prohibited from interexchange services, equipment manufacture, data services, and other markets. Likewise, the parent company, AT&T, was disallowed from reentering the local telephone market, but retained the ability to provide long-distance service. Other, preexisting local telephone companies came under much of the new regulation. The regional telephone companies are called *Local Exchange Carriers* (LECs). The regions they service are called *Local Access and Transport Areas* (LATAs). Long-distance companies are called *Interexchange Carriers* (IXCs or IECs).

Local Connections

Before we get too far into the subject, let's recall the objective: we need to run a wire from your organization's data communications equipment to the data communications equipment of your Internet service provider. If the two of you are within eyeshot, you might lay a piece of fiber or twisted pair cable beneath the asphalt separating you, and be done with it. More likely, however, you are going to rent some wiring from a company that does wiring for a business—the phone company.

In the simplest scenario, Figure 4-1, you and your Internet service provider are located close to one another; you both share access to the LEC's network through the same central office (CO). Two lines are run—one from each of you—and

---

* New legislation, including the *Telecommunications and Deregulation Act of 1995*, is opening up the telephone marketplace to new ventures, and less regulation.

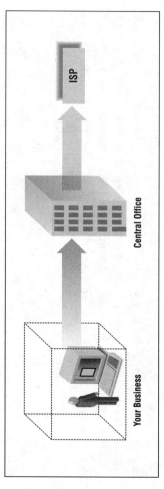

Figure 4–1: Local connection

permanently routed through the telco network. Two flat recurring charges will apply: the charge for your access to the CO, and the charge for the ISP's access (these circuit legs are called channel terminations).

Connections Between COs

For more widely separated connections, as in Figure 4-2, we will add another leg to stretch the circuit between central offices. This will introduce a new, distance-sensitive component to the monthly bill; in addition to the termination charges, your bill will reflect a separate tariff* for channel mileage (or kilometerage, I suppose). The farther apart the endpoints, the greater the charges will be.

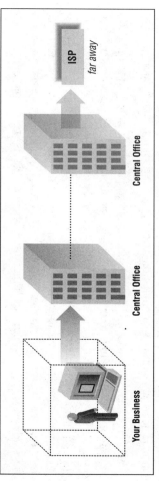

Figure 4–2: Connection to a more distant ISP

Note that in both scenarios—this and the previous one—we are asking the same LEC to connect you to the Internet Service Provider. Naturally, for this to be possible, the LEC has to serve a geographical area containing both of you (the *Local Access and Transport Area*, or LATA). Suppose, however, that you are bringing in a connection from a location far away, not serviced by the LEC. In that case, you

---

* Exchange carriers file *tariffs* with regulatory bodies, proposing rates for particular services.

will need the services of another kind of exchange carrier—an Interexchange Carrier (IXC).

Connection Through an IXC

One of the tenets of the legislation of 1984, and its subsequent updates, is that LECs must accommodate IXCs. In particular, if a long-distance telephone company wishes to make its services available through the local telephone company, that wish has to be satisfied; LECs do not have the right to deny interconnection. Furthermore, LECs are required to provide a uniform level of connectivity to all comers. This will prevent a LEC from favoring one IXC over another. In some cases, the interconnection is physically located on the LEC's premises.

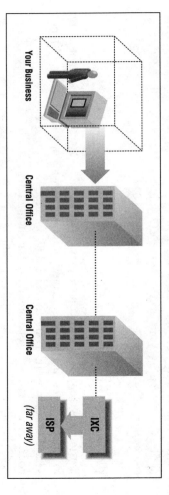

Figure 4–3: Internet connection through an IXC

As an example, say that you will be connecting through an IXC (examples are LDDS WorldCom, Sprint, MCI, etc.) to a remotely located Internet Service Provider. The first requirement is that the IXC have a presence through an LEC central office within your LATA—hopefully somewhere nearby. Your connection to that ISP will go through a *special access* unswitched circuit, that begins with your LEC, crosses the LEC's network to an interconnect with the IXC, and then makes the long-haul run to the other side. Traversal of the remote LEC network takes place in reverse.

Several charges come into play: as before, you have to pay the LECs for channel termination—both between the final destinations and the closest CO, and between a (possibly different) CO and the IXC, as shown in Figure 4-3. Also as before, these are flat-rate charges. On top of that, you have to pay the LECs for channel mileage between COs. Last, you will have to pay distance-sensitive IXC charges for the long-haul connection.*

---

* Note: when you are contracting for Internet service, there can be other charges too, such as "port" charges. We'll get to these later.

CAPs

The LEC is involved with your connection because they own the wiring out in the street and up on the poles. If you want to connect to your IXC, you have to go through the LEC. One of the reasons for the intense regulation of LECs is that the wiring provides the basis for a monopoly; if other companies aren't allowed to sell services through the LEC's wiring, they won't be able to compete for your business.

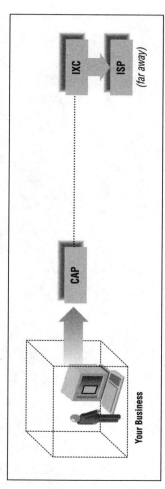

Figure 4–4: Connection directly through a CAP to an IXC

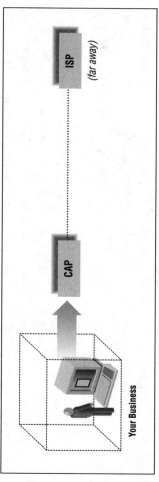

Figure 4–5: Connection directly through a CAP to an ISP

In some metropolitan areas, it is possible to hire yet another kind of carrier, called a *Competitive Access Provider* (CAP) (or *Bypass Carrier*), to provide links between your office and your IXC (Figure 4–4), or even directly to your Internet Service Provider (Figure 4–5). CAPs operate private networks, independent of the LEC, with wires run through everything from abandoned mine shafts to sewers to telephone poles, and up and down the glass and concrete towers of central business districts. CAPs are not subject to the same level of regulation as the LEC, and have much greater flexibility in negotiating connections. When shopping for a long-haul connection, you should seek out CAPs in your area. They may save you a bundle.

Public Data Networks

In addition to dedicated line data services, most LECs operate public Frame Relay, SMDS, or ATM networks, as depicted in Figure 4-6. These provide a "cloud" through which you can exchange traffic with another office, or with a (nearby) Internet Service Provider.

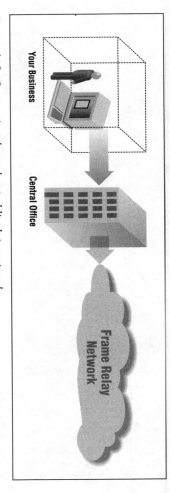

Figure 4-6: Connection through a public data network

Depending on your locale, the connection tariff may be fixed—you may pay one price for access to the network (at a certain speed), regardless of the starting point (provided that the customer is within the network service area). Or you may pay for an access circuit with a mileage charge—just like a regular DDS or T1 connection, except that the circuit has only one access leg. Public networks can be a bargain. And, for the time being, the load on many of these new thoroughfares is low; you can get a lot of performance for the price.

Connection Type

As you can see, there is a variety of possibilities. Most of the circuits we discussed above were *point-to-point*, meaning that we could find two distinct terminations for the connection. Only the last scenario was significantly different; with public data networking, we share physical networks with others. In graphic terms, our connection to the circuit disappears into a cloud.

Of course, you and your prospective ISP will have to use the same network strategy; the methods you choose for trading data must be compatible. We haven't talked about data link protocols yet, but let me suggest that you can often look at the protocol specified by the ISP to predict which kind of data circuit you will have to buy. If you will be connecting via HDLC, PPP, or even SLIP, for instance, then the circuit is definitely going to be point-to-point. In a logical sense, you will have to hire the phone company to string a data line from here to there—"there" being the location of the access provider's POP.

If the link protocol is Frame Relay, on the other hand, then a connection into the telco's shared network is often all the physical connectivity you will have to buy. I need to warn you, though, that there's a little bit of grey area; you might purchase Internet service that is described as "Frame Relay," yet still have to buy a point-to-point link. It's not that there's some disagreement over what constitutes Frame Relay service. Rather, the ambiguity has to do with the location of the network. Some access providers operate *private* Frame Relay networks; you may still have to purchase a point-to-point link out to their POP, before you can jump into their shared network.

Circuit Parameters

Of course, we should be able to say a bit more about the circuit than where it terminates. We also need to describe its speed and specify how data will be encoded and framed for transmission. Naturally, both ends of the link have to be compatible and match the capabilities of the terminating data communications equipment.

Bandwidth

Table 4-1 shows some common connection speeds. Interestingly, many of the kinds of connections you may consider will be adaptations of voice channel circuitry to the job of carrying data. A 56 Kbit/S DDS (Dataphone Digital Service) line, for example, is actually a single 64 Kbit/S voice channel.* *Clear 64* is another (fairly rare) single channel connectivity option that, unlike vanilla DDS, provides the full 64 Kbit/S channel bandwidth. Likewise, the two B channels of an ISDN connection are 64 Kbit/S voice channels. We call this basic 64 Kbit/S rate of speed *Data Speed 0*, or DS0.

Faster connections, such as T1 (DS1) and T3 (DS3) lines, are groupings of DS0 channels. In a T1 circuit,[†] 24 channels provide a total bandwidth of 1.536 Mbit/S, or 1.344 Mbit/S of usable bandwidth (on a 1.544 Mbit/S connection), depending on line encoding. Similarly, European and Asian E1 circuits are composed of 32 voice channels, providing a total 2.048 Mbit/S. A 43 Mbit/S T3 circuit (44.736 Mbit/S, nonchannelized) is built from 672 voice channels. Effective data rates on T's of more than 64 Kbit/S are possible because data communications equipment *multiplexes* information across multiple 64 Kbit/S channels, to combine bandwidth.

You may sense a jagged granularity to the units of bandwidth offered by these circuits; speeds make an abrupt jump from 64 Kbit/S (DS0) to 1.54 Mbit/S (DS1), and beyond. It makes sense when you consider the underlying purpose; DS1 and DS3

---

* The missing 8 Kbit/S goes toward line synchronization, as we will see in Chapter 14, *Physical Networks*.

† To be precise, DS1 is the speed. T1 is DS1 multiplexed over copper.

links form trunks for bundling telephone conversations together and ferrying them from place to place. You might prefer an intermediate speed for your data connection—say, 256 Kbit/S. However, you will still have to purchase a circuit providing *at least* the bandwidth you need, plus the bandwidth you *don't* need—enough to bring you up to the next closest raw increment.

Table 4-1: Common Circuit Speeds

Label	Data Speed	Circuit Speed
DDS	9.6 Kbit/S - 56 Kbit/S	64 Kbit/S
Clear64 (DS0)	64 Kbit/S	64 Kbit/S
B-ISDN	64 Kbit/S * 2 + 16 Kbit/S	144 Kbit/S
Fractional T1 (AMI)	56Kbit/S - 1.288 Mbit/S	1.544 Mbit/S
Fractional T1 (B8ZS)	64Kbit/S - 1.472 Mbit/S	1.544 Mbit/S
T1 (DS1) (AMI)	1.344 Mbit/S	1.544 Mbit/S
T1 (DS1) (B8ZS)	1.536 Mbit/S	1.544 Mbit/S
Inverse Multiplexed T1	N * 1.536 Mbit/S	N * 1.544 Mbit/S
T3	43.008 Mbit/S	44.736 Mbit/S
OC-1	49.536 Mbit/S	51.84 Mbit/S
OC-3	148.608 Mbit/S	155.52 MBit/S

As an example, say that you are planning a 256 Kbit/S (fractional T1) link to the Internet. You will pay the ISP proportionally less for the traffic (hopefully). However, you are still going to have to purchase a T1 circuit. This is because the difference between full T1 service and fractional service isn't a function of the speed of the physical connection. Rather, it has to do with choices programmed into the data communications equipment. *Fractional* T1 or T3 service utilizes just *some* of the available channels; you are going to have to purchase a full "T" regardless. The equipment on both ends of the connection agrees on which channels are ignored (or used for other purposes, such as voice), and which are designated for data. From these, a fractional link is assembled.

As you might guess, there are actually ways to extend bandwidth beyond the basic increments. ISDN subscribers, for instance, often *bond* channels together to create a faster circuit. Similarly, for connections beyond DS1 speeds, it is sometimes an option to *inverse multiplex* T1 lines; several T1 circuits can be combined side by side to provide an N * DS1 speed connection. Scaling quickly comes into play, however. DS3 speed circuits are only about four to six times the cost of a DS1 speed line; at some point you would make the jump to T3.

Data Link Rate Commitments

Often, when we talk about a fractional "T," we are also considering a point-to-point data link protocol (such as PPP or HDLC), joining the endpoints together. The formula for deciding how much service you can expect through the connection (at least through the last leg) is straightforward: the maximum bandwidth of the link is the same as the physical circuit speed. If you have a T1 connection, you should expect T1 connectivity across the link. Likewise, if you order fractional "T" service, your point-to-point bandwidth will be some multiple of 64 Kbit/S, less than the circuit maximum of 1.544 Mbit/S.

Frame Relay, SMDS, and ATM connections provide an additional twist to the notion of subrate service. As above, you might contract for less-than-circuit-speed Internet traffic. However, the restriction may be imposed by data link protocols, rather than by the physical circuit; performance is a function of a software-enforced, *committed information rate* (CIR). I might, for instance, purchase a 256 Kbit/S frame relay link, to be provided over a full T1 circuit. The good news is that if the network is generally quiet, I can zoom ahead of my committed rate and take advantage of a rate ceiling (maximum burst rate), possibly extending as far as the speed of the physical network. If the activity level is high, on the other hand, the network is allowed to discard some of my traffic in order to keep control over congestion; my guarantee only extends up to the committed rate.

Anyway, to reiterate: data link protocol-enforced bandwidth limits are soft; my traffic can burst beyond the subscribed rate to either a burst rate or the full capacity of the "T" (provided the downstream network has bandwidth to spare). A physically limited, fractional "T," on the other hand, has no such ability to burst beyond the programmed data rate. There can be hybrids too, as you might guess. You *could* use data link protocols such as Frame Relay or ATM over fractional "T"s.

Encoding and Framing

Circuit speed can depend on other parameters too, such as line *encoding*—the method by which data are represented on the wire. In North American DDS and T1 circuits, the common encodings are AMI (*alternate mark inversion*) and B8ZS (*binary 8 bits with zero supression*). Each delivers a different effective circuit bandwidth as a function of its ability to provide data, and to maintain synchronization with the remote end of the connection. E1, in Europe and elsewhere, uses an encoding method called B3ZS (*binary 3 bits with zero suppression*). T3 circuits use B3ZS too. ISDN connections use an interesting encoding scheme known as 2B1Q (*2 binary, 1 Quaternary*) that stuffs two bits into each bit-time.

Framing is the method by which data communication equipment marks data boundaries, and buries status information within the bit stream. The framing can be simple, as with the single channel of a DDS connection, or more complicated, as with a multiplexed "T." North American T1 links are generally framed using methods known as ESF (*Extended Super Frame*), or D4 (or Superframe) channel bank framing. T3 circuits conduct traffic using M13 multiplexor framing, or newer, C-bit Parity framing. Very-high-speed optical links use a variety of framing methods, though SONET optical framing is the one we care about most.

Encoding and framing techniques are interesting by themselves (*I* think). We will explore them in Chapter 14. On the more practical side, however, it is important that you know which options describe your physical connection. These will be dictated by the circuit you choose, and must be supported by the equipment you buy.

Data Communications Equipment

Several pieces of data communications equipment will take up residence on your end of the link. Physical ownership of the equipment depends on the arrangement you have with your Internet access provider. In some cases, the Internet service provider leases pieces as part of the service. In others, subscribers are required to supply their own equipment. In many cases, the subscriber's choice is limited to the brands the access provider is familiar with; you will need to settle the brands issue at the outset.

DDS and T1 Equipment

As depicted in Figure 4-7, DDS or T1 connections will have the following three pieces:

- Network termination
- A CSU/DSU
- A router

The *network termination unit* is a device that the exchange carrier installs on-site—typically within a wiring closet. It regenerates the signal coming from the street and aids in running diagnostics on the carrier's physical network. The device belongs to the exchange carrier; you don't have to pay for it.

The location of the network termination unit or wall jack coincides with an administrative boundary called the demarcation point, or *demarc*. With respect to the physical connection, everything outside—before the demarc—is the exchange carrier's responsibility. Everything after the demarc is your responsibility (or your Internet Access Provider's, depending on your arrangement).

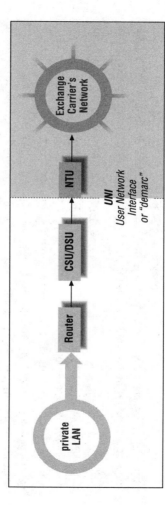

Figure 4–7: DDS and T1 physical network components

The next piece of equipment in the chain, the CSU/DSU (*Channel Service Unit/Data Service Unit*), isolates your network from your exchange carrier's network. It also recovers the timing, low-level framing information, and data passed from the network termination point. If the signal is multiplexed (like T1), the CSU/DSU recombines the channels into a single (or perhaps multiple) data stream. CSU/DSUs are specific to the general circuit type. A DDS CSU/DSU will not be interchangeable with a T1 CSU/DSU, for instance.

The CSU/DSU, in turn, sends a synchronous data stream to the router—into a *serial port*. The router interprets the data stream in accordance with the wide area networking protocol selected by the person who programmed it. It could be configured to expect one of a PPP, HDLC, or Frame Relay encapsulation, for instance. There will be at least one other port on the router, which will interface to a LAN of some sort—Ethernet, Token Ring, etc. Traffic from the serial port gets forwarded to the LAN port, completing your Internet connection. Of course, a lot more happens on the router as well. We will talk about router programming later on.

Note that it is possible that other kinds of equipment will fill or supplement the role of the CSU/DSU at your site. Really, one of the CSU/DSU's biggest jobs is multiplexing; your equipment might even be called a *multiplexor*. It's also possible that you will have a T1 *channel bank* in your wiring closet, for telephone service. Again, this is a kind of multiplexor. In some cases, it is possible to peel off one or several DS0 lines from the channel bank for data—particularly when the same company that provides your phone service will be providing your Internet connection.

T3 Equipment

A T3 link comes into your site on two coaxial cables—one for each direction of service. Assuming that you aren't multiplexing other kinds of information over the connection (such as voice or video) these cables terminate directly into your DSU (no CSU required). Otherwise, the T3 service might first be broken out by a multiplexor into component channels—say, multiple T2's—and then fed to a variety of devices upstream. It's also possible that you might order T3-speed (DS3) service, yet have it delivered over other media, such as microwaves or optical fiber, as in Figure 4-8. These would terminate into a device—a *terminal*—to be converted into a DS3 signal, and then to be fed into your DSU. Your DS3 service might even be delivered via SONET.

At T1 speeds, we hook the CSU/DSU and router together using a serial V.35 connection. At higher speeds, we often join the DSU and router via an HSSI (High Speed Serial Interface), or even a SCSI interface.

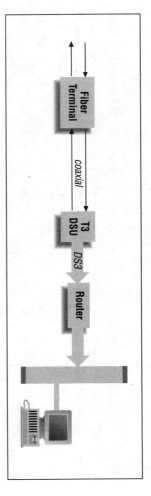

Figure 4-8. DS3 connection delivered via fiber

The sophistication of the DSU may depend somewhat on the kind of traffic you plan to move through it. With ATM and SMDS connections, the router and DSU *may* cooperate in managing the wide area networking protocol across the HSSI. The standard interface between them—called a DXI (data exchange interface)—splits responsibility for higher and lower portions of link processing. Proprietary exchange interfaces exist as well. It is also possible to have a clear digital connection between DSU and router; the router will manage the data link protocol without help from the DSU. We will explore these issues in detail in Chapter 14.

Ordering a Circuit

For most installations, the time it takes to get the physical circuit in place puts a lower limit on how fast you can get onto the Internet. You can get a CSU/DSU, router, and server in place within a couple of weeks, but exchange carriers often need a month and a half to get a line installed.

Dedicated connections are typically handled by the exchange carrier's business data services unit. You describe the kind of service you need, the endpoints, and in some cases the data link protocol. The framing and encoding methods have to be supported by the circuit, so one often learns from the carrier what these will be, rather than the other way around. At the same time, your carrier may ask for information describing your CSU/DSU. In particular, they may want to know:

- *Facility Interface Code*—this describes the CSU's framing capabilities—DDS, D4(SF), or ESF.

- *Service Order Code*—this describes the kinds of data representation the CSU supports (AMI/B8ZS).

- *USOC Jack*—the kind of jack (RJ48S, RJ48C, RJ48X) required.

The carrier may also wish to know the model, make, and FCC registration number for the equipment.

Be aware that if you plan to change circuit technologies in the future—say that you will one day be migrating from DDS to T1 service—this is essentially the same as canceling one circuit and ordering another. Only in those cases where you will be making incremental use of available raw bandwidth—say, moving from a fractional "T" to a full "T"—will you be able to preserve your circuit installation investment and reuse data communications equipment.

Monthly and one-time installation charges will be quoted according to a schedule, and may include a mileage component (see above). If you are ordering a longhaul circuit, the bill can include components from both companies—the LEC and IXC. There may also be special construction charges involved if the LEC has to make an extra effort to bring a circuit out to you.* These extra charges can be substantial, by the way; make sure that you are aware of them in advance.

An exchange carrier's business data services unit can usually generate a quote within a few days. If you wish to negotiate, understand that charges fall into two general categories: those that are set by tariff, and those that are set at the discretion of the carrier. As we saw earlier, tariff-derived charges are less negotiable—the carrier is charging set rates.

Data service, like telephone service, is provided on credit. If you are a new business, or if you haven't established a credit rating, the exchange carrier may require a deposit before the circuit is ordered. A little bit of advice from someone who has been there: don't assume that because you filled out the appropriate paperwork, the circuit will arrive on schedule. If your application gets hung up in accounting, you may not know about it for several precious weeks. Call and check on your own data circuit—even if it was ordered on your behalf by the ISP. Each circuit comes with an order number that you can use to track its progress.

---

* Businesses can be charged extra to cover the cost of running a circuit. Individuals typically cannot.

Router Configuration

Now that we've discussed the ISP and the circuit, we'll discuss how you make the circuit work. We'll start with the router, because that's the connection between your network and the rest of the world. Router programming can be one of the most intimidating parts of bringing up an Internet connection, particularly if you have never done it before. It's not that routers are exceedingly ugly, ill-tempered, or shoot sparks. The trouble is that, for most people, routers are a new experience. The programming environment is unlike any other, each brand is different, and the little available guidance is often burdened with acronyms and assumptions about your knowledge of the subject. At the same time, it is impossible to dismiss the need for some basic understanding; we have to know "something about network protocols" in order to program the router.

Unfortunately, "something about networking protocols" turns out to be more than hand-waving; the next chapters, 7 through 12, are devoted to programming the serial port alone. Understand, I neither want you to pop a blood vessel nor go off muttering in disgust. So before we go another step, allow me to provide a map of the chapters ahead (Figure 5-1), and make some suggestions about how you might approach the material. Setting out from here, the remainder of this chapter gives an overview of router programming, and provides a few concrete examples. In particular, we will look at configurations for cisco, Livingston, and Morning Star routers.* Even if you don't own one of these brands, the material should give you a taste for *how* a router might be programmed, and may even offer functional templates that you can follow.

Chapter 6, *OSI Networking Layers and IP*, provides a primer on ISO network layers and IP networking. Chapters 7, 8, 9, 10, 11, and 12 go into detail about the specific

---

* The decision to demonstrate these brands was arbitrarily dictated by those I had hanging around.

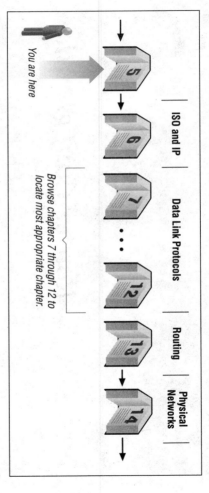

| ISO and IP | Data Link Protocols | Routing | Physical Networks |

Browse chapters 7 through 12 to locate most appropriate chapter.

You are here

Figure 5-1: Road map to upcoming chapters

network and link layer protocols that routers trade over serial connections. The material is necessarily detailed; consider that if you are going to program the port, you will need to understand what the router manual is telling you. The good news is that you will typically only need to understand *one* serial link protocol and *one* variety of physical network; the rest will apply to other peoples' connections. Therefore, unless you are especially interested in the spectrum of networking technologies, or fascinated by acronyms in general, you might want to focus on the material that applies to *you*, to the exception of the material that does not—for example, read one of the link layer chapters, and skim the rest.

Chapter 13, *Routing*, briefly discusses routing. Chapter 14, *Physical Networks*, talks about a variety of physical network technologies. Only one of these is likely to underpin your Internet connection. As with the link layer information, you might skim through Chapter 14 to find the technology that applies to you.

By the way, you may not actually have to program your own router; ISPs sometimes supply the equipment, in which case it usually comes preconfigured. Regardless, consider that if you own it, then you will one day want to tinker with it; it is a good idea to become acquainted with the router even if it isn't your job to get it working.

The Big Picture

Routers are devices that join logical networks together. Computers living on one network will forward traffic to a router in order to reach computers living on another.

In Figure 5-2, the PC labeled **X** on network **1**, for instance, would depend on router **A** to forward traffic to the PC **Y**, on network **2**. Similarly, if PC **X** needed to

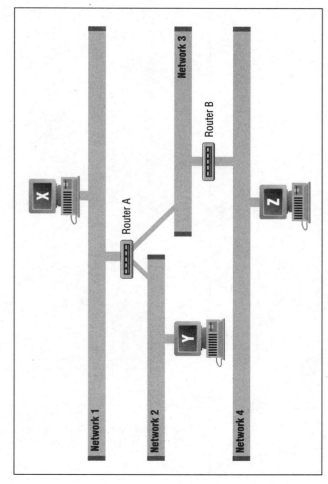

Figure 5–2: Routing between networks

reach PC **Z** on network 4, it would again forward traffic through router **A**. It would then be up to router **A** to further forward the traffic through router **B**.

Forwarding decisions are based on *routing tables*—lists routers keep that say "where to go next." Depending on how routers are configured, they may build their tables dynamically or by trading information with other routers, or the tables may be statically "wired" in advance by the administrator. Hybrids are possible too.*

From our point of view, the most interesting configuration looks like the picture in Figure 5-3. We have a LAN, connected through a router to an ISP's POP, and then out to the Internet. The router on the "near" side will have two interfaces (perhaps more). One will connect to the local LAN. The other will typically be a serial interface, connected to a CSU/DSU, and then out through a dedicated circuit to the ISP. Traffic through the serial port will flow over one of a variety of wide area networking or data link protocols. If you haven't considered them before, you might

---

* It is important to note that routing decisions are based on *network numbers*. This distinguishes a router from another device—called a *bridge*—which forwards traffic based upon low-level hardware (or "MAC") addresses.

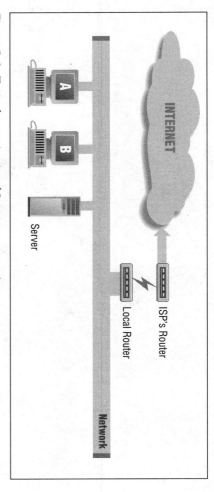

Figure 5–3: Typical organizational Internet connection

be surprised to discover that so many protocols could be so different from one another:

PPP

A point-to-point, multi-protocol link technology, in use over every conceivable medium. PPP endpoints can negotiate network parameters, and, optionally, can authenticate their peers as communications proceed.

X.25

A "reliable" public data network technology featuring private virtual circuits, virtual calling, and per-packet charging. Though generally operating at slower rates than some of the other serial interface protocols we will consider, X.25 is ubiquitous in many parts of the world.

HDLC

Both a point-to-point and multi-party link-layer technology, HDLC provides reliable, acknowledged transfer across dedicated links.

Frame Relay

This is a cost-effective, lightweight, many-to-many, medium-speed, virtual-network, link-layer technology. Frame Relay is supported by almost all exchange carriers (telephone companies), and most of the private networks of some ISPs. It's tunable too; bandwidths are a function of the protocol and can be changed repeatedly over the life of the circuit.

ATM

This is virtual circuit, fast packet technology. Traffic of all kinds—data, voice, video—is chopped into 53-byte cells, interleaved, and conducted over very high-speed media. The bandwidth, behavior, and destination of each virtual circuit can be tuned.

SMDS

SMDS is a high-speed metropolitan-area networking technology that behaves like a LAN. Traffic is cut into 53-byte packets and distributed over a limited (typically) geographic area.

SLIP

SLIP is a simple data link protocol for conducting IP traffic over point-to-point links. SLIP is being rendered obsolescent by PPP. It's still frequently used for dial-in connections, but most new dedicated point-to-point links use PPP.

Other technologies that you might think belong in this list—ISDN, T1 connectivity, SONET—are actually physical network layers, and so would be paired with link layer or wide area network protocol from the list above. You might use PPP in combination with ISDN, for instance, or Frame Relay in combination with a T1 circuit. The pair you will ultimately settle upon is typically dictated by your ISP; you run what they run. If you haven't decided upon an ISP yet, you have the following luxury: You can decide whether to let the ISP choose the wide area networking protocol, or you can let the protocol choose the ISP.

Your router—situated between your ISP's network and your LAN—will need attention in four separate areas:

LAN Interface

The local network interface must be configured using an address from one of your registered IP networks and a network mask that matches that of the other equipment sharing the segment.

Serial Interface

The serial interface must use the same data link protocols (as in the list above), and the same encapsulation method as the remote (ISP's) router. Depending on the protocols chosen, you may need to program logical circuit identifiers, and associate these with IP addresses. This can get a little complicated; we cover serial interface protocols in upcoming chapters.

Routing

The router needs to know where to forward every packet that washes up on one of its interfaces. The simplest configurations use static routing—routing tables are manipulated by the administrator. More complicated installations employ dynamic routing—routing updates are traded between locally connected neighbors.

Access Lists

A router should be secured to discourage unwanted or malicious traffic. We accomplish this with access lists that sort out traffic on the basis of source, destination, and type.

The last item—access lists—is covered conceptually in Chapter 16, *Internet Security*, and by example in Appendix A. The first item—programming the LAN interface—won't demand any more mental effort than setting up a network interface for any of the other devices on your LAN; you need to choose an address and network mask, and perhaps a frame type (e.g., 802.3 or Ethernet). Again, the syntax may be foreign, but the networking elements will be familiar. We will see examples later. As for the remaining two topics—serial link protocols and routing—well, that's what the next eight chapters are about. For now, let's see what these beasts look like.

A Few Sample Router Configurations

Let me start by admitting that we are getting a little bit ahead of ourselves; the configurations below make use of concepts and terms that we haven't discussed yet—virtual circuits, point-to-point connections, default routes, and more. Still, I think it is important to get a glimpse of the finished product, before wading into theory. Keep in mind that you can always visit this section twice—once now, and once again after looking at the later chapters.

Some routers have rich command sets; there can be many ways of asking one router to do the same thing. Likewise, there can be a choice of programming interfaces. Many can be programmed via a Telnet session; some (Bay, cisco, Livingston, to name a few) have optional PC or X-based configuration GUIs; some (such as Imatek) use front panel configuration. In the next few pages, we will visit the command-line programming environments for a few router brands—namely Morning Star, Livingston, and cisco. Again, this may not provide enough detail for you to avoid looking at the manual or the chapters ahead. But it will give you a feel for the kinds of things you need to tell a router (any brand).

cisco

Let's start with cisco and a bare-bones configuration for a 2500 series router, running feature set 10.3, IP support only. Router environment and electrical requirements will be packed with the router; I will assume that you can provide space and power. For the data connection, the router needs a serial cable with a special connector (ordered from cisco). The other end goes into your CSU/DSU with a standard V.35 connector (typically).

To initially program this router, connect a terminal to tty port 0 and apply power. Upon first boot-up, the router will offer a set of configuration questions, including host name, addresses, etc. You can go through the setup questions if you like; this will get you most of the way there. Or, you can skip the questions and program the router manually, as I have done in the following section.

The cisco router's command interface has two basic levels: an unprivileged mode, and a privileged, "enabled" mode. You first connect to the router without configuration privileges, as evidenced by the prompt, for example "Router>". To enter the privileged mode, type **enable**. The new prompt should be similar to "Router#". A password may have been set, in which case you will have to enter it before being allowed to proceed (try "cisco"). Whenever you wish to return to the previous mode, type **exit**.

Individual cisco router configuration commands may be global—applying to the whole router—or specific, applying to a particular interface. When programming, you'll change levels often—briefly narrowing your focus to, say, the Ethernet port, or a serial port, and then popping back up for a more global view. Likewise, the commands that you enter when configuring a particular interface will be specific to that interface. Here's an example of a command that sets a port's IP address:

`ip address 198.252.200.1 255.255.255.0.`

No particular port is implied; we already selected an interface before setting its IP address. If we make a mistake, we can back out gently; the negation of most commands is "*no <rest of command>.*" For instance, the inverse of the above command would be:

`no ip address 198.252.200.1 255.255.255.0.`

If you're in a jam, you can always type **help**, or enter a "?" to view the possible completions for a command in progress.

To edit the configuration, you would type **conf t** from enabled mode. The prompt would change to Router(config)#. At that point, you could make configuration changes that apply to the whole router. To address a particular interface from within configuration mode, you would type **int** <*port selection*>. For example, one might enter "**int e 0**" to address Ethernet port 0, or "**int s 0**" for serial port 0. Similarly, real and pseudo terminal lines are addressed as **line** <*port selection*>, for example, **line vty 0**. To leave an interface, or to exit configuration mode altogether, you would type "**exit**."

```
!
version 10.3
!
hostname Router
!
enable password cisco
!
no ip domain-lookup
!
interface Ethernet0
 ip address 198.252.200.1 255.255.255.0
!
```

```
interface Serial0
ip address 192.168.10.118 255.255.255.252
!
interface Serial1
no ip address
shutdown
!
ip route 0.0.0.0 0.0.0.0 192.168.10.117
!
line con 0
line aux 0
line vty 0
 login
 password cisco
line vty 1 4
 login
 login
!
end
```

In the preceding example, we see a simple cisco router configuration. We begin by assigning an address and network mask to Ethernet port 0. On serial port 0, we choose cisco's implementation of HDLC as the encapsulation method (High-Level Data Link Control, explained in chapters ahead). You don't actually see HDLC specified; HDLC is the default.

Notice that we specified a particularly narrow network mask when setting the serial port's address. This mask defines a subnetwork with just two usable addresses—"117" and "118." The practice is common for point-to-point links. Consider that only two addresses are necessary, one for each end of the link. Next, we add a default route. And last, we set a password for the console, and then enable a login. The following sequence of commands will program the configuration above:*

```
Router> en
Router# conf t
Enter configuration commands, one per line. End with CNTL/Z.
Router(config)#enable password cisco
Router(config)#no ip domain-lookup
Router(config)#int e 0
Router(config-if)#ip address 198.252.200.1 255.255.255.0
Router(config-if)#ex
Router(config)#int s 0
Router(config-if)#ip address 192.168.10.118 255.255.255.252
Router(config-if)#ex
Router(config)#ip route 0.0.0.0 0.0.0.0 192.168.10.117
Router(config)#line vty 0
Router(config-line)#line vty 0
Router(config-line)#password cisco
Router(config-line)#login
```

* You may also need to bring the interface(s) "up" the first time you use them. When addressing interface serial 0, for example, issue the command **no shutdown** to bring the interface "up."

```
Router(config-line)#ex
Router(config)#ex
Router#ex
```

Provided that you are happy with the configuration, you may save it to nonvolatile memory by entering **wr** at the (config) prompt. Likewise, you can verify the saved configuration by typing **wr t** (write terminal). For the record, I should mention that I wouldn't use the router configured this way—there are no access lists; the router is not secured. We will look at access lists in Chapter 16.

Morning Star

Morning Star Technologies manufactures multi-protocol routers that have become popular solutions for Internet connectivity. The product line has several router styles, including single and dual Ethernet "firewall" versions. The idea behind the "firewall" routers is that you might hang a Web server off one Ethernet port and protect it with one set of access lists, then connect your LAN through the second port and protect it with a second set of access lists. Some stand-alone Morning Star routers save their configurations to flash memory. Others use a floppy. As with the cisco router, you perform initial programming of the Morning Star router through a serial port and a terminal session.

The programming environment is UNIX-like; there is a directory containing boot and configuration files, such as would be found in /etc on a UNIX host. Likewise, configuration changes are made with a text editor, then scratched to RAM, to be further committed to flash memory or floppy when satisfactory. The following example shows the contents of bare-bones copy of *rc.boot*, the boot-time configuration file for a Morning Star Express router. In this case, we are connecting a single PVC through a Frame Relay connection (more about this coming up).

```
ifconfig lo0 127.0.0.1
ifconfig enet0 198.252.200.1 netmask 255.255.255.0
frd addr 192.168.11.11 netmask 255.255.255.0 56000 tty0 ignore-cd
arp -s 192.168.11.1 tty0:101
route add default 192.168.11.1
inetd
getty tty1 38400 nowait respawn timeout 60
```

Other portions of the Morning Star programming environment—access lists, specifications, routing protocol configuration, passwords, etc.—live in their own configuration files. Like the *rc.boot* example, these are edited and saved into the UNIX-like filesystem.

Livingston

Livingston Enterprises, Inc. routers have also become a popular solution for full-time Internet connectivity. The company manufactures several varieties of *Portmaster* products, including a dual Ethernet "firewall" router, conceptually similar to the Morning Star dual-Ethernet router, described earlier.

The Livingston router is fairly easy to program. The environment is (as usual) unlike the others we have seen; we don't change levels as router programming proceeds (like cisco), nor do we edit a configuration file (like Morning Star). Rather, fully qualified commands are entered one at a time, gradually approaching a completed configuration. Help is available at all times in VMS-style typed requests (e.g., *help set gateway* . . . .).

```
telnet <router>
ComOS - Livingston PortMaster

login: !root
Password: <return>
Command> set password passwd
Command> set ether0 address 198.252.200.1
Command> set ether0 netmask 255.255.255.0
Command> set ether0 routing off
Command> set s1 network hardwire
Command> set s1 address 0.0.0.0
Command> set s1 destination 192.168.12.100 255.255.255.0
Command> set s1 protocol PPP
Command> set s1 mtu 1500
Command> set s1 routing off
Command> set gateway 198.168.12.100
Command> save all
```

As with the other two routers, you would perform initial configuration of the Livingston IRX router through a serial port and a terminal session. As an example, the above commands program a statically routed, full-time PPP connection. Again, we will expand on the configuration in upcoming chapters.

Other Brands

If you skimmed through the configurations above, you should have started to notice a common configuration pattern. The only missing step is access lists, which we will cover in Chapter 16. For most installations, the steps will be the same:

1. Set the LAN Interface address.
2. Set the serial interface's data link protocols, framing, and endpoint identifiers (if applicable).

3. Set up a static route pointing to the access provider's router.

Of course, it's very easy to state the steps so plainly. But I also know what it's like to be mired in a confusing command set, a difficult manual, or an impossible technology. The best defense is knowledge, so let's forge into the chapters ahead, get some background information, and help you set up the serial port.

6

OSI Networking Layers and IP

Your router documentation's wide area networking sections will talk about OSI concepts like *link layer* and *network layer* protocols (so will I). We have to develop these definitions in order for our upcoming discussions to be meaningful. It is also important to understand a little about IP networking. Accordingly, we will approach IP by example. We will look at Internet Protocol (IP) operating on a LAN, starting with applications, and working our way down to the wiring. This will make it easier to identify those IP components that are portable to a wide area network—and those that have to stay behind on the LAN.

The OSI Reference Model

The universal standard for network comparison is the OSI reference model.* It describes seven peer-protocol layers, as shown in Figure 6-1. The idea is that all primitive networking functions can be ascribed to one of these layers, and that a carefully crafted set of protocols might be able to stack neatly, such that you could swap out functions at one level without modifying any of the others.

Furthermore, because the complexity of lower layers is hidden from higher layers, network peers could conduct a conversation at the same level, yet remain bliss-fully ignorant of all that lies below. An application, operating at the top layer,

---

* The *Open Systems Interconnection* (OSI) Reference Model is a product of the *International Standards Organization* (ISO), a group of government and private standards bodies, formed in 1946 to promote international standards. The model itself is nearly two decades old. At one point, there was a degree of industry commitment to migrate to a set of OSI-based local area networking protocols and applications, partly because of a U.S. government (DOE) requirement (GOSIP) that vendor products comply with OSI standards. For various reasons, including the complexity of OSI-based protocols, and the suitability of existing protocols (such as IP), plans for wholesale migration to OSI-based LANs collapsed in the early 1990s. However, many components of the networking effort are still active, including X.500, X.400, and link-level protocols.

Figure 6–1: OSI reference model

might say: "Here's the letter 'E'. Send it to my friend." Layers below worry about how the information is to be prepared for transmission (Should it be encrypted? converted to a neutral format?), how the conversation is being conducted (virtual connection? connectionless?), where the message should be forwarded next (routing), how to encode the data for transmission, and how to access the physical network.

    <link hdr><net hdr><trans hdr<...<'E'>...>trans trailr>net trailr>link trailr>

As a consequence, the message becomes more and more encapsulated as it works its way from top to bottom; each layer (perhaps) adds its own envelope to the data passed from above. If we stick a probe on the physical medium (network), we might see the letter 'E' fly by, sandwiched between the headers, flags, checksums, and trailers of each layer it has traversed.

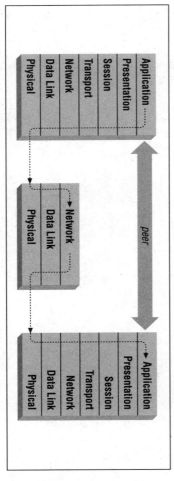

Figure 6–2: Networking traffic through an intervening gateway

The reverse process takes place at the destination; the encapsulation added by lower levels is stripped off until the message finally arrives at the peer—"Here's the letter 'E'."

Figure 6-2 illustrates how a message might traverse the protocol layers as it moves from an application on one host to an application on another. In this scenario, the message comes to rest briefly on a host en route between the source and destination hosts. There, it scales a few protocol layers—a couple of skins of encapsulation are shed, and then immediately grow back. The picture reflects a simple path between two networks connected through an intervening gateway.

IP Networking

We care about the OSI model because many of the technologies that we will discuss are described in terms of this model. At the same time, we care about IP networking, because that's what we are trying to do—move IP traffic from one place to another. We're in a little trouble: IP layers don't map directly to the OSI reference model. IP has four layers—a process layer, a host-to-host layer, an internetwork layer, and a network access layer. If you looked at the two models side-by-side, they would line up roughly as shown in Figure 6-3.

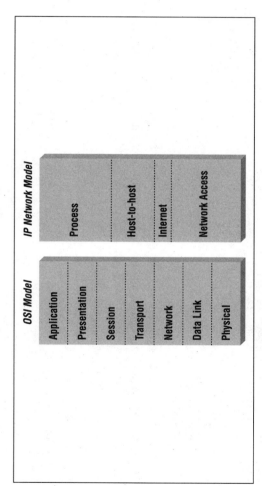

Figure 6–3: OSI model compared with IP model

The trick, then, is to be able to map what we need to know about wide area networking protocols onto what we need to know about IP. I can't think of a better way to approach the problem than by example. Accordingly, let's take the scenario above, and look at how the letter 'E' might be sent from one host to another through an intermediate gateway, via Internet Protocols on an Ethernet LAN. When we're done, we should be able to see how IP and the OSI model relate to each other. As a by-product, we should get an inkling about which parts of IP operating on a LAN are transportable across the link between routers. You may scratch your head part way through, but hang on. This is going to help make the upcoming chapters make sense.

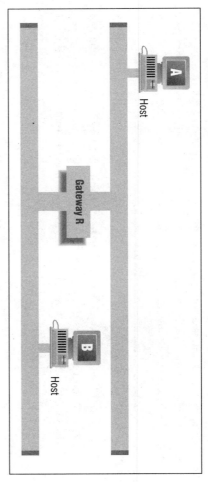

Figure 6–4: Two hosts, A and B, separated by gateway R

Our letter 'E' starts its journey from within an application (say, *Telnet*) running on computer A, as depicted in Figure 6-4. In OSI terms, it works its way down to the transport layer, traveling through presentation and session layers on its way to the bottom. As we have seen from the OSI/IP diagram above, IP networking doesn't have presentation and session layers *per se*. However, intermediate manipulation of the data, such as conversion to an external data representation, or a cursor mapping, could take place within the application. Or perhaps the connection might be check-pointed, or the characters might be grouped for block transfer, as part of the terminal line discipline. In an OSI-conforming network, these could be presentation layer and session layer functions, respectively.

TCP

Once we reach the transport layer, we can again find some common ground between the OSI model and IP networking. Our example application, Telnet, uses the TCP transport in the host-to-host section.* Assuming that we have already established a connection, Telnet hands the 'E' to TCP, which encapsulates it within a *segment* that begins with a TCP header. The header includes fields for source

---

* Generally speaking, we could choose from a number of IP transports, although the most likely choices are *TCP* (Transmission Control Protocol) or *UDP* (User Datagram Protocol). TCP is a *connection-oriented* transport protocol. Applications wishing to communicate via TCP must first establish a connection with an application running on a remote host. TCP service is *reliable*; data arrive in order and don't get lost. UDP, on the other hand, is an example of a *connectionless* transport protocol. There is no formal connection establishment, nor does the transport protocol intercede to guarantee delivery. In either case—TCP or UDP—we identify the participants by *port numbers*, so that once a datum arrives, it can be directed to the appropriate application. See Chapter 16, *Internet Security*, for more discussion of IP transport protocols.

port number, destination port number, checksum, sequencing, parameters and options flags. The last portion of the segment contains the data—the letter 'E.'

```
<TCP header<'E'>>
```

TCP bundles the segment together with a little more information that details the recipient host IP address, the sending host IP address, the transport protocol (TCP), and the segment length. TCP then hands the package to IP for delivery.

There's a little more going on here than packet diagrams explain: in hand, we have a message bundled within one of several possible transports (TCP, UDP, some less common protocols). In TCP's case, the transport provides the illusion of a reliable, stream-oriented network. The underlying IP network layer, on the other hand, carries no such guarantees;[*] it will be up to the TCP layer to keep track of the data sent and received, and to pester IP to redeliver segments as necessary.

IP

As we move from TCP to IP, we start to cross over into the parallel OSI network and IP internet layers, as shown in Figure 6-5. IP has its own header format—separate from TCP—which includes delivery options, control information, checksum, and source and destination IP addresses. There's also fragment information; the original TCP segment may have been fragmented so that the IP *datagram* will be within size limits. A field within the header describes whether the IP datagram contains a fragment, and where it would fit at reassembly time.

```
<IP header<TCP header<'E'>>>
```

Yet another field within the IP header describes the kind of transport the IP datagram is carrying—TCP in our case. This is necessary so that IP knows which transport protocol to hand the encapsulated segment to when it reaches the other side. Should the segment be handled by TCP, UDP, etc.?

The IP header does *not*, however, record the port numbers the applications are using—it doesn't care. Port numbers are a transport level concern; at this point they are buried within the encapsulated TCP header. Note that the IP (network) layer is often the point where we draw the line when preparing traffic for other types of media. The layers below may vary, although everything from IP upward often stays the same.

---

[*] It may be the case that *everything* is running on top of a reliable network technology—such as X.25—in which case IP will actually inherit guarantees from below.

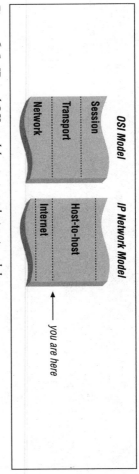

Figure 6–5: IP and OSI models compared at network layer

Routing

Here we have to make a decision: where to send the IP datagram next? If the IP destination address is on a directly-connected network, then the datagram can be hand-delivered to the recipient host. If, on the other hand, the destination is a remote network, then IP will have to locate a gateway through which to forward the datagram. Here's where *routing* comes into play.

Typically, the operating system keeps a table of destination networks, metrics (distances), and next hops along the way. This *routing table* is maintained either statically (by hand) or automatically (by *routing protocols*). IP checks the routing table to see where a datagram goes next—either to its final destination on a directly-connected network, or to a gateway, such as **R** in Figure 6-4.

Like a gopher poking its head out, to decide which direction to burrow, our 'E' message is going to climb its way back to the IP layer upon arrival at **R**. It has to. IP routing decisions are made at the IP layer; lower levels don't know about the routing table. Once the next hop—**B**—has been identified, the datagram will again descend protocol layers for delivery.

ARP

We're faced with a problem: The IP addresses are at too high a level for use over Ethernet. The question is: How do we translate the IP address we have in our hand into a low-level address appropriate for the network medium? Consider the difference between an IP address and an Ethernet address. The former is arbitrary; you choose an interface's IP address when you configure the machine's networking software. The actual network interface, on the other hand, has a unique *Media Access Control* (MAC) address, assigned at time of manufacture. We need some way to cross over from the IP address space to the medium address space—in this case, a way to map IP addresses to Ethernet addresses. We might do it via a table, or we might have a software (or firmware) mechanism for "discovering" the address mapping.

IP devices operating on Ethernet (and other selected media) discover MAC addresses by a mechanism called ARP (*Address Resolution Protocol*). Each host keeps a cache of the MAC addresses of devices it finds on directly connected networks. If one IP host wishes to communicate with another for which it has no MAC entry in its table, it broadcasts an *ARP request* containing the IP address it is trying to resolve. The host owning the IP address (or a proxy) responds to the broadcast with the matching MAC address. MAC addresses in hand, the two Ethernet-based hosts can now communicate.*

Datagram Delivery

As we concern ourselves with actually moving packets across the local area network, we start to cross into the IP network access layer, and soon into the OSI data link layer, as depicted in Figure 6-6.

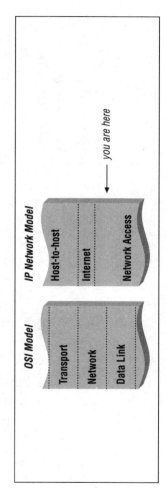

Figure 6-6: IP and OSI models compared at the data link layer

Our example assumes an Ethernet LAN, although the issues we must deal with are similar for many kinds of networks. To start, we have to think about how we will identify the contents of the datagram once it reaches its destination. We have already considered a similar problem when we talked about identifying which of several IP protocols a packet carried—TCP, UDP, etc. On the LAN, we have to be able to tell which of several protocols (IP, IPX, DECnet, etc.) a packet carries, and how the LAN is supposed to behave.

We have standards to fall back upon. The data link layer has two subdivisions, as shown in Figure 6-7: *Logical Link Control* (LLC) and *Media Access Control* (MAC). In the case of Ethernet, and many other networks, the LLC sublayer interface is specified by standard IEEE 802.2 (and later, ISO 8802-2:1989). The standard defines several common interfaces between higher-level protocols, such as IP, and the networks they will ride upon—Ethernet, Token Ring, and others. The idea is

---

* A host coming online may make an unsolicited broadcast of its MAC address, in order to seed other hosts' ARP caches.

Figure 6–7: Subdivisions of data link layer

that a higher-level protocol expecting to communicate through one of these interfaces will know how datagrams are to be packaged, and how the underlying network is supposed to behave. Furthermore, the IEEE 802.2 LLC interfaces are medium-independent; the underlying network may be one of several types (Ethernet, Token Ring, FDDI, etc.), but the LLC definition will be the same. This means that the same networking code can be used for all kinds of physical media.

There are four LLC network service abstractions. The one we care about, labeled *Type 1*, describes an unacknowledged, connectionless service; there are no return receipts, and data may be lost. On the surface, this sounds like a broken network, although in fact raw media behave this way. And LLC Type 1 matches our requirements for IP well. If reliable connectivity is desired, it can be provided by higher-level protocols, particularly TCP.

For the record, *Type 2* (or LLC2) is connection-oriented; a logical connection is formally established by participating nodes, and data transfers are acknowledged by receipts. *Type 3* describes a network that provides receipts but does not establish a logical connection. *Type 4* provides all of the above services together.

Within the LLC, we encapsulate multiprotocol data into frames, then label them with *service access points* (SAPs). These SAPs—source and destination—identify the protocols from which a packet has come, and to which a packet must be delivered upon reaching the other side. Just before transmission, your IP datagram will be encapsulated within an LLC segment—SAPs and all—and passed down to the MAC sublayer for delivery.

<LLC header<IP header<TCP header< 'E' >>>

SAP values are defined for a number of common upper-level protocols. However, in a few instances later in the chapter (though not in the current IP-over-Ethernet example) you will see a *SubNetwork Access Protocol* (SNAP) segment added as a supplement to link layer encapsulation methods (such as LLC).

```
<LLC header<SNAP header<user data>>
```

In the case of LLC, a SNAP segment is used when no SAP definition exists for the encapsulated user data protocol. In general, this might occur for one of several reasons: standards organizations haven't agreed upon a SAP identifier for the upper-level protocol in question; there is no room in the SAP field for another protocol value; or perhaps you are working with something nonstandard and need your own access point. SAP definitions are universal. SNAP header information, on the other hand, can be local to your organization—it can be tailored. I tell you this because it comes up in the chapters ahead.

MAC Level Access and Framing

Now it's time to move the data across the network. At this point, we can ignore all vestiges of IP networking. We have a hardware-level MAC address for the destination host or for a gateway. We have some data—the IP datagram—though we no longer care about its contents. The whole job is to package the datagram into an Ethernet packet (a *frame*), and deliver it across the network.[*]

We are now at the bottom of the data link layer. As with Dante's Inferno and the higher networking layers, we have to package the data so we can cross to the next lower world. In the case of Ethernet, we start the frame header with a preamble— a sequence of alternating bits that will provide synchronization. Following that, we have a frame delimiter, source and destination (MAC) addresses, data, and a cyclic redundancy check for error detection.

```
<Ethernet header<LLC Header<IP header<TCP header<'E'>>>Ethernet CRC>
```

Again, all of the other segments we have assembled are embedded within the Ethernet packet, and within other segments—like Russian dolls, or the layers of an onion. The unbundling takes place when we reverse the process, and climb up through protocol layers.

---

[*] The name *Ethernet* refers to a standard published by Digital, Intel, and Xerox, in 1980. 802.3, an IEEE standard published later, modified the Ethernet specification slightly. The proposal was that those using Ethernet would eventually move over to accommodate the new standard. It never happened; you may find 802.3 traffic (typically LAN filesystems) mixed together with Ethernet traffic on the same network. People usually don't differentiate between them in conversation; both are colloquially called Ethernet.

Physical Layer

The ultimate object is to take the bits of the assembled packet and toggle them down the wire to the host waiting on the other side. There are two facets to the process: physical network access and data representation.

Access concerns the method by which we establish our right to transmit across the network. With a token ring network, for example, we wait for the "token" to come by before we are permitted to speak. Ethernet uses a less civilized access method called *Carrier Sense, Multiple Access with Collision Detect* (CSMA/CD). A host wishing to communicate across an Ethernet network first listens to see if another host is already transmitting. If it finds that the network is quiet, it sends its packet. At the same time, the sending host also listens to hear if somebody else might have taken the same opportunity to transmit. If two (or more) packets collide (become garbled), both hosts back off for a while, and then try again. Eventually, everybody gets an opportunity to say their piece.

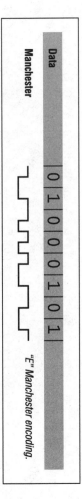

Figure 6–8: Manchester encoding

Data representation is the method by which we distinguish bits from one another. Naturally, the method depends partly on the medium. An optical fiber, for instance, would probably use varying light intensities or modulated frequencies. Ethernet is electrical; signals are bi-level—high or low. Bits are modulated onto the network using what is known as *Manchester* encoding, as shown in Figure 6–8: every bit-time contains a state transition. A "zero" bit contains a state transition from high to low in the middle of the interval. A "one" bit contains a low to high transition in the middle of the interval. In this way, every bit-time is guaranteed to contain a state change, which, consequently, provides a carrier—a signal that a receiving host can grab onto.

Why We Are Here

Okay, now I have you in the basement, watching water drip from the pipes. Why did I take you here? As I mentioned previously, I wanted to illustrate a few networking concepts, including encapsulation, address resolution, fragmentation, framing, and encoding. Though we may be looking at variations, all of these concepts are transferable to the wide area networks we will discuss. Furthermore, we will see situations where we have to make choices in features like encapsulation and framing, or have to play games with ARP in order to make a network function. I had to define these concepts so that I could discuss them in the chapters that follow.

Most important, I wanted you to understand what happens to IP at the various protocol layers. Particularly, I wanted to provide a glimpse of the reasons why the higher layers—TCP, UCP, and much of IP—can remain untouched across the range of wide area networks we will discuss. Though we may repeatedly swap out the pieces on the bottom, your computers will have no idea whether their IP traffic is being routed over Ethernet, or two cans and a string (and that's good).

PPP and SLIP

When you think of PPP (*Point-to-Point Protocol*) or SLIP (*Serial Line Internet Protocol*), dial-up connectivity probably comes to mind. That's because both protocols have been widely used for part-time Internet access over analog modems. However, there is nothing inherent in either protocol that requires the connections to be temporary; SLIP and PPP can be used for full-time links as well. SLIP is becoming less common; it lacks the nifty link negotiation features that are part of PPP. However, it works, and you *can* use it—even between routers.

Both protocols, PPP and SLIP, are solutions for two-ended links—site **A** connected to site **B**, as shown in Figure 7-1. This makes them suitable for any kind of two-ended physical network technology—analog modem connections, connections between routers over leased lines, and even for ISDN. Other possibilities exist too: PPP traffic can also be conducted over virtual circuits, such as an X.25 connection, or a Frame Relay link, described in upcoming chapters. The basic requirements are the same: the number of participants must be fixed at two, and the link must be full-duplex. According to some reports, PPP is becoming increasingly common in these high-end applications.

PPP

The object of the game is to move network traffic—particularly IP in our case—from one end of the link to the other. PPP does this by encapsulating network layer protocols, such as IP, IPX, DECNET, etc., within its own frames, then ferrying them transparently to the other side. Once there, the traffic is unbundled and sent on its way. To the user of a particular protocol (say, IP) a PPP link appears to be for their exclusive use. In reality, PPP packets of many flavors may share the link; multiple protocols can be active simultaneously.

How PPP Works

A PPP link establishes itself in phases. The connection begins with an exchange of *Link Control Protocol* (LCP) packets. These provide a mechanism for the two ends of the link to shake hands and agree upon link configuration parameters. They might decide the maximum length of a frame, for instance, or agree upon whether they will use compression for PPP frame elements. These LCP packet exchanges may continue—interspersed with data packets—for the life of the connection, to monitor (LQM), or to signal changes in the link's state.

Once the PPP link is established, it can be optionally authenticated. This might not be so important for dedicated digital lines. However, for dial-ups—where anybody can attempt a connection—an authentication ability built into the link layer is convenient. It provides a way for the network to reject unsolicited callers. Two separate authentication mechanisms are available: *Password Authentication Protocol* (PAP) and the *Challenge-Handshake Authentication Protocol* (CHAP). PAP is like a login password sequence—invoked once at the start of a session. The petitioning end of the link repeatedly sends the authenticating end an ID and password pair until the connection is approved (at which point the connection is established) or failure is declared, and the link is terminated.

The second protocol, CHAP, provides a stronger authentication mechanism. The volley starts when the authenticator sends its peer a challenge. Both participants calculate a response to the challenge. The authenticator then compares the response it gets from its peer with the answer it has generated locally. If the answers match, the authenticator sends a positive acknowledgment back to the petitioning end of the link. If not, the authenticator may (optionally) tear down the link. CHAP authentication isn't limited to the initial greeting; authentication can take place repeatedly within a single session.

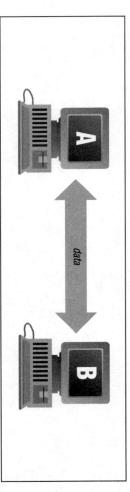

Figure 7-1: SLIP and PPP are for two-ended links

Having gotten beyond PPP link establishment and authentication, activity turns to the individual network layer protocols that PPP encapsulates. These may be many in number, but as a prerequisite each has to be represented by a *Network Control Protocol* (NCP), embedded within your PPP implementation. The NCP's job is to negotiate the protocol-specific particulars of the point-to-point link. Taking IP as an example, we might need to establish the addresses for the two link endpoints, or agree upon header compression options.

NCP chatter takes place in tandem with other traffic on the PPP link, and may occur all the time the PPP link is in operation. As new network layer protocols join in, their individual NCPs must likewise negotiate network connection, status, and layer-specific details.

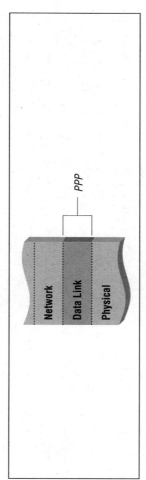

Figure 7–2: PPP operates at the data link layer

Eventually, we arrive at the end of the hors d'oeuvres. Once a protocol's NCP has established a connection, the two endpoints can trade traffic at the data link layer (Figure 7-2).

As I mentioned earlier, the various protocols that travel the link—IP, IPX, etc.—remain oblivious to one another. However, if you look at the whole picture, you will see multiprotocol exchanges, alongside LCP and NCP messages. Fields in the PPP header identify the protocol each data packet carries, and make it possible to break them out appropriately at the receiving end.

<PPP header><IP header><TCP header><data>>padding>

Okay, let's stop for a second and look at what we have. There's an encapsulation method: different protocols can be bundled into PPP segments. We have a link management protocol (LCP) (this is essential; it gives us a way to look out for the network's own well-being). Notice that we *don't* have any notion of PPP routing, or even PPP link addresses. This is the nature of the protocol. There are only two endpoints; link-level addresses aren't necessary.

The only things we are missing are techniques for framing data for transmission across the physical layer. A frame header and trailer will provide the necessary additional information that the endpoints need, to be sure that the data have arrived intact.

```
<Frame header><PPP header><IP header><TCP header><data>>padding><frame trailer>
```

As you might guess, PPP isn't dependent on any particular physical frame format; any standard that gets the PPP segments across the intervening network gap will do. However, the most commonly used frame format is a derivative of HDLC (described in an upcoming chapter), tailored for point-to-point links.

Vanilla HDLC is designed for synchronous networks only. But since PPP's adaptation has to run over synchronous and asynchronous networks (modems, in particular), the HDLC-like framing has been extended. To start, the PPP framing supports both bit and byte boundaries. Consider that modems operate solely on bytes—not bits; therefore byte boundary padding is required. Furthermore, PPP's HDLC-like framing has provisions for embedded flow control.

If you are using PPP for asynchronous communications, you will probably find that your documentation mentions an *asynchronous control character map*, used for escaping control characters. This will apply if, for instance, you are depending on XON/XOFF flow control between modems on two ends of the link. The danger is that either character—XON or XOFF—could be embedded within data passing through the link, which would cause them to be interpreted as flow control. The 32-bit asynchronous map describes, via bit positions in the map, which of the first 32 characters will be "escaped," and sent transparently through the link. An asynchronous map of 0xA0000,* for example, marks the 17th and 19th characters (XON and XOFF) for special treatment. Longer character maps (up to 256 bits) are possible too, although the receiving end of the link will limit its scope to the first 32. At any rate, it is important that asynch maps on both ends agree as to which characters are to be escaped, or whether asynch maps will be used at all.

Configuring PPP

When setting up a PPP link, you will need to choose values and settings for a number of parameters. I can't describe the exact commands your router will use, although I can list a few common setting choices. In many cases, you can just accept the defaults.

Choose IP encapsulation

Depending on your PPP installation, IP encapsulation may be implied or enabled by default.

---

* 0xA0000 = 0b10100000000000000000.

Example—Livingston and PPP

The following commands depict a statically routed, full-time PPP connection through a Livingston IRX router:

```
telnet <router>
ComOS - Livingston PortMaster

login: !root
Password: <return>
Command> set password passwd                              (1)
Command> set ether0 address 198.252.200.1                (2)
Command> set ether0 netmask 255.255.255.0                (3)
Command> set ether0 routing off                          (4)
Command> set s1 network hardwire                          (5)
Command> set s1 address 0.0.0.0                           (6)
Command> set s1 destination 192.168.12.100 255.255.255.0 (7)
Command> set s1 protocol ppp                              (8)
Command> set s1 mtu 1500                                  (9)
Command> set s1 routing off                              (10)
Command> set gateway 198.168.12.100
Command> save all
```

We begin by setting the local Ethernet address and network mask. Next, we disable routing broadcasts to the internal network (assuming static routing on the local LAN). Then we tell the router that s1 will carry a hardwire (not a dial-up) link; serial port 1 (s1) is configured to use a V.35 connector on the back of the unit. On the sixth configuration line, we set the serial line destination address (192.168.12.100) and netmask to match the remote ISP's router. Notice that, in this case, we *didn't* set our own address (we used 0.0.0.0); instead, we learn the local address from the far router during PPP link negotiation (we could have set it if we liked). Starting at line seven, the protocol is set to ppp, and the maximum transfer unit (largest packet) is set at 1500 bytes. As last steps, we set up a static default route, and then save the configuration to nonvolatile memory.

Select IP addresses

PPP endpoints can operate with or without their own IP addresses, and each endpoint may choose independently. One possibility is that you could choose two addresses from a a distinct IP network or subnetwork—dedicated to the link between the sites. On the other hand, you may choose to "borrow" the address of another interface on the router, terminal server, or computer hosting the PPP software, and assign *it* to the link; the local side of the link could have the same address as the Ethernet port on your router, for instance. This conserves addresses and simplifies routing a bit. Yet another possibility is that you could assign the remote end of the link an address taken from your in-house LAN. This is a common method for connecting remote personal computers. You may choose to assign addresses dynamically—either via a script or via bootp (or DHCP) (not covered here). We also need to play a few games with ARP and routing. I will elaborate, addressing possibilities momentarily.

PPP fields compression

You may independently ask PPP to compress the frame's protocol field, or address and control fields.

Enable Link Quality Monitoring (LQM)

Each end of the PPP link may independently negotiate LQM to babysit the connection. LQM is based upon LCP exchanges, particularly *echo-request* and *echo-reply* commands.

Configure TCP header compression

TCP headers can be compressed at the endpoints, as long as both ends agree. Header compression is valuable when the TCP segment contains very little data. An example might be a keystroke from a Telnet session—the girth of the header is much greater than that of the encapsulated data; header compression helps.

Choose the MTU

The *maximum transfer unit* is a measure of the longest packet you will allow across the PPP interface. You might accept the default (1500 bytes). Shorter MTUs will bias a connection in favor of short, bursty communications (such as keystrokes) to the disadvantage of long packets, such as those that make up a file transfer. During link negotiation, the PPP endpoints will agree upon the ultimate MTU size.

Configure authentication

Not all PPP implementations support CHAP or PAP. However, you may want to look into connection authentication.

Configure or disable asynchronous character mapping

If you are using PPP over a modem line, you may choose to configure asynchronous character mapping (described above) to escape flow control characters. If using hardware flow control, on the other hand (recommended), you will probably want to disable asynch character mapping.

Demand-Dialing

PPP connections over dedicated links will establish themselves automatically, under LCP. However, dial-up connections (including PPP over ISDN) begin with a phone call. You may need to configure a telephone number and a *chat* script to place the call, and log into the remote server. Likewise, you will have to configure time-out criteria to decide when an idle link should be closed down. This can be a little tricky; background activity—such as network time updates—have to be excluded from the list of services that keep the link alive.

As you know, PPP is a popular solution for remote networking of Macs or PCs. In practically every remote dial-up configuration, the link is set up so that the PC borrows an address from LAN on the other side of the access provider's router or terminal server.

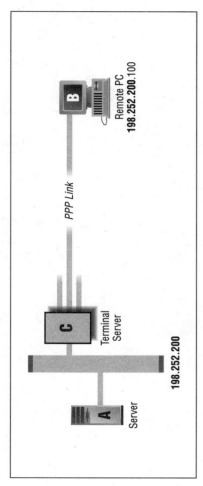

Figure 7–3: Connecting a remote node via PPP

Having a valid address isn't enough, however. We also have to play a few tricks on the LAN. For one thing, we need to manage the illusion that the remote PC is directly connected to the LAN. Referring to Figure 7-3, server **A** believes that it can hold a direct conversation with the PC **B** because both share the same IP network number. That means that the first time **A** wants to raise **B**, it is going to "ARP" **B**'s MAC address. The problem is that ARP depends on broadcasts, but broadcasts won't cross over to the serial link; **B** can't respond. But if **B** could respond, what would be the right answer to the ARP query? In other words, where should **A** send traffic in order to talk to **B**? The answer, as you can guess from the picture above, is that **A** should send its IP datagrams to **C** in order to reach **B**.

Because **B** can't speak for itself, some other machine on the LAN will have to respond to ARP queries on **B**'s behalf; another machine will have to provide *proxy ARP* for **B**. It could be the server (**A**), the terminal server (**C**), or any other machine on the LAN.

The actual commands you need to set up proxy ARP will depend on the host filling the role. On most UNIX machines, the appropriate command is:

```
arp -s <IP address> <MAC address> pub
```

The MAC address for Ethernet will be twelve hexadecimal digits, cut into groups of two, separated by colons (e.g., xx:xx:xx:xx:xx:xx). Other media will have different style MAC addresses. You can generally find the MAC address of the appropriate machine (such as C in the picture above) by typing:

```
ifconfig <network interface name>
```

on a UNIX host, or by typing the following command from another (different) UNIX machine on the same network:

```
arp -a
```

A table of recently ARPed MAC addresses will be produced. As a last resort, you can typically look at the network interface card to find the MAC address; there should be a label.*

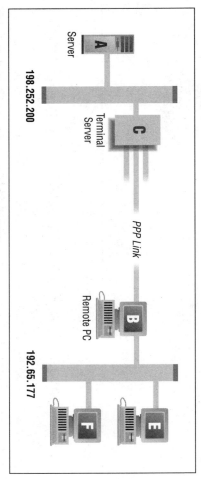

198.252.200

Server

A

Terminal
Server

C

PPP Link

Remote PC

B

192.65.177

F

E

Figure 7-4: Interconnecting networks via PPP

Perhaps you need to connect a larger community of users. Figure 7-4 shows several hosts—a network—on either side. The left-hand side of the PPP link is configured with C's address; the right-hand side has B's address; neither PPP endpoint has its own address. This can be a little confusing at first. If there were a separate subnetwork joining the computers, we would be able to compare this to a LAN, and immediately appreciate how it works. In this case, however, it might help to imagine that we start with a composite host, **C-B**, made of Silly Putty, then pinch it on both sides, and stretch it apart. The strings that remain are the PPP connection.

---

* Token ring users: be careful, the MAC address can often be configured by the administrator; the one written on the card may be incorrect. Check with the network card diagnostics.

SLIP

Serial Line Internet Protocol (SLIP) is different from PPP, particularly in terms of its limited scope: SLIP is solely for the transport of IP datagrams over point-to-point links; other protocols are not supported.[*]

The frame format (such as it is) is simple; there is no header, no error checking, and no protocol identifier. IP datagrams are merely fragmented, if necessary, and pushed down the serial link to the other side. If packets are lost, it is up to higher-level protocols (such as TCP) to recover. This might have been a tenuous proposition once; analog modems—a hang-out for SLIP—didn't come with built-in error correction. These days, the data returned from analog modems are error-free.

How SLIP Works

SLIP (rfc1055) defines four special characters: END, ESC, ESC_END, and ESC_ESC. The END character's function is simple: it marks the end of a packet crossing the SLIP link. The trouble is that the same character that stands for "end" might also appear in the middle of the SLIP conversation—as data. To guard against this possibility, ESC, followed by ESC_END, is substituted whenever END appears in the data stream. On the other side, they are reconverted to the original value. Likewise, the ESC character has to be protected; a sequence of ESC followed by ESC-ESC is substituted for it.

Configuring SLIP

SLIP is used mainly for dial-up IP networking over analog lines. It is less configurable than PPP, and lacks the built-in authentication and link management capabilities of PPP. However, in terms of performance, SLIP and PPP are similar. Let's look briefly at the parameters you may configure for a SLIP connection:

Select an IP address

Typically, you would assign the remote end of the link an address borrowed from your in-house LAN. You may choose to assign addresses by hand, or pass them out dynamically—either via a script or via bootp (or DHCP) (not covered here).

Configure TCP header compression

TCP headers can be compressed at the endpoints (rfc1144). Both ends must set/unset this option together.

---

[*] Technically, you could run other protocols over SLIP, either by encapsulating them into IP packets, or by running a separate "SLIP" link, carrying a different protocol.

Choose the MTU

The *maximum transfer unit* is a measure of the longest packet you will allow across the SLIP link. You might accept the default (1006 bytes). Again, both ends must agree.

Demand-Dialing

You may need to configure a telephone number and a *chat* script to place the call, and log into the remote server. Likewise, you will have to configure time-out criteria to decide when an idle link should be closed down.

As with PPP, we also need to play a few games with ARP and routing. That is, we need a host on the LAN to agree to provide proxy ARP for the remotely-connected host, and we need to place a default route on the SLIP client so that it can find its way back out. Of course, you may have more than a single host at the other end of a SLIP connection; whole networks can be linked together. The picture becomes only slightly more complicated. Look back at the discussion of PPP.

8

Frame Relay

Say that you have a large, geographically distributed company, or perhaps a data service that needs to reach customers over a broad physical area. In either case, the challenge is to link the central office to the branches or customers in a cost-effective fashion, and at reasonable levels of performance. There are two main ways to go about it. You could construct your own private network from point-to-point links—every connection would terminate back into the main office—or you could hop onto a shared service, such as an X.25 public data network. The problem is that option one is expensive, and option two is often slow (and sometimes expensive). This creates a window of opportunity for other kinds of pooled network technologies, particularly *Frame Relay*.

Frame Relay is a packet-switched,* link layer, wide area networking protocol. As with PPP, we think of Frame Relay connections in terms of point-to-point links, except that in this case the endpoints are *virtual*—two sites can *appear* to have a dedicated connection, but they may actually share networking hardware and wiring with many others. Furthermore, there can be many links terminating at the same port, as shown in Figure 8-1. This makes Frame Relay valuable in wide area networks with multiple participants; an organization can have a virtual many-to-many network, yet only have to purchase a single connection per office.

Each Frame Relay link is organized as a *permanent virtual circuit* (PVC), administered from a central Frame Relay switch, or switch network. A PVC is associated with one or more pairs of numerical *data link connection identifiers* (DLCI)—endpoints—that permanently identify a virtual path through the Frame

---

* *Packet switching*: data are blocked into segments and transferred across a network according to an embedded addressing scheme. Packets—units of data—interleave to share the network. Contrast this to a circuit-switched network, where the medium is held captive to a single data conversation as long as the circuit is open.

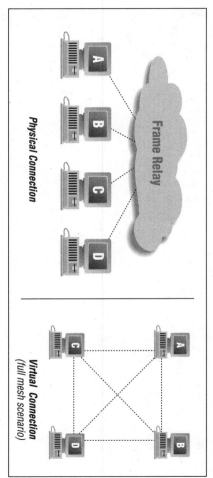

Physical Connection

Frame Relay

Virtual Connection
(full mesh scenario)

Figure 8-1: Physical versus virtual connections

Relay network. The path may simply be two connections serviced from the same Frame Relay switch (a pair of DLCIs, as shown in Figure 8-2), or it may traverse a larger, combined Frame Relay network; you can join multiple PVCs together.[*] The destination of a frame leaving your network is fixed in advance—there is no notion of "dialing around."[†]

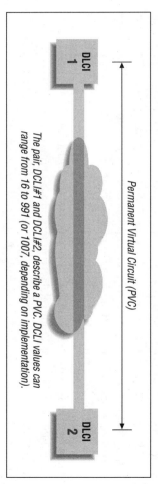

DLCI
1

Permanent Virtual Circuit (PVC)

DLCI
2

The pair, DCLI#1 and DCLI#2, describe a PVC. DCLI values can range from 16 to 991 (or 1007, depending on implementation).

Figure 8-2: DLCIs describe virtual endpoints

Each PVC can be configured with its own *Committed Information Rate* (CIR); the network will give priority treatment to a preallotted amount of bandwidth (if it's actually available . . .). Demand beyond the CIR is marked "discard-eligible"; traffic can be dropped on the floor at times when there isn't sufficient bandwidth to spare. If spare capacity *does* exist, on the other hand, a PVC can burst out beyond

---

* Frame Relay standards specify an interface only; a Frame Relay switch often "backs into" another flavor of wide area network, such as an ATM backbone.

† Frame Relay standards provide for a *switched virtual circuit* (SVC)—a connection that can make-and-break like a telephone call. However, SVC service has not established itself as a wide area networking alternative.

the CIR to the maximum rate available under the physical network connection, or up to a CIR ceiling. The CIR gives network users a way to enjoy some of the bandwidth guarantees of a dedicated circuit, plus some additional headroom, without sacrificing the economy of a shared network.

Current Frame Relay implementations operate at speeds up to 2 MBits/second. Upcoming implementations will operate at DS3 speeds. Frame Relay's variable frame size and rate commitment capability make it suitable for data traffic—typically LAN traffic. Frame Relay is not particularly suited to low latency or time-dependent traffic, such as voice or video—especially over congested media. However, companies have been using Frame Relay for these applications anyway. It's available almost everywhere, it works, and it's cheap; connections tend to be priced in a fashion that's independent of distance.

How Frame Relay Works

Frame Relay is an "unreliable" link technology, operating in the data link layer (Figure 8-3); the job of assuring data delivery is left to higher-level protocols. This actually suits Internet traffic well. If you consider that IP (and others) already has provisions for reliable delivery (TCP/IP), guaranteed exchange in the Frame Relay network would be redundant—and it would make the network perform more slowly.

Frame Relay packages data into variable length (HDLC-derived) frames. Each frame begins with a header that includes the fields needed for transmission over the physical layer: a flag to mark the start of a frame, the destination DLCI, and some control and discard-eligibility information.

<FR header<Information Field>FR trailer>

A trailer provides an error check for the data contained within the frame, and a flag to mark the end.

It takes very little effort to initiate a Frame Relay connection. Once the PVC has been programmed into the switch, any valid frame sporting a legal DLCI number will be transferred to the other side; no connection set up or negotiation is required. However, Frame Relay connections are usually conducted under control of an accessory *Link Management Interface* (LMI).

The Frame Relay LMI plays a role analogous to the LCP (Link Control Protocol) described under PPP. It can participate in link bring up, by notifying the remote end about an available PVC, or about PVC additions and deletions after the link has been established. The LMI can also provide diagnostics and a heartbeat, to verify that the link is operating. Consider that without the LMI, a lost PVC would look the same as a quiet connection, with no data transfer; you might not know a

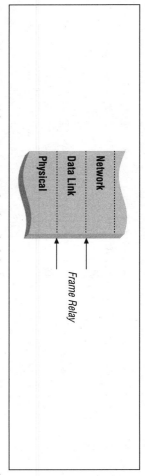

Figure 8-3: Frame Relay operates in the data link layer

failure had occurred. DLCI 0 (or 1023, depending on implementation) is reserved for LMI transfers between the user's equipment and the Frame Relay network. *

IP over Frame Relay

Frame Relay, as described so far, provides a mechanism for moving "stuff" across a PVC. The transfers don't have to be any more qualified than that;† we may use a PVC for any kind of data, as long as the timing requirements aren't too stringent.

However, there are mechanisms for encapsulating—and fragmenting, if necessary—multiprotocol data for exchange over an individual PVC. In the case of IP, rfc1490 defines the most commonly used method:‡ IP data are fitted with a special subheader that signals the presence and nature of the encapsulated information.

Figure 8-4: Rfc1490 encapsulation

Figure 8-4 shows the layout of an rfc1490 encapsulated IP datagram. Header fields (particularly the *Network Level Protocol ID* [NLPID]) signal that IP data are present.

```
<FR header><rfc1490 hdr><IP datagram><FR trailer>
```

---

* There are three different LMI specifications in use: specification, ANSI T1.617 Annex D, and ITU-T Q.993 Annex A. Choose one to match your provider's network.

† A device called a *Frame Relay Assembler/Disassembler* (FRAD) can be used to glue various kinds of data streams together across a Frame Relay network. Typically, a FRAD adds the "reliability" component left out of Frame Relay, taking care to buffer, acknowledge and retransmit lost frames.

‡ If using cisco routers, you'll find another—cisco-specific—encapsulation (default) method available.

Example—cisco and Frame Relay

This an example of a simple Frame Relay configuration on a cisco router. A single PVC is defined on serial port 0:

```
interface Ethernet0
  ip address 204.255.73.1 255.255.255.0
!
interface Serial0
  ip address 192.168.10.118 255.255.255.252
  encapsulation frame-relay IETF
  frame-relay lmi-type ansi
  frame-relay interface-dlci 101 IETF
!
interface Serial1
  no ip address
  shutdown
!
  ip route 0.0.0.0 0.0.0.0 192.168.10.117
!
line con 0
  password passwd
  login
```

The first two lines configure an Ethernet port on the local LAN. Then, we instruct the router to speak Frame Relay with rfc1490 encapsulation, and an ANSI-type LMI on serial port 0. This end of link is assigned a circuit end-point identifier—DLCI 101. The route command forwards all traffic destined for places other than the local LAN through the Frame Relay PVC.

Everything—NLPID, Control, and IP datagram—gets stuffed into the information field of a Frame Relay frame, then passed to the other side of the PVC. Once unbundled, it is up to the remote machine to dispense with the datagram as appropriate. Note that Frame Relay is a link-level protocol; any routing that has to take place is directed by higher-level protocols, such as IP. It might be an IP routing decision, for instance, that causes your traffic to take one PVC rather than another.

Configuring Frame Relay

Let's go over some of the parameters you might have to configure when setting up a Frame Relay connection. I won't cover all of the possibilities; particularly, I won't discuss SVCs. However, I will list relevant parameters for a typical PVC for routed Internet access.

Example—Morning Star and Frame Relay

This is a bare-bones Frame Relay configuration for a Morning Star Express router, borrowed from Chapter 5:

```
ifconfig lo0 127.0.0.1
ifconfig enet0 198.252.200.1 netmask 255.255.255.0
frd addr 192.168.11.11 netmask 255.255.255.0 56000 tty0 ignore-cd
arp -s 192.168.11.1 tty0:101
route add default 192.168.11.1
inetd
getty tty1 38400 nowait respawn timeout 60
```

We start by configuring the local loopback and local Ethernet interface. Line three invokes a copy of the Frame Relays daemon (frd), sets the local address (192.168.11.11), line speed, and interface (tty0); tty0 corresponds to the V.35 connector on the back of the unit.

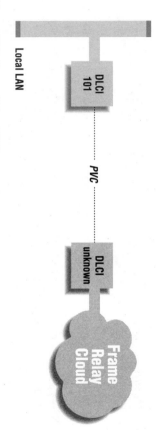

Figure 8–5: Frame Relay PVC

On line four, we seed the router's ARP cache to associate a Frame Relay DLCI (this is provided by the network operator or by the ISP) with a remote IP address (Figure 8-5). This way, whenever the router wishes to exchange traffic with the remote end of the serial link—192.168.11.1—the MAC address translation will refer to the PVC. Note that we don't know the DLCI at the far end. The Frame Relay switch keeps track of both DLCIs; the endpoints only need to know their own. Finally, we add the far end of the PVC as the default gateway. A few other commands follow—an invocation of inetd, and a getty (login prompt) for tty1.

Choose an encapsulation method

For routed Internet traffic, you will have to enable IP encapsulation, then choose an encapsulation frame type. Typically, you would make a selection corresponding to rfc1490 encapsulation.

Assign addresses and masks

Your end of the Frame Relay link needs an IP address and associated network mask. Often, access providers peel off a 2-bit subnetwork mask (255.255.255.252) for each PVC. This gives two usable addresses in a four-address subnet—the second and third (the first and last are reserved for broadcasts). One is assigned to their end of the link; the other is assigned to yours. A PVC runs between them. The address assignments will come from your access provider.

Assign DLCIs to the PVC(s)

Each PVC has a local DLCI associated with it, provided by your access provider. If you are running LMI, then you may not need to specify the DLCI; the Frame Relay switch can learn its DLCI from LMI messages. Note that you may have a reason to run multiple PVCs (e.g., one for general traffic, and one for USENET news); each needs a separate DLCI. Typically, one maps DLCIs to IP addresses.

Add an ARP entry

You may need to add an ARP entry to your router so that lower-level network protocols can "discover" the PVC assigned to the address for the remote end of the Frame Relay link. Again, the syntax depends on your router.

Assign a committed information rate

Each PVC has a CIR associated with it. No PVC should have a greater CIR than the capacity of the physical link. Choosing a CIR that is a fraction of your total link capacity gives you a way to play off one PVC against another; when a particular PVC exceeds its CIR, your data communications equipment will mark it "discard eligible," so that other kinds of traffic have preference.

Enable/Disable LMI

In most cases, you will want to run LMI to keep watch over the link, to assign DLCIs, and to return status. Again, there are several LMI schemes. Yours has to match your provider's.

Configure TCP header compression

You may wish to compress TCP headers. This will create slightly smaller frame lengths for TCP/IP sessions. Check with your access provider's settings.

As with PPP, you may also need to plant a static route on your side of the connection. This will direct internal traffic out to the Internet Frame Relay link. In some cases, your access provider may ask you to supply routing updates over the link. These may not actually be used to trade routing information. After all, the access provider doesn't expect you to be adding new networks without telling them. Rather, routing updates may be used to keep a vigil on your end of the link; their absence indicates that the connection has gone down.

Example—Addressless cisco Frame Relay

Here's another cisco router example. We are defining a single Frame Relay PVC on a subinterface of serial port 0:

```
interface Ethernet0
ip address 198.252.200.1 255.255.255.0
!
interface Serial0
no ip address
encapsulation frame-relay IETF
frame-relay lmi-type ansi
interface Serial0.1 point-to-point
ip unnumbered Ethernet0
frame-relay interface-dlci 101 IETF
!
interface Serial1
no ip address
shutdown
ip route 0.0.0.0 0.0.0.0 Serial0.1
!
line con 0
password passwd
login
```

The first two lines configure an Ethernet port on the local LAN, and assign an address for the router. Next, we turn our attention to the router's serial port. Frame Relay allows multiple logical circuits to terminate into a single physical endpoint. Correspondingly, we can take a single physical router port and treat it as if it is composed of a number of logical subinterfaces. This explains why you see settings for `Serial0` (physical), and `Serial0.1` (logical), above. If we had more logical connections terminating on the same port, we could configure `Serial0.2`, and so on. The subinterface inherits the settings of the parent, so our selections for the physical port also apply to the subinterfaces. Above, we have specified IETF/rfc1490 encapsulation (as opposed to cisco's encapsulation), and an ANSI-type LMI on serial port 0.

Next, we turn our attention to the subinterface, configure a Frame Relay PVC, and associate it with a DLCI (101). In this case, we are not assigning an address to the PVC. Rather, we will treat the endpoint as if it had the same address as port Ethernet 0. Similarly, on the *route* command a few lines below, we do not specify an address for the default route. Instead, we use the name of the subinterface that connects us to the ISP. This is called *addressless* port configuration. Note that we could have also used numbered endpoints. However, addressless configuration can be a convenience when you don't have spare network numbers for the link between routers.

X.25 and LAPB

Imagine, as we did at the start of the previous chapter, that you need to trade data with many partners. In fact, make it hundreds of partners. Perhaps you are collecting point-of-sale information from credit card units, or monitoring lottery ticket distribution. Again, there are two basic approaches for tying all of these partners back to your site: you could perhaps make hundreds of point-to-point links. They wouldn't even have to be full-time links; modems could intermittently dial your site and trade data. *Or*, each of the partners could locally jump into a public data network and forward information back through a *single* physical connection (at your end—one physical connection, many virtual connections).

Like Frame Relay, discussed in the previous chapter, X.25 provides this kind of many-to-many network connectivity.* The notion of Permanent Virtual Circuit (PVC)—a fixed, established path through the network—applies, as does the notion of a *Virtual Call* (VC)—an on-demand, "dialed" connection. However, unlike Frame Relay, X.25 extends farther up the ISO reference model ladder, into the network layer; traffic can be routed between X.25 nodes by X.25 protocols. There's flow control too. Furthermore, X.25 connections are "reliable"; packets don't get lost, and are guaranteed to arrive in order (this is a function of X.25's data link protocol—LAPB).

There's something you have to give up in trade for all of these features; flow control and reliable packet delivery require that the X.25 endpoints (and often the intermediate switches) acknowledge, buffer, route, forward, and possibly retransmit every frame that comes through. This slows data transfer and adds latency. If the network is wide—containing many "reliable" hops—the delay and performance penalties paid in exchange for reliable delivery can really add up.

---

* X.25 can be used in a point-to-point mode as well.

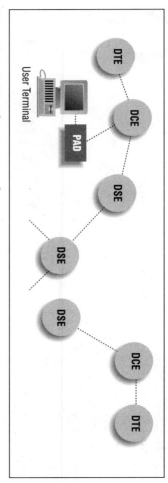

Figure 9-1: X.25 wide area network

"Why, then," you may ask, "do people use X.25 for IP connectivity—particularly if they could choose Frame Relay (or even ISDN)?" The answer is that X.25 has provided a solid and very featureful public data networking environment for a long time. The first round of X.25 standards is almost 20 years old, and the user community is large, especially in Europe. By the same token, X.25 networks have increased in performance over the years; modern X.25 connections run at speeds of 56 Kbits, 64 Kbits, and even 2 Mbits. Taken altogether, X.25 can still provide a cost-effective slow-to-medium-speed connection to the Internet. Service is ubiquitous in many countries, and hardware is readily available. One can more affordably trade smaller amounts of data with X.25. And X.25 can do things that Frame Relay is very new at—particularly on-demand, switched virtual connections.

How X.25 Works

The ITU-T (CCITT) "X.25 suite" of protocols details *interfaces* for three layers of the ISO model: physical, data link, and network (Figure 9-3). The standards are described in terms of *Data Terminal Equipment* (DTE) to *Data Communications Equipment* (DCE) connectivity (computer to modem) (Figure 9-2). The standards don't necessarily illuminate the network on the other side of the X.25 DTE-to-DCE connection; it could be anything. Consider that it doesn't really matter what's back there, as long as the connection to your equipment behaves as you expect it to. The preceding figure depicts intermediate hops as *data switching equipment*, or DSEs. In many cases, the intermediate hops (Figure 9-1) will share X.25 protocols (and an internal exchange standard, X.75). But again, X.25 is an interface standard; the internal network may well be built upon other protocols.

The physical layer interface for X.25—the wire—is described by standards X.21 or X.21 *bis*. This is roughly equivalent to EIA RS-232C running at a maximum speed of 19,200 baud (synchronous). Of course, this is pretty slow by today's standards. Accordingly, other media have been adapted to X.25 as well.

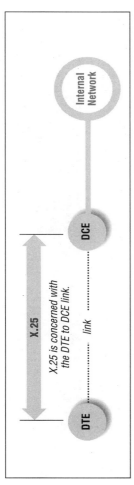

Figure 9–2: X.25 describes DTE to DCE link

The second layer—the X.25 data link layer—uses a protocol called *Link Access Procedure Balanced* (*LAPB*) is a relative of HDLC. The link level procedures and frame layout are similar to HDLC's (described below), so I won't duplicate the discussion here. The quality of LAPB that we care about is its built-in reliability; data delivery is guaranteed by procedures (acknowledge, retransmit, etc.) residing in the LAPB link layer. Compare this to the Frame Relay discussion in the last chapter: Frame Relay made no guarantees; it was up to higher-level protocols (such as TCP) to detect lost data and request retransmission.*

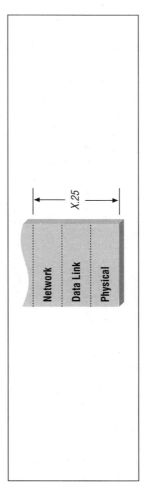

Figure 9–3: X.25 operates in the lowest three OSI layers

Let's stop a moment and see where we are. So far we have talked about a physical connection and a link layer protocol. These will get our traffic from the local network to the X.25 interface. We still need a mechanism for moving the data to someplace far away—across the public data network. This is where the third (network) layer of X.25—called *Packet Layer Procedure* (PLP)—comes into play.

The preceding figure shows a network-level X.25 PLP segment. This would be encapsulated within a link-level X.25 LAPB frame, and then passed across the network. I show it to you so that you can see how X.25 channels are identified: we have PLP logical channel group numbers (16 possibilities) and logical channel

---

* X.25 can also ride on other link layers, including LAPD (ISDN) and 802.2 LLC. We'll see some of this later on, when we talk about ISDN.

Format ID	Logical Channel Group	Logical Channel	Packet Type Specific	Data or Control Information
Header				**Data**

Figure 9-4: X.25 PLP segment

numbers (256 possibilities), specifying 4096 possible concurrent network-level connections. Your link to a *specific* resource (say, Internet access provider) would be identified by one of these group number/channel number pairs. As with Frame Relay DLCIs, these pairs have local significance only; they refer to *your* end of the network. (The receiving end will probably address you through very different-valued group and channel parameters.) Furthermore, the group/channel values may change from session to session depending on the nature of the connection. Virtual Calls, for instance, will be allocated group and channel numbers on the fly (at the time a connection is established). Accordingly, PVC parameters can be configured into your data communications equipment in advance.

Within the PLP packet format (Figure 9-4), there are two subtypes: data packets and control packets. Control packets provide flow control, error indication, and call set up. Virtual Calls (VCs) make extensive use of control packets for "dialing," ring indication, call acceptance, forwarding, and completion. *Call Request* and *Call Incoming* forms of control packets embed a "telephone" number—a VC identifier (X.121) of up to 14 digits—in the data field. With this, the network will create a routed path for the call when the connection is first requested. From then, until the circuit is torn down, a VC is indistinguishable from an X.25 PVC. Note that PVCs actually require little support from control packets. No call set up is necessary; the PVC operates continuously.

As with other kinds of protocols that we have looked at, X.25 data packets can contain *anything*. In some cases, the contents are identified by the connection itself—a particular PVC or VC may be known to carry a certain kind of traffic—perhaps a terminal session. Often, however, the payload is encapsulated network traffic (such as IP). In this case, the data need a wrapper so that the receiving end knows what protocol is contained within, and can tell whether the data have been fragmented.

IP Over X.25

Rfc1356 describes several methods for multiprotocol encapsulation under X.25, particularly for virtual calls. For IP, two possibilities are presented: IP encapsulation on a per-virtual-circuit basis, and multiplexed IP encapsulation, wherein the virtual circuit may be shared with other protocols, in addition to IP.

```
<LAPB hdr<PLP hdr<multiprotocol hdr<encapsulated data>>LAPB trailer>
```

In the first case, the *Call Request* command that an X.25 virtual circuit provides tells the receiving node that the remainder of the conversation will encapsulate IP; no further identifying headers are needed. In the second case, each PLP packet carries a tag that describes its contents. This way, the remote end of the link can pick the IP packets from the IPX packets, and so on.

Configuring X.25 and LAPB

Again, for our purposes, the most interesting configuration is the one that carries IP traffic. Let's take a look at steps for configuring an X.25 PVC or VC for IP:

Assign X.25 to an interface

X.25 requires the use of a synchronous, serial interface for a standard connection. Depending on your requirements, you might also choose to run X.25 over some other kind of network medium (using *Connection-Mode Network Services* [CMNS]), or on top of another protocol, such as TCP/IP (called XOT, rfc1613). Again, your access provider and vendor data can provide details.

Choose an IP encapsulation method

You will need to specify that IP is to be used over the interface, and select an encapsulation method. Often, you will choose rfc1356 encapsulation, nonmultiplexed.

Configure an X.121 address

Each X.25 interface that will place or accept VCs will need an X.121 address. This will be mapped (in our case) to an IP address. A single interface may have multiple X.121 address aliases.

Associate an IP address with an X.121 address

Often, your end of the link will have one of two addresses borrowed from a 2-bit IP subnetwork. The other end of the link—the provider—will have the other address. The IP address you set on your end of the link will be associated with your X.121 or X.25 PVC address.

Associate an IP address with an X.25 PVC

If you are setting up a PVC (instead of a VC circuit), you will need to associate an IP address with the PVC.

Set Timers and flow control parameters

LAPB timers and flow control values should be set per instructions from your access provider.

X.25 is a network-level protocol with its own routing capability. This makes it possible for an X.25 packet to find its own way from one end of the public data network to the other. However, from an IP standpoint, a handful of X.25 virtual circuits looks like a handful of network interfaces—some traffic goes down one VC, and some goes down another. Accordingly, you may need to set up IP routes to map networks to virtual circuits. This will instruct some virtual calls to go one way, and some to go another—based on their X.121 addresses.

Asynchronous X.25 Connectivity

It's possible that you will use X.25 in a different fashion. So far, we have discussed the DTE-to-DCE interface standards, and some of the traffic make-up for X.25 exchanges. Much of this is cast in terms of a synchronous X.21 (or RS232C) interface to the public data network. However, you may be connecting through, say, an analog modem to another kind of device that we haven't talked about yet—a *Packet Assembler/Disassembler* (PAD) (Figure 9-5). A PAD provides an alternate interface to traffic on an X.25 network.

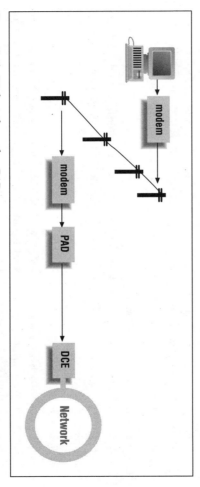

Figure 9–5: Dial-up through a PAD

All the physical, link, and network level details are left to the PAD. All *you* see are the data being traded with the other side. Of course, you could use such a connection for something boring, such as a serial terminal connection (login:). On the other hand, you *could* use it to encapsulate another link layer protocol, such as PPP. In that case, your connection will behave no differently than a direct point-to-point circuit (except that it will probably be a bit slower).

10

ATM

The qualities you look for in a data communication environment depend on what you are trying to accomplish. In the preceding chapters, we looked at encapsulating LAN traffic for transport over packet-switched wide area networks. It's important to recognize that we have humble needs; Internet traffic isn't particularly demanding. Performance can be lumpy and intermittent, and it really won't seem any different from what you are already used to—as long as the aggregate bandwidth is okay.

Other applications have more rigorous requirements. For example, digitized voice—as carried by the local telephone company—has moderate bandwidth requirements (64 Kbits or less), but stringent timing requirements; if a "packet" of digitized voice failed to arrive on time, your phone conversation would suffer a gap. Likewise, if the latency is too great (1/10 of a second is too much), exchanges become painfully halting; people step on one another in conversation. (If you have participated in a phone call over a satellite link, you will know what I mean.) Digital video, to take another example, has higher bandwidth requirements than voice, though it can be slightly more forgiving in terms of timing.

Traditionally, we have approached bursty, LAN-like data exchanges with time-shared media and variable-length frames. Wide area networking solutions we have investigated so far—PPP, X25, and Frame Relay—all fit into this category. These protocols have the quality of utilizing the network in proportion to their data requirements: if there's a lot of data to move, then the frames are "wide." Conversely, single characters—such as those generated from a terminal session—will produce very short frames. Because packet technologies only "speak" when they have data to exchange, multiple sessions can share the network. Voice, on the other hand, has enjoyed dedicated channels; a guaranteed, *synchronous* slice of bandwidth is devoted to each phone line. Whether the dedicated bandwidth is used effectively or not is another matter; someone can express undying love for you; you can listen, or you can drop the phone into your sock drawer and leave the room; either way, the same amount of telephonic resources is consumed.

The question is: How does one find a data communications technology that is good for applications in each camp, and for the spectrum in between? To answer, imagine how we might try to run both kinds of traffic—voice and LAN—over the same wire. One possibility is that we split the available bandwidth into reserved slots and dole these out for specific applications, as in Figure 10-1.

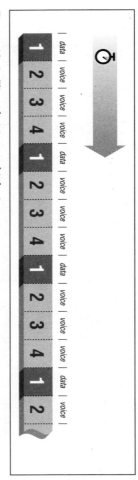

| data | voice | voice | data | voice | voice | voice | data | voice | voice | data | voice |
|1|2|3|4|1|2|3|4|1|2|3|4|1|2|

Figure 10-1: Time division multiplexing

At first glance, it looks as if this might do the job. Variable-length, packetized LAN traffic can be dropped into the data slots—fragmented if necessary; voice conversations (or whatever) can ride the remaining slots. It works, but notice that we lack some efficiency: the preset allocations for data and voice cannot expand dynamically, and temporarily quiescent slots go wasted.

It turns out that the technology we are discussing—called *Time Division Multiplexing* (TDM)—isn't new at all. T1 service that you might buy, for example, is based on TDM. In the case of a T1 circuit, there are twenty-four 64 kbit/S slots; you may use all, some, or none of them for data. We also call this technology *Synchronous Transfer Mode* (STM) because each allocation unit can be identified by its position in the cycle.

Now imagine that you cut the slots loose, so that they were no longer identified by position. Moreover, imagine that you cut out the distribution requirements altogether—any cell can appear at any time (Figure 10-2). Suddenly the picture is very different: you can have eight data cells, followed by a single voice cell, followed by three data cells, a gap, and then another voice cell. The distribution and order of the cells can be a function of the demand on the network, and the requirements of the applications. Of course, we have a new problem to contend with: if any kind of cell can appear at any time, we need some way to tag them so we know where they go—we have to add a header.

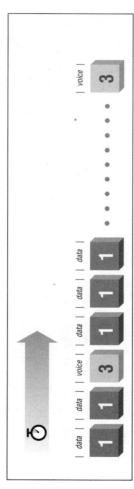

Figure 10–2: Data encapsulated into individual cells

These are the basics of *Asynchronous Transfer Mode* (ATM). Each *cell* is 53 bytes long—48 bytes of data plus a 5-byte header. Because the cells have a fixed size, it is (relatively) straightforward to construct hardware that can process them very quickly. ATM switches and networks are already available with capacities of hundreds of megabits per second. Because the transfer rates are high, and the cells are small, it should be possible to accommodate time-sensitive data (such as voice) even while large LAN-style data transfers are taking place. The trick is to design a network that can both provide and enforce different flavors of communication services, and to make them flow together seamlessly. As we'll see, ATM offers up to four "abstractions" into which different flavors of traffic fit. These range from *isochronous* (constant bit rate) circuits with many of the characteristics of a TDM connection, to variable bit rate circuits with the characteristics of Frame Relay.

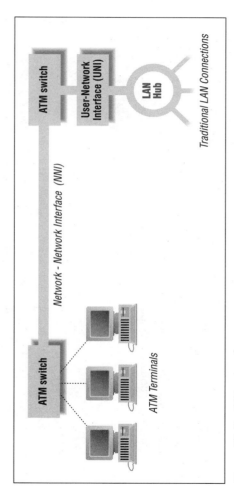

Figure 10–3: ATM network

Where would you use ATM? The technology has already found a place as a backbone technology for large, and sometimes distributed, networks. If you are shopping for a very-high-speed Internet connection, you *might* find an access provider extending ATM to you (though it might be SMDS, described below). Proponents suggest that ATM could become a LAN alternative too, replacing slower Ethernet and Token Ring technologies with gigabit connectivity (Figure 10-3).

Will ATM be used extensively for voice or video? It is difficult to predict. Timing requirements for voice are very tight; current circuit-based voice technologies blindly relay digitized signals from point **A** to point **B**; no sophisticated data switching is involved. With ATM, on the other hand, each packet header is previewed at each way station. Accordingly, a long-haul, multi-hop ATM network could introduce delays, or even lose data, particularly if the network is busy.

If all goes as its champions' plan,* ATM will be the technology that will underpin *Broadband ISDN* (B-ISDN), a plan for the universal network of the future. This would be a seamless mix of video, voice, and data technology coming right to your house, probably via optical fiber. As a user, you would subscribe to an array of ATM services, requesting link qualities that match the jobs at hand. If you were moving voice data, for instance, you would want a connection with tight timing and a certain minimum bandwidth guarantee. For a LAN interconnect, on the other hand, you would be looking for a chunk of bandwidth, though perhaps looser timing would be okay. The question is: Who should worry about all of this stuff? We have already divorced ourselves from higher-level protocols, such as TCP. And the link-level protocols we have investigated so far have been suitable only for data because of their variable length frames, and their disregard for timing or (perhaps) lost frames.

Fortunately, in the case of ATM, the details of providing a variety of connection types, and of arbitrating between them, are pushed down into the ATM protocols—even partway into the physical layer. The idea is that you—the user—can pretend an ATM connection is a circuit, and forget about it—just as you might ignore the time division multiplexed nature of a T1 connection.

How ATM Works

The ATM network model is split into data and control functions. Hierarchically they're the same; they share the same functional divisions, and behave similarly. Accordingly, I'm going to disregard the fact that they are sometimes treated separately, and skinny the discussion down to a simple, two-dimensional, layered picture of ATM networking.

As I mentioned previously, ATM offers a variety of network abstractions, ranging from time-dependent transfer to something more like a packet-switched data network. The illusion is managed by a link layer interface called the *ATM Adaptation Layer* (AAL), as shown in Figure 10-4.

---

* ITU-T, ANSI, ETSI, ATM Forum, and others

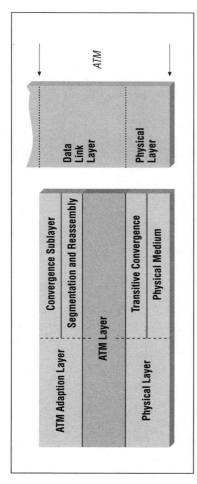

Figure 10–4: ATM compared to OSI model

There are four AAL possibilities:

AAL Type 1

Type 1 traffic flows with a *constant bit rate* (CBR), and a timing relationship between the sender and receiver. The link is connection-oriented (and reliable), meaning that no data is lost, and everything arrives in order. A type 1 connection would be suitable for encoded voice transfers.

AAL Type 2

In contrast to type 1 traffic, type 2 traffic does not feature a constant bit rate. Everything else is the same; the connection is reliable, and there is a timing relationship between sender and receiver. Type 2 connectivity would be suitable for video.

AAL Type 3/4

Type 3/4 is for *variable bit rate* (VBR) traffic with no timing relationship. You could choose between connection-oriented and connectionless service. Depending on your requirements, either of these could be suitable for wide area networking of LAN traffic.

AAL Type 5

AAL Type 5 is similar to type 3/4 (VBR), except that a multiplexing function has been left out; data are not interleaved under control of the AAL. Instead, duties such as multiprotocol encapsulation are left to other link technologies that use ATM as a virtual circuit. This makes the ATM connection more efficient, because it leaves housekeeping to the endpoints. If you are connecting for Internet service via ATM, you will most likely be riding on a type 5 AAL.*

---

* For recommendations about implementing multiprotocol encapsulation, see rfc1483, "Multiprotocol Encapsulation over ATM Adaptation Layer 5." See also ITU-T I.555, Bellcore TA-NWT-001115, ATM Forum B-ICI 1.0, and Frame Relay Forum documents for descriptions of Frame Relay over ATM.

Again, the AAL type you choose depends on the nature of the traffic that you are moving across the network.

The Gory Details

All of the ATM Adaptation Layer choices—Type 1 to Type 5—can be split into higher and lower functional groups called the *Convergence Sublayer* (CS), and *Segmentation and Reassembly* (SAR) (look at the picture again). The complexity and girth of the subfunctions depend on the complexity of the AAL they make up. The convergence sublayer serves as the interface from higher-level services to the ATM network—giving the network a personality. IP or Frame Relay, to take a couple of examples, might talk directly to an AAL convergence sublayer, providing link-level frames populated with enough information so that the embedded protocols can be recognized on the other side.

Just below the convergence sublayer, the segmentation and reassembly (we called it fragmentation earlier) sublayer chops information into 48-byte cells, and—when working in the reverse direction—glues them back together.

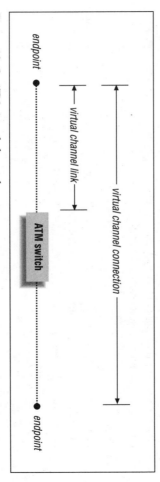

Figure 10–5: ATM virtual channels

Passing now below the AAL layer, the *ATM Layer* provides functionality we have seen in the link layers of other networking technologies, plus some we might attribute to a physical layer. To start with, the ATM Layer is responsible for keeping track of virtual circuits, and for authoring the 5-byte cell header. There's a little new terminology to cope with: a single, one-way data connection is called a *channel*. Groupings of channels form a *path*. Single, one-hop connections are called *virtual channel links*. A *virtual path link* is a group of channel links sharing the same endpoints (Figure 10-5).* You can concatenate links into multiple hops to create longer *virtual channel connections* or *virtual path connections* (Figure 10-6).

---

* You might consider these cousins of X.25 and Frame Relay PVCs and VCs.

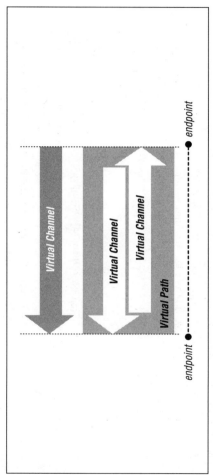

Figure 10–6: ATM virtual paths

The ATM Layer tags channels and paths with identifiers (VCIs and VPIs) that iden-tify the traffic from one hop to the next. The identifiers ride in the 5-byte ATM cell headers; the 48-byte AAL payload is cemented onto the end (Figure 10-7).

In operation, cells are switched through the network, visiting hubs in turn. Cells bearing identifiers for a locally terminating ATM path or channel get pulled from the network and passed up to an appropriate AAL. Others have their tags (VCIs and VPIs) rewritten to values appropriate for the next leg of the journey, and then scoot along. In the big picture, all of this is hidden; an AAL process on one ATM switch holds a conversation with an AAL process on another; both are ignorant of the workings below.

Figure 10–7: ATM cell

The ATM Layer manages other functions too, including the multiplexing and prior-itizing of ATM cells. Depending on the nature of the subscribed service (the AAL type), the ATM layer must choose which cells are the next to go, and (perhaps) which ones will be lost due to congestion problems.

At the bottom of the ATM model, the physical layer standards include methods for framing data for transmission over physical media, for detecting errors, and for adapting the frame rate. Notice that some of these jobs—framing and error detec-tion—have crept down into the physical layer; we have called these data link layer functions in the past. Part of the reason for this change is that much of the lower-level ATM link functionality is cast into networking hardware; the physical layer deals with fixed-size frames, and these are switched, typically, not by link layer software, but by network hardware. ATM proposals and specifications offer several network media possibilities, including SONET, DS3, FDDI, and others (more about these later).

ATM DXI

You might purchase an ATM interface or a router that handles all of the ATM layers—link layer to physical layer—natively. However, you can also find hybrids. ATM standards provide an auxiliary interface abstraction between DSUs and Routers, called a *Data Exchange Interface Protocol* (DXI). DXI splits ATM functionality between a custom ATM DSU and a capable, multiprotocol router.

Figure 10–8: ATM DXI

The DSU is responsible for lower-level ATM functions—cell assembly/disassembly and virtual channel handling. AAL interfaces to higher-level protocols are available on the router. The two devices—router and ATM DSU—communicate and manage their interfaces via an HDLC-derived frame, across the DXI.

Using ATM for Data Transfer

For our purposes, the two most important uses of ATM are transfer of IP, and Frame Relay (encapsulating IP). Again, we can segregate things—IP or Frame Relay on the top, and ATM on the bottom. The question is: "What do we need to do to glue the top and bottom together?"

Starting with Frame Relay, let's inventory what we have to work with: IP layers, Frame Relay encapsulation, and frame generation will all have taken place before we get to the ATM network. We will have Frame Relay DLCIs in hand, plus some desired network qualities, such as a committed information rate (CIR) and a tolerance for unreliable service. We *may* be running a management protocol (LMI). ATM, then, has to provide the following: a certain bandwidth guarantee and something that looks similar to a Frame Relay permanent virtual circuit.

It turns out that ATM AAL Type 5 provides the appropriate transfer mechanism; service is simple, lightweight, and unreliable. Bandwidth guarantees can be managed at the interface to the ATM network. Traffic marked as exceeding the Frame Relay network's CIR can be marked by a similar congestion control mechanism (called *cell loss priority*) as it enters the ATM network.

ATM networks have native support for semipermanent virtual channels and paths. Two channels back to back (one for each direction of traffic flow) can form a conduit for Frame Relay PVC traffic over ATM. A second set of channels would accommodate the Frame Relay LMI. Both sets—glued together—form an ATM virtual path for Frame Relay. Translation from one world to the other—DLCI to Virtual Path Identifier (VPI)—can take place at the network interfaces. You—the subscriber—will have to perform the mappings when you configure the network. After that, the operation will be "hands-off."

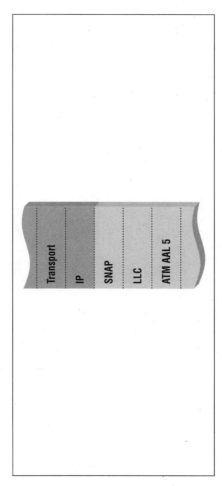

Figure 10-9: IP networking over ATM

Other Frame Relay over ATM scenarios are possible; multiple Frame Relay PVCs could be included within a single set of ATM virtual circuits. In this case, a *Frame Relay Bearer Service* within ATM would be responsible for PVC multiplexing over a single set of ATM circuits.

IP Over ATM

Now let's consider transfer of IP over ATM, such as you might use in-house someday. Most of what we need we inherit from IP: all the business of transport encapsulation (TCP, UDP, etc.) will have taken place already, and IP routing will have decided where to go next with a datagram—at least in terms of an IP address (Figure 10-9). A customized AAL Type 5 will provide a useful network abstraction; IP already assumes that the underlying network is unreliable. Two transfer possibilities present themselves. The first is that a route could be associated with a particular ATM virtual circuit (called *VC Multiplexing*—see rfc1483). This is a simple way to go because we can essentially treat the ATM network as a collection of point-to-point IP pipes. A routing decision will choose one of these pipes, and forward the data to its next hop.

On the other hand, you might imagine scenarios where you would want IP to be more closely tied to the ATM network. Use of the network as a very fast LAN, for instance, will require us to provide LAN-like data structures and services; we need the functional equivalent of a data link layer, including SNAP and LLC shims (for multiprotocol data encapsulation), and an *ARP* protocol equivalent, so that we can translate IP addresses into virtual circuits. Now it gets tricky; at the lower levels, LAN traffic is typically connectionless—anybody can address a packet to anybody else at any time. Under ATM, on the other hand, we have virtual circuits. Dynamic any-to-any connectivity will require that VCs be created and torn down on the fly, left in place for long periods of time, or something in between.

ATM standards provide for virtual calling; VCs can be created by the network, on demand. Nodes have addresses (like phone numbers). Via ATM signaling, one node can "place a call" to another. This could be the basis for on-the-fly any-to-any connectivity. To complete the picture, however, we have to be able to "ARP" other nodes. Remember, we start with an IP address. We need to turn this into something we can use over the ATM network. Unfortunately, we're at a disadvantage, since there is no notion of a broadcast—we can't make a single request to everyone on the network, all at once. Instead, participating ATM nodes will have to be collected into a list. ARP requests will then be resolved against the list (this list will be handy for routing broadcasts, too). Upon finding an IP-to-"phone number" address translation in ATM's "ARP directory," we can create a virtual circuit (or use an existing one), and contact the corresponding node directly.

As I mentioned before, LAN-like connectivity is one of the envisioned uses for ATM. If you look around, you can find adaptors that allow you to use an ATM network as a LAN. But beware: it is (perhaps) a little early. In fact, let me make this a global comment: the features we have discussed may not be available in your case. Though ATM is rich with standards and proposals, much is still a work in progress. This may push you toward single-vendor ATM solutions, compromise, or an implementation different from what I have described. Furthermore, it's not clear that ATM will ever be put to some of its proposed uses; I wouldn't even venture to guess its impact over the next couple of years. Lastly, ATM hardware is still fairly expensive. Tread lightly.

Configuring ATM

Let's look at some of the parameters you will need to configure for an ATM connection. As you now know, ATM can have many personalities. However, our purpose is to establish an AAL5 ATM PVC connection for routed Internet traffic, either directly from a router, or through an ATM DSU over a DXI connection. Accordingly, I would like to focus on this configuration, somewhat to the exclusion of others. In fact, even the steps below are an oversimplification; you will find that ATM has a plethora of knobs to twiddle. I have mentioned just a few here.

Associate an IP Address(es) with an ATM Interface

Your end of the link will have an IP address, and a subnet mask as directed by your access provider. You need to assign these to an ATM interface on your router.

Create a PVC(s)

Your access provider will also have set up virtual path identifiers (VPIs) and virtual channel identifiers (VCIs), which you will bundle into one or more PVCs. Typically, you can choose the PVC numbering as you please. PVCs will be associated with ATM interfaces, and hence with the IP address(es) you have configured for those interfaces.

Choose an ATM Abstraction and IP Encapsulation

At the same time as the PVC(s) is configured, you will select the ATM Abstraction Layer—AAL 5, in our case—and choose an IP encapsulation method, most likely 802.2 LLC SNAP encapsulation of IP, as per rfc1483.

Configure Broadcasts

PVCs may be individually configured to forward broadcasts to the IP address on the other side. You will need this feature if you are going to allow dynamic routing.

You might choose *not* to configure broadcast capability over the PVC to your access provider, or through other PVCs you might have set up, which means you won't be able to "ARP" or share routing information. In this case, you will need to populate your router with static routes, and perhaps seed your ARP cache as we did with PPP, earlier. This way, you can trick traffic bound for hosts on the other side of the ATM PVC into crossing the link.

11

SMDS

Data rates of 1 to 2 megabits per second are going to seem pretty slow in the not-too-distant future. The technology, and in many cases the infrastructure, for moving information at tens of megabits per second are all around us, especially in metropolitan areas. Some of this infrastructure belongs to the local exchange carriers, and some belongs to competitive access providers, some belongs to interexchange carriers, some belongs to cable television companies. Regulatory changes are making it possible for all four groups to go after the same customers, which suggests that the high-speed, metropolitan area networking (MAN) market is going to become very explosive over the next few years.

What happens next is a topic ripe for discussion. I think that when we get to the point where we have a significant portion of the Internet community tied together at 10+ Mbit/S rates, new applications will move in to take advantage of the bandwidth. That will effectively cut the Internet community in half: the haves, and the have-nots. There will be some kinds of Internet exchanges that will be off-limits, even to people with T1 access. My next prognostication is that this will precipitate a large-scale migration to multimegabit network technologies; within a few years, we will all have 10+ Mbit/S Internet access. It may be carried over fiber, coax, or even twisted pair. It all depends on the telecommunications infrastructure in your area.

Link layer technologies are already lining up for the job. ATM, which we discussed in the previous chapter, is one possibility. Some of the point-to-point protocols we are discussing (PPP, HDLC) could do the job too, though point-to-point links are deprecated in the MAN environment because each requires a separate interface and a separate wire (or fiber). Another possibility is *Switched Multimegabit Data Service* (SMDS). SMDS provides a high-speed link protocol with the economy of a public data network, along with the properties of a LAN.

Viewed from a few miles up, SMDS appears to have qualities in common with ATM-based connectivity; SMDS runs over high-speed circuits, data are segmented into 53-byte cells, and subscribers connect back to a central hub.

Figure 11-1: SMDS network

As we get closer, however, we find a very different set of protocols, different methods, and a different philosophy—SMDS is much more like a multiaccess LAN than like a public data network.

For starters, conversations are connectionless; we don't have Frame Relay or ATM link layer notions of virtual circuits. Rather, each SMDS station, or group of stations, carries a unique address,* like nodes on a very large LAN. Similarly, if you want to talk to somebody, you merely need to address traffic to them—again, like a LAN. Users can exchange data in variable-length packets up to 9188 bytes long. These are broken into ATM-sized cells for transfer across the network, as we will see later.

An SMDS hub can accommodate aggregate transfer rates of many tens of megabits per second. DS0 (64 Kbps) and DS1 (1.54 Mbps) speed connections are provided at full bandwidth. SMDS subscribers can reserve a bandwidth slice—an *access class*—for higher-speed connections. This could give you a fractional DS3 (45 Mbps) connection, or better. Allocations are parceled out from the network centers, subject to limits imposed by the speed of the medium that brings SMDS into the building. Connections run back to a central site over a variety of physical media, including twisted pair, coax, and even optical fiber (particularly on top of SONET framing, described in Chapter 14, *Physical Networks*). The back-end, hub network can be anything; it might be an ATM switch, or a fancy router—it depends on the rest of the network architecture (Figure 11-1).

---

* Per specification ITU-T E.164

Internet access via SMDS is already available in some cities. If you need a high-speed connection, this is a great way to go. SMDS bandwidth is generally reasonably priced, and the hardware is relatively affordable. Furthermore, SMDS is *supposed to be* a stepping stone to ATM. Some of the data communications equipment and the media could be preserved if you were to switch one day. Of course, anything could happen; SMDS could be around for a long time.

The Gory Details

The SMDS specification comes from Bellcore. It is fashioned upon a subset of IEEE 802.6—a standard that describes a *Distributed Queue Dual Bus* (DQDB)* architecture for high-speed, connectionless, metropolitan area networks (MANs). The idea behind 802.6 is that a locale might run the optical buses from building to building to form a city-wide network, supporting many different flavors of traffic—from data transfer to time-sensitive exchanges, such as voice. Multiple DQDB networks could be linked together, if desired, to form a larger public data network. SMDS borrowed a lot from the DQDB standard, but left the dual bus behind; high-speed connections run in a star configuration, anchored at a central hub.

SMDS has a three-layer *SMDS Interface Protocol* (SIP) that starts at the OSI link layer and extends all the way down to the physical layer. The protocol describes everything from an interface to the network layer, down to framing and media access.

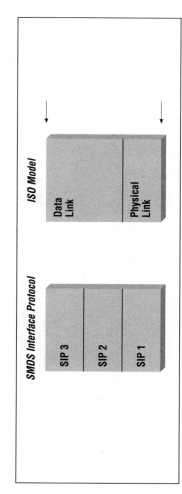

Figure 11-2: SMDS compared to OSI model

The top layer (Figure 11-2), *SIP 3*, accepts an LLC frame from a higher-level protocol (say IP, at the network layer). This frame will include data from the higher-level protocol, plus (typically) some extra (LLC/SNAP) information to identify its

---

* DQDB is two counterrotating optical buses, similar to FDDI, except that DQDB is not token-based.

contents. The frame may be up to 9188 bytes in length, upon being passed to SIP 3 level.

The SIP 3 layer adds a header and a trailer to create a longer segment, called a *Level 3 Protocol Data Unit* (L3_PDU). The header contains a variety of fields, including source and destination addresses. Each address is 8 bytes in length, including zone and country codes, and a 10-digit E.164 decimal address—like a phone number. Other fields provide error control, versioning, and padding.

```
<L3_PDU header<LLC Header<encapsulated data>>trailer>
```

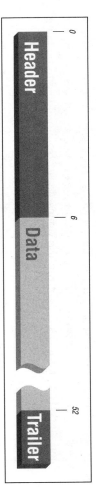

Figure 11-3: SMDS level 2 protocol data unit

Next, upon graduating from SIP layer 3, the L3_PDU gets chopped into 44-byte chunks—from head to tail. Each gets its own 7-byte header and 2-byte trailer (Figure 11-3). This new, smaller segment is called an L2_PDU. The header includes control information, a sequence number, and an identification field. Some of this is necessary for message reassembly. Consider that the 10-digit address and country code get minced up along with everything else—they can't be used to identify the source or destination of the 53-byte cells. Instead, the SIP 2 layer provides sequence numbers and a sufficiently unique message identifier so that the original datagram can be reconstructed when it reaches the other side.

The bottom level, SIP 1, interacts with the transmission medium, providing appropriate framing and timing. Because there are several SMDS-compatible framing/access standards—DS0, DS1, DS3, and others—there are several SIP 1 varieties.

SMDS and IP

As I mentioned above, an SMDS network can behave like a LAN; IP can run on top of SMDS transparently. We need a little bit of glue, however (Figure 11-4).

Recall that in a LAN environment, every node has the ability to spontaneously communicate with every other; no circuit set up is necessary. As a prerequisite, hosts need to know *how* to address other hosts. In the case of SMDS, what we need is a method by which IP hosts can translate IP addresses into E.164 addresses, so that they can communicate; we need a way to perform *address resolution*. On a LAN, IP address resolution is typically performed by *Address Resolution Protocol* (ARP); the host wishing to translate an IP address into a

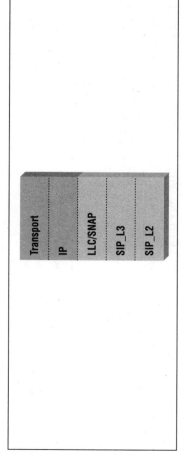

Figure 11–4: IP networking over SMDS

corresponding MAC address broadcasts an ARP query. Somebody else on the LAN—typically the host owning the IP address—responds with its MAC address, so communications can begin.

SMDS lacks a bona fide broadcast mechanism. Instead, IP layer ARP functionality is provided via SMDS *address groups*—multiple SMDS nodes listening to a single E.164 group address, in addition to their canonical addresses. This is also called a *logical IP subnetwork* (LIS). When an ARP broadcast goes out to the hosts in the group, each can compare the IP address requested with its own. If there's a match, the lucky node will send its E.164 address back to the requesting host. Likewise, routing broadcasts can be distributed to the group, using the same mechanism.

Regular IP transfers are SMDS-node-to-SMDS-node. LLC and SNAP headers identify and encapsulate IP within SIP_L3 frames. Again, this allows the receiving end to tell what the SIP_L3 segment carries, and which higher-level protocol is next in line to handle the user data.

SMDS DXI

As with ATM standards, SMDS provides an additional interface abstraction between DSUs and Routers—called a *Data Exchange Interface Protocol* (DXI) (Figure 11-5). This makes it possible to split SMDS functionality between a specially constructed SMDS DSU and a capable, multiprotocol router. The other alternative would be to have a monolithic, dedicated unit; that could cost more, and would certainly be less modular.

Lower levels—SIP 1 and SIP 2—are handled by the SMDS DSU. Longer, HDLC-derived frames pass across the DXI. The router implements SIP level 3 encapsulation. This is very likely the scenario you will employ if you connect to the Internet via an SMDS network.

Figure 11–5: SMDS DXI

Configuring SMDS

As we have seen, SMDS is more LAN-like than Frame Relay, X.25, or ATM. That means that we won't have to configure virtual circuits or paths between you and your access provider. Rather, we will set your site up to look like a node on a very large LAN. There is some behind-the-scenes work; we'll have to take a few steps to map IP-flavored features, such as broadcasts and "ARP," to the SMDS network.

Set an interface for SMDS encapsulation

You will have to tell your router that a particular interface will be conducting SMDS traffic (with an SMDSU, probably).

Map an IP address to the interface

Your router's SMDS interface will have an E.164 (1+10 digit) address, supplied by your access provider, plus an IP address—also from your access provider. A command on your router will map the E.164 address to the IP address.

Set a broadcast address

The broadcast address corresponding to the IP address you configured in the last step must be mapped to an SMDS multicast group. This way, "ARP"'s and routing broadcasts can reach each member of your logical IP subnetwork. As with your own (unicast) address, the multicast group will be specified by an E.164 address.

Enable ARP and/or routing

The choice of whether to enable broadcasts for ARP and routing will probably come at the suggestion of your access provider. Note that it is possible that you won't have any other nodes to share IP broadcasts with; if the SMDS connection is being treated more like a point-to-point link than a LAN, then routing and "MAC" (ARP) addresses may be statically configured. In that case, you may either populate your own ARP table or direct ARP queries to an ARP server—possibly one belonging to the access provider.

One attraction of SMDS is that multiple offices in a metropolitan area might join in, and share high-speed, LAN-like connectivity. At the same time, one or more of these offices might enjoy a connection to the Internet through the access provider's own backbone. SMDS equipment can be flexible in this regard; you may set up a single interface as a participant within multiple logical IP subnetworks.

12

HDLC

If you have been bushwhacking your way through these network protocol chapters, then you have probably started to see a pattern: almost every link protocol seems to have borrowed something from HDLC (*High-Level Data Link* protocol). In particular, many of the frame types we have looked at—LLC, PPP (native), Frame Relay, LAPB, and others—have been based on HDLC frame formats. Part of the reason for HDLC's successful breeding is that it has been around for a long time; HDLC became an ISO standard in 1979. Over the years, the protocol has been enhanced. HDLC is still in common use, though some of its older features have been deprecated.[*]

Unlike some of the more exotic standards we have talked about, HDLC is used solely for data communications over variable-length frames. It operates over synchronous media, such as digital leased lines, for both point-to-point and multidrop connections. It's also reliable; each HDLC frame is acknowledged at the receiver. This means that higher-level protocols can assume that all information sent across the network has arrived intact. For IP, that's a little bit of overkill. However, the overhead may be negligible for single-hop links. Accordingly, you may find that your Internet access provider offers HDLC between their point of presence and your router (MCI and Sprint both do).

---

[*] An HDLC connection you might use today is *balanced*—any participant has privileges to initiate a conversation. In the past, there was a distinction—primary versus secondary—between the link endpoints.

How HDLC Works—The Gory Details

As with many other link layer protocols, there are procedures and supervisory functions for establishing and maintaining a data link. PPP has similar functions (LCP), as does Frame Relay (LMI). Because HDLC communication is reliable, end-points have to maintain a collection of state variables and buffers to keep track of the conversation.

Traffic is exchanged over three frame types: *Information frames* (I-frames), *Supervisory Commands/Responses* (S-frames), and *Unnumbered Commands/Responses* (U-frames). I-frames carry user data from one point to another, plus acknowledgments for previous frames headed in the other direction. S-frames carry independent acknowledgments and retransmit requests, and provide flow control. U-frames extend the repertoire of commands by borrowing space from the sequence numbers that normally accompany HDLC frames.

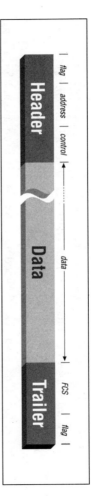

Figure 12-1: HDLC frame

The HDLC frame format shown in Figure 12-1 is identical to LAPB, which we discussed earlier, when looking at X.25. The flag field carries a unique bit sequence (0111110) that marks the start of a frame. The address field contains a *station* address. The use of the address field changes, depending on whether the frame is a command, or a response to a command (more about this in a second). The control field manages the frame types—I, S, or U—and provides a mechanism for polling. The FCS field contains a cyclic redundancy check. A final flag closes out the frame.

Notice that there is just one address field, even though it takes two link participants to hold a conversation. You might wonder how this could work. How can stations identify who is talking to whom if there's just one address field? Consider that each individual conversation is asymmetric; one station asks for something and the other responds. The exchange goes something like: "Fred, I want to start a conversation." The response is analogous to: "This is Fred. Okay, I am holding a conversation." (Fred heard a cry in the dark, and responded. However, Fred doesn't know whom he is talking to.) As the conversation continues, the secondary's job is to keep track of, and announce, the status of its end of the connection, for example, "This is Fred, I just received frame number 4."

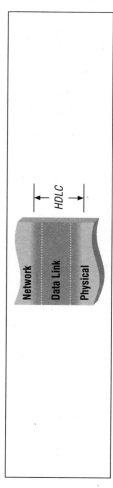

Figure 12-2: HDLC operates primarily in the data link layer

Information frames may creep ahead of acknowledgment—HDLC maintains a window.* Furthermore, multiple frames may be acknowledged at once, or acknowledgment may be embedded within frames fulfilling other functions. Eventually, a conversation closes down formally, or under an error condition; HDLC operates under the supervision of timers. If an event fails to transpire—say an acknowledgment takes too long—a timer will expire, and link recovery procedures will come into play.

In addition to frame format and procedures, HDLC standards concern themselves with preparing frames for transport over the physical media (Figure 12-2). In particular, HDLC implementations watch bit sequences for long strings of successive "1" bits. Whenever five "1"s occur in a row, HDLC stuffs in a "0." The reverse process takes place on the receiving side. This accommodates a common digital encoding method called *nonreturn from zero inverted* (NRZI). NRZI exhibits no state changes for successive one bits; without the zero insertion, a sequence of "1"s might otherwise appear to be a carrier-less, dead connection.

IP Over HDLC

IP datagrams can be encapsulated under HDLC. Again, a variety of methods is available. We could use LLC/SNAP or PPP, for instance, to transfer multiprotocol data. If the link is dedicated to IP, on the other hand, transfers can be unembellished; datagrams may be encapsulated without multiprotocol headers.

Configuring HDLC

The parameters you will need to configure for a dedicated, point-to-point HDLC link may be very few. Timer settings, addresses, protocol encapsulation, and HDLC link mode may be assumed, or negotiated by the endpoints.

---

* Some router vendors' (cisco, Bay) implementations of HDLC don't support the HDLC window.

Example—cisco and HDLC

This example shows a simple router configuration using cisco's own HDLC implementation:

```
!
interface Ethernet0
ip address 198.252.200.1 255.255.255.0
!
interface Serial0
encapsulation hdlc
ip address 192.168.10.118 255.255.255.252
!
interface Serial1
no ip address
shutdown
!
ip route 0.0.0.0 0.0.0.0 192.168.10.117
!
line con 0
password passwd
login
!
end
```

We begin by assigning an address and network mask to Ethernet port 0. On serial port 0, we choose HDLC as the encapsulation method. If we had chosen nothing, this would have been the default. Notice that the narrow network mask on the serial port allows for just two addresses—"117" and "118." This is a common practice for point-to-point links; only two addresses are necessary—one for each end of the link. Next, we add a default route. And last, we set a password for the console, and enable a login.

Choose HDLC encapsulation

First, you need to tell your router that one of its serial interfaces will run encapsulated IP traffic over a (synchronous) HDLC link. Note that if you don't choose encapsulation, HDLC may be the default.

Assign an address and network mask to the interface

Each end of the link will have an IP address and an associated network mask. Often, the link endpoints will be part of a 2-bit subnetwork, with two usable addresses—one for the access provider, and one for you.

Set the HDLC link mode, timers

You probably won't have to worry about setting the HDLC link mode, but for the record, you would typically choose *Asynchronous Balanced Mode* (ABM). This tells the router that either side of the link can initiate a conversation, without asking the other's permission.

Choose an IP encapsulation method

The IP encapsulation method is another setting you probably won't have to fuss with; IP may be ferried via the HDLC link directly, without multiprotocol encapsulation. However, other possibilities exist. Your encapsulation scheme will have to match your access provider's.

As with PPP, and other point-to-point link services, you will have to think about routing for the HDLC link, and perhaps consider providing proxy ARP to speak for the remote end of the link. See the previous discussion about PPP for more details. Also, check with your access provider.

13

Routing

Well, I guess I jumped the gun a little—we have already taken a few shots at routing in the preceding chapters. Still, it can't hurt to shore up the discussion, even at the risk of repeating myself in some spots. Picture, again, the simple connection between a user's network and the Internet: on the near side of the connection, we have the in-house LAN and all of its associated computers. On the far side, we have the ISP's network and the rest of the Internet.

The goal is seamless desktop Internet connectivity.[*] The question is: Which way does traffic have to go? Consider that every IP packet generated within the LAN has one of two general destinations: somewhere else on the internal LAN, or out on the Internet. Only a few networks—perhaps just one—will be "inside." Most destinations will be out on the Internet; there are hundreds of thousands of networks out there. Of course, it would be ridiculous to have to tell every router within the local LAN how to reach every one of several hundred thousand networks. Instead, it makes sense to lump the most heavily traveled destinations together, and declare the path to be the *default route.*

For instance, PC **A** in Figure 13-1 would use the path through router **X** for its default route. This would make **X** the *default gateway* for **A**.[†] Similarly, PC **E** would use router **Y** as its default gateway, trusting that **Y** knows how to deliver packets anywhere they need to go. And notice that just as the PCs need default routes, the routers themselves need to maintain destinations of last resort. For instance, router **X** has to know that traffic bound for the great wide Internet has to be forwarded to the ISP's router on the far side of the serial link.

---

[*] In Chapter 16, *Internet Security*, we introduce a firewall into the picture.

[†] PC **A** may not know anything about internal routes, such as the path to PC **F**. However, the first time it tries to use router **X** to reach **F**, **X** will respond with an ICMP redirect message that says that the best route to **F** is through **Z**. **A** is supposed to respect this message, and redirect traffic accordingly.

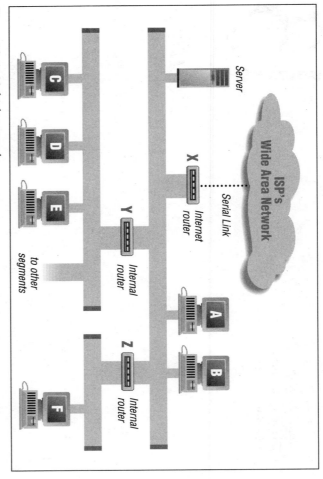

Figure 13–1: Multiple networks

The mental picture that should come to mind is one of tributaries and streams all coalescing into a common river, as in Figure 13-1. Traffic bound for the Internet may have to make its way across multiple internal networks before finding its way to the organization's Internet router, and out the door.

Static Routing

Hopefully, your in-house network is in reasonable shape, and ready for IP traffic. I'd hate to be the one who introduces a monkey wrench into the works, though frankly it happens often, and usually with smaller organizations. One possible problem is that the network may be served by a single LAN server with multiple interfaces. Perhaps each PC in the organization can log into the server okay, but the server may not be prepared to route IP traffic from one segment to another.[*] Another possible hitch is the use of unregistered IP network numbers; traffic from the Internet can only route to registered networks.[†] Anyway, assuming that you can make your network function similar to Figure 13-1—routing IP between segments, or using just a single segment—I am going to proceed.

---

* If we are talking about Novell, then you can get an NLM that will route IP.

† You can avoid the problem of address migration by installing a nonrouting proxy firewall.

How do we supply default routes to all of the PCs and routers on your network? Brute force is one method. We can manually set routing tables so that default routes for all internal computers and routers point "downstream," to the next router nearest to the Internet. We call this (and other flavors of manual table manipulation) *static routing*. The attraction is that it's easy to set up—though perhaps a bit inflexible.

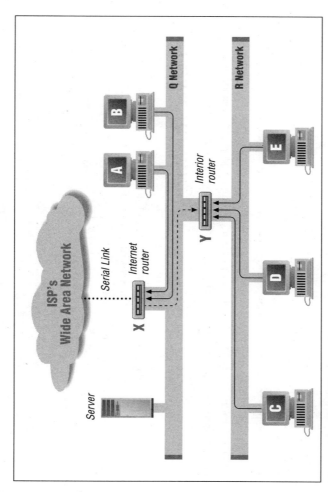

Figure 13-2: Default routes

In Figure 13-2, PCs **A** and **B** and router **Y** would have static default routes that send outbound traffic to router **X**. Similarly, PCs **C**, **D**, and **E** would have default routes pointing to **Y**. Router **X**'s default route points toward the ISP's router on the far side of the serial link. Additionally, **X** would need a routing entry that points back toward **Y** for destinations on network **R**.

How do you specify default (and other) static routes? The IP stacks for PCs will typically have a spot in the configuration menu where you can specify one or several default gateways. As examples, Microsoft's stack's default gateway is chosen under *network setup*; Trumpet Winsock can be configured in *trmpwsk.ini*; Novell's LAN workplace stack is configured in *net.cfg*. On a UNIX machine, we add a default route with the *route* command:

```
# route add default [IP address of default gateway] 1
```

The lone "1" represents a *metric*—a measure of "how far" away the gateway is, with a "1" meaning "close by." On a router, we may specify the default route using an address (and netmask) of all zeros. For example, on a cisco router:

```
ip route 0.0.0.0 0.0.0.0 [IP address of downstream router]
```

And, as I mentioned earlier, we would also need routes back to any other internal networks. In the last figure, for instance, we should have a route back to network **R** from router **X**.

```
ip route [network R] 255.255.255.0 [IP address router Y]
```

I mentioned it briefly before, but I should probably reiterate: I am operating under the assumption that the ISP expects you to route traffic through them via default routes; they don't expect you to be listening for dynamic routing updates from them, nor supplying any of your own. This may not be true in your case; you may need some form of dynamic routing between you and the ISP. Check.

Dynamic Routing

Routers (and computers) can learn from other routers about paths to networks far away. A modest handful of distinct routing protocols—methods for trading routing information—will probably be supported by your router.* Some of these protocols depend on periodic state broadcasts—every 30 seconds, router **X** tells everyone on the local segment about all of the networks it can reach (RIP, IGRP). Other protocols employ update messages; information is exchanged only when a route changes (OSPF, IS-IS). And different interfaces can typically run different routing protocols, or none at all. In any case, the goal is the same: maintain the local routing table. When the dust has settled, the information a router collects dynamically may be functionally identical to that which you would have entered by hand, except that you won't have had to go through the bother.

Regrettably, it is way beyond the scope of our discussion to explore the configuration of dynamic routing within your organization. And, going out on a limb a little, if you aren't using dynamic routing already, then static routing, as discussed earlier, will probably do the job—at least long enough for you to bring up an Internet connection. If you *are* using dynamic routing, then I have just a few more points to add, particularly regarding default routes.

The default routes that we manually added to a router, before, would also play a part in a dynamically routed environment. However, rather than supply a default route to each router along the way, we only need to supply one—to the router

---

* Look for *Routing in the Internet*, by Christian Huitema, published by Prentice-Hall. You might also seek *TCP/IP Network Administration*, by Craig Hunt, published by O'Reilly & Associates.

closest to the Internet. This would be propagated dynamically, along with local routing information. A machine several hops away would use the propagated default route to find its way back to the Internet. If it turns out that your organization has multiple connections to the Internet, then multiple default routes can be propagated; internal routers will choose the closest.*

Note that PCs and other computers that are not listening to routing updates will still need configuration of default routes. As before, the correct choice is a directly-connected router along the path to the Internet connection.

Exterior Routing

For the record, routing information passed between medium and large ISPs is maintained using a different set of routing protocols than you would be likely to use, either within your organization or between your organization and your ISP. These *exterior* routing protocols trade reachability information between independent, interconnected groupings of networks, or *autonomous systems*.

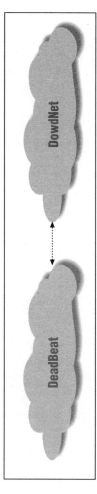

Figure 13–3: Routing between autonomous systems

DeadBeat, the fictitious ISP introduced in Chapter 3, *Choosing a Service Provider*, would be an example of an autonomous system (AS).† DeadBeat would advertise reachability for its customers' networks using an exterior routing protocol, particularly *Border Gateway Protocol, version 4* (BGP-4). This information would pass, by arrangement, to other AS's, such as the fictitious and potentially disastrous Dowd-Net, shown in Figure 13-3. The updates would include a list of networks reachable within DeadBeat, and possibly some reachable through DeadBeat.

---

* It may be the closest router to the Internet from within the organization, though that doesn't make it the closest router to the destination . . .

† AS registration is through the InterNIC.

14

Physical Networks

In 1962, telephone companies began migrating to digital technology for voice communications. There are a number of reasons to favor digital transmission over analog. It's less noisy, and digital equipment can recover a signal far better than analog equipment can. Furthermore, the circuitry is cheaper, and digital conversations are easier to multiplex. The downside is that it takes more raw bandwidth to transmit a digitized voice—64 Kbit/S versus the equivalent 8 Kbit/S for analog technology.* Still, the trade-offs pay for themselves in better service and easier signal handling.

Today, practically all of a telephone company's infrastructure is digital: connections between telephone company offices are conducted digitally. So is long-haul connectivity between carriers. Telephone service to your place of work is probably digital as well. Perhaps the only place you will encounter analog telephony is in the loop between the phone company's *central office* or *feeder plant* and your house. And even this will become digital in the next few years.

Anyway, it's not surprising that many of our choices in connectivity have their roots in digital telephony; data services have borrowed from an infrastructure whose central purpose has been the transfer of digitized voice signals. Accordingly, the terminology, bandwidth increments (typically Nx64Kbit/S), and the equipment used for data connections have a lot in common with voice communications.

In this chapter, we are going to look at some of the physical networks that might underpin your Internet connection. The material here is a complement to the

---

* By the way: the phone company's 64 Kbit/S equals 64,000 bits per second. People who work too much with computers (like me) may automatically assume that 64 Kbit/S equals 65,536 bits per second.

material in the previous chapters. We have examined link layer technologies; now we will examine the networks that they ride upon.

Low-Speed Lines

Let's start with a look at some lower-speed physical networks, operating in the 64 Kbit/S to 128 Kbit/S range. There are slower connections available; you might connect to the Internet via a 28.8 Kbit/S analog modem,[*] or even over a 19.2 Kbit/S synchronous X.25 connection. However, I'm going to assume that if you are shopping for a new, full-time connection today, then you are going to be interested in higher speeds.

56K Leased Lines

The entry point for full-time, dedicated circuits is *Dataphone Digital Service* (DDS)—a private line, 4-wire, 56Kbit/S offering introduced by AT&T in the mid-1970s. DDS (people often simply call it 56K service) is inexpensive, ubiquitous, and, unfortunately, nonexpandable. In reality, the line speed is 64 Kbit/S, not 56 Kbit/S; DDS rides upon a single (DS0) voice channel. However, a portion of the bandwidth (8 Kbit/S) is given up for endpoint synchronization, as we'll see in a moment. If you are purchasing a full-time, 56 Kbit Internet connection—for Frame Relay, PPP, HDLC, or anything else—the underlying service is almost certainly going to be DDS.

How DDS works

The physical wiring that carries a DDS circuit is copper pairs, just like regular (analog) telephone service, except that the usual signal conditioning devices (called "loading coils") and taps will have been removed between the central office and your site.[†] Because DDS travels over copper, and because copper wiring is sensitive to external effects, it is important that the data stream be represented in a way that won't exacerbate any unwanted electrical properties. Furthermore, we want the signal to be easily recoverable. Accordingly, DDS typically employs an encoding scheme known as *Alternate Mark Inversion* (AMI), shown in Figure 14-1.

A bit stream is modulated onto a line under control of a precise clock; "0" bits are indicated by a bit-period without a state change; "1" bits are indicated by a pulse. The polarity alternates—first positive, then negative—with each successive "1."

---

[*] Not to disparage analog modem technology; a high-speed modem is an amazing device, cramming multiple bits into each bit-space via frequency, amplitude, and phase encoding.

[†] A loading coil causes energy to concentrate in the voice frequency range, at the expense of higher frequency components. This makes conditioned lines unsuitable for higher-speed digital communications.

Data						
Alternate Mark Inversion	0	0	1	0	0	1	1

The letter "E"
AMI encoding.

Figure 14-1: AMI encoding

This gives AMI two good properties. First, it ensures that there is a net zero DC component on the wire. Consider that if pulses of the same polarity were repeated, the line could charge up like a big capacitor, making continued pulse recovery difficult. Second, pulse inversion improves noise detection. Induced pulses (from lightning, for instance) aren't expected to respect AMI's encoding scheme; whenever we see two sequential pulses of the same polarity (called a *bipolar violation*) we can identify it as line noise.

There's still a problem: a long string of zeros won't cause *any* pulses. This, in turn, can lead to a loss of synchronization between the transmitting and receiving ends of the line; the receiver has to see *some* activity to keep in synch. To compensate, DDS data communications equipment inserts a "1" bit after every seven data bits, thus assuring a pulse.* This is where the 8 Kbit/S gets lost.

Interestingly, almost all of the 64 Kbit/S is available for voice communication. Bit insertion *does* occur, though it happens only every once in a while, and in the second least significant bit of the sampled voice; the result is too subtle to hear. Of course, a data stream couldn't stand for that; a "1" versus a "0" makes all of the difference in the world.

DDS equipment

I'm sure that the lady from the phone company will enjoy a cold drink, if you offer one. Pleased, she will leave behind an RJ-48 telephone jack, like a shiny prize. This will be called the *demarcation point*, or "demarc." It's the spot at which the telephone company's equipment (and responsibility) ends, and the *customer premises equipment* (CPE) begins. There should be a network termination unit (NTU) at the demarc too—a digital signal processor (DSP) for equalizing the DDS signal and restoring its pulse shape. If the NTU isn't directly connected to the RJ-48 jack, then it is probably tucked around the corner. It's there somewhere.[†]

---

* Not to muddy the water, but you can also have in-band signaling on a DDS line. In this case, the eighth bit is a "0," but the signal code will contain a "1" bit, which fulfills the need to have a state change.

† Alternatively, the physical interface to the NTU may be via a DB-15 connector.

You or your Internet access provider will be responsible for supplying a box called a *CSU/DSU* (Channel Service Unit/Data Service Unit) that plugs directly into the RJ-48 jack. As the "/" in the name hints, the box contains two parts: a channel unit that speaks to the telco network, and a data unit that speaks to data terminal equipment (DTE)—your router. Often, you will hear people say just "DSU" or "CSU" for short. Technically, you can buy CSUs and DSUs separately, so the term CSU/DSU is appropriate for a single unit that combines both parts. Figure 14-2 shows the path from the "demarc" to your router.

We already have a notion about the CSU/DSU's function: its job is to recover a stream of bits from an AMI encoded signal, and forward it to the router (or some other kind of DTE). Likewise, the CSU/DSU AMI-encodes information traveling in the other direction, back out to the DDS circuit, and on to the Internet. Technically, the "CSU" portion is required for T1 and DDS links;[*] it isolates the carrier's network from yours.

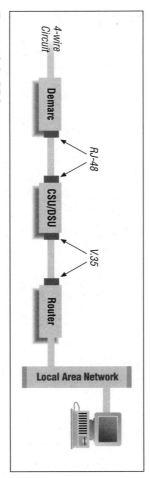

Figure 14-2. DDS connector

The connection from the CSU/DSU to the router will be through a second interface, often sporting an industrial-looking V.35 connector (Figure 14-3). A cable will join this connector to an identical one on the back of your router. The traffic on the cable will (typically) be a synchronous serial connection. Other possibilities include RS-232 or RS-442 signals, and DB-25 connectors. The CSU/DSU you buy may be minimally configurable—preset for 56 Kbit/S AMI encoding. Or it may have options for alternate encoding, multiplexing, or speeds lower than 56 Kbit/S—such as 19200, or 9600. It depends on the brand and the cost.

Via the Network Termination Unit, the telephone company has the ability to test their circuitry all the way up to the demarc. The CSU/DSU will probably also have a selector switch for choosing between normal operation and one of several test modes. During circuit turn-up, or when there is trouble on the line, you may be asked to place the CSU/DSU into one of these test modes, so that the telephone

---

Figure 14–3: V.35 connector

company can troubleshoot the connection right through to the CSU. Particularly, you may be asked to set the CSU/DSU into *digital loop test* mode (Figure 14–4).

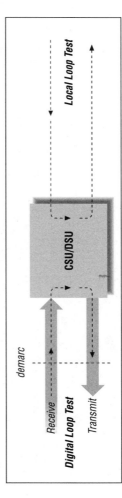

Figure 14–4: CSU/DSU loop tests

This will allow the telco to send a test pattern down to your CSU/DSU, and compare the stream coming out the other side. It's also possible to place the CSU/DSU in *local loop test* mode for checking the connection between the DTE (your router) and the CSU/DSU.

The front of the CSU/DSU will have several lights, including RD (receive data), SD (send data), CD (carrier detect), and NS or INS (indicators to tell whether you have DDS service). There may be loopback indicators as well. In normal operation, the service light should be lit (or a "no-service" light extinguished, depending on the CSU/DSU), and the RD and SD lights should be glowing dimly—even if no data is being transmitted. Why should they glow? Recall the discussion about bit insertion, earlier; insertion causes *some* activity on the line, even when no data are being exchanged.

Clear channel capability

It is possible (though not particularly likely) that you may hook up to the Internet over a DDS connection with *Clear Channel Capability* (CCC) (the service is called *Clear 64*). In a CCC link, the requirement for injected "1" bits is obviated by an encoding standard, B8ZS, that replaces AMI. Recall the problem: too many zero bits in a row could cause loss of synchronization over the DDS circuit. To counter, the CSU inserts a "1" every eighth bit. That "1" provides the needed line activity, but it takes a whack out of the bandwidth—56 Kbit/S, in lieu of 64 Kbit/S. It would be really nice to have that bit back.

Figure 14–5: B8ZS encoding

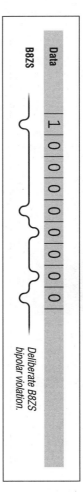

B8ZS (Bipolar with 8th zero substitution, Figure 14–5) gets over the 1's density problem in a different way. Rather than blindly stuffing the eighth bit, a B8ZS-capable DSU watches the bit stream for occurrences of eight "0" bits in a row. When the pattern appears, the CSU substitutes a pair of deliberate bipolar violations. Normally, these bipolar violations would be tagged as line noise. However, the remote CSU watches carefully for the pattern, and reconstitutes the eight "0"s whenever it appears.

Again, you can't typically choose which service—DDS versus Clear Channel—you will use; your equipment has to match the capabilities of the rest of the circuit.

Configuring a DDS connection

DDS circuit setup is straightforward. Let's trace the steps:

Configure the CSU/DSU data rate and line encoding
   Almost certainly, the configuration will call for a 56,000 bit rate, AMI encoding, and slave clocking. Typically, your choices will be made via DIP switches at the back of the unit. Note that you may need to have the switches set before power-up; the CSU/DSU may read the settings just once per power cycle. Some less expensive CSU/DSUs may be permanently wired for 56000/AMI.

Connect the devices together
   The CSU/DSU will probably come with an RJ-48 cable. Connect this between the unit and the demarc. Also connect the CSU/DSU to your router via a synchronous serial (V.35) cable. Note: you may need to order this separately.

Interface your router to your LAN

Your router will look like just another host on your LAN. Connect as appropriate. Note that some routers come with only an AUI port; you may need an adapter to interface with 10BaseT or thinnet.

Configure your router

Your router will use one of the link layer protocols described in the last chapter. Configuration may be cryptic, unfortunately. The good news is that your access provider will likely help you with your initial configuration. You can also find some help in the previous chapter. Additionally, check with your access provider to see if they will require routing updates from you. Most access providers route statically; others trade routing information with their customers. Also, see if your access provider will be monitoring the router via SNMP; likewise, this may need configuration. You will probably want to program access lists (security) into the router as well. See Chapter 16, *Internet Security*.

Basic Rate ISDN

A shovelful of earth may contain creatures—bacteria, rhizopods, and mycelium—stuff that's practically edible—even delicious. Likewise, you might pull a network cable from the wallplate, and be lucky enough to sample a few higher life forms. With several types of media, data link layer components are native residents of the physical network layer. Sometimes the medium and the link protocols are interdependent to the extent that you will never find them living apart. Still, one often refers to the physical connection by the name of the wire rather than by the names of its tenants, just as one might talk about dirt without hinting at hors d'oeuvres.

Anyway, that's my excuse for introducing *ISDN* (Integrated Services Digital Network) in this chapter, rather than in the last. Primarily, we are talking about a physical network connection, though some data link layer concepts tag along for the ride, as we'll see later. We will talk about *Basic Rate* service now, and touch upon *Primary Rate* service a little later.

In its raw form, a Basic Rate ISDN link consists of three separate channels: a 16 Kbit/S signaling channel, called the *D channel* (delta), and two independent 64 Kbit/S data channels, called *B channels* (bearer) (Figure 14-6). You can pump whatever you like over the bearer channels—you could have voice on one of the B channels, and network traffic on the other. You can even *bond* the channels together, to achieve higher data rates; the two B channels could work together to provide a 128 Kbit/S connection, for example. The D channel is available for data movement, too, though you typically share the channel with call setup and signaling functions.

The B channels (and even the D channel, in a sense) behave like telephone lines, with the ability to receive inbound calls, and to dial out. You might *want* to use an ISDN connection for a full-time Internet hook-up. However, the lines are usually tariffed such that a full-time, dedicated digital connection (such as DDS) will be more cost-effective—particularly if you stay on line for 50 or so prime-time (day rate) hours per month. (ISDN typically costs 1 to 7 cents per minute, plus monthly charges.) You will probably find that an ISDN data connection will be best suited for intermittent Internet access, in lieu of a dial-up modem connection. You will also find that ISDN availability is spotty. Even if you're located in an area where it is available, your ISP may not be.

A few words about perspective before we continue. This is a book about getting hooked up to the Internet; accordingly, I am approaching ISDN from a pretty narrow point of view. However, ISDN is general purpose; we can hook up other devices to the network, beside computers. For instance, if I have a digital telephone, and you have a digital telephone, I can call you, and we can chat—digitally, from end to end via ISDN. At the same time, our computers can talk—over the second B channel. Or if we like (and if we have the equipment) we can trade digitized video.

Here's where people sometimes get mixed up about ISDN: it's not a segregated system; it's part of the telephone company network. If you have an old-fashioned, Bakelite, rotary phone, I can *still* call you on my shiny new, probably expensive, and possibly carcinogenic, digital phone. Your end of the conversation will be analog, but my end will be digital. And as we will see further on, there's even a way for you to hook up your old analog telephones, and your analog modem, to the ISDN line. You could, in fact, eliminate analog telephone service altogether, yet retain the ability to call out for pizza. *

Anyway, the point is that you might want to buy an ISDN connection someday anyway—even if you don't use it for your Internet connection. Consider how different that makes this section from the rest of the chapter: you wouldn't have any other reason for buying a DDS connection, would you? Basic rate ISDN

---

* See also *Using ISDN*, by James Y. Bryce, published by QUE.

Figure 14-6. ISDN 2B+D

connections are going to become common for many types of information transfer. That being understood, forgive my narrow-minded approach. Though I might like to wax poetic about the possibilities of high-speed data transfer from your house to mine, I have a job to do here.

How basic rate ISDN works

If it was a trick to move 56 Kbit/S over a DDS circuit, then it must be a real challenge to move 144 Kbit/S (2B+D) over the starling-covered wires hanging from the pole outside your window. According to standards (ANSI T1.601.1992), the signal may have to travel as far as 18,000 feet (5.5 kilometers) without regeneration. The AMI encoding scheme that we looked at previously *could* be used, though a terrific amount of raw bandwidth would be necessary, and distances would be limited (we need to go both directions over two wires, probably by interleaving the flow of traffic). Instead, basic rate ISDN circuits (typically) use an encoding* method known as 2B1Q (*2 Binary, 1 Quaternary*).

2B1Q works by stuffing two bits into each bit time; bit pairs are represented by a single, four-level value known as a "quat."

Table 14–1: Bits versus quats

Bits	Quat
00	−3
01	−1
10	+1
11	+3

Table 14-1 shows the correlation between bits and quats. Labels ({−3, −1, +1, +3}) signify distinct quat values. To be precise, they're labels only; they don't necessarily represent signal levels. I suppose I could choose a more illustrative example, but I have gotten used to the letter "E." Figure 14-7, shows its representation in quats.

The ISDN connection is encoded similarly. Repeatedly, and in succession, the contents of the two B channels and the single D channel are rolled into "quats," and toggled down the ISDN wire pair—B1, B2, D, B1, B2, D, and so on.

Okay, now we have a way to move the 2B+D ISDN channels across town. However, you may have noticed that this only covers our requirements in one direction; data has to go both ways—we have to share the wiring with two distinct

---

* ISDN standards are still young enough that there are variations in implementation. Line encoding methods, for example, can differ from country to country, and phone company to phone company.

signal streams. The solution is a device called a "hybrid." It allows bidirectional communication over a single wire pair.*

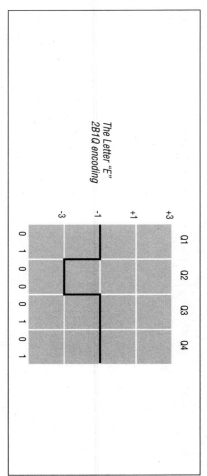

Figure 14-7: The letter 'E' 2B1Q encoding

The hybrid is a relatively low-tech device—a compound inductor, with some impedance matching, connected between the "transmit" and "receive" lines of your data communications equipment. At your receiver, the hybrid cancels out the information that you are sending, as you send it. This way, your equipment doesn't hear the things it says, but *does* hear the information coming from others on the line. Likewise, the connection on the remote end is balanced by a hybrid. The illusion is that a single wire pair is acting as two pairs, between the two endpoints.

Still, there's a problem. It's the hybrid's nature to bounce echos back from the remote end of the link. To counter this, ISDN terminations have to have built-in echo suppression: an inverted copy of the transmitted signal is delayed and re-applied at the receiver to cancel the returning reflection.

Of course, none of this is *your* problem. Your data communications equipment (described later) takes care of encoding and recovering the 2B1Q stream, and of providing access to the 2B+D channels. Typically, you will be interested in the highest level of service—the applications that run over the line. Still, I'd like to jump up just a level or two, and take a few more minutes to describe the link and network layer concepts that live on top of an ISDN connection.

---

* Hybrids are not new; a hybrid is what allows your present, two-line analog telephone to both send and receive at the same time.

The D channel

D channel conversations control B channel connections. A suite of ISDN Call Control messages (per ITU-T Q.931) provide for call setup, teardown, ringing, status indication, transfer of user information, etc. It is a Q.931 message that delivers the hang-up blow to a vinyl siding salesman, for instance. At the same time, the D channel can support low-bandwidth user data applications, particularly applications riding on top of X.25 (see Chapter 9 for a description of X.25).

The glue that holds the conversations together is a link layer protocol for the D channel, called *Link Access Protocol, D Channel*, or LAPD. If you read the last chapter, then this next tidbit won't be a surprise: like practically every other link layer protocol we have looked at, LAPD is a descendant of HDLC, and—more directly—a descendant of LAPB (of X.25 fame). Your equipment and the central office switch trade LAPD frames all the while your connection is active.

You can hang as many as eight* separate devices from an ISDN line. From a data link point of view, this means that we have to be able to support multipoint addressing. Accordingly, you will find that the LAPD address field contains a subfield called the *terminal endpoint identifier* (TEI). Each of the eight possible devices will be known by one of these TEI's. Your digital phone will have one, for example, as could the termination point for your B channel data connection (a terminal adapter, described later). You may be required to configure each TEI by hand, or it may be configured automatically, by the network.

In addition to the TEI, each LAPD frame address field also contains a *service access-point identifier* (SAPI). The SAPI parameter tells what flavor of traffic (what network layer protocol) the LAPD frame is trading with the device indicated in the TEI field. This is the distinction between, say, Q.931 Call Control messages, and other types of traffic, such as X.25 or Frame Relay—all being conducted over the D channel.

A (SAPI,TEI) pair is unique on your ISDN link; it defines a particular D channel conversation between one of your devices and the central office switch. Notice, however, that the pair has *local* significance only. In order for my digital phone to call your digital phone, we are going to need network-wide addresses. We have to work our way from the local, LAPD data link layer addresses to wider, grander, more global telephone company addresses.

We begin with a "telephone number." Your carrier will assign at least one *Directory Number* (DN) to your ISDN line, and probably two—one for each B channel (you could get as many as sixty-four). With these, I can place a call, or calls, to you. Still, the DNs are not quite sufficient. The network also has to choose the

---

* You can have more than eight devices if you place them behind a PBX.

correct device—digital phone, video, etc. You may have multiple devices, and if I put a voice call through, I certainly don't want to pop into your computer!

To further discriminate between connection possibilities, the phone company will assign you one or more *Service Profile IDs* (SPIDs) to match the devices you have online.* In some cases, you will program a SPID directly into each device—perhaps via a setup program, or from a keypad. In other cases, SPID programming won't be necessary. Rather, devices will be identified with DNs; the first one to pick up an incoming call wins. Upon initialization, devices report their SPIDs to the telephone company switch, and in return, the switch assigns them TELs (provided the TELs aren't defined by hand, as mentioned above).

Okay, so now I have a way to place a digital telephone call to you—all the way across the telephone company network. First, my digital telephone connects to the switch. The switch knows what kind of device I am calling from because I have already offered my SPID. Furthermore, the switch can track my D channel (Q.931) conversation because it has a local (TEI, SAPI) pair. Next, I pass your phone number to the switch, and it locates (via your SPID) a device on your ISDN link that is suitable to accept the call—namely, your digital telephone. The switch then conducts a D channel conversation with your ISDN telephone, on your end of the link (it makes your phone ring . . .). If all goes well, a B channel is allocated from my end to your end, and we get to talk.

Shopping considerations

The functionality of the 16 Kbit/S D channel depends upon a separate network, independent from the telephone company's primary voice network. This separate network—called *Switching System 7* (SS7)—routes the Q.931 call setup messages, plus some other kinds of traffic as well. However, not all telephone companies have a functional SS7 infrastructure in place at this time. In those cases, the signaling has to occur in-band—within the B channels. The unfortunate side effect is that this will drive the available bandwidth down to 56 Kbit/S per channel. You might want to check into this with your carrier before you leap. At the very least, you will have to be sure that your ISDN equipment will support in-band signaling in the interim.†

Another thing to check into is the telephone company central office switch type. You will need to be sure that your ISDN equipment can talk to their switch. In most cases, National ISDN-1 (NI-1) compatibility (from Bellcore) will be sufficient. However, there are still cases where *Custom ISDN* interfaces are in use; you might

---

* Often, the SPID looks just like a DN with a few more digits attached. For instance, an NI-1 SPID might look like 01xxxxxxx001, where the x's represent your DN.

† Availability of the full 64 Kbit/S of bandwidth is called *Clear Channel Capability.*

have to interface directly with central office switches, such as the AT&T 5ESS, or Northern Telecom DMS-100, using native, protocols. Also check to see what revision of switch software the carrier supports. Again, if your equipment doesn't complement their network, you can't use it.

Other questions you may want to ask:

Is X.25 support included?

X.25 capability probably won't be included as part of a baseline, basic rate ISDN connection. In fact, it may not be available at all through your carrier's network. Check with the carrier.

How many DNs do I get?

You will get at least one DN (phone number). This is enough to allow multiple B channel connections. In some cases, the telephone company will give you two DNs as part of the package. You may even purchase more—up to 64. This would make it possible for you to, say, run multiple businesses with multiple phone numbers, from the same ISDN line.

How many Call Appearances (CAs) do the DNs get?

A Call Appearance is a logical connection to one of your DNs. B channels can only support a single connection at a time. However, you can have multiple calls in the air simultaneously. One call can be on hold, for example, another can be "ringing," another can be active—all at the same time.

Are Electronic Key Telephone Set (EKTS) functions enabled?

EKTS provides PBX-like functionality to the line—call transfer, forwarding, etc. This may cost extra.

Does the ISDN connection support functional signaling?

Most switches will support *functional signaling*. This gives your equipment the option to transfer signaling information—such as the keystrokes that make up a telephone number—in blocks, rather than passing them down the line one at a time (called *stimulus signaling*).

By now you are probably saying, "Does this have to be so difficult?" I admit that I introduced more variables than you will likely need to understand in order to get your connection up. You won't have to pay too much attention to link layer components—TEI and SAPI, for instance. Hopefully, however, you will have the benefit of the bigger picture. I think that's important because ISDN connectivity is very new to many people, some of whom are phone company employees. The more you know going in, the less time you will have to spend debugging the connection.

The B channels and data

As we have seen, the 64 Kbit/S B channels are available for all kinds of exchanges—voice, video, and data. We have yet to get specific, however, about routed Internet traffic. I'd hate to blow a good punch line, but here it is: the encapsulation method you will probably use for moving IP traffic across the B channel is Point-to-Point Protocol (PPP). Calling it universal would be a stretch, however. In some spots, particularly in parts of Europe, you may find IP over ISDN encapsulated within HDLC. Take a look at the previous chapter for clues about configuring either one.

As you know, a single B channel will give you a 64 Kbit/S routed (or bridged) Internet connection. In some cases the channels can be *bonded* at a low level, to create a common 128 Kbit/S circuit. As an alternative, it's also possible (and perhaps preferable) to employ something called *PPP Multilink Procedure* (rfc1717). This will create a composite channel via extensions to PPP.

ISDN equipment

Somehow, I managed to make it all the way to the end of the ISDN section without introducing the hardware. I have to confess that I did it on purpose, because there's yet another bucket of acronyms to swallow, and they go down like roofing nails. I prefer to take them one at a time.

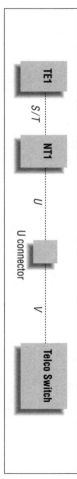

Figure 14–8: ISDN equipment

Figure 14-8 shows a simple arrangement. We have some *reference points*—S, T, U, and V, and some functional boxes—TE1 and NT1—plus the phone company's ISDN switch. It can get more complicated, too, as we will see in a moment. First, let's take a moment to investigate what runs over the wires.

The V reference point corresponds to the twisted pairs coming from the telephone company. This is where we will find the 2B1Q traffic that we discussed earlier in this section. The *U connector* is a jack that the telephone company installs at your home or place of business. The 2B1Q signals cross through the U connector to the NT1.

The *NT1* (Network Termination 1) converts the 2B1Q signals to AMI (see the DDS section for a description) for transport over the S/T interface, shown in Figure 14-8. This gives the S/T interface qualities it needs to support multiple drops (remember, there can be up to eight devices), and it makes the signal recovery circuits in the ISDN devices cheaper, because AMI is easier to decode.

I should stop a second for a few clarifications. Subscribers in North America will be generally responsible for providing their own NT1 (and everything else in the ISDN circuit). Furthermore, the NT1 will need a local power supply, and possibly a battery backup. This is in contrast to a regular analog telephone connection, which is powered remotely, by the phone company. In much of the rest of the world, the phone company supplies the NT1 (and power)—the U interface is hidden from the subscriber.

TE1 (Terminal Equipment type 1) denotes a piece of ISDN terminal equipment. It might be a digital phone, a router, or a direct ISDN connection into your computer. In any case, the TE1 device will speak directly to the telco switch via the ISDN link.

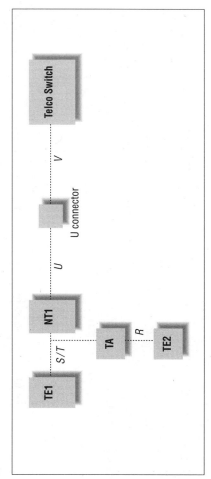

Figure 14-9: ISDN equipment with terminal adaptor

In Figure 14-9, we have a new reference point, **R**, between a *TA* (Terminal Adaptor) and a *TE2* (Terminal Equipment type 2). A TE2 is a device connected to the ISDN network that *doesn't* speak ISDN protocols. Rather, a TE2 depends on a TA to translate ISDN traffic into a form it can use. A simple scenario might be an analog telephone (the TE2), going to a TA that converts digital voice traffic into analog voice signals.

It's also possible that the TE2 will be a computer—perhaps communicating with the TA asynchronously, over a serial port. Why would you hook a computer up this way? Well, there's no good *long-term* reason for it (except money perhaps), but it is possible that you already have the data communications software and hardware you need for an asynchronous serial connection (basically, a 16550

UART and a protocol stack). The setup steps for this kind of configuration are detailed later.*

The (practically certain) possibility that the asynchronous line will deliver data to the TA at a different rate than the TA uses to talk to the ISDN switch raises the specter of yet another protocol, this time for *rate adaptation*. Consider that if the TA can't send data downstream at full speed, it is going to have to "packetize" it for the remote computer. Likewise, the remote computer will have to recognize that the data is arriving in packets, and reassemble it. In ISDN's short useful lifetime, there have been two standards for rate adaptation—V.120, which basically stuffs extra bits into the data stream, and V.110, which creates packets. V.110 is almost gone, at this point; V.120 support should be part of any data TA you might buy.

The complement of devices you will purchase depends on your needs, of course. In North America, you might buy a combination NT1 plus TA, in one box. You could hook TEIs to this as desired, and perhaps also hook in one or two analog telephones. In other parts of the world, the NT1 comes with the telco service. After that, it is up to you to mix and match TEIs and TAs as your budget allows.

Configuring basic rate ISDN

As you know, ISDN can serve a variety of purposes. However, let's go over some specific configurations for a typical organizational ISDN data link—first via a router, and then through a TA connected to an asynchronous PPP connection.

Install the NT1

In North American installations, the phone company will install a U interface. Connect your NT1 to the U, and connect a power supply to the NT1. You might want to place the NT1 power behind a UPS so that you won't lose in-progress connections during temporary power glitches.

Connect the AMI side of the NT1 to the router

Your router will have one or more basic rate ISDN interfaces. These will connect to the multi-drop, 4-wire, AMI side of the NT1 via modular (probably RJ11) jacks.

Assign SPIDs

If your telephone company assigns you data SPIDs, then you will have to program these into the router in order to communicate with the central office switch. It is possible that your connection will work without a SPID(s); it depends primarily on the switch type.

---

* You may see sales literature that calls the TA a *digital modem*. This is a misnomer.

Configure TEI negotiation

Recall that the switch identifies individual devices on your ISDN link by their terminal endpoint identifiers (TEIs). These are different from SPIDs; a SPID describes a service; the TEI describes a device (TE) providing the service. At some point, the central office switch will need to either assign or discover the TEIs associated with your SPIDs. This can occur when you first power up the TEs, the first time the device receives a call, or statically—the TEI can be hand-configured into the TE. Whichever the case, you must configure your router to match the telco central office switch's expectations.

Select a switch type

You must select a switch type that matches the telephone company's central office switching equipment. Typical North American choices are NI-1, AT&T 5ESS, and Northern Telecom DMS-100. Other parts of the world may use other switch types; check with your access provider.

Configure encapsulation

Depending on your requirements, you may configure one of several encapsulation methods—most likely PPP or HDLC. If your router is to place on-demand, dial-up network connections, then you will have to configure IP address mappings and chat scripts as well. Also, you may want to configure multilink PPP, if supported; this will give you a higher bandwidth connection.

If you are connecting through a TA and an asynchronous serial port, rather than a router, then your steps will be more like the following:

Install the NT1

Connect your NT1 to the U interface, and connect a power supply to the NT1. Note that in some countries, the phone company provides the NT1.

Connect your TA to the AMI side of the NT1

The 4-wire, multidrop, AMI side of the NT1 connects directly to your TA. Note that many TAs feature a second port for connection of analog telephones, modems, and fax machines.

Assign SPIDs

Your telephone company will assign you SPIDs for voice and data connections. You will need to program these into your TA. Note that it is possible that your connection will work without a SPID(s) (but may require that you program DNs into the TA). Check with your provider.

Configure TEI negotiation

Configure TEI negotiation to match the expectations of the central office switch (see the ISDN/router checklist above for more details).

Select a switch type

You must select a switch type that matches the telephone company's central office switching equipment. Typical North American choices are NI-1, ATT 5ESS, and Northern Telecom DMS-100. Other parts of the world may use other switch types; check with your access provider.

Choose/enable rate adaptation

Because data will be flowing into the TA at a speed different from that at which the TA will feed the data through a B channel, you will have to choose a rate adaptation method. ANSI V.120 is the most likely choice. Both ends of the connection must support it.

Configure bonding if desired

You may wish to bond B channels for a higher-speed connection. TAs on both ends of the link must support bonding; look into this before you purchase the TA.

Configure protocol encapsulation

Dial-up connections through your computer's serial port will be conducted using asynchronous PPP. The TA will convert this to synchronous PPP, encapsulated within V.120 frames.

From your computer's point of view, an ISDN-based connection through the asynch port will look no different from a fast modem. Typically, the Hayes AT command set will be supported—dialing will be just the same as you are used to. You must, however, have a 16550 class UART in your computer to support the higher data rates.

New Devices

Expect new networking devices and media over the coming years—things we haven't heard of yet. Furthermore, don't be surprised if some of the "new" media I describe here never quite take off. The trouble is that economics, ease of use, and availability play a much greater role in establishing markets than great standards. [*] Basic Rate ISDN may become a classic example. Though the technology is here, it is taking a long time to root itself. Tariffs are higher than for analog phones; equipment costs more; there are interoperability questions. In the meantime, 28.8 modems work really well, albeit much more slowly. And they're cheap. People are not abandoning their modems in droves.

What might be coming? Cable modems, for one, are already making their way into the market. These are broadband, asymmetric, high-speed devices that you plug

---

[*] I owned 8-track tapes, and quadraphonic stereo equipment. I should know about great standards that never take hold.

into the cable television system. We call them *asymmetric* because the bandwidth in one direction is much greater than the bandwidth in the other. This will suit most people's Internet access requirements quite well: you send a URL, and you get back a great pile of data; the inbound traffic is much greater than the outbound traffic. And these devices operate in the *10 to 30 Mbit/S range!*

Another interesting new offering is ADSL (*Asynchronous Digital Subscriber Line*). This is a twisted-pair technology that transmits data over an asymmetric allotment of bandwidth, as cable modems do. Data flows at a rate of 6 Mbit/S in one direction, and 64 Kbit/S in the other. Again, this is perfect for surfing the Internet; a small request goes out, and you get buried in data. However, it might not be appropriate if you plan to maintain a Web server.

Medium-Speed Lines

Like lower-speed connections, medium-speed connections—in the 1.5 Mbit/S to 2.0 Mbit/S range—are based upon digital telephony. In fact, the two families are more than closely related; a DS1 (or "T1")* circuit is no more than a large handful of DS0 (64 Kbit/S) circuits. Again, the original purpose was the transport of digitally encoded voice communications. The same circuits are available for data transport too—both in full and fractional forms.

T1

As with DDS circuits, a T1 or fractional T1 connection can be the foundation for a variety of link level protocols, including Frame Relay, PPP, and HDLC. You can also find T1 speeds used for low-end SMDS connections. And as we will see later, T1 connectivity underpins another flavor of ISDN, called *Primary Rate ISDN.*

How a T1 circuit works

A T1 connection bundles together twenty-four *time division multiplexed* 64 Kbit/S channels over a 4-wire copper circuit, for a total bandwidth of 1.536 Mbit/S. An E1 circuit—in Europe, Africa, and other parts of the world—carries thirty-two 64 Kbit/S channels, totaling 2.048 Mbit/S. In both cases, channels are "time-sliced" onto the wire; in rotation, each channel gets an 8-bit time slot. A full T1 data connection will make use of all 24 slots; a fractional T1 will use just some of the slots. In some cases, you may divide the slots up—some for data, and some for voice

---

* The term *DS1* (data speed 1) describes the bandwidth of the circuit. A *T1* circuit is a particular implementation of DS1 connectivity—namely time division multiplexing over copper. You will often hear "T1" when people really want the less specific label "DS1." I'll be talking about copper too, so I will make the same mistake—I'll say "T1" or "E1," even when it's not as precise as it might be.

(as in Figure 14-10). For data-only connections, the circuit can be run *unchannelized*—no time division multiplexing is performed on the signal.

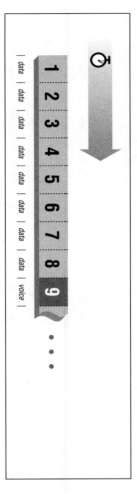

| data | data | data | data | data | data | data | data | voice | • • •

Figure 14-10: Time division multiplexing

That's the big picture. As you have probably guessed—especially after the discussions of DDS and Basic Rate ISDN—there's a little more to encoding and recovering a T1 signal than the hand-waving treatment I just gave it. Particularly, the signal needs to be framed appropriately, so that data communications equipment on the receiving end can tell which slot is which.

How would you go about marking the beginning of the T1 rotation? You *might* place a flag sequence at the head of each frame. This could be a unique bit pattern, like the flags that appeared at the head of the HDLC-derived link layer frames we discussed in the last chapter. The pattern would give the data communications equipment at the receiving end something to latch onto. The trouble is that one flag per frame would be overkill; once the transmitting and receiving ends are in synch, they don't drift very far apart very quickly; synchronization doesn't have to occur at the same frequency as the frame pattern.

Rather than spend precious time transmitting a complete synchronization pattern, T1 frame formats spread the flag over multiple frames—stealing one bit per frame. This means that it takes a while before a complete flag can be extracted from the frames whizzing by. But as I hinted a moment ago, once synchronized, the two ends stay pretty well in synch.

In the case of the most current T1 format—called *Extended Superframe Format* (ESF)—the synchronization flag is 6 bits wide, and repeats every twenty-four frames.* You may wonder what ESF does with the other 18 stolen bits. It uses them for error checking and link supervision. The equipment you would buy today will probably support both styles of framing.

As for T1 encoding, there are two approaches: AMI and B8ZS. Recall that for lower-speed, DDS circuits, we had to give up 1 bit in 8 to maintain synchroni-

---

* You might also see D4 (Superframe), channel bank framing.

zation. In a T1 circuit, on the other hand, AMI has long been used *without* injecting "1" bits. It's not that the "1"s-density problem doesn't exist for higher speed lines. Rather, an AMI-encoded T1 circuit expects the 24 DS0 (64 Kbit/S) channels to adhere to the "1"s-density rules. Provided they do, the T1 circuit inherits the appropriate "1"s-density.

Still, that leaves a problem. If the twenty-four channels are data, they are going to have to shoulder the injected "1" burden, which will reduce them to 56 Kbit/S apiece. This will make the total effective T1 bandwidth 1.344 Mbit/S, in lieu of 1.536 Mbit/S. To benefit from the full connection bandwidth, a T1 circuit needs to use B8ZS encoding. Again, this is called *Clear Channel Capability*, and will probably be part of your Internet link.

In contrast to T1, European E1 (CEPT) framing *does* contain a flag at the beginning of the time slice rotation. There's also a complete CRC for the frame, and some signaling information. Furthermore, the line encoding scheme is different; E1 lines use a format called *High Density, Bipolar 3 zeros suppression* (HDB3). Like B8ZS, HDB3 guarantees a sufficient number of pulses on the wire to maintain synchronization, regardless of the data being transmitted. Any string of four "0"s is replaced with an intentional bipolar violation.

Again, you get what the other side serves you—AMI versus B8ZS, ESF versus D4; you usually don't have a choice. Most of the CSU/DSUs you might purchase are flexible enough to accommodate several formats, though you should be sure to check in advance.

T1 equipment

As I mentioned earlier, a T1 or E1 link can serve several purposes. Your company's telephone service may come over a subset of a T1 link's twenty-four channels, for instance. This would (might) leave the remaining channels available for Internet connectivity. Of course, the equipment you would use to handle data and voice simultaneously would be pretty sophisticated, and more expensive than the equipment for a data connection alone. But if you already own it, you might as well see if you can use it. *

One such piece of equipment would be a *channel bank*. This is a multiplexor that converts analog telephone conversations to digital (and vice versa) for transport over the T1 link. You can often borrow some channels for data connectivity as well. These will be bundled together, shipped across your T1 line, and broken out and fed into a CSU/DSU at the other end.

---

* The "gotcha" is that your Internet service will probably have to come from the same company that provides your phone service. See Chapter 2, *Service Options*.

It is also possible that you might have a device specifically labeled a *T1 multi-plexor*. The multiplexor takes mixed rate information and bundles it into T1 channels. As with the channel bank, a T1 multiplexor will let you "peel off" several channels for partial T1 speed connectivity to the Internet.

Anyway, I throw these things out as possibilities, though I won't be exploring them further. The connection we're most interested in looks very much like the DDS circuit described earlier—a Network Termination Unit, a "demarc," CSU/DSU, and a router (Figure 14-11).

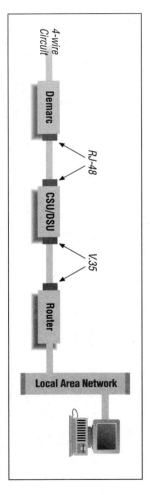

Figure 14-11: T1 circuit

Likewise, the high-level functionality of the boxes is similar. We have network termination at the "demarc"; the incoming signal will be regenerated one last time before passing through to the CSU/DSU. Joining with your internal network, we will have a router capable of supporting the link level protocol dictated by your access provider. The biggest differences will be in between—in the T1-capable CSU/DSU.

The T1 CSU/DSU will differ from the DDS CSU/DSU in several ways. For one thing, it will be more expensive—about four or five times as expensive. It will also be more configurable, allowing for various frame formats, line encodings, and partial or full T1 data framing. As with DDS, the CSU also provides isolation (required) from the telephone company's network.

As we saw earlier, a B8ZS ESF T1 connection provides for network signaling, embedded within the frames. Some of the associated status information will be available through indicators on the front of the CSU/DSU. This may help you debug the data connection in times of trouble. Typical indicators include:

Loss of Service

When an insufficient number of "1" bits (pulses) are received, the CSU/DSU may declare the circuit to be out of service.

Yellow Alarm

A yellow alarm indicates a transmission problem at the *remote* CSU/DSU. A specific bit pattern will identify the alarm; the mechanism differs depending on the frame format. Of course, for the remote CSU/DSU to signal an alarm, the basic T1 circuit has to be operational.

Loss of Synchronization

If the CSU/DSU can't locate the synchronization flag over some number of frames, it will indicate that it lost "synch" with the remote CSU/DSU.

Red Alarm

A red alarm indication warns that the CSU/DSU has lost synchronization over a longer period of time.

Bipolar Violations

This indicator warns that (unintentional) bipolar violations have been detected on the circuit.

There may be test indicators on the CSU/DSU as well. These will be illuminated when you place the CSU/DSU into one of several loopback test modes. The functionality of the loopback tests is analogous to those of the DDS equipment, discussed earlier.

Configuring T1 and fractional T1

The physical portion of the T1 circuit shouldn't take you too long to configure. I have found that the biggest problem is interpreting the manuals that come with the equipment. Somehow, digital communications equipment manuals have avoided the trend toward being readable.

Configure the CSU/DSU Data Rate and Line Encoding

The telephone company will be able to tell you the line encoding and frame type you will be using. These will be configured via DIP switches at the back of the CSU/DSU. Note that you may need to have the switches set before power-up; the CSU/DSU may read them just once per power cycle. Be sure to configure the CSU/DSU for full or fractional T1 speeds, depending on the circuit you have purchased.

Connect the Devices Together

The CSU/DSU will typically come with an RJ48C or RJ48X cable (this has to match your demarc). Connect this between the unit and the demarc. Also connect the CSU/DSU to your router via the synchronous serial (V.35) cable. Upon power-up, the synch light should glow (wait a second). If not, double check the switch settings, and—failing that—check with the phone company.

Connect Your Router to Your LAN

The router you are using for Internet connectivity may come with one or two LAN connections. Some of the "firewall" routers on the market are logically two routers in the same box. The first interface is for a private LAN; the second is for a public (information server) LAN.

Configure Your Router

Your router will use one of the link layer protocols described in the preceding chapter.

Primary Rate ISDN

We looked at basic rate ISDN connectivity several sections back. Another form of ISDN connectivity, called *Primary Rate ISDN*, may also be available in your area. As with basic rate ISDN, the Primary Rate circuits serve multiple purposes—digitized voice and data travel over the same wires. The protocols and the methods are the same as well: there are B channels for data, and a D channel for signaling. In fact, the only significant difference between basic and Primary Rate ISDN services is the speed of the D channel (64 Kbit/S), and the number of B channels (23).

For anyone who is still sore from climbing over the last mountain of ISDN acronyms, I have some very good news: the circuit that would bring a Primary Rate ISDN to your place of business is none other than a T1 connection (or an E1 connection); there is nothing new to learn. One of the 64 Kbit/S channels will carry the D channel LAPD frames for Q.931 signaling, and X.25. The others—B channels—may be allocated as desired. Some may be used for data; some may be used for voice; the number and distribution can change dynamically. And as with basic rate service, B channels may be bonded for higher bandwidth applications.

Would you purchase a Primary Rate ISDN circuit solely for Internet access? Probably not. But you might purchase one for your phone services, and let ISDN connectivity to the Internet tag along for the ride. Again, ISDN is going to be primarily for intermittent access—at least for the time being. A dedicated circuit will probably be less expensive for full-time Internet presence.

High-Speed Lines

High-speed networks form the foundation for some of the newer wide area networking protocols we examined in the last chapter—particularly ATM and SMDS. You *can* run point-to-point protocols over a fast network, of course, though you will find that high-speed Internet connections will be cheaper via shared, wide area networks. The reason is simple: high-speed equipment and lines are costly. An Internet access provider is going to save a bundle (so will you) if they share the wires (or fibers) with other forms of traffic. Like you, they will probably be subscribers to a metropolitan network maintained by a third party; like you, they are interested in purchasing a single physical link into the network.

What is considered to be a high-speed connection? There are no official guidelines, of course, though we are definitely in the high-speed bracket at fractional and full DS3 (T3) speeds (44.736 Mbit/S). And even that level of capability is a sliver of what is possible. The high end of the standardized scale—OC-48—will operate at speeds of almost 2.5 Gbit/S.

I won't belabor the high-speed network designs to the same extent as I did DDS, ISDN, and T1 connectivity—it is very unlikely you will be using this book alone as your guide. When the network costs start to exceed the budgets of small companies, consultants magically appear. So, assuming that you will be in good hands when it actually comes time to plug the network together, I would like to offer the next few pages as a short road map through higher bandwidth links, and the acronyms that travel with them.

T3

Like a T1 connection, a T3 link carries time division multiplexed data.* Again, it can be voice or information traffic; the network doesn't care. Equipment at either end bundles the traffic together and ships it across the link. It is up to the receiver to demultiplex it appropriately.

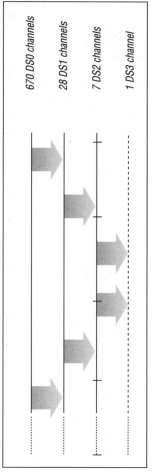

670 DS0 channels

28 DS1 channels

7 DS2 channels

1 DS3 channel

Figure 14-12: Aggregation of channels in a channelized DS3

Just as a T1 (DS1) circuit was constructed from a bundle of DS0 channels, a T3 circuit is (logically) constructed from a hierarchy of lower bandwidth slices (see Figure 14-12). Twenty-four DS0 channels form a DS1; DS1s are taken—four at a time—and grouped into DS2s; seven DS2s are combined to form a DS3. This gives us six hundred and seventy-two (672) 64 Kbit/S channels to work with, or a

* The label "*T3*" is misused in the same way that T1 often is. What we really want to say is *DS3* (Data Speed 3); T3 refers to DS3 bandwidth over copper.

combined bandwidth of 43.008 Mbit/S. The missing bandwidth (remember, the circuit speed is 44.736 Mbit/S) goes toward synchronization, connection management, and error detection.

Common devices for multiplexing data across a T3 link include the M13 multiplexor. This device combines 28 DS1 channels into a single DS3 stream (Figure 14-13).

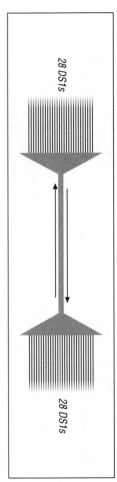

28 DS1s

28 DS1s

Figure 14-13: M13 multiplexors

A companion multiplexor can restore the 28 DS1s on the other side. You can imagine that an M13 multiplexor would be useful for "trunking" multiple T1s for transport between telephone company offices.

Likewise, some T3 DSUs—such as you might use for a T3 data connection—support *M13 framing*. Additionally, most newer T3 data equipment will support a framing format called *C-bit Parity*, offering better link diagnostics and performance monitoring. Data connections may be further run unchannelized; data may be aggregated into higher bandwidth chunks, for custom data applications.

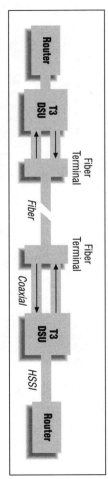

Router

T3
DSU

Fiber
Terminal

Fiber

Fiber
Terminal

Coaxial

T3
DSU

HSSI

Router

Figure 14-14: Unchannelized DS3 connection

The connection between T3 sites may be any of a variety of technologies, including fiber optics, microwaves, or coaxial cable. DS3 service may even be conducted over SONET, described later. Typically, service enters the facilities through a "terminal," is converted to electrical signals, if necessary, and fed to a T3 DSU via a pair of 75 ohm coaxial cables (one going in each direction), terminating in BNC connectors (Figure 14-14). The downstream link between the DSU and router may be an HSSI (*High Speed Serial Interface*), a V.35 connection, or even SCSI or differential ECL.*

DS3 speed networking is pretty fast. Consider that a standard-issue Ethernet backbone runs at 10 Mbit/S. A company will have to have a higher bandwidth in-house network, or some heavy voice requirements, to make a sensible case for DS3 Internet connection—if you can find one. Still, the cost for the circuit isn't as great as it might be. A T3 connection can be priced on the order of four to six times that of a T1 connection—for thirty times the raw performance.

SONET and SDH

You may shop for a "T3" link, yet actually purchase an optical link carrying a DS3, or higher-speed signal. Dedicated optical connections are becoming very inexpensive (in relative terms) thanks to advances in (single mode) fiber technology, electronic optical emitters (such as laser diodes), and LSI circuitry—for multiplexing, signal recovery, and error correction. Even so, the optical link and associated equipment may be proprietary in nature.

Recent movement in the direction of broadband wide area networking (particularly ATM and SMDS) is helping to push standardized physical network technology along. The most significant examples are *Synchronous Optical Network* (SONET), promoted by Bellcore and published as an ANSI standard, and its ITU-T counterpart *Synchronous Digital Hierarchy* (SDH).

Table 14–2. SONET Carrier Designation

SONET Carrier Designation	Mbit/S
STS-1/OC-1	51.84
STS-3/OC-3	155.52
STS-9/OC-9	466.56
STS-12/OC-12	622.08
STS-18/OC-18	933.12
STS-24/OC-24	1,244.16
STS-36/OC-36	1,866.24
STS-48/OC-48	2,488.32

Table 14-2 shows the defined bandwidth range for SONET networks. In the not-too-distant future, OC-192 should be a standard as well. SDH network speeds are the same, beginning at the 155.53 Mbit/S mark. You can see that there are two tags (STS and OC) associated with each speed. The STS (*Synchronous Transport Signal-level*) designation describes the signal over electrical media; the OC (*Optical*

---

* Differential Emitter Coupled Logic (ECL) provides a fast-switching, low-impedance, power-hungry interface with good noise immunity.

Carrier-level) designation describes the same signal after conversion to optical media. Many SONET devices terminate the optical signal locally; there is no conversion to an electrical carrier. Note that the low-end connection—SONET OC-1—is sufficient to carry a DS3 signal.

A SONET-based network is accessed via terminal equipment (a router, in our case), which feeds into a SONET multiplexor, which in turn drives line termination equipment, and the optical carrier. In Figure 14-15, the terminal equipment (TE) may constitute one of a number of *virtual tributaries*—lower-speed interfaces into the SONET MUX. The data contributed by the tributary could be broken out at the other side, by demultiplexing on the far end.

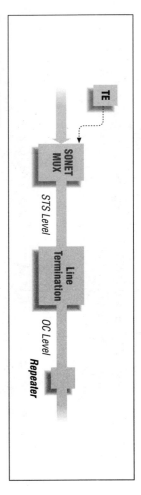

Figure 14-15: SONET equipment

SONET is meant to be flexible. From the user's point of view, a SONET network provides a certain amount of subscribed bandwidth. This may be a subrate—less than the network is capable of. The remaining bandwidth need not go wasted, however; other traffic may share the network as well. It's up to the multiplexors to combine channels, and populate the STS-level signal.

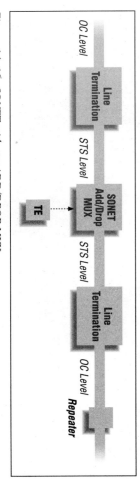

Figure 14-16: SONET with an ADD/DROP MUX

Here's where SONET gets really nifty. The ability to add and drop channels from an already multiplexed carrier is built into the standard. Compare this to adding or dropping a channel from a T3 link: we have to demultiplex the whole signal, change its contents, and remultiplex it. This can get expensive; T3 mux/demux equipment costs tens of thousands of dollars. With SONET's add/drop capability, on the other hand, you could add a trivial 1.54 Mbit/S channel to a SONET network as it passes near your place of work. Your terminal equipment would forward its contribution to an *Add/Drop Multiplexor* (Figure 14-16). As the signal passes through, the multiplexor modulates the signal into the STS frame, and adjusts a set of header pointers that tell the next multiplexor down the line where the new (and old) data can be found. Similarly, an add/drop multiplexor can altogether delete a channel from the STS frame. An Internet connection via a SONET link would probably be carved into a sub rate channel, using these very methods.

15

Connection Turn-Up and Debug

Well, it's Prom Night. You've got your corsage, your blue polyester suit with a white ruffled shirt, and a black satin cummerbund.* Your date is MCI, or Sprint, or UUNet, or somebody. They're calling at 9:00 to turn up your circuit, and route traffic to your site. Are you ready?

We covered a lot of ground in the preceding chapters; we touched upon everything you need to think about. But while we wait for your date, I thought we might go through a checklist to make sure that you didn't miss something. At the same time, we'll talk a little bit about circuit troubleshooting, wide area networking, debug, and IP routing problems—just in case something that happens on Prom Night becomes an issue later on.

Circuit Turn-Up

Circuit turn-up usually takes place in stages. Naturally, the telephone company has to install your connection before anything can happen. The wiring is run, and back at the central office(s) electronic switching equipment is programmed so that you and your ISP can trade traffic. It is possible that sometime between then and turn-up day, a CSU/DSU on the far end will come to life, and attempt to trade framing information with the CSU/DSU on your end. At the appointed hour on the appointed day, you and a representative of your ISP will talk on the telephone, and finish the configuration. Typically, the ISP will only be interested in reaching your router at first; follow-on configuration issues, such as USENET news setup are usually tackled later on, and often by other personnel.

---

* I went to proms in the late 1970s. That should help explain the clothing . . . .

Pre-Turn-Up Checklist

Of course, you can hire an ISP to do *everything* for you—plug in the equipment, configure the router, and monitor the circuit, in which case little in this chapter will matter. On the other hand, you may be responsible for everything—including keeping after your ISP. For those of us who do have to get bits under our fingernails, let's review a list of pre-turn-up day tasks.

Step One—Verify hardware

As a first step, let's review hardware to make sure that you have all of the pieces you need—cables, CSU/DSU, and router—plus space and power.

1. Verify that your CSU/DSU matches the requirements of the circuit, and that you have selected framing, clocking, and encoding settings appropriately. You can get the settings from your ISP, or the telephone company. In some cases, you may specify preferences—D4 versus ESF framing, for instance.

2. Verify that your CSU/DSU-to-demarc cable has the correct pin-outs. Be careful here; there can be several cable and jack types—particularly for T1-speed circuits (RJ48C vs. RJ48X). Check with your CSU/DSU documentation.

3. Verify that you have a cable sporting the right V.35 connectors, or HSSI connectors to go between your CSU/DSU and router. Also, be aware that data communications equipment often ships *without* the cabling you need. Furthermore, some vendors use proprietary V.35 connectors; you may have to order a special cable.

4. Be sure that you have prepared the LAN on the internal side of the router, particularly if you are erecting a firewall. You may need a wiring hub, or a piece of thinnet, for instance. If the firewall is the *only* piece of equipment on the LAN, then you might want to consider purchasing a single piece of twisted pair cabling, with the pairs reversed (a loopback cable); this will save you from purchasing an extra hub.

5. Check to be sure that you have an appropriate adapter to connect your router to your internal LAN or firewall LAN. Many routers come with AUI ports alone; you may need to convert this to twisted pair or thinnet.

6. Verify that you have the power you need close to the demarc, and that your internal LAN has a drop nearby. It is a good idea to keep the cable runs to the CSU/DSU and router as short as possible.

You can connect the equipment together and apply power before the circuit is actually turned up.* In fact, having the CSU/DSU in place ahead of time can sometimes save a step; the ISPs can see that the circuit is operating end-to-end before the day of the phone call. Likewise, keep an eye on the CSU/DSU front-panel lights. You may see them change as the time for tune-up approaches.

Step Two — Verify router configuration

It is going to be difficult to be sure that you have the router configuration correct until you actually get to put the router into service. However, you can verify *some* of the settings, and be pretty sure about the rest:

1. Check to see that your router's LAN port is functioning, and that hosts on your LAN can reach the router without problems (ping). In particular, make sure that the LAN IP address and netmask are correct, and check routing back into the internal network. Of course, LAN connectivity doesn't require that the connection to the ISP be operating; you can test LAN connectivity far in advance.

2. Review your serial port configuration. Do you have the correct IP address and netmask for your end of the link? If you are running a virtual circuit (Frame Relay, X.25, or ATM), do you have circuit endpoint identifiers in place, and mapped to IP addresses? Look at the status of the serial interface (e.g., *show int s0*) to see if it says something like "connecting." If it says "down," then you may need to bring the interface "up" before it will be ready to accept a connection from the other side.

3. Review your router's routing table entries. Does the default route direct all nonlocal traffic toward the ISP's remote router? Do you need to stuff your router's ARP cache with an entry that directs traffic across the serial link?

4. If you have access lists, it will be a good idea to leave them "off" until you are sure the link is functioning.

Be aware that if you are running a nonrouting firewall, then you may not be allowed to ping through, and will be even less likely to be able to run a traceroute. However, you *can* run all of these tests from the firewall itself. The firewall will have a foot in your internal LAN, and share a network with the Internet router. The firewall should be able to reach any destination.

---

* Note that, technically, you may be required to attest to the carrier that the equipment on your end of the link meets requirements, and that you are qualified to operate it. Your T1 CSU/DSU manual may include an affidavit template for submission to your carrier.

The Turn-Up Phone Call

I have been involved in circuit turn-ups that have taken less than five minutes, and in others that have taken many days. A lot has to go right, frankly, for the turn-up to go quickly. The phone company has to have the circuit configured, you have to have your equipment set up correctly, and the ISP has to have their act together. As I mentioned above, you should connect your data communications equipment together in advance, so that the telephone company and ISP can perform some testing before the big day.

Depending on the ISP, you may deal with one person in one place, or with multiple people, in multiple places. Larger ISPs operate networks independently of their Internet service. To take an example, MCI provides Frame Relay services for private intracompany communications. They use the same Frame Relay network to provide Internet services. This means that service turn-up is a two-step process: the Frame Relay group brings up a PVC, and the Internet group routes traffic over the PVC. Fortunately, the process is pretty well-oiled.

Telnet into your router before the call, and check to see that everything looks OK. You might sample the status of the serial interface to see if it reports being "up" or "established," as might be the case if the ISP began configuring their end of the link before your appointment.* A periodic "ping" to the ISP's remote router will also give you a hint about changes in the circuit's status.

Eventually, the phone will ring. The first thing that the ISP will want to do is review your configuration with you. You may be absolutely prepared, but they don't know that, of course, and may ask some surprisingly elementary questions. At the same time, they are used to addressing start-up issues, and they *do* work for you, so you should take the opportunity to pursue anything you are not clear about. Note that these people are likely to be some of the best networking folks in the ISP's staff. You may never get a chance to talk to them again—your follow-on calls may go to a separate support group—so take advantage of the time.

Once you and the ISP's representatives have sorted out the serial connection, IP connectivity between routers should follow immediately. You can then begin testing your reach out to other destinations—first *within* your ISP's own network, and then out into the greater Internet. There's really not a lot more for you to do—other than "ping"—once IP is moving between routers. It's up to the ISP to see that your traffic routes across their network correctly.

---

* On a Livingston router, check the interface by typing **show s1** (assuming s1 is the link to the ISP). On a cisco router: **show int s0**. On Morning Star, type **ps aux**, and look at the process list, or type **dmesg** to look for announcements that might have scrolled by.

At the point when you can reach arbitrary Internet destinations from your router, you should then Telnet to your firewall, or an internal host, and try connecting to Internet sites from there. There is an important difference between attempting connections from your router, and attempting them from a host on your LAN: router traffic emanates from the serial port's address. To be sure that traffic is reaching your site correctly, you have to attempt a connection that starts from the near side of your router's LAN port.

Once the connection appears to be working, you can thank the ISP's representative, and gingerly declare that you don't need her help any longer. You might, at this time, make appointments for other services you may need—a USENET newsfeed, nameserver hosting, or SNMP monitoring. For most ISPs, the first "ping" marks your anniversary date—they start charging *now*.

Troubleshooting

Internet links go up and down all the time. I've never heard that such a person exists, but I wholeheartedly believe that there is a fellow in a yellow hardhat who motors from city to city, maniacally plunging his backhoe into the asphalt in attempts to sever optical cables.

At any rate, it can seem as if your connection has gone down, when the trouble is, in fact, several hops removed from you. The biggest problem (or advantage, depending on your viewpoint) is that everything beyond the demarc belongs to someone else; your ISP or exchange carrier has to get involved when the circuit goes belly up. The first sign of trouble is usually backed-up mail, or a loss of outbound access, though it may be your telephone ringing (people become addicted to the Internet very quickly . . .). Before you get on the phone to the ISP, you can do some basic fault isolation:

1. Verify that your link is down. Begin by attempting to "ping" a site connected to the Internet via a competing ISP. Often, this will be the site of a friend—a site that you know is "up." Preferably, you will have its IP address handy (as opposed to its domain name). This will eliminate the possibility that your nameserver has crashed, and that users are taking this to mean that the link is down. Try a few other destinations as well.

2. Next, attempt to ping your ISP's Web server. Again, use an IP address if possible, not a domain name. If you can reach their Web server, but cannot reach out into the great Internet, then you may assume that they are having a problem in one of the exchange points, or within their own network.

3. If you cannot reach your ISP's Web server, try pinging the far side of the serial link joining your router to your ISP's router. It would probably be best to try

this directly from your router. That will eliminate the possibility that your own router has gone down, or that you have an internal routing problem.

4. If you get no response from the far side of the serial link, then either your ISP's router has failed (or they have purposely taken the link down), or the circuit between you has failed.

You might also cut out a few steps by walking over to your equipment and taking a look at the lights. Check for alarms on T1 CSU/DSUs, or a "no service" light on a DDS CSU/DSU. Likewise, you can check the status of the router's serial interface. The link protocol should be "up" or "established."

Once you have determined that the connection really *is* down, you will want to contact your ISP. They, in turn, will want to run their own tests. In many cases, they will ask you to place your CSU/DSU into loopback mode, so that they can perform end-to-end testing. If their tests succeed, then they may declare that the problem is on your end; from their point of view, they can reach all the way up to your router, but not into the router itself. (Of course, this discounts the possibility that *their* router might be suffering a link layer problem.) If the loopback test fails, on the other hand—if they cannot reach your CSU/DSU—then somebody (you or the ISP) will have to contact the primary exchange carrier. They will open a service ticket, and perform circuit testing.

What *can* go wrong? I don't know if we are especially lucky, but we *have* been hit by lightning; that in itself altered the function of some of our equipment. We have also had some intermittent problems—particularly with a CSU/DSU. Everything looked great most of the time. Occasionally, however, the device would get timid, and stop talking to the router. Of course we thought it was our ISP's fault. . . .

Ping and Traceroute

Ping and *traceroute* are two *really* useful tools for debugging your Internet connectivity. They can be found on most UNIX hosts, with equivalent versions available on routers, and within personal computer IP environments. The first of the two tools—*ping*—uses an ICMP echo request/reply pair. Provided the remote site allows ICMP through, you may "ping" them to see if they are alive.

Traceroute operates on a different mechanism altogether: IP packets carry a *time-to-live* (TTL) parameter. By convention, a packet's TTL is decremented every time the packet crosses an IP gateway (router). Once the TTL reaches zero, the last gateway in the path returns an ICMP "time expired" notice to the host that was the original source of the packet. TTL "time expired" notification provides a method to squash packets trapped in routing loops. Consider that if there were no TTL accounting, lost packets could bounce between routers for days, or even months. Traceroute exploits TTL accounting by sending out UDP/IP packets with successively longer TTLs. Gateways along the way return "time expired" notices—one for each hop in the journey. When the last UDP packet reaches its final destination, an "unreachable port" message is returned, and we have a complete journal of the hops along the way.

```
% traceroute www.atlantic.com
traceroute to www.atlantic.com (205.246.144.102), 30 hops max, 40 byte packets
 1  wisper.atlantic.com (198.252.200.1)  3.523 ms  3.443 ms  3.374 ms
 2  serial.hartford.ct.psi.net (38.1.10.219)  47.063 ms  29.238 ms  29.457 ms
 3  leaf.net218.psi.net (38.1.10.2)  52.541 ms  75.248 ms  89.242 ms
 4  38.1.2.19 (38.1.2.19)  74.805 ms  72.889 ms  63.246 ms
 5  s1-mae-e-f0/0.sprintlink.net (192.41.177.241)  127.309 ms  75.57 ms  234.058 ms
 6  s1-dc-8-H1/0-T3.sprintlink.net (144.228.10.41)  75.848 ms  295.938 ms  338.443 ms
 7  s1-dc-6-F0/0.sprintlink.net (144.228.20.6)  57.845 ms  62.261 ms  74.932 ms
 8  s1-pen-1-H2/0-T3.sprintlink.net (144.228.10.34)  69.054 ms  80.909 ms  166.661 ms
 9  s1-pen-8-F0/0.sprintlink.net (144.228.60.8)  195.849 ms  97.765 ms  107.532 ms
10  s1-berlin-2-s0-T1.sprintlink.net (144.228.68.18)  107.035 ms  85.211 ms
    177.863 ms
11  205.246.144.102 (205.246.144.102)  80.85 ms  98.474 ms  78.565 ms
```

The traceroute output shown here details a trip across PSI's network, through MAE-East (an exchange point operated by MFS Datanet), and out through Sprint's network. There were eleven hops along the way. You can see host names on the left, and their associated IP addresses, shown in parentheses. In cases where no reverse DNS look-up was available, the IP address appears twice. The times (in milliseconds) to the right describe the round trip delays for three separate probes.

16

Internet Security

I used to have a job constructing nuclear power plant simulators. Each simulator was a full-sized replica of a real power plant control room, complete with controls and indicators. Behind the scenes, computers acted in lieu of the plant; water temperature gauges went up, steam pressure gauges went down, and imaginary radioactive water poured onto the floor.

The power plant operators would take their training on the simulators. This gave them a chance to test their skills in dangerous situations, without endangering the public. Out of sight of the trainees, the instructor would tell the computers to model a stuck check value, power failure, or steam pipe rupture. The trainees would then scramble about, working to keep the plant safe and under control.*

We had a game to play when no training was in progress. One person would be in charge of keeping the plant running. The other would try to cause trouble by shutting down pumps, and closing valves. The odds were in favor of the bad guy; at the very least, he could cause a reactor scram. The game would have been much easier if I could have belly-bumped my opponent out of the control room, and locked the door behind him. No knob or switch would have been as effective as the door to the room where the simulator was housed.

Likewise, in Internet world, a single "door" is the best method for securing your own network against the outside world, and keeping people away from your pump and valves. The downside is that if the door is too rigid, it will be difficult for *you* to pass through as well. As is the case with many disciplines, firewall construction is full of trade-offs.

---

* I'm told that the Nuclear Regulatory Commission has a rule that says that plant operators are not allowed back into the control room for a period of 48 hours after simulator training. The reason? They might forget where they are, and get a little too playful with the steam generators or pressurizer.

In this chapter, we are going to look at Internet firewall construction. I'm going to approach the subject clinically—no paranoia, no stories of corporate sabotage, and no dead people. I will begin by describing a firewall, and differentiating between the things a firewall can do for us and the things we have to handle by other means. Following that, we will look into specific firewall configurations, tools, and auditing procedures—progressing from basic to sophisticated. In some ways, this discussion is going to be like taking a bus to the bad end of town. We will go through a lot of neighborhoods on the way, and make a few stops. The meanest among us will ride the bus to the end. Anyway, my goal is to provide you with a firewall recipe you can live with, and to do it in a reasonable amount of time. If you need more, you can find whole books (good ones) that have been written on the subject.* For the ever-suspicious, these will provide some strong motivation for security. Many of these references cover, in detail, material that I will only touch upon.

What Is a Firewall?

Lots of configurations of routers and computers travel under the legend *firewall.* What we are usually talking about is a barrier to keep unwanted traffic from traversing our internal network (Figure 16-1). Ideally, an unauthorized Internet traveler will not be able to get through our firewall, nor discover any information that we wish to keep secret.

Typically, we construct firewalls using a combination of tools and techniques, including:

- Control of basic network information (or intentional misinformation). By restricting the host and routing information available to the rest of the world, we can make it difficult to discover or reach computers on the other side of the firewall.

- Access lists. Like the hosts of an exclusive party, we can fashion elaborate lists of invited network guests. Routers come with primitives that allow us to choose traffic according to its origin, destination, and service type.

Similarly, at the host level, we can insulate (many) network services with *wrapper* programs. These take the place of daemons, such as FTPD and telnetd. When a connection request comes in, the wrapper is invoked. Once it has determined that the request is from an "approved" source, the wrapper "execs" the appropriate daemon, which handles the connection.

---

* For starters, see *Firewalls and Internet Security,* by Cheswick and Bellovin, published by Addison-Wesley, and *Building Internet Firewalls,* by Chapman and Zwicky, published by O'Reilly & Associates.

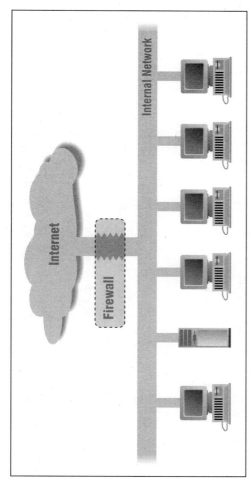

Figure 16–1: Internet connection with a firewall

- Proxies. For tighter firewall configurations, we can erect proxy servers to intercept, examine, and forward traffic for a deliberately sanctioned set of applications or network services. *Circuit-level* proxies work at a low level, logging and forwarding packet traffic, with little insight into the information being exchanged. *Application-level* proxies unbundle and forward requests; the proxy server typically understands the form of the information being transferred, and can keep more comprehensive logs.

Several of these devices depend on a cycle of identify-and-trust: we identify the source of the traffic, and then decide if it should be allowed to pass. Of course, it is important that a firewall be configured properly so that only those Internet exchanges we trust can make their way through. A more subtle hazard accompanies the first part of the cycle—identification. I may say, "Network X is allowed to have conversations of type Y with local host Z." But how can I be sure that I'm really talking to network X? Perhaps X is an imposter. Questions like these push firewall configurations into grey areas; we not only have to pick and choose among our friends, we also have to mistrust them.

Securing your network against the stick-wielding mob is the main goal. But you can aim a firewall in the other direction too—at your own community. A firewall can limit the kinds of Internet services that people within the organization can reach. Likewise, it can collect logs of their activity.

There are a lot of things a firewall can't do, of course. It can't recognize that someone in your company is mailing out the Secret Sauce Recipe. Nor can it distinguish between a data file and a virus-laden virus scanner. Firewalls operate at a lower level, typically, allowing or denying network activity according to its origins, destinations, and type—not its content. Assuming that we have the ability to pick from among a group of computers and services we can trust, we have to hope that their owners are trustworthy as well.

This brings us to a fine spot to elucidate a point: a firewall is not a security policy. It is merely a tool for securing a machine or a network. You can use a firewall to enforce certain aspects of a security policy. However, there are some "big picture" questions that your organization will have to grapple with first. Never start by arguing over the configuration of the firewall. Begin by identifying policies.

Configurations

Imagine a street lined with compact economy cars, keys tossed trustingly among the coffee cups, cat hair, and newspapers on the passenger's seat. There could be one exception near the corner—a shiny new red Maserati—locked, full of Doberman pinschers, and wearing an anti-theft device on the steering wheel. Which is the more tempting target? It depends on the thief, of course. But most of us will agree that one economy car is much like another, and all are pretty boring. The sports car, on the other hand, might be fun to drive.

The moral is that there is great protection in anonymity and boringness. If I don't notice that you're there, or expect to find anything interesting, I probably won't waste my time trying to bust into your site. On the other hand, a lightly protected, boring site is a good place from which to stage attacks on other sites, and cover up one's tracks.[†] In either case, yours is not the gold ring of all Internet sites; *some* protection may be enough to drive the pernicious elsewhere. I tell you this so that you will understand why I might look the other way if you chose less-than-state-of-the-art firewall protection. "Good" protection can provide an annoyance factor, without making Internet access cumbersome, and without requiring a full-time firewall administrator. And "good" protection is really that—*good*. You need to weigh the trade-offs yourself, but you shouldn't dismiss a minimalist firewall configuration out of hand.

* Actually, this is *sort of* true. You can find add-ons that will scan traffic, and do something (e.g., not deliver a piece of mail) if it looks like trouble.

† As one reviewer put it, "crooks boosting a car for use in another crime may *want* an econobox; they're less conspicuous."

A Minimalist's Firewall

A minimalist's firewall consists of a combination of router access lists, service wrappers, and self-policing (Figure 16-2). For our purposes, I will assume that you have a single server acting as a mail hub, Web server, DNS server, etc.

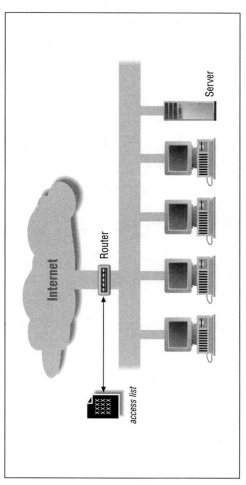

Figure 16-2: A minimal firewall

We want to:

- Allow people within the organization to reach the Internet from their desktops.

- Allow people on the Internet to reach our Web server, mailhub, etc.

- Make it impossible for people on the Internet to contact machines on our network, other than the server.

The devil is in the details, of course, but this captures our goals pretty succinctly. Let's begin by configuring the router.

Router Access Lists

Every IP packet that passes through your Internet connection, router, and network has a header that tells something about its origin, destination, and, in many cases, purpose.* Figuratively speaking, you could slide your glasses down your bony, thin nose and peer into the header of each packet as it whizzes by. You would notice a mix of different IP packet types, pertaining to different IP transports—

---

* Non-IP traffic has packet headers too, of course. We only care about IP here.

particularly TCP, UDP, and ICMP packets. Their relative proportions and destinations would be a function of the applications running on the network; some of them we will recognize as belonging to well-known services, such as Telnet or FTP. Others may be trading between applications we hadn't considered. For our purposes, the differences between them are significant, because the way they are used has bearing on the way we apply filters to them. Let's start with a look at TCP traffic.

TCP/IP

You often hear people use "TCP/IP" to describe the whole ball of wax—TCP, UDP, etc. What they should really say is simply "IP" (Internet Protocol). TCP is just one of a number of possible IP transport protocols. For most people, the misusage doesn't matter. In our case, however, the features of each transport are important.

We call TCP a *reliable, connection-oriented* protocol, meaning that for the applications that speak to one another via TCP, the data exchange behaves as if it were conducted over a dedicated circuit. From the application's point of view, it appears that all data arrive intact and in order. In reality, packets do get lost, and they can get out of order. It is up to the networking software to put things right before forwarding the information to the program waiting to receive it.

TCP/IP conversations start with an exchange of basic information. Typically, the calling computer opens a connection on a local TCP port numbered above 1024, and heads out into the network to make contact with the callee.* The remote destination is often a *well-known service*—located on a port number in the range below 1024. Here, the caller expects a warm reception from a network application, hosted by the callee. For example, SMTP mail conversations are typically conducted on port 25. If I wanted to contact your computer to deliver mail, I would expect to be able to connect to port 25 and speak with your mailer daemon. Telnet, to take another example, listens on port 23.† The combination of addresses (caller and callee) and port numbers (the caller's high-numbered port and the callee's well-known port) provides a tuple by which we can uniquely identify a conversation.

To actually begin the TCP/IP conversation, the caller sends a *SYN* (synchronize) packet, containing the destination address and port, and the source address and port. This is accompanied by a sequence number, which is used to track the ordering of data in packets to follow. The callee replies to the *SYN* packet with an *ACK*, *SYN* (acknowledge) packet, and the conversation is established. Data packets are

---

* Port numbers for each transport (UDP, TCP) range from 1 to 65,535. Note that there is no particular connection between like-numbered ports on different transports. Port 50/TCP wouldn't have anything in common with 50/UDP, for instance.

† Look at */etc/services*, which lists service types and their associated port numbers and transports.

forwarded and "ACKed" until the connection is eventually closed by one or both parties.

From the point of view of a router, there is a wealth of information with which to scrutinize a TCP session. If I wanted to prevent TCP connectivity from the outside world to a particular service (say Telnet), I could instruct the router to drop any incoming packets (or outgoing packets, depending on whether I'm considering the external or internal network interface) with destination port 23. Another possibility would be to selectively drop *SYN* packets. This would prevent the initial hand-shake, and likewise prevent the TCP conversation from getting started in the first place. I could loosen my grip a little too, and permit certain kinds of traffic to reach certain computers. For instance, I might want to prohibit connections to port 23 on all computers except one—a machine open to the public.

The rules that describe how packets should be filtered, known collectively as *router access lists*, are programmed directly into the organization's router by a net-work administrator. Typically, access list programming occurs in two steps: a set of rules is assembled, one at a time, and then applied all at once to a router interface. Routers can have multiple network interfaces—many more than the two implied in Figure 16-2. Accordingly, there can be multiple access lists in use on a given router.

It would be nice if I could just give you a rule set and move on.[*] The trouble is that rule syntax and filtering mechanisms can vary greatly between router vendors. Some brands only apply rules to packets leaving an interface; others can filter traf-fic traveling through an interface in either direction. Some watch for *SYN* packets; others are easier to program for source/destination pairs. Perhaps fortunately, the array of possibilities is going to force us to take a few minutes to really understand how we would go about crafting a set of rules. Whatever the capabilities of the router, the exercise of setting up access lists starts the same way: by considering the kinds of traffic we want to allow through the router, into our network.

Table 16-1: A Set of Access Rules

Transport	Allow	Source Port	Dest Port	From Addr	To Addr
!ip	in, out	source-route		0.0.0.0/0	0.0.0.0/0
!any	in	any port	any port	198.252.200.0/24	198.252.200.0/24
tcp	syn, in	any port	80 (httpd)	0.0.0.0/0	198.252.200.3/32
tcp	syn, in	any port	70 (gopher)	0.0.0.0/0	198.252.200.3/32
tcp	syn, in	any port	23 (telnet)	199.100.201.0/24	198.252.200.3/32
tcp	syn, in	any port	23 (telnet)	192.65.177.3/32	198.252.200.0/24

---

[*] Maybe I can... Appendix A contains sample access lists for a few router types.

Table 16-1: A Set of Access Rules (continued)

Transport	Allow	Source Port	Dest Port	From Addr	To Addr
tcp	syn, in	any port	25 (smtp)	0.0.0.0/0	198.252.200.3/32
tcp	syn, in	any port	119 (nntp)	129.5.160.14/32	198.252.200.3/32
tcp	syn, in	any port	21 (ftp)	0.0.0.0/0	198.252.200.3/32
tcp	syn, in	20 (ftp-data)	high-numbered	0.0.0.0/0	198.252.200.3/32
tcp	syn, out	any port	any port	0.0.0.0/0	0.0.0.0/0
tcp	syn, in	any port	1025-65535	0.0.0.0/0	198.252.200.0/24
udp	in	53 (domain)	53 (domain)	0.0.0.0/0	198.252.200.0/24
udp	out	53 (domain)	53 (domain)	198.252.200.0/24	0.0.0.0/0
tcp	syn, in	any port	53 (domain)	199.100.105.2/32	198.252.200.3/32
icmp	in, out	redirect		0.0.0.0/0	0.0.0.0/0
icmp	in, out	any		0.0.0.0/0	0.0.0.0/0

Table 16-1 shows a reasonable first cut at a set of rules, using a format and some addresses that I have chosen for illustration. I have made an assumption that the router can filter packets heading through the network interface in either direction. It might not be true for your router, in which case you will have to spread the send and receive rules over access lists for two interfaces—incoming and outgoing.

Each packet coming through the router is checked against each rule, in order. The first rule that matches takes precedence. If we get to the bottom of the access list without a match, the packet is rejected. Note that this implicit rule—packets that don't match any rules are rejected—might have to be added explicitly for some routers. For others, the presence of any access list is a choice for default rejection of unvouched-for packets.

The "from" and "to" fields use a syntax that describes an address template, followed by the number of significant address bits. For example, an address such as 198.252.200.3/32 describes one particular host; all 32 bits of the address count. A template like 198.252.200.0/24, on the other hand, specifies a whole class C network. By the same convention, a "from" field of "0.0.0.0/0" tells the router that no bits in the address specification are significant; all addresses match.

The first rule in the list above says, "Don't accept (indicated by the '!') any IP traffic with source-routing enabled." I'll explain what this means shortly, but for now let me just say that it is important that this rule appear near the top of the list, because it has to be applied to every packet that comes through.

The second rule in the list says, "Reject traffic coming from my network, destined to my network." The rule is a little peculiar: How could traffic from and to our network appear on both sides of the network interface? One possibility is that packets on the Internet side of the interface contain deliberately spoofed source addresses, to make it *appear* as if the traffic originates locally. This would allow a trickster to take advantage of any special trust afforded hosts on the local LAN. By prohibiting conversations with yourself, you can avoid this well-known security hole.

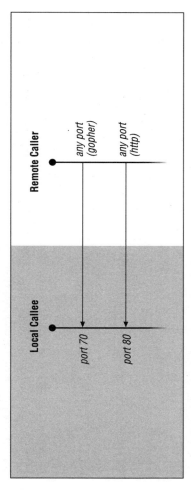

Figure 16–3: Web and gopher connections

The next two rules allow inbound (in) TCP connections to ports 80 and 70, *httpd* and *gopherd*, respectively (Figure 16-3). Additionally, we will allow *SYN* packets through. This makes it possible for computers on the Internet to initiate conversations to daemons on those ports. Again, the router you are using may not be able to distinguish *SYN* packets from others, in which case you will have to drop the "SYN" check for conversation initialization.

| tcp | syn, in | any port | 80 (httpd) | 0.0.0.0/0 | 198.252.200.3/32 |
| tcp | syn, in | any port | 70 (gopher) | 0.0.0.0/0 | 198.252.200.3/32 |

As I described just a moment ago, the "to" field of "198.252.200.3/32" tells the router to restrict traffic to a single address, 198.252.200.3; the "32" says that all bits in the address are significant. Taken together, the two rules state that TCP traffic is allowed on ports 80 and 70, from anywhere, to just one host: 198.252.200.3.

| tcp | syn, in | any port | 23 (telnet) | 199.100.201.0/24 | 198.252.200.3/32 |
| tcp | syn, in | any port | 23 (telnet) | 192.65.177.3/32 | 198.252.200.0/24 |

Just below the gopher and http specifications, telnet rules describe who will be allowed interactive logins. The first of the two rules says that any host on class C network 199.100.201.0 may initiate a telnet session with host 198.252.200.3. The second rule says that one particular host—192.65.177.3—is allowed to make a telnet connection with *any* computer on our class C network 198.252.200.0.

| tcp | syn, in | any port | 21 (ftp) | 0.0.0.0/0 | 198.252.200.3/32 |
| tcp | syn, in | 20 (ftp-data) | high-numbered | 0.0.0.0/0 | 198.252.200.3/32 |

The rules for SMTP and NNTP connections (which I will skip) are analogous to the Telnet, httpd, and gopher rules we have looked at so far: we limit whom we will allow to start an inbound conversation. FTP rules, on the other hand, require extra consideration because FTP sessions actually consist of two connections—a control connection and a data connection. As with the other applications we have considered, the outgoing FTP user process first allocates a high-numbered port, and then contacts a remote host—this time on port 21. Through this control connection, the user can log on, set transfer options, etc.

Figure 16–4. Outgoing FTP sessions

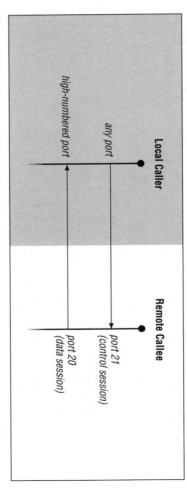

When there is data to transfer—a file to be moved, or a directory listing to be viewed—the FTP user process sets up a listener on a high-numbered port. The remote computer then makes a connection originating from port 20, back to the caller's high-numbered port. Now we have two connections open. The first is used for control of the conversation; the second is used for data transfer.[*]

Our rules have to deal with two cases: inbound and outbound FTP sessions. For inbound connections (Figure 16-5), we will have to allow remote computers to initiate conversations on our port 21, but *only* to our server; other machines on our network will not be allowed to serve FTP sessions. Likewise, the server has to be able to start a return conversation, originating from our port 20, and destined for their high-numbered port.

Outbound FTP (Figure 16-4) sessions give us a more troublesome risk. Allowing computers on our network to reach out to the Internet on a high-numbered port is

---

* There is an FTP primitive (*PASV*) that allows the user process to open both connections, outbound. This would reduce the security risk associated with opening high-numbered ports for inbound connections. However, *PASV* isn't universally supported by FTP daemons.

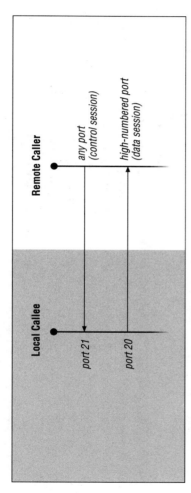

```
    Local Callee                    Remote Caller

        ●                               ●
                                           any port
        │                                  (control session)
 port 21│
        ▼
        ●───────────────────────────────●
                                           high-numbered port
        ▲                                  (data session)
 port 20│
        │
```

Figure 16–5: Incoming FTP sessions

no big deal. It's the return (data) connections that are the problem. In order to accommodate the return connection from an outbound FTP session, we have to make a hole in the firewall to allow computers on the Internet to *initiate (SYN)* return conversations to high-numbered ports on our network. It may not be FTP we are worried about, by the way: once we allow conversations to be started on high-numbered ports, we have to assume that other, unsanctioned applications might be listening for connections up in the stratosphere as well. A pernicious remote user could force an outgoing connection through port 20, with no intention of conducting an FTP session.

As we skip to the bottom of the list, we find a few rules with broad-brushstroke port specifications:

| tcp | syn, out | any port | 198.252.200.0/24 | 0.0.0.0/0 |
| tcp | in | any port | 1025-65535 | 0.0.0.0/0 | 198.252.200.0/2.4 |

The first rule says that any computer on our network is allowed to start a conversation with any remote computer we choose, for any TCP service (provided, of course, that they let *us* in). In other words, there are no restrictions on outbound conversations. As you might guess, you can apply limits here too: rules can restrict internal network computers' access to remote Internet services. Typical scenarios might be enforcement of a corporate-wide ban on IRC traffic (Internet relay chat), or restrictions to certain Web sites.

The rule that follows (1025-65535/tcp . . .) is necessary if computers on our LAN are to be able to hold conversations with computers on the Internet. Recall the way a TCP conversation is initiated: the caller connects locally to a high-numbered port, and heads out across the network to make contact with a well-known service (low-numbered port) on a remote computer. In order for the callee to respond back to the caller, we have to make a provision for return traffic on high-numbered ports. TCP traffic is allowed from anywhere, to anywhere on our network, provided that it is bound for a high-numbered port, and provided that it isn't the start of a conversation (a *SYN* packet).

There are yet a few more rules in the list, and other issues to talk about. I will return to these later. At this point I would like to collect our bearings, and make sure we know where we are headed. The access lists rules we have looked at up to this point are for filtering TCP/IP traffic only. The rules are reasonably straightforward: we monitor who started the conversation (us or them), and where the traffic is bound. But we have other types of traffic too, particularly UDP traffic, which is a little more difficult to filter, and so represents a bigger security problem.

UDP/IP

UDP/IP conversations differ from TCP/IP conversations in several ways. From an application's point of view, UDP is an unreliable transport; nothing in the networking software guarantees that packets won't get lost, or arrive out of order. The problems of verifying the data and making sure they are received fall on the applications trading UDP data. Furthermore, the cycles of establishment, transmission, and acknowledgment that are characteristic of TCP are missing from UDP; the program has to take care of establishing its own conversations and keeping them alive. This all sounds horribly cumbersome, and it can be. Still, UDP does have its advantages: network conversations are lightweight; no synchronization and no "ACKs" are necessary. For many kinds of exchanges, UDP can cut down on traffic.

Unfortunately, the features that make UDP efficient also make it very difficult to secure. For one thing, it is difficult to read the intentions of an inbound UDP packet. Is it the response to a request, the start of a new conversation, or unsolicited data? Conversations have no discernible beginning or end, so it is difficult to tell "who asked whom for what." Furthermore, UDP queries and responses often take place on the same port, or no particular port, in some cases, which renders the low/high port number filter split that we used with TCP meaningless. Likewise, UDP exchanges are relatively easy for the malicious and criminally insane to hack into. There is no DATA-ACK cycle, and the networking software isn't keeping track of sequence numbers; fake packets are much easier to inject into the conversation stream.

UDP filtering isn't wholly impossible. The challenge is that it takes more than a snapshot of network traffic to decide whether a UDP packet deserves to pass through. Really, we need to keep track of whole conversations. I might, for example, notice a request leaving my network for a remote host on port 53 (DNS). I could reasonably expect a response from the remote computer, again on port 53, a short time later. A packet that just shows up out of the blue, on the other hand, might be one we'd toss. This is the problem we have with UDP and router-based access lists: routers are typically pretty stupid. They don't remember the traffic they have seen—they don't keep "state" (by design, actually). Consequently, there is no way to tell a router to allow traffic from only those computers with whom we initiated the conversation.* Anyway, given our limited ability to filter UDP traffic, we should probably consider shutting most of it off. We will probably want to leave port 53 open for DNS queries, provided we are maintaining our own nameserver.

udp	in	53 (domain)	0.0.0.0/0	198.252.200.3/32
udp	out	53 (domain)	198.252.200.3/32	0.0.0.0/0
tcp	syn, in	53 (domain)	199.100.105.2/32	198.252.200.3/32

You will see that I have made provisions for DNS in the access lists just given. In this case, the access lists support iterative DNS queries from just one computer behind the router—the nameserver at 198.252.200.3 (Figure 16-6). All other UDP ports are shut down.

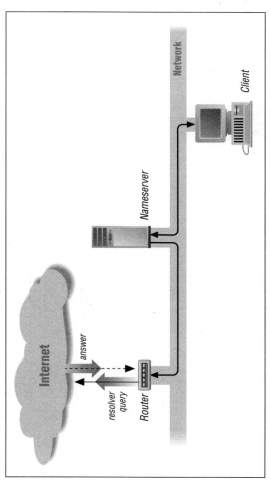

Figure 16-6: Client sends queries to internal nameserver

Notice that I poked a hole for TCP at port 53, in addition to the UDP hole at port 53. You may recall my earlier claim that there is no set correlation between UDP and TCP port numbers. In this case, however, the nameserver just happens to listen on both parts; requests to UDP port 53 are for DNS look-ups; requests to TCP port 53 are for *zone transfers*—the update of a secondary nameserver from the primary.

---

* Some firewall packages, such as *Firewall-1* from Checkpoint Software, can keep track of UDP conversations. More about this near the end of the chapter.

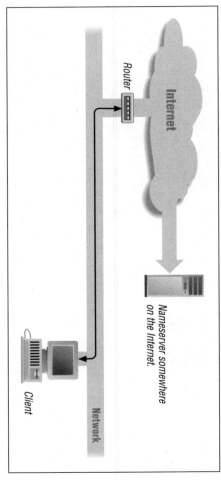

Figure 16-7: Client sends queries to external nameserver

There is a second possibility as well: hosts on your internal LAN might query against an external nameserver living out on the Internet (Figure 16-7). Typically, this external server would be a computer belonging to your access provider, and provided as a convenience. The implications to the access lists are significant: LAN clients making recursive queries to an external nameserver will require the ability to go out on (fairly random) UDP ports numbered above 1023. This means that you will have to tear a fairly wide, probably unacceptable, gash in your UDP filtering.

A third (very secure) possibility is a minimally configured internal nameserver that forwards all of its requests to a specific external nameserver. This can reduce the ease with which someone might deliberately feed your computers bogus domain information, and thereby redirect outbound traffic. We will see a specific example of a forwarding nameserver configuration in the next chapter.

Anyway, we have a few ways to accommodate DNS exchanges. What services do we give up by turning down the screws on other flavors of UDP traffic? NFS, RPC services, upcoming video and voice applications, to name a few. You *can* poke holes for some of these too (if you can guess the port numbers), though every service you let through weakens your firewall just a little bit more.

ICMP

A third IP protocol to think about is ICMP (*Internet Control Message Protocol*). Like UDP and TCP, ICMP rides on top of IP. However, unlike the other protocols, ICMP is an integral part of IP; you can't have IP without it. ICMP's purpose is to trade status messages between IP gateways and hosts. An ICMP message might say something about the reachability of a remote host, a destination's difficulty in keeping up with traffic, or preferred routes between two points, A and B. Because the status messages ICMP carries help to smooth operations, sites will typically allow ICMP to reach into their network, or, at the very least, to reach their firewall.

ICMP packets are categorized into a handful of types, each responsible for delivering a different kind of message. You are probably familiar with the UNIX *ping* command. Ping is based on two ICMP message types: *echo* and *echo reply*. As network primitives go, these ICMP exchanges are fairly harmless. The greatest potential danger is that someone could use ping to probe your network, looking for hosts.* Other message types, particularly *destination unreachable* and *source quench*, offer opportunities for mischief; perniciously generated ICMP messages can shut down connections. Still, you would want these message types to be allowed through. There is one ICMP message type, however, that presents enough of a security problem that you will probably want to filter it out: ICMP *redirect* messages.

ICMP redirect messages are designed to allow routers to suggest better routes to local network hosts. To understand how it works, say that I'm one of several routers on your LAN. Your computer might send a packet to me, to be forwarded to some far-off network. Because I am trading routing information with other routers, however, I might know that you would be better off directing traffic through my sibling router "A," rather than through me (Figure 16-8).

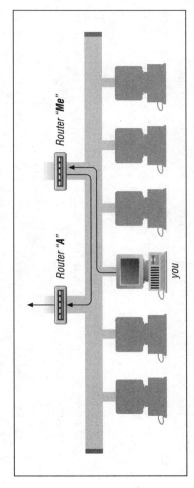

Figure 16–8: ICMP redirection

I could send an ICMP redirection message that told you so. Your computer would then adjust its routing table to take advantage of the suggested path.†

Redirection to take advantage of better routes represents a legitimate use for ICMP redirect messages. But you could imagine nefarious uses as well. If we shared the

---

* On the other hand, a remote site could launch a ping storm and bring your network to its knees. Filtering to prohibit connections from the remote site would be an appropriate response.

† If your computer was listening for such messages. . . . Technically, it is required to (rfc1122).

same LAN, for instance, I could issue a bogus ICMP redirect message to divert your traffic to my computer. ICMP redirect messages could also play a part in more elaborate traffic theft. By a combination of counterfeit routing broadcasts and (perhaps) ICMP redirect messages, I might be able to trick routers between your network and mine into directing particular kinds of traffic to me. I could then masquerade as the remote network you *thought* you were connected to, and perform salacious acts with the purloined data.

Because of the potential for ICMP redirection abuses, many routers are configured to disallow redirect messages. You will likely want to disallow such messages too. ICMP redirection is typically turned off at the router via a single directive, such as "no icmp redirect." See your router manual, or look at the sample configurations in Appendix A.

Source routing

There is yet another facility, global to all types of IP traffic (TCP, UDP, ICMP, and others), that represents a sizable security hole. Like ICMP redirection, *source routing* provides a mechanism for absconding with traffic. It works like this: within the IP packet header one can embed specific instructions for moving traffic from site "A" to site "B." That is, you can tell the routers along the way to ignore what they *think* they know about reachability to remote networks, in favor of what you have hard-coded into the packet header. By agreement, the recipient has to return responses via the reverse, source-routed path.

In a trustworthy network, source-routing is a tool that you would like to have at your disposal. It would give you a way to choose a path that you *want* traffic to take, perhaps to debug a problem, to avoid congestion, or to keep unneighborly data transfers off the main network thoroughfare; routing is controlled by the endpoints. The danger is that source routing can also be used to impersonate remote hosts, and abuse any special trust afforded to them. For instance, say that you have tuned your router access lists to deny remote telnet sessions from all computers except for one, located halfway around the world. If I *knew* the address of that computer, I could (potentially) source-route packets from my network, in the next building, to yours. By choosing the same network address as the trusted computer, I could slip through your router.

Source-routing can be controlled by instructing your router to reject packets with the source-routing flag turned on. As with ICMP redirection, source-routing is typically disabled with a single directive, such as "no source-route" (I have it as rule number one in my table, given earlier). Again, check with your router manual, or review the samples in Appendix A.

The completed access list

Gathering everything together, we have a set of access lists that will close the big security holes, and limit traffic to a few selected services. In summary, we are looking to:

- Disallow source-routed packets.

- Carefully poke holes for TCP traffic.

- Shut down most or all UDP traffic.

- Disable ICMP redirection.

Don't forget to choose a good password for the router!* Depending on the nature of traffic on your network, you may want to turn down the screws on other TCP ports as well. X11 traffic, for instance, is conducted on ports in the 6000/TCP through 6100/TCP range. By filtering access to those ports, you can protect the user's X sessions from being hijacked by X-cons. Likewise (for Sun users) Open-look traffic, starting at 2000/TCP and extending upwards a couple of ports, should be protected. If you are running other kinds of IP applications, such as database servers, you should protect their port numbers too.

The rules we have cobbled together describe what it is we want to do, but how can we apply them? As I mentioned above, different brands of routers require different approaches to access lists. I have basically assumed the best-case scenario, where we can apply any type of filtering to any interface. If it turns out that your options are limited, you will have to take the rules and bend them so they match the tools that you have. For instance, if your router only allows you to filter outgoing packets, you will have to split the list into two pieces, and apply some of the rules to one interface, and some to another. Or perhaps your router can't discriminate between *SYN* packets and other types. That's workable too, though you will have to filter traffic according to source, destination, and port number alone.

Application Wrappers

Applications on the server can be fitted with a form of access lists too. As with routers, you can limit connectivity to certain services according to the origin of the request. *Wrappers*, as they are called, replace the standard daemons with small programs that check inbound connection requests against access parameters, and, when satisfied with the identity of the caller, exec the real daemon. A wrapper for the telnet daemon, for example, would be started by *inetd*† when a terminal session request comes in on port 23/TCP. The user would experience a brief delay as

---

* Actually, the right thing to do is limit the hosts that can log into the router, via access lists.

† *inetd* is a super-daemon that listens on many ports at once. It was introduced into BSD 4.3 to tame the wild sea of daemons that resulted when every new network application had to answer for itself.

the wrapper software scurried about, verified permissions, performed a reverse DNS look-up on the connecting host, and logged the connection.

An alternate method would be to replace inetd altogether with a smarter program that knows something about access lists and logging; in essence, inetd and the wrappers would be rolled into a single program. An example of the "wrapper" approach is a suite of tools called *TCP Wrapper*, written by Wietse Venema, at the Eindhoven University of Technology. A popular inetd replacement is *xinetd*, by Panagiotis Tsirigotis of the University of Colorado.* Why use wrapper programs? Assuming that we have installed the router access lists we created above, the only computer on our network that will be reachable from the outside is our information server. But it's sitting out on the deck, just waiting to be tampered with. One of the biggest dangers of the minimalist firewall we have constructed is that if the information server is somehow breached, it will provide a clever miscreant a starting point from which to hack the rest of the internal network.

Like talcum powder sprinkled beside the basement door, wrapper programs will mark the trails of animals that have forced their way through. You can tell where they came from, when they connected, and what service they connected to. More importantly, wrappers will reveal questionable patterns of activity, such as repeated connection attempts. Additionally, the log file entries that wrappers create provide a valuable supplement to the logging messages that come from the services themselves (login, ftpd, etc.). And if you care to go further, you can also use wrappers for triggers. You could, for example, have a wrapper send you email when a particularly uncivilized user connects to violate the system.†

Installing TCP wrapper

Along with the *TCP Wrapper* package, Wietse Venema provides a wonderful description of how the replacement daemons work, how to build and install them, and how they can be applied. I might just let it go at that, except that an overview will give us insight into the workings of the wrapper programs, and of *inetd* itself. Furthermore the ideas are portable; you can apply the same concepts to the various service wrappers and *inetd* filters available. In fact, we will be looking at another wrapper program later in this chapter. To begin, let's look at */etc/inetd.conf*, the configuration file for *inetd*. Each line of the file describes a different service, including the owner, its path, an argument list, and a few parameters to describe the type and behavior of the connection. *inetd* learns from this file upon boot-up which ports it should watch, and what it should do when a connection comes in.

---

* *TCP Wrapper* can be found at *ftp://cert.org/pub/tools/tcp_wrapper*. *xinetd* can be found at *ftp://mystique.cs.colorado.edu*.

† Of course, this gives the attacker a switch with which to remotely shut down your computer....

Service	Socket	Protocol	Wait/Nowait	User	Server	Arguments
nntp	stream	tcp	nowait	root	/usr/sbin/in.nntpd	nntpd

For instance, the line above (snipped from *inetd.conf*) says that when a TCP connection comes knocking on the nntp port (119),[*] *inetd* should spawn a copy on *in.nntpd*, the USENET news transfer daemon. Notice that the correlation between the port number and the program that gets spawned isn't fixed (except by convention); you could choose to run almost anything in response to a connection at port 119. In particular, you could choose to replace invocation of the NNTP daemon with invocation of a wrapper program.

Service	Socket	Protocol	Wait/Nowait	User	Server	Arguments
nntp	stream	tcp	nowait	root	/usr/sbin/tcpd	/usr/sbin/in.nntpd

The line above shows how a replacement entry in *inetd.conf* might look. In lieu of the server program, we have told *inetd* to spawn */usr/sbin/tcpd*—the wrapper program. As arguments, we have passed the name of the real server and any arguments the real server might need. When a connection comes in for port 119, it is the wrapper program that gets started. Once it has performed its access checks, and taken any actions required, it execs the real server program and disappears.

The wrappers can be built and installed by a different method as well. Server daemons (*ftpd*, *telnetd*, etc.) can be segregated into their own, private directory. Copies of the wrapper are then put in place of the server daemons, causing the wrapper to be invoked instead of the actual service. *inetd.conf* is left unmodified, meaning that inetd is unaware of the changes. Once the wrapper (*tcpd*) has verified an incoming connection, it then looks among the segregated collection of daemons for the appropriate server.

In either configuration, the actions of the wrappers are under the control of two files: */etc/bosts.allow* and */etc/bosts.deny*. An incoming connection is first checked against the specifications in *bosts.allow*. If none of the rules matches, control flows over to *bosts.deny*. If none of the specifications matches, access is granted.

A configuration file entry has the form:

```
services:hosts[:action]
```

The leftmost field specifies a list of services. The middle field describes a host (or groups of hosts) to be allowed or denied access to those services. The third field, if included, contains an auxiliary action to be taken when the first two fields match.

---

[*] Where did I get the 119? */etc/services* associates the names in the left hand column of *inetd.conf* with service names.

As a quick example, let's say that we want to prohibit all connections to our server with the exception of the following:

- We will allow NNTP traffic from two sources—computers on our own network and our newsfeed (*nntp.deadbeat.net*).

- We will allow Telnet connections from anywhere, with the exception of one network—the source of some worrisome probing.

To start, we need to specify sanctioned connections in *hosts.allow*:

```
in.nntpd:198.252.200.0/255.255.255.0,nntp.deadbeat.net
in.telnet:ALL EXCEPT 192.65.177.0/255.255.255.0
```

In the second configuration file, *hosts.deny*, we disable all other connections:

```
ALL:ALL
```

Wildcards (*s, and the word ALL) and a complement operator (EXCEPT) allow us to express any combination of services. In every case, connections will be logged via the *syslog* facility.

Note, though, that the specifications aren't foolproof. As with router access lists, we have to assume that we can trust the information that is available to us. In the "allow" rule above, for example, I said that I would accept connections from any computer on class C network 198.252.200.0. But again, my filtering criteria are open to spoofing. Similarly, the reverse look-up on the newsfeed *nntp.deadbeat.net* could theoretically be faked.

The good news is that the veracity of remote connections doesn't have to be accepted opaquely. You can run cross-checks against what you have been told. For instance, a reverse DNS look-up (address to host name) could be followed by a forward look-up (host name to address), to see if the information jibes; presumably, the address found on the forward look-up will be the same as the source address of the connection. Beyond that, systems can cooperatively share connection information using the *IIDENT* system.* Again, check with the excellent documentation that comes with the TCP Wrapper package.

Care of the Server

The linchpin in the security scenario we have been considering is the Internet server. If the malevolently curious break into the server, they will have free (IP) rein of the rest of the network.† Service wrappers will provide an audit trail and a

---

* See rfc1413.
† It could be really bad. If I got onto your server as root, I could (perhaps) snoop packets on your LAN. If the Secret Sauce recipe flew by, I'd have it.

first line of defense. However, the greater part of server protection comes down to choices in system administration and self-policing.

For starters, we want to limit the number of active server accounts to very few—typically an administrator or two. This will keep both friends and strangers from having a look at the machine's configuration, and from obtaining copies of sensitive information (such as the password file and service access lists). The less outsiders know about the way your site security is administered, the better.

We also need to take basic steps to assure that we have plugged the known leaks (see "CERT," further on), and to make sure that files and directories carry appropriate permissions. Incidentally, you might assume that because your release of the operating system is relatively recent, the holes will have been plugged by the vendor. Dull surprise: vendor software distributions can be way out of date (often years). Besides, new security liabilities are unearthed all the time. Even if your operating system revision is a few months old, you may have missed the latest hole.

System audits

We begin by auditing the directory and file permissions. Frankly, this part of the job could be pure drudgery, not unlike putting up storm windows. Fortunately, there are several excellent audit tools that automate the process of walking through the file system and flagging potential problems. They can also catalog "signatures" (see *"Tripwire,"* below) of important executables to make sure that they aren't subsequently tampered with.

When auditing a UNIX file system, we want to make sure of the following:

- *Setuid** permission is limited to a small subset of well-known applications.
- System directories are owned by an appropriate administrative user (often root).
- System configuration files are writable exclusively by root, and in some cases unreadable by others.
- Scripts are writable only by their owners.
- Passwords are secure.

---

* An executable with *setuid* (set user ID) permission temporarily grants the person running it the privileges of the program's owner. For instance, if I placed a copy of csh in my home directory with *setuid* permission enabled, you could run the program and have full access rights to my files. Analogously, a program can have *setuid* permission enabled, giving the person who runs it temporary membership in the associated group.

- Users' home directories are writable only by their owners.

- Anonymous FTP is set up securely.

- System executables haven't been tampered with.

- Devices have appropriate permissions.

Certainly, an audit isn't limited to these chores, but this captures the sense of what we are trying to accomplish.

The best known of the automated system audit packages are the TAMU *Tiger Scripts* and *COPS*. Each is good for one-time audits and routine inspections. The output in both cases is a report detailing security problems found. Neither package adjusts file permissions; it is up to the administrator to review the output of the audits and make fixes as necessary.

TAMU

The Texas A&M University (*TAMU*) Tiger Scripts are very easy to use. They can be untarred and run in-place for a drive-thru system audit, or installed under */usr/local* for periodic, scheduled file system checks. A configuration file chooses which of the variety of tests are to be run, and which options to apply. Out of the box, the Tiger Scripts cover most of the tests in the list above. A hook into *crack* extends the scripts further by adding a password cracking facility. This can be run against your own password file to determine if any of your users has chosen a weak password.*

The Tiger suite also comes with an interface to a database of digital signatures for the binaries of some common operating system releases. The digital signatures work like this: In advance, important files are passed through an algorithm to create a (nearly) unique signature that identifies the file. The signature might be a checksum; a CRC or the output of a more complicated polynomial; or a hash function. At verification time, if the digital fingerprint of a particular system file doesn't match the recorded value, the signature checker raises a flag, indicating that the file either is out of date (has been superseded by a later release), or has been tampered with. Again, the software takes no action when a suspicious system file is found. It is up to the administrator to decide what to do.

For completeness, I should tell you that the Tiger Scripts are actually just a portion of a larger suite of tools called the *TAMU Security Package*. In addition to the auditing tools, the package contains a nifty PC-based packet filtering facility and a collection of network traffic logging tools. It's a bit of a digression to discuss them here, but these tools could fit into your bag of tricks so I will.

---

* *Crack* can be retrieved from *ftp://ftp.cert.org/pub/tools/crack*. TAMU tools are at *ftp://net.tamu.edu/*.

Recall that we discussed the problem with filtering UDP applications—it is difficult to tell whether an incoming packet is a response to a request, unsolicited traffic, or someone jimmying the lock. In order to monitor UDP traffic effectively, one has to keep a record of ongoing conversations—one has to keep "state." Routers typically don't keep state, which makes them weak filters for UDP exchanges. The TAMU Security Package includes a packet filtering tool, *Drawbridge*, which, unlike a router, keeps a cache of current connections so that it can tell something about the nature of UDP traffic, and deny unspoken-for connections. The tool is staged on an X86 platform with two network interfaces; one connects to your internal network, and the other connects to the outside world—just like a router.* In addition to its UDP features, Drawbridge has a broad range of TCP capabilities as well.

The other piece of the security package—the TAMU network monitoring tools—is a (Sun-based) collection of programs and scripts for logging and analyzing network traffic data. Like the packet filtering facility, the logging tools operate with a bit of intelligence, recognizing conversation initiation, responses, and closure. The challenge is that even though the logging tools try to deal in terms of sessions, just a few hours of network monitoring can create a mountain of data. Accordingly, the logging facilities also come with data reduction scripts for making sense of the gathered information.

The complete collection of TAMU monitoring tools is available via FTP, with the exception of a program called *netwatch*, which is designed to recognize patterns of pernicious behavior in network traffic. Because it might be valuable for crackers to understand the workings of *netwatch*, TAMU makes it available by request only.[†]

COPS

Like the *TAMU Tiger Scripts*, the *Computer Oracle Password and Security* system (*COPS*) is a collection of tools for auditing your UNIX host for security liabilities. COPS is also relatively easy to run, and produces a detailed survey of your system, including file access permission problems. The set of features doesn't match the Tiger Scripts exactly; COPS contains a few security checks that the Tiger Scripts lack, and vice versa.

One very interesting tool that differentiates COPS is the *Kuang* expert system. The Kuang expert system asks the question, "Given the file and directory permissions

---

* The difference is that this tool acts as a *bridge*. That is, the same logical network appears on each side of the device. Compare this to a router, where different networks are present on opposite sides.

† Since we're in a digression, let me digress even further. Another really useful tool for watching network traffic is *tcpdump*, available from the Lawrence Berkeley Laboratory, Network Research Group, *ftp://ftp.ee.lbl.gov/tcpdump-*.tar.Z*. You should find 30 minutes some time to sit in front of a tool like *tcpdump* to get an idea of how much traffic is on your network, and what sorts of information is being traded. I think you would find it fascinating.

on this system, could a user obtain root privileges?" You might imagine "bunny" scenarios, where somebody has left the *passwd* file world-writable, making it possible for anyone to eliminate the root password. Kuang could recognize this. More potently, Kuang is designed to determine the answer to the question, given a sequence of misconfigured or carelessly protected files and directories, that could *indirectly* lead to a security hole.

There are two versions of Kuang included with COPS—a perl version, and another which is a combination of C and scripts. The perl version is newer, and has extra features. In either case, it may take a little perseverance on your part to customize the expert system to your host. Configuration is buried in the scripts, and the output can be a little cryptic. The tool is interesting nonetheless.

You can get a copy of COPS from *ftp://cert.org/tools/cops/cops_104.tar.*

Tripwire

The Tiger Scripts and COPS both contain tests for verifying that system binaries and critical files haven't been tampered with. In the simplest case, checksums are calculated and squirreled away for comparison during future audits. More complicated digital signatures might be derived from a hash function (such as *MD5*).

The danger is that simple digital signatures can be forged; a file modified for subversive purposes could be further modified to reproduce the same signature as the original. This would make changes invisible to a file system integrity check. Stronger signature methods, on the other hand, make forgery a more difficult proposition. The most elaborate signatures can't be reverse engineered, and would take an impractically long time to duplicate by an exhaustive search.

Tripwire is a newer package that provides a flexible and sophisticated set of tools for maintaining digital signatures for important system files, and for performing file system integrity checks. A number of signature types are supported, right out of the box. The tools are extensible too, so you can add new signature types as desired. You can find Tripwire at *ftp://ftp.cs.purdue.edu/pub/spaf/COAST/Tripwire.*

SATAN

In the Spring of 1995, Dan Farmer (COPS) and Wietse Venema (TCP Wrapper) released a set of tools for remotely *probing* hosts and networks for security holes. This is a big step beyond auditing for errors in files permissions, or looking for a configuration *faux pas.* SATAN actually mounts a remote probe of the computer under test. It can be aimed at whole networks as well.

The results of a SATAN session include details about the daemons present, hardware, network topology, and security liabilities. It will even help you pick at potential holes to see if you are at risk. SATAN scans for:

- NFS security holes
- NIS password file access
- *rexd* access
- sendmail problems
- TFTP permissions
- Remote shell access
- Unrestricted X server access
- FTP server vulnerabilities

All of these problems are well documented, and can be prevented by the steps we have already taken in this chapter. The danger, of course, is that SATAN makes it easier for strangers to survey computers that *haven't* been audited. Accordingly, you should be wary of unprotected computers. You can get a copy of SATAN from *ftp://ftp.win.tue.nl/pub/security/*.

Catch Your Breath

We have covered a lot of material in this chapter, and for better or for worse, it isn't over yet. The good news is that we now have in hand all of the pieces we need to build the most basic firewall (Figure 16-9):

- We have secured the network router with access lists.
- We have secured the server with application wrappers.
- We have performed a comprehensive system audit.

And we learned a lot along the way—information that we can use in the coming sections. Before taking another step, though, I think we should drop our bags, take a breath, and see where we are. For some of you, we may have gone far enough; the firewall we have built may be sufficient protection for your purposes. Others will want to proceed. At any rate, a few words are in order about what's good and what's lacking in this firewall.

Recall the goals that we set for ourselves. We wanted to:

- Allow people within the organization to reach the Internet from their desktops.
- Allow people on the Internet to reach our Web server, mailhub, etc.
- Make it (almost) impossible for people on the Internet to contact machines on our network, other than the server.

In terms of flexibility, this firewall rates high; we can allow any kind of traffic through. Provided you have opened the proper ports at the router, desktop computers will be able to reach directly into the Internet for any kind of application—

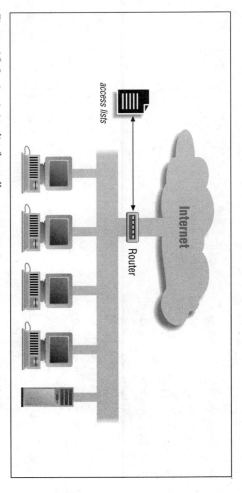

Figure 16–9. A minimalist firewall

Web, gopher, FTP, CUseeme, audio, whatever. Likewise, holes we have punched into the router access lists will allow incoming connections to servers (httpd, gopher, mail, etc.) we have enabled on the UNIX host. And again, the same access lists will also prevent inbound connections to other computers on the network.

There are some bad points to consider, though. First, the network topology is opened up for the world to see. Because there are direct exchanges between internal computers and hosts on the Internet, each host has to be at least partially visible to the outside world, and hence more open to probes. Second, where there is some complicity between parties on the inside and outside, it may be possible to tunnel protocols that would otherwise be restricted by the router access lists.* This would essentially neutralize the firewall.

The biggest problem, as I mentioned above, is that the server makes a very shiny prize for a cracker. Once the server is compromised, the rest of the network is opened up—router packet filters can't do anything to keep the cracker from exploring the computers inside. Restricting logins helps a lot. But the danger increases as you add more facilities, such as WWW services, gopher, etc. These things can be hacked, and from time to time people do manage to break them.

So given all these caveats, who might be able to use this firewall? Well, *some* firewall is better than *no* firewall, so anybody who would otherwise have chosen to do nothing should at least take the steps we have discussed so far. For many organizations, a minimalist firewall will be sufficient because they are not generally open in the first place. A small company, for example, may have little or no IP

---

* Network traffic can be encapsulated within other network traffic, passed through a firewall (on a high-numbered port, perhaps), and de-encapsulated on the other side. This is one form of *tunneling*.

CERT

In November, 1988, Cornell graduate student Robert T. Morris released the "Internet Worm" out into the network. The Worm was a cleverly constructed, multifaceted beast, taking advantage of "trusted" hosts, casual passwords, and security holes in two UNIX utilities—the *sendmail* daemon (on VAXes and Suns), and *fingerd* (on VAXes). Once it set up camp on a new machine, it would copy over the pieces it needed and begin anew. Within a few hours, the Worm choked a huge portion of the Internet.

One month later, DARPA established the Computer Emergency Response Team (CERT) at the Software Engineering Institute on the campus of Carnegie Mellon University, and gave it the role of Internet security watchdog. Likewise, the Defense Communications Agency established a Security Control Center to do the same jobs for the Defense Data Networks. Other response teams were established as well.

The problem is this: because so much of the Internet structure is replicated, a new kind of breach discovered at one site is instantly a threat to the whole community. Accordingly, it is essential to get word about new crackers' tricks out quickly, so that people can gird their networks against them. CERT plays a central part in this process, acting in the role of the watchtower herald. They gather information about security problems, alert the Internet community, and recommend prophylactic measures. In some cases, network vulnerability is discovered before crackers get to it. In others, CERT's actions are precipitated by a crisis. (You can subscribe to CERT security advisories. Send a request to *cert@cert.org*. You can also find the complete collection of CERT advisories online at *ftp://cert.org*.)

As you might guess, general announcements of new security holes have a downside: once you tell the world that a hole has been found in a network program—even if you don't tell precisely how the hole can be exploited—you bring it to the attention of other potential crackers, who might have otherwise missed it. You might even find your site under attack by someone who learned of your vulnerability from a CERT bulletin. Your first reflex might say be to say, "Don't advertise the holes." It's a problem that the security community agonizes over. How should a vulnerability be reported? And if nothing were said? Holes would never get plugged.

networking in-house. Rather, they may share all of their internal data using protocols such as IPX (Novell) or NetBEUI (Microsoft),* neither of which is routed through the Internet. Just keep an eye on the server!

A Slightly Better Firewall

Ready for more? As we have seen, the biggest chink in the armor of a minimalist firewall can be the information server. Typically this will be a UNIX machine running a mail daemon, Web server, gopher server, and the like. Proper access to the services generally isn't a security problem. The risk is in the possibility that someone will gain access to the login shell on the server, and from there gain access to the rest of your network.

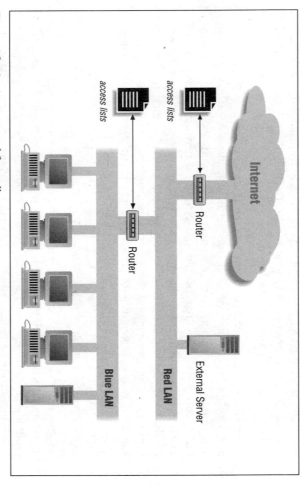

Figure 16-10: An improved firewall

A simple and very powerful improvement to the minimalist firewall comes from the addition of a second router, as in Figure 16-10. Essentially, this allows us to put the information server outside of the organization, behind a separate secured router. Think about how this would help: The inside router's access lists can say, "No traffic is allowed in; all traffic is allowed out." The rules are simple—there are

---

* Watch out! More and more LAN Manager-style file sharing will be taking place over IP networks, and this will be routable.

no exceptions.* The beauty is that even if the Morlocks drag the information server down their hole, they are no closer to your internal LAN than they were before. In short, compromising the information server does not compromise the company LAN. Of course, the outside router can continue to protect the server, as in the single-router setup we looked at previously.

In popular terminology, the outside LAN is called the *red* LAN. The internal LAN is often called the *blue* LAN. Naturally, your internal network may be more complicated than this, but the overall picture doesn't change; the rest of your network can be considered the blue LAN.

What is the downside of the two-router configuration? The first negative that probably comes to your mind is cost: routers cost money. Realize that the routers don't have to be identical. You might choose a lower-end model for the external connection. The router doesn't have to be exceptionally speedy. This is because the external (WAN) connection will be relatively slow compared to your internal network speeds. Likewise, you only need two interfaces—one WAN and one LAN. The internal router, on the other hand, has to support LAN-speed traffic through both (or many, perhaps) interfaces.

Other options include the purchase of a three-interface "firewall" router, like the *Livingston IRX Firewall Router,* the *Morning Star Firewall Router,* or any multi-interface router. Logically, these devices are arranged as two routers in a single box (Figure 16-11).

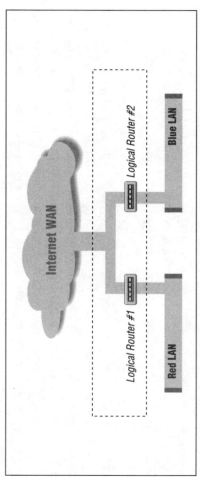

Figure 16–11: A firewall router

Each supports two sets of access lists and two separate LAN interfaces—one for the "red" LAN and one for the "blue" LAN. And because you don't have to string them together serially, you have more control over what kinds of traffic reach each

---

* Well, except for FTP return connections, maybe. Though it sure sounded powerful when I said it.

LAN; restricting a certain flavor of traffic from the red LAN doesn't preclude allowing that same flavor of traffic to reach the blue LAN. Best of all, the cost is less than what you would pay for two individual routers.

Notice, however, that even though the two-router configuration is an improvement over the single-router configuration of the minimalist firewall, some of the same liabilities exist. Your network is open to mapping, and it will still be possible for people to tunnel traffic. But if you asked me what I thought about it, I'd say, "I like it." Though I'd probably consider a heavier-duty firewall, given something valuable to protect.

Heavy-Duty Firewalls

You might imagine that the definition of a firewall would get tighter as you move toward higher-scale solutions. It doesn't really. High-end packet filters, circuit-level gateways, and application proxy servers all fall under the "firewall" moniker. You have to educate yourself a little, to be able to decide what you want. Saying "I want an expensive firewall" unfortunately isn't enough. Besides, you can pull together a very high quality firewall for peanuts, provided you don't mind doing a little work. If you have decided to spend money, on the other hand, you should first decide what kind of firewall you need, and then pay to get back some transparency. Anyway, we will look at both solutions—build-it, and buy-it.

Proxies

I feel a dumb analogy is in order. Let's try this: say that you are the manager for the CyberSlugs, the most popular rock band in the world. The band is so popular that they are mobbed wherever they go, and the press is constantly trying to get photographs of them out around town. The CyberSlugs have a secret studio where they can go to write and record their music. They need complete isolation from the press and their fans in order to get their work done. Accordingly, it is your job to make them as unobtrusive as possible.

Here's the problem: the band constantly needs things like guitar picks and cassette tapes. But since they can't be seen in town, you have to shop on their behalf. From the point of view of the people who frequent the music store, this makes you a peculiar fellow. Why does one person, who doesn't even seem to be a musician, need 36 pairs of drum sticks and 15 high-E guitar strings for one evening?

We know what's really going on: you are acting as a proxy for the members of the CyberSlugs—taking orders and filling them in town. From the outside, all purchases appear to come from the same person. Not only do the people in town have no idea the CyberSlugs are there, but with you acting as their proxy, no one will ever find them. You are a firewall.

This silly analogy has done its job, and the illustration isn't so far off. For an Internet connection, a proxy-based firewall (Figure 16-12) demonstrates the same qualities:

- All transactions appear to emanate from a single host.
- The details of the internal network are hidden from view.
- There is no other way to get through to the computers inside.

Topologically, the proxy firewall server sits between the outside world and the internal network. It has two network interfaces—one foot in each world—but it doesn't pass any packet traffic between them.* Rather, the firewall runs *proxy servers* that take requests from machines on the internal network, log them (optionally), and then send duplicate requests out the other side, to the Internet. Data coming back are again intercepted and re-sent to the client waiting inside.

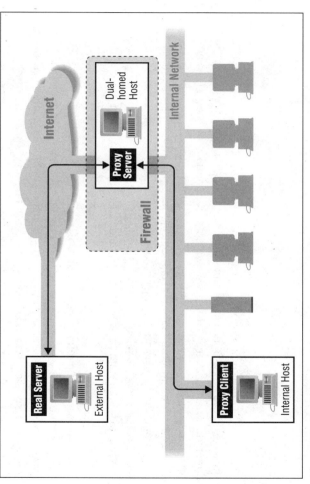

Figure 16-12: Using a proxy server

At first glance, it sounds as if there must be some elaborate connection accounting and multiplexing taking place. Typically there's not. Rather, the proxy servers

---

* Terminology: the two interfaces make the computer a *dual-homed host*. A dual-homed host config-ured to be a firewall is often called a *bastion host*.

spawn children to handle individual requests. The children each open two sets of "protocol,address,port" tuples—one on the inside, and one on the outside. They often aren't even aware of the other, proxied conversations taking place.

Circuit-level proxy servers

Proxies can be staged at different levels. A *circuit-level* proxy is based upon a collection of subroutines that are replacements for system socket library calls.* An IP application modified to use these routines is forced to direct network I/O requests through a daemon that lives on the bastion host firewall, rather than attempt them locally. The good thing about this kind of proxy is that any program you have source code for can be modified relatively easily. You merely replace a few of the calls with compatible counterparts, recompile, and relink. Of course, if you don't have the source code, this isn't going to be so easy. The best known circuit-level proxy is *socks*, available from *ftp://ftp.inoc.dl.nec.com.*

Application-level proxy servers

In contrast to circuit-level proxies, *application-level* proxies take a broader view of network traffic, typically handling whole transaction requests, such as an FTP session, an HTTP "get," or a telnet login. Clients forward requests to the proxy servers running on a bastion host. The proxy servers then repackage the requests, make contact with the appropriate Internet resources, and eventually return the result back to the internal LAN.

Depending on the firewall implementation, clients of application-level proxies (such as Web browsers, graphical FTP tools, etc.) may have to pose their requests to proxy servers differently than if they were making contact with the Internet on their own behalf.† Fortunately, application-level proxy firewall support is now natively supported by many client packages, including Mosaic, Netscape, and others; you don't have to sacrifice the best browsers just because you are operating behind a firewall. Additionally, there are some application-level proxy firewalls that can handle unmodified requests; no special client is required.‡

---

* You can also have circuit-level gateways that don't require proxy routines. An example would be the BorderWare firewall, described below.

† Actually, this is true of graphical clients. Command line applications, such as Telnet or FTP, can use proxy servers without needing modification.

‡ Examples are Gauntlet and BorderWare.

Internal Network Addresses and Proxy Firewalls

For many organizations, there's a side benefit to using a proxy firewall that may be as important as network security. Because the firewall completely masks details about the internal network, there are no restrictions governing IP address assignments inside. This can be terrifically important for an organization that has "borrowed" an unregistered IP network, and proliferated it throughout the LAN or WAN. Consider the alternative: after the fact, a company could go to the InterNIC and request a valid IP network number to replace a "borrowed" address. It gets tricky, however, if the assumed network was an unregistered class A or class B. These classes are in short supply, and the InterNIC is reluctant to give them up. Rather, they are likely to respond with a block of class C addresses, to be spread around the organization.

Suddenly, the conversion costs a lot more than the weekend of hair-pulling that typically accompanies an address change. A corporate network built upon an assumed class A or class B network may be topologically inappropriate for multiple class C networks. It might be bridged, for instance, where it now needs to be routed; it could cost a lot of time and money to reconfigure the LAN to support the new set of addresses. Internet access through a proxy firewall avoids the address problem altogether; internal addresses can be left alone. Typically a single legitimate class C network is all that is necessary for connection between the firewall and the Internet.

As you may have guessed, there is one little problem associated with using a "borrowed" network: there is a chance that you will one day need to reach the organization that actually "owns" the network. Because of the routing tables on your firewall, however, you will never be able to exchange traffic with the network's legitimate owner; all traffic for the borrowed network will be redirected back to your own LAN.* To solve the problem, three networks have been set aside by the Internet Assigned Numbers Authority (IANA), for use on firewall-isolated LANS. There's one for each of classes A, B, and C:

```
10.0.0.0        (class A)
172.16.0.0      (class B)
192.168.0.0     (class C)
```

Having these network numbers available gives you the option of switching from an illegal network to a reserved network, without forcing you to make changes in the network topology.†

---

* Actually, you could add host routes to your firewall's routing tables, on a case-by-case basis.
† See rfc1597. I should also mention that the idea of using nonroutable network numbers, such as these, isn't universally embraced. The danger is that you may one day want a routed network; perhaps you have multiple connections to the Internet, or wish to use applications for which no proxies exist; see rfc1814 too.

Building a Proxy Firewall

So let's say the decision to erect a proxy Internet firewall has already been made. We still have to decide whether to "build it" or "buy it." Probably the strongest reason for building your own firewall is cost: a commercial firewall for a company of 100+ users can range in cost from $15,000 to $100,000 USD, after the hardware is figured in. I have some favorites at the lower end of the price scale, but for many folks, even a $15,000 price tag would be too much. If you are working on a shoestring budget, and if you feel comfortable with your UNIX expertise, you might consider assembling your own firewall.

Before I proceed, I should mention that the idea of constructing your own firewall isn't universally embraced by firewall dogma. "Leave that stuff to professionals," you sometimes hear. But I give you more credit than that, especially if you got this far in the book. Besides, you won't be creating a firewall from scratch. Rather, you will be customizing a set of tried and tested firewall tools. Just be careful.

The TIS Toolkit

As I mentioned above, you can design a proxy firewall using either circuit or application-level proxy servers. Likewise, you can choose from a variety of contributed software components, available out on the Internet. By far, the most popular and most complete collection is the *Trusted Information Systems (TIS)* firewall toolkit from Trusted Information Systems of Glenwood, Maryland. The TIS suite includes application-level proxies for WWW, FTP, Telnet, gopher, and others, a secure front-end for sendmail, service wrappers, and a facility for channeling certain types of traffic through the firewall (for news, perhaps). Trusted Information Systems markets the TIS toolkit, with additional features, under the name *Gauntlet*, but they also make it available, in source code, via anonymous FTP.* Within limits, TIS grants you permission to use the toolkit within your own organization, at no charge. This makes it a great place to start. In the next few sections, we are going to take a look at configuring and using the TIS toolkit for your firewall.

Bastion Host Preparations

Before installing the toolkit, we need to think a little bit about the computer it will run on. To start with, it has to be a UNIX machine. It may be tempting to look around the office for an orphaned computer. Just remember that because the bastion host has to be intimately involved with each request made of the Internet, it probably needs to be more powerful than a cast-off Sun 3, or a 386. Likewise, the bastion host should have a fair amount of memory—at least 16 Megabytes or

---

* Connect to *ftp://ftp.tis.com* for the toolkit and for more information.

more. On the other hand, don't be afraid of a high-end PC. 486s make great fire-wall machines: fitted with localbus network and disk controllers, high-end PCs can be faster than dedicated-purpose UNIX workstations.*

Of course, you are going to need two network interfaces—one for the Internet side, and one for the internal LAN. The trickier part is disabling packet-forwarding between them. Here's the problem: UNIX kernels often come shipped with packet-forwarding enabled. This means that once you add a second network inter-face, the computer will happily assume the role of a gateway (router), which is precisely what we *don't* want. To shut off packet-forwarding, we need to build a new kernel with forwarding disabled. Unfortunately, the details are going to be specific to your brand of computer, so I'm afraid I can't help you too much with this. But find out how to configure a new kernel, and look at the configuration parameters for a switch that disables packet-forwarding between interfaces.

Once the new kernel is running, see that both interfaces are configured, and that the routing table has been stuffed with entries for both the internal and external networks. A default route needs to be stuffed into the table as well. Typically, this points towards the external (Internet) router.† You will also want to disable dynamic routing; comment out any invocations of *routed* or *gated* from within the /etc/rc files. This will prevent the bastion host from advertising reachability to net-works on one side to hosts on the other.

You can test that packet-forwarding has been disabled by trying to ping through the bastion host.

Figure 16-13 represents a test scenario. Tell both *host 1* and *host 2* to use the bas-tion host as their default router. Make sure that *hosts 1* and 2 can each ping the bastion host. Then *attempt* to ping *host 1* from *host 2*. If the kernel build was suc-cessful, no traffic should go through. Note that the test is inconclusive if you merely try to ping the bastion host's far interface (the one on the other side) from *host 1* or *host 2*. Many kernels are happy to accept traffic for any of the machines' network addresses, regardless of which interface packets arrive on.‡

There's only one more thing to do: secure the bastion host against unwanted logins, security holes, and extraneous services. How do we do that? We audit the computer using the same tools we discussed several sections ago, when creating a minimalist firewall. When that's done, we are ready to install the toolkit. We will talk more about the implications of running information services on the bastion host, below.

---

* In fact, one of our favorite firewall platforms is a 486 or Pentium running Linux.

† See the *ifconfig* and *route* commands.

‡ Technical note: such a machine is said to conform to the weak endsystem model, described in rfc1122.

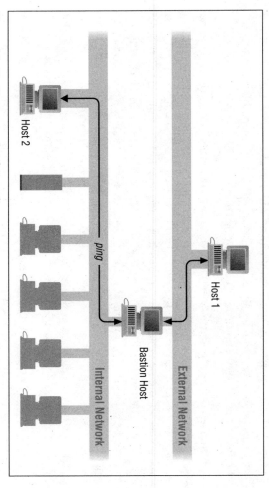

Figure 16–13: Testing packet forwarding

Using the TIS toolkit

The TIS toolkit comes as a number of independent modules, many of which share a common configuration file. You don't have to install them all; you can rummage through the modules for the ones you need. The installation instructions and overview that come with the toolkit are excellent, so I won't spend time duplicating the information here. However, I would like to take you for a quick tour of the different tools, so you can understand the problem each one solves.

SMAP

If you telnet into port 25 on your UNIX machine, you will probably find the *sendmail* waiting to take your order. If you like, you can strike up an *SMTP* conversation. Below is the record of a conversation I had with a sendmail daemon just a little while ago:

```
220-daisy.deadbeat.net Sendmail 8.6.10/8.6.10 ready at Sat, 3 Dec 1995 15:19:21 -0500
220 ESMTP spoken here
helo maddie.atlantic.com
250 daisy.deadbeat.net Hello maddie.atlantic.com [198.252.200.31], pleased to meet you
mail from:<dowd@atlantic.com>
250 <dowd@atlantic.com>... Sender ok
rcpt to:<dowd@daisy.deadbeat.net>
250 <dowd@daisy.atlantic.com>... Recipient ok
data
354 Enter mail, end with "." on a line by itself
hello!
```

```
250 PAA01977 Message accepted for delivery
quit
221 daisy.deadbeat.net closing connection
```

I asked the daemon to deliver a message for me. Of course, I didn't need to wrestle directly with the sendmail. I could have run one of the many available mail tools, and let it do the talking. But "telnetting" right into sendmail sets the stage for our security discussion—it's sort of like asking God to deliver a letter. If I can get Him to track through the neighbor's begonias on the way out, I will have really done some damage.

sendmail is a terrifically capable mail transfer agent. But it is also fairly complex, and on many machines it runs with root privileges. The goal for a cracker is to get sendmail to do something it isn't supposed to do, and thereby gain control of the machine. The current version of sendmail (8.7.5, as of this writing) has no known holes in it, but past versions have been cracked to obtain root access. The Internet Worm exploited a problem with sendmail's interactive *DBUG* function.

The TIS toolkit contains two tools that help insulate sendmail from the evil-minded. *SMAP* is a replacement for the sendmail daemon. It listens on port 25, and mimics the responses that sendmail would give to a remote mailer attempting to deliver mail. Talking to SMAP, my SMTP conversation above would look very much the same. The difference is that instead of talking with a program that could actually deliver my mail for me (sendmail), I would instead be speaking to an unpriviledged, unsophisticated order-taker (SMAP). SMAP collects the message envelope and body, naively says "Thank you very much," and sets the message aside for later processing. For additional security, SMAP runs chrooted in its own directory; there is little opportunity to break it.

Once SMAP has gathered the pieces of an incoming mail message, it drops them in a spool directory. A second program, *SMAPD*, periodically wakes up, logs the messages, and hands them off to sendmail (not running as a daemon) for delivery. Of course, it is up to sendmail to decide whether the message is actually deliverable—SMAP doesn't have a clue. The implication is that it can take a little longer for mail to be delivered, or bounced (minutes instead of seconds). This is because sendmail only has a shot at it every once in a while, when SMAP runs through its cycle.

Telnet-GW and Rlogin-GW

Other TIS tools have closer interaction with the user than SMAP. Say, for instance, that you start up a Telnet session from your desk, hoping to connect out to a computer on the Internet. Being behind a nonrouting firewall, there is no way for you to reach your destination directly. Instead, you have to connect to a proxy server running on the firewall, and tell it where you want to go. It's sort of like jumping into a cab, and asking the driver to take you somewhere, except perhaps that the proxy server has more of the demeanor of a state cop than a cabby.

The two remote terminal session proxy servers that come with the TIS toolkit are *Telnet-GW* and *Rlogin-GW*. They sit on the firewall, accepting connections to ports 23 and 513, respectively. Both run without special permissions, chrooted into an area where no harm is likely, should they be cracked. Using *Rlogin-GW* you can actually skip the intermediate conversation by supplying both a user name and host when you connect to the proxy server, e.g., `rlogin firewall -l dowd@maddie.atlantic.com`.

The rlogin and Telnet proxies can face both directions, by the way—toward the Internet and toward the internal network community. A set of access lists in a central configuration file decide who will be allowed to pass through the proxy, to the other side. The TIS toolkit also comes with extra facilities for user authentication, via one-time challenge response passwords, and electronic tokens. These can be invoked at connection time, forcing users to prove their right to pass.

FTP-GW

Like the Telnet and rlogin gateways, *Ftp-GW* provides a proxy service for remote FTP sessions. Actually, FTP is a little more complicated than remote terminal connections. You may remember this from earlier in the chapter, when we looked at router access lists: FTP sessions include two connections—a control stream and a data stream. Both connections have to be proxied.

Again, as with the remote terminal sessions, FTP sessions can be configured for challenge by authentication mechanisms, such as one-time passwords. Likewise, all connections are logged, and certain sources and destinations can be "blacked out" via access lists. Additionally, individual FTP primitives can be selectively disabled, allowing for intentionally broken FTP service.

Http-GW

Http-GW is another of the TIS firewall application proxy servers. It forwards requests from Web browsers on the internal LAN to HTTP servers, gopher daemons, and FTP sites on the other side of the firewall. The nifty thing about Http-GW is that Web clients don't even have to be "proxy aware"—you can use any old browser you like. The difference is that a "proxy aware" client knows that a firewall is in place, that all traffic has to be directed through it, and that URLs have to be specified completely. Other, naive clients assume that they can contact Internet servers directly. Provided you tell your browser to connect to Http-GW for the first access, Http-GW will rewrite all the pointers returned to you in the documents it fetches. These rewritten pointers will direct all of your subsequent accesses back through the firewall. In short, any browser can (theoretically) work.

As with the other proxy servers in the TIS toolkit, Http-GW features connection logging and access lists.

Plug-GW

You may have applications for which there is no proxy server available. For instance, USENET news transfers (NNTP) are not supported by a proxy in the toolkit. For these cases, TIS provides *Plug-GW*, a pass-thru for traffic to another computer, on the other side of the firewall. Of course, in the case of USENET, you *could* run a copy of *nntpd* on the firewall, and process news locally. However, this potentially weakens your security a bit—all applications carry some liability (not to mention that it would slow down your firewall). Instead, you might consider making your news hub a machine on the internal LAN, reachable only through Plug-GW. As with the other tools, Plug-GW supports access lists and connection logging.

Netacl

In addition to the nice selection of proxy servers, the TIS toolkit comes with its own application wrapper, very much like TCP Wrapper, described earlier. The wrapper, *Netacl*, takes the place of daemons in *inetd.conf.* When a connection request comes in, it is Netacl that gets invoked—not the daemon. Netacl can then either "exec" the appropriate daemon, or dump the caller, depending on what its rules tell it to do. Again, all connections are logged.

Netacl has some terrific additional features as well. Via configuration files, you can ask it to run processes chrooted to a particular directory. This will prevent a (yet undiscovered) security hole in a particular daemon from being used to break into the system.[*] Furthermore, you can invoke different daemons, depending on the network source address, and destination. This would allow you, for instance, to provide two different forms of *finger* service—one for the inside world and one for the outside world.

Think about this: with all of these proxy servers listening on the well-known ports for FTP, Telnet, rlogin, etc., how do you connect *to* the firewall? Consider that if you try to Telnet in, you will be intercepted by Telnet-GW; you can go someplace else, but you can't actually log into the firewall. The same is true of the FTP server, and others. If the server is configured with proxies alone, there is really no way to access the firewall.

---

[*] Of course, you have to prepare the chrooted area so that the daemon can find all of the data files and devices it needs.

There are three ways to approach the problem:

1. You can leave it that way; if the system console is the only way to reach the firewall, you can be that much more confident that nobody will get in.

2. You can provide Telnet access on some other (inconspicuous) port, and protect it with access lists.

3. You can use a tool like Netacl to allow Telnet sessions from certain hosts, but provide the proxy server interface to the rest.

The third alternative will make it possible for an administrator or two to take care of the machine from their desktops, rather than having to walk into the computer room (or closet, perhaps) and log in at the console. The danger of spoofed addresses returns, though: if a remote user can convince Netacl that they are "telnetting" from a trusted address, they will be greeted by a regular login prompt, instead of the proxy server. Again, you can protect the login with challenge/response passwords or electronic tokens, if you wish. And of course, if properly configured, the router will be able to recognize when people from outside the organization are trying to get into the firewall by using local source addresses.

A Proxy Firewall and Information Servers

Well, what have we accomplished? Using the TIS toolkit, and a secured host, we have created a conduit for (limited) traffic between the local network and the Internet. But look what's missing: we have no information servers! If the Internet were a dance, we'd be a wallflower.

One possibility is that we could run information servers, such as gopherd and httpd, directly on the firewall. Again, taking advantage of Netacl's ability to provide different services on the same port, we could make it so that incoming connections raise Web or gopher servers, but outgoing connections are greeted by a proxy agent (such as Http-GW). * Likewise, anonymous FTP could be staged on the firewall for serving files to the outside world (TIS even includes some custom code for this).

There are a few problems though; as I mentioned previously, every extra application running on the firewall is a security liability—another potential hole. And depending on the size of the company, the firewall may already be busy enough ferrying data to and from the Internet; it probably doesn't need more to do. Here's a different approach: why not stage a separate information server, outside the bastion host? Figure 16-14 shows this configuration.

---

* You might also look at CERN's HTTPD. It's a nice package that can act simultaneously as a proxy agent and a server of documents. Connect to ftp://ftp.w3.org.

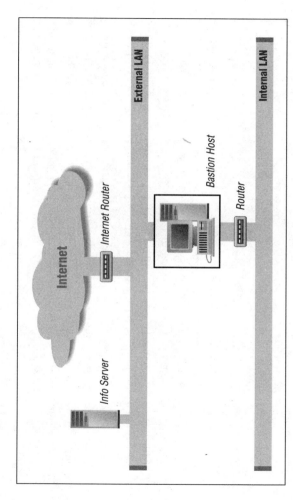

Figure 16-14: Information servers outside the firewall

This second computer—the information server—typically doesn't have to be very powerful. A midrange PC or a Mac will often do. Consider that because you are behind a Internet WAN connection, there is only so much data outsiders can suck off the machine. In relative terms, 56 Kbits (or even T1, for that matter) is a pretty slow network connection; a slow computer can keep up. In many cases, organizations can find an orphaned machine to fill the information server role. If you have a UNIX machine handy, you can configure and secure it using the same tools we applied to the minimalist firewall server, described above.

DNS and a Nonrouting Proxy Firewall

Now we must be finished: we have a complete Internet site solution, we have proxy servers for our internal users, we (perhaps) have an information server off to the side, and our network is secured. Time for a beer? Sorry. We're not quite done; we still need a strategy for domain name service. Here's why:

Suppose that after all of our firewall preparations, we set the bastion host up as the domain name server for the organization, put on a silly grin, and went home. What tempest might fill the log files that night? Remember that the bastion host has one foot in the Internet and one in the internal network, meaning that it can reach any computer, inside or out. Accordingly, any host addresses—inside or out—returned by DNS will work. The trouble is that the same does not apply to the rest of the universe. Hosts on the inside of the firewall, for instance, will receive valid

addresses for computers that the firewall ultimately prevents them from reaching.[*]
Likewise, computers on the Internet trying to speak with hosts on the private LAN
will find them unreachable.[†] Of course, *unreachability* from the outside is what
we hoped for when we built the firewall. However, we still want to be able to
gather electronic mail; MX records must direct SMTP traffic towards the firewall, so
it can be forwarded to internal machines.

All of this suggests that we need a split strategy for DNS—a private nameserver for
the firewall, and an external nameserver for the rest of the world to use. In fact,
three nameservers even makes sense in some cases, depending on whether you
also need to provide DNS to machines isolated behind the firewall.

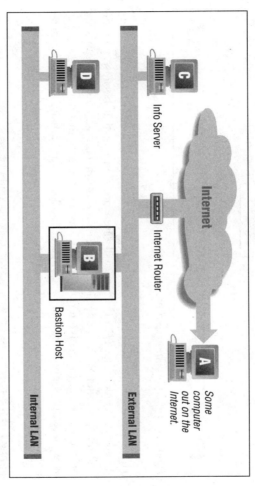

Figure 16–15: DNS behind a proxy firewall

To understand why this has to be so complicated, let's think about "who needs to
know what" in the picture above. Don't bother about which machines actually
serve the DNS information. We'll worry about that later. Instead, consider the con-
sumers of DNS data. We have three classes of machines: computers out on the
Internet, the bastion host, and computers within the organization.

---

* Note: this applies to the TIS toolkit proxy implementation. One *can* use external addresses through
Gauntlet, and other transparent firewalls.

† Or worse... if you have borrowed someone else's network number, your traffic could be directed
toward their network, wherever they may be. This is discussed in more detail later.

DNS for computers on the Internet

We want to be stingy about the information we provide to the outside world; there is no reason to tell strangers (such as host "A" in Figure 16-15) about computers that lurk within the firewall (such as "D"). At the same time, we probably have some computers that we wish to advertise, including the information servers (like "C"), and the mail hub ("B," the bastion host).

An external nameserver providing this information to the rest of the Internet would need to be configured with each of the following:

Addresses for information servers

Addresses for information servers, such as *www.deadbeat.net*, *gopher.deadbeat.net*, etc. need to be visible to the Internet. Often, these domain names will resolve to a single IP address (an information server) via DNS canonical names.

MX records for the organization's mail

Mail for the company can be collected via MX records (e.g., **.deadbeat.net*, and *deadbeat.net*). Usually, the MX records will point to the bastion host, which forwards mail for delivery inside.

A reverse look-up (in-addr.arpa) for the bastion host

A valid in-addr.arpa record should be served for the bastion host because it will be proxying connections to many Internet resources—some of which may require address-to-name resolution for security.

Nameserver records

The external nameserver should also list the addresses of the primary and secondary external nameservers.

localhost records

Forward and reverse look-ups for 127.0.0.1 (localhost) should also be served.

Again, notice that we completely left out information about hosts behind the firewall. A few MX records are the only clue that there might be other computers on the private network.

DNS for the bastion host

By contrast, the bastion host has different requirements than the hosts of passersby on the Internet. It needs to know the names and addresses of the machines inside the firewall (Like "D"), for log files, security, and auditing. If there are other SMTP mail hubs within the organization, the bastion host may also need access to internal MX records. Naturally, the bastion host also has to be able to resolve external DNS references, just like other Internet hosts. Remember, this machine has a foot in each world. It has to be able to see computers on both sides.

A DNS configuration to serve the bastion host includes the following:

The organization's domain

All addresses—internal and external—for the organization's domain, plus reverse records, should be available to the bastion host. This includes machines inside and outside the firewall.

MX records for internal mail hosts

Computers responsible for handling their own SMTP mail, or mail hubs within the firewall, should be represented by MX records visible to the bastion host.

localhost records

Forward and reverse look-ups for 127.0.0.1 (localhost) should be served to the bastion host as well.

DNS for computers inside the firewall

Again, depending on the complexity of your network, you may not need internal DNS service. If you have a single SMTP mail hub (probably the firewall), for instance, or if your computing environment is made up primarily of proxy clients, IP traffic will be directed toward the firewall anyway—DNS will not be used to decide how to reach other computers. Internal DNS becomes important when there is a rich IP environment *inside* the firewall. To supply DNS to computers behind a firewall, we need the following:

Addresses for internal resources

All internal addresses (even blocks allocated via bootp or DHCP) should have names and reverse records visible from the internal nameserver.

MX records for internal mail hosts

Computers responsible for handling their own SMTP mail, or mail hubs within the firewall, should have MX records on the internal nameserver.

MX records for all mail beyond the firewall

All electronic mail traffic for destinations beyond the firewall should be directed to the bastion host via wildcard MX records.

localhost records

Forward and reverse look-ups for 127.0.0.1 (localhost) should be available from the internal nameserver.

Modified root information

The internal name server should believe that it is authoritative for the top of the DNS tree (root), and that the hierarchy begins with the organization's own domain. *deadbeat.net*, for example, might be the top level domain inside the firewall. Any nameserver look-up that can't be resolved within the *deadbeat.net* domain will be answered with "host or domain unknown."

Consider what would happen if instead of answering "host unknown," the internal nameserver supplied valid addresses for computers on the outside: after successfully completing the nameserver look-up, the internal host would attempt to make contact beyond the firewall, and, after some delay, fail. Either way—"host unknown" or a failed connection—we'd be disappointed. However, it would take a lot longer in the second case.*

Nameserver placement

The details of setting up the DNS data files—both internal and external—are covered in Chapter 17, *Domain Name Service*, so I won't go over it again here.† However, a few words about where to place the nameservers would probably be a good idea. Several permutations are possible.

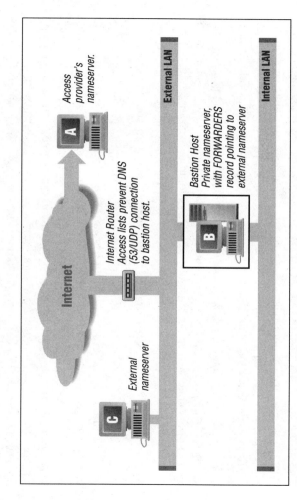

Figure 16–16: Firewall DNS with two nameservers

For starters, let's say that you have a pretty uncomplicated IP network, and that you need DNS service for just two communities—the outside world, and the bastion host. The external, spartan, DNS information could be served from your information server ("C"), if you have one, or from your access provider's equipment. This external nameserver would be your official DNS primary for the organization, registered with the InterNIC. I normally recommend that people maintain their

---

* Again, this applies to the TIS toolkit. A transparent proxy server firewall will be able to connect, given an external IP address.

† In fact, if you find this all too confusing, you might set the discussion aside for now, and look at Chapter 17. Much of what we are discussing is laid out there in cookbook form.

own primary nameservers, rather than leave them with the access provider. However, in this case, the DNS information being provided is very basic, and not likely to change often. That is, the flexibility we give up by having the primary administered elsewhere won't be a big inconvenience.

The nameserver for the bastion host can run *on* the bastion host. Remember, however, that the goal is to keep this information out of the hands of the Internet public. That means that, via router access lists, we want to prevent DNS queries (UDP/53) originating from the Internet from reaching the bastion host. But this gives us a problem: if we don't allow any requests inbound on port 53, how will the bastion host make its own outbound DNS queries?* One answer is that we can use a *forwarders* directive in the bastion host nameserver to tell DNS to send unresolved queries outside, to a particular host—either to the information server or to the access provider's own nameservers (Figure 16-16). The answer, when it comes back, will always be from one of those two machines, and can therefore be filtered. The other possible answer is "We've engineered this thing to death. Let's just let the bastion host make its own DNS queries, and be done with it." In that case, people *can* learn information about hosts beyond the firewall (if they set their nameserver to point to the firewall), though it doesn't become any easier to reach them—they're still tucked behind the firewall.

Now let's add one more (as in Figure 16-17), internal DNS server, for use only by hosts on the private company LAN.

Really, this is an easy addition—we can leave the other two nameservers pretty much alone. The internal nameserver is prepared using the records described earlier. You will find a concrete configuration example in Chapter 17.

The one possible twist is that we might want to set up zone transfers between the internal nameserver and the bastion host for private LAN data. This would relieve us from updating two separate DNS databases each time a change was made to the internal network. There's one exception here, though: we want the bastion host and internal nameserver to consult separate MX records for reachability to the outside world. Wildcard MX records for Internet destinations probably shouldn't be shared.†

Take a breath! To summarize up to this point, the external nameserver primary is either the information server living on the red LAN, or the access provider's own

---

* Recall the discussion about UDP filtering. It would be difficult to tell whether an incoming packet was the response to a request by the bastion host, or a request *to* the bastion host. Shutting off inbound DNS requests is tantamount to shutting off outbound requests.

† They *could* be shared, as long as the wildcard MX records served inside had an extremely low priority. The trouble is that there are computers living on the Internet with address records alone—no MX records. These would become unreachable because MX records pointing to the bastion host would suggest this as the ultimate destination.

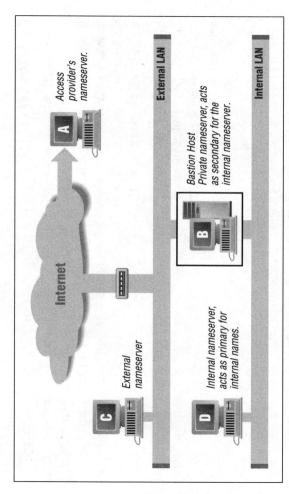

Figure 16–17: Firewalled network with three nameservers

nameserver host. The private nameserver for the bastion host server runs on the bastion host.

Just in case you missed it, the various nameserver configurations I described are in support of the TIS Toolkit, running nontransparent proxies. If you have a transparent firewall (that doesn't have its own, multiple nameservers), you might want to do it a little bit differently. Here's why: if the proxy servers are transparent, then internal machines will need to resolve addresses for hosts out on the Internet—they had no use for external addresses when using nontransparent proxies. This means that the internal nameserver will be able to share a nameserver with the bastion host.

Overall, I hope it is clear what we are trying to accomplish. Using multiple domain nameservers, we can provide local pictures of network information. Machines on the Internet, on the internal LAN, and the bastion host can be individually lied to about the network's structure. This will add security, and make the firewall more transparent. If, on the other hand, you got lost in the discussion, please don't feel bad. This is pretty convoluted stuff. You should be able to follow the DNS templates offered in Chapter 17 and achieve the same results.

Third-Party Firewalls

"Good grief!" you might say. "After all of that, why would I ever want to build my own firewall?" There are plenty of reasons for not rolling your own, including money, time (which equals money), and your own lack of familiarity with the environment. You probably wouldn't want to make firewall construction your first big incursion into the UNIX world—there's a lot of assumed knowledge in even the most basic projects.

Anyway, whatever the reasons, we still have another option: *buying* a firewall. The good news is that there are some high quality firewalls on the market. Some of them are fairly priced, too. I list a few possibilities, below, though this isn't a complete list by any means. *

Gauntlet

Trusted Information Systems (Glenwood, Maryland), the folks who were kind enough to provide the TIS toolkit we discussed previously, market a complete firewall solution known as *Gauntlet*. Gauntlet is based on the toolkit, with extensions. As we have seen, the toolkit provides a broad range of application proxy servers for many of the Internet information tools that organizations want to run.

Gauntlet's pricing is moderate, and the firewall software is mature and secure. Note that this is one of the few firewalls that has been subject to the scrutiny of the Internet community. Other firewalls are proprietary; source code isn't available for inspection.

BorderWare

The *BorderWare* firewall from Border Network Technologies (Toronto, Ontario) is a complete firewall *and* information server solution. The firewall provides transparent circuit-level proxies and application-level proxies for Internet applications; no proxy clients are necessary. Computers within the organization treat the BorderWare firewall as the default router.† When packets arrive, the proxies unbundle, log, and forward requests out to the Internet. The internal network infrastructure is completely hidden from view. Accordingly, illegal addresses can be used. All traffic is subject to source/destination/service rules, much like router access lists.

BorderWare also comes with Web, FTP, USENET news, and mail servers. Everything is configured via a GUI front-end. For security, firewall logins are not

---

* Cathy Fulmer maintains a good, up-to-date roster of firewalls at *http://www.waterw.com/ ~manowar/vendor.html*.

† In fact, a BorderWare firewall can *replace* your external router.

possible. Currently, BorderWare runs exclusively on Intel X86 platforms. Pricing is moderate.

Firewall-1

Firewall-1, from CheckPoint Software Technologies Ltd. (Israel), is a different sort of firewall than BorderWare or Gauntlet; it is an intelligent router, rather than a proxy server. You will recall previously that we discussed the challenge of applying packet filters to different kinds of traffic—TCP, UDP, etc. Vanilla routers have a problem with some protocols because they can't remember what they have seen. Firewall-1, on the other hand, keeps complete connection histories for all of the traffic that passes through it. It can therefore tell the difference between an unsolicited inbound connection and the response to a request from a machine within the organization.

Additionally, the latest versions of the product can rewrite IP addresses, and provide site-hiding. Firewall-1 is managed via a GUI (X-based) frontend. As with the other firewalls, it has a complete set of alarms and logging functions. Pricing is moderate. A Windows NT version is available.

ANS Interlock

Interlock, from Advanced Networks and Services (AOL) (Elmsford, NY) is a comprehensive suite of services, built around application-level proxies. Interlock includes support for HTTP, Gopher, FTP, Telnet, X, SMTP mail, and network time. Other applications—USENET news, arbitrary UDP and TCP clients—are supported by passthroughs. As with other firewalls, logging, alarms, and challenge/response identification are supported.

Interlock has an additional feature: end-to-end encryption. One firewall can share information with another through (DES) encrypted traffic. This kind of ability is available on certain brands of routers, but on few firewalls, making Interlock a notable exception. The platforms are IBM (AIX) and Sun. Pricing is high.

Raptor Eagle

Eagle, from Raptor Systems, is an application proxy firewall with sophisticated alarming and logging capabilities, packaged behind a comprehensive GUI. Windows NT and UNIX versions are available. As with a few of the other firewalls mentioned so far, this firewall is completely transparent; applications don't even need to know it exists. Also, the firewall performs site-hiding, rewriting addresses on the way out. Pricing is moderate.

17

Domain Name Service

I have a copy of the *Scientific American Cyclopedia of Formulas*, published in 1911. It's great if you need to remove a ring from a swollen knuckle, grow mushrooms in a dresser drawer, or rid your home of Buffalo Moths. These days, some of the ingredients are kind of hard to come by; the book expects you to find compounds like uranium nitrate and cyanide at the pharmacy. Still, it's hard to gripe; everything is in one place. Even if I have to make friends with a weapons dealer to manage Buffalo Moths, at least I have a solution.

This chapter and the next, after the same fashion, will be a collection of formulas for name service and mail configuration. Here's what we are going to cover:

• Basic domain name service (DNS) configuration

• Name service for isolated networks and nontransparent firewalls.

• Name service for transparent firewalls.

• Multiple domains

• sendmail configuration

• Aliases

• Gateways to LAN mail systems

• POP (Post Office Protocol)

• Site-hiding

This will give us an infrastructure upon which to build other applications, such as Web service, gopher service, news, anonymous FTP, and so on. Appendixes C through F say a few words about FTP, Web, mail, and USENET news service. Unfortunately, this is also where we get off. *Managing Internet Information*

Services, published by O'Reilly & Associates, provides a comprehensive follow-on; the book contains in-depth discussions about FTP configuration, http daemons, mailing lists, and more. If you would like more information about the topics in this chapter, please see *TCP/IP Network Administration*, and *DNS and Bind*, also published by O'Reilly & Associates. Likewise, if you need help with UNIX, you might look into *Essential System Administration, Second Edition*, also from O'Reilly & Associates.

The Server

Network infrastructure services—particularly name service and mail—have to be staged somewhere—on a server. Usually, we are talking about a UNIX machine, though it is possible to run network services on other operating systems, such as MacOS, Windows 95, or Windows NT. My experience is that though the interface may be slightly different, the jargon will be the same. So even if you are configuring, say, OS/2, the discussion here should be helpful.

In any event, we need a server. Be careful though: sometimes there's a temptation to nominate a working computer for the job, à la "This machine will run our payroll *and* be our Web server." That's not really a good idea, for two reasons: First, the information server will be a site for development and experimentation; you probably don't want critical applications vying for serious use of the server while everyone else is having so much fun. Second, there is a security risk: when you open up the server to the Internet, you are inviting random people to stop by. If, by chance, somebody cracks your machine, it would be better if they found nothing you weren't willing to give away in the first place.

Figure 17-1 shows a common secured network configuration. An external LAN is home to one side of a firewall and to an information server. In this case, domain name service for the Internet would be best located on the external information server, perhaps alongside a Web daemon, gopher daemon, etc. The firewall, on the other hand, could manage electronic mail. In fact, this is a natural spot for mail because the firewall is easily reachable from both the inside and the outside.

A simpler network configuration, like the one shown in Figure 17-1, may have all services—mail, DNS, news, Web, etc.—running on a single information server; one machine can usually manage the whole job. You should be moderately generous with memory and disk space. Sixteen megabytes of memory is a good start. You can even get away with less sometimes—it depends on the machine architecture (RISC platforms typically require more memory), and the server activity level. Likewise, a modest amount of disk space is usually fine—500 MBytes is usually enough for a Web server and related tools. If you are going to run news, plan on a few gigabytes.

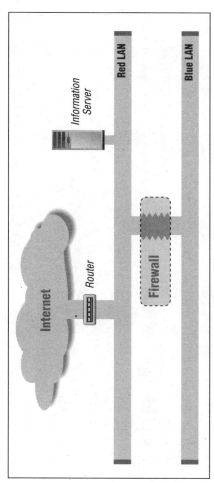

Figure 17–1: Secured network configuration

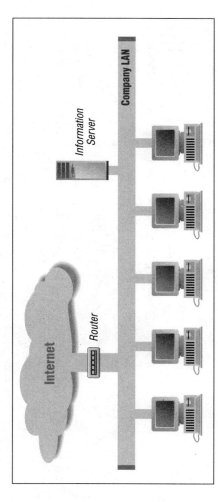

Figure 17–2: A simpler network configuration

You will need software too. A UNIX operating system release typically comes equipped with support for domain name service (DNS) and sendmail (though it may be old and in need of replacement). Other services (e.g., POP) may not be included in your operating system distribution at all—you may have to build them from source code.

As you probably guessed, you can begin erecting network information infrastructure pieces long before the Internet connection comes in. In all but a couple of cases, the services that we set up in advance will be fully configured to serve the Internet when the circuit is turned up. And even for those services that behave differently on or off the network, we can prepare a pair of configurations, one for now and one for later. We'll begin with DNS.

Domain Name Service

In a nutshell, *Domain Name Service* (DNS) is the facility that converts names that humans are comfortable with (for instance, *bart.deadbeat.net*), into a form that computers can use (like 198.252.200.10). It goes the other way, too: an IP address can be translated into a domain name. DNS is a hierarchical, distributed system, fastened together by a chorus of pointers from parents to children. For a site coming online, the goal is to glue into the hierarchy so that people can find you and your information services by name. Without DNS, your computers would be known only by their numerical IP addresses.

To take an example, say a company named *"GizNiz"* wants to get onto the Internet with the domain *gizniz.com*. A couple of steps are required:

1. The *GizNiz* company has to provide for primary and secondary *nameservers.* These are computers that are prepared to answer questions like *"What machine accepts mail for gizniz.com?"* and *"What is the address for www.gizniz.com?"* The primary nameserver is the authority; the secondary, as needed, clones information (in what is called a zone transfer) from the primary, and acts as an alternate resource.

2. The *GizNiz* company has to register its domain with the InterNIC (this was discussed in Chapter 2, *Service Options*). In this way, *gizniz.com* becomes part of the domain hierarchy. When a computer out on the Internet goes looking for information about *gizniz.com*, it will eventually find its way to the primary or secondary nameserver, which will then be able to answer specific questions about *GizNiz* hosts.

Many Internet Service Providers (ISPs) (not all) will be happy to handle both steps—nameserver maintenance and domain registration—on your behalf when you order an Internet connection. Depending on your requirements, you may eventually choose to migrate responsibility for the primary nameserver back to one of your own computers, to be administered locally. I argued in favor of this in Chapter 2. Leaving the job of domain administration with the carrier may sound convenient. However, when you need to make a change—perhaps to add a new host to the domain—you will have to contact the ISP and ask for an update; it just takes longer.* Furthermore, a few access providers' nameservers are notoriously overloaded; your site may appear to be unaccessible to outsiders if the ISP's nameserver times out while answering someone's request for your address.

Anyway, assuming that you do decide to maintain your own primary nameserver, you are going to need to run a copy of the named daemon (*named*) on the

---

* There's a notable exception to my argument. If you are operating behind a proxy firewall, you may never need updates to your DNS zone information. More below.

machine that is registered with the InterNIC as the primary nameserver (and on the secondary, too, though I'll assume that it is located somewhere else).* The executable for the daemon can typically be found in one of */etc, /usr/etc/,* or */usr/sbin.* Often, it will be started automatically at boot time from one of the "rc" files in */etc* or */etc/rc.d.* Let's take a walk through the named configuration files, to understand how the daemon works.

Named Data Files

The actions of *named* are controlled by a boot file, called *named.boot,* usually found in the */etc* directory. Below, we have a basic *named.boot,* describing a machine that is acting as a primary nameserver for three domains: *gizniz.com* and a couple of reverse (*in-addr.arpa*) domains (I'll explain these in a moment).

```
;
; type        domain                        source file
;
directory     /etc/named.data  ; running directory for named
;
primary       gizniz.com                    db.gizniz
primary       0.0.127.in-addr.arpa          db.127.0.0
primary       200.252.198.in-addr.arpa      db.198.252.200
cache         .                             db.cache
```

The `directory` directive near the top of the boot file tells the daemon where to find DNS zone definitions. In this case, the directory specified is */etc/named.* Another common choice is */var/named.* It really doesn't matter which you choose, as long as the "db" (zone) files can be found there. You may need to create the directory before you can populate it.

Forward zone definition

Appearing a few lines from the top of *named.boot,* the first primary declaration tells the daemon that you are keeping data for the zone *gizniz.com* in the file *db.gizniz,* and that the daemon will be the primary nameserver for the data. *db.gizniz* might look like this:

```
gizniz.com.    IN    SOA    server.gizniz.com. root.server.gizniz.com. (
                           1       ; Serial number
                           10800   ; Refresh every 3 hours
                           3600    ; Retry every hour
                           604800  ; Expire after a week
                           86400 ) ; Minimum ttl of 1 day

               IN    NS     server.gizniz.com.
               IN    NS     server.provider.net.
```

* UNIX machines usually run the *Berkeley Internet Name Daemon* (BIND). People usually just call it the "name daemon," and refer to the whole ball of wax as "DNS."

```
;
localhost          IN    A     127.0.0.1
;
router             IN    A     198.252.200.1
server             IN    A     198.252.200.2
host1              IN    A     198.252.200.3
host2              IN    A     198.252.200.4
;
www                IN    CNAME server.gizniz.com.
gopher             IN    CNAME server.gizniz.com.
ftp                IN    CNAME server.gizniz.com.
;
gizniz.com.        IN    MX 10 server.gizniz.com.
server.gizniz.com  IN    MX 10 server.gizniz.com.
```

This is often called a *forward* zone definition because it describes how names can be translated into addresses (a *reverse* zone definition goes the other way). The record at the top of the file designates the nameserver as the *Start of Authority* (SOA)—the true source of information—for the domain. The SOA record also contains some loosely labeled numeric parameters. I'll go over each one briefly:

- The *serial number* keeps track of changes in the data, and (by incrementing) signals to secondary (and other) servers that the zone data has been changed and should be re-cloned (a zone transfer is in order). When you change information in the data file, you should also increment the serial number.

- The *refresh* value tells secondary servers how many seconds to wait before resampling the primary's serial number to see if the zone data has been modified. Zone transfers from primary to secondary won't occur if the serial number does not change.

- The *retry* parameter tells a secondary nameserver how many seconds it should wait between failed attempts to pull a zone transfer from the primary.

- If too much time goes by between successful zone transfers—more than the *expire* parameter specifies—the secondary will stop returning data, and will instead answer DNS requests with "server failed."

- The last parameter, *minimum*, tells all clients of DNS information how long they should honor a cached piece of information administered from this zone file. A value of 7200 seconds, for instance, would say that any information you receive about the *gizniz.com* domain should be considered valid for 2 hours. After that, it's time for another DNS look-up.

Now let's look at the records within the zone definition:

```
gizniz.com.        IN    NS    server.gizniz.com.
gizniz.com.        IN    NS    server.provider.net.
```

The two NS records, shown above, describe hosts that are acting as nameservers for the domain. In this case, we have listed server.gizniz.com (presumably, the machine we are configuring now) and server.provider.net, the secondary nameserver borrowed from your ISP.

Next, we have address (A) records for particular hosts within the *gizniz.com* domain. Because we have declared in the SOA record that the zone data describes *gizniz.com*, an entry like "host1" is assumed to have the "gizniz.com" part tacked on.*

```
localhost    IN    A     127.0.0.1
;
router       IN    A     198.252.200.1
server       IN    A     198.252.200.2
host1        IN    A     198.252.200.3
host2        IN    A     198.252.200.4
```

The address records above set IP addresses for hosts named router.gizniz.com, server.gizniz.com, and so on. The localhost record (localhost.gizniz.com) has been included for the benefit of programs that perform interprocess communication through the local loopback.

```
www      IN    CNAME    server.gizniz.com.
gopher   IN    CNAME    server.gizniz.com.
ftp      IN    CNAME    server.gizniz.com.
```

Farther down in the *db.gizniz* file, CNAME records describe canonical names (aliases) for server. These say that any requests for names www.gizniz.com, gopher.gizniz.com, or ftp.gizniz.com should be answered with the address of server.gizniz.com.

Last, we have MX (mail exchange) records for *GizNiz*. These say that any mail bound for the *gizniz.com* domain, or for the server in particular, should be sent to host *server.gizniz.com*. The "10" marks a preference; we could have nominated other hosts to accept mail for *gizniz.com* with lower or higher preference (the lower the number, the higher the preference). Another MX record might be appropriate here too:

```
gizniz.com.            IN    MX    10    server.gizniz.com.
server.gizniz.com.     IN    MX    10    server.gizniz.com.
```

```
*.gizniz.com.    IN    MX    10    server.gizniz.com.
```

This says that mail bound for any *GizNiz* host should be sent to the server. This would be useful if the server was acting as an inbound mail hub for many independent hosts within the *gizniz.com* domain. As we'll see in the next chapter,

---

* You can see that in some of the records I have specified *fully qualified domain names*—the host name and the "gizniz.com" part are coupled together. In others, I have just used the host name. Because we are creating a zone definition for *gizniz.com*, we can specify hosts either way—long version or short version; the suffix is appended if the domain name is not fully qualified. Be sure to note, however, that fully qualified domain names end with a period.

choices we make when configuring *sendmail.cf* have a relationship to the MX records we advertise, here, under DNS.

Reverse zones

Next, we turn to *reverse domains*—so-called because they describe translations in the other direction—from IP addresses to names. Our boot file, *named.boot*, tells the nameserver that it is the primary for two reverse domains: *0.0.127.in-addr.arpa.* and *200.252.198.in-addr.arpa.* Note the formula here (ignoring the *in-addr.arpa* portion): the IP addresses are turned around, so that they are specified with the most specific portion appearing on the left. This places them in the same general form as the forward zone information that we looked at previously. As with the forward zone, we will create reverse zone definition files that designate our nameserver as the *Start of Authority* for the domains:

```
0.0.127.in-addr.arpa.    IN    SOA    server.gizniz.com. root.server.gizniz.com. (
                                        1        ; Serial
                                        10800    ; Refresh every 3 hours
                                        3600     ; Retry every hour
                                        604800   ; Expire after a week
                                        86400 )  ; Minimum ttl of 1 day
                         IN    NS     server.gizniz.com.
```

```
0.0.127.in-addr.arpa.    IN    NS     server.gizniz.com.

1                        IN    PTR    localhost.
                         IN    PTR    loopback.
```

This copy of *db.127.0.0* can be copied almost verbatim, except that the NS record should be changed to list your nameserver. Notice that for reverse mappings we are using (PTR) records in lieu of the address (A) records we used in *db.gizniz*. By translating these, the nameserver will return names; when it is asked to translate 127.0.0.1 (actually, 1.0.0.127.in-addr.arpa) the answer will be localhost.

Now looking at file *db.198.252.200*, which follows, we see a PTR record corresponding to each of the address (A) records contained within *db.gizniz*. Again, our nameserver is listed as the *Start of Authority*:

```
200.252.198.in-addr.arpa.  IN  SOA  server.gizniz.com. root.server.gizniz.com. (
                                      6        ; Serial
                                      10800    ; Refresh every 3 hours
                                      3600     ; Retry every hour
                                      604800   ; Expire after a week
                                      86400 )  ; Minimum ttl of 1 day
```

```
200.252.198.in-addr.arpa.  IN  NS   server.gizniz.com.

1    IN    PTR    router.gizniz.com.
2    IN    PTR    server.gizniz.com.
3    IN    PTR    host1.gizniz.com.
4    IN    PTR    host2.gizniz.com.
```

By the way, you *could* operate without providing reverse domain information. However, computers on the Internet attempting to translate your addresses into a domain name will come up empty-handed. This gives you a certain amount of anonymity, but there is a price to pay. For security reasons, many sites log the names of computers that connect to them. If the reverse domain information is available, logging proceeds pretty quickly. If the domain isn't registered or available, however, it takes a while for the reverse look-up to timeout. This sometimes translates into frustrating delays for the users on your own network; connections to Internet resources will seem to take forever. Users may even be refused access to resources. Some sites' policy is to disallow connections from hosts lacking reverse DNS records.

Cache file

The last line in *named.boot* references a file called *db.cache*, which lists the names and addresses of servers that can provide lists of root nameservers in the DNS hierarchy. Here's the reason for it: look-ups are hierarchical. When you ask the nameserver for a domain translation that it hasn't handled recently (say *www.atlantic.com*), it may have to start with the most fundamental question: i.e., "Who's in charge of *atlantic.com?*" The search starts at the top of the DNS hierarchy, and works its way down. The nameserver begins by querying one of a number of "root" nameservers to learn who is authoritative for *atlantic.com*. From there, it will contact the *atlantic.com* nameserver and ask about *www*.

The *db.cache* file lists the root nameservers:

```
.                       3600000   IN  NS  A.ROOT-SERVERS.NET.
A.ROOT-SERVERS.NET.     3600000       A   198.41.0.4
.                       3600000       NS  B.ROOT-SERVERS.NET.
B.ROOT-SERVERS.NET.     3600000       A   128.9.0.107
.                       3600000       NS  C.ROOT-SERVERS.NET.
C.ROOT-SERVERS.NET.     3600000       A   192.33.4.12
.                       3600000       NS  D.ROOT-SERVERS.NET.
D.ROOT-SERVERS.NET.     3600000       A   128.8.10.90
.                       3600000       NS  E.ROOT-SERVERS.NET.
E.ROOT-SERVERS.NET.     3600000       A   192.203.230.10
.                       3600000       NS  F.ROOT-SERVERS.NET.
F.ROOT-SERVERS.NET.     3600000       A   192.5.5.241
.                       3600000       NS  G.ROOT-SERVERS.NET.
G.ROOT-SERVERS.NET.     3600000       A   192.112.36.4
.                       3600000       NS  H.ROOT-SERVERS.NET.
H.ROOT-SERVERS.NET.     3600000       A   128.63.2.53
.                       3600000       NS  I.ROOT-SERVERS.NET.
I.ROOT-SERVERS.NET.     3600000       A   192.36.148.17
```

You can see a typical *db.cache*, here. Each root nameserver (signified by the lone ".") is listed along with its IP address. You probably noticed that we *haven't* designated our nameserver as a primary for the root server data. Instead, via the cache directive, we doped the nameserver's database with root server records (hints) to last the life of the process.

Root server data creeps over time; new nameservers come online, and addresses can change. For that reason, you should occasionally (every few months) fetch a new list of root servers, and incorporate it into *db.cache*. Updated information can be found at *ftp://rs.internic.net/domain/named.root*.

Resolver

As its name suggests, domain name service is a service, and therefore has clients. On a UNIX machine, we collectively call these clients "the resolver." There's nothing we can really shake a stick at; the resolver isn't a program or process. Rather, it's a set of library routines that translate host names into addresses, and addresses into host names. Programs call resolver routines. The resolver routines, in turn, talk to nameservers.

Under UNIX, the behavior of the resolver routines is controlled, in part, by a file called *resolv.conf*, kept in the */etc* directory.

Here, we have a minimal *resolv.conf*. It specifies the local domain name to the resolver routines. The resolver will append the domain name to host names before passing them to the nameserver for resolution. For instance, if I ask for the address of *host1*, the resolver routines will try the look-up as *host1.gizniz.com*, first, before falling back to *host1*. Similarly, a look-up like *bart.specials.com* will be attempted as *bart.specials.com.gizniz.com*, before being passed on unadulterated. This may seem like a waste of effort, but it allows the resolver to catch local subdomains first, before attempting resolution outside.

It is also possible for *resolv.conf* to include a nameserver specification:

```
domain gizniz.com
nameserver 198.252.200.3
```

This tells the resolver to bounce queries off the nameserver process located at the specified address, instead of using the localhost (127.0.0.1). This would be useful in situations where you have a central machine acting as the nameserver; you can aim the other machines' resolvers in the central machine's direction. Note that, depending on the operating software, the nameserver directive may be necessary even if you are using the local host's nameserver:

```
domain gizniz.com
nameserver 127.0.0.1
```

As you probably know, addresses can be resolved by other means, including the host table (*/etc/hosts*), or *NIS*. In some cases, you have to take extra steps to force resolver routines to use DNS for resolution. It depends on the brand of computer. Some have an extra hostresorder directive for *resolv.conf*; others depend on a separate configuration file. On a Sun, you may be required to run NIS, or make changes to your shared C libraries.*

Testing the Resolver

Once you have set up *resolv.conf*, you can test your nameserver. Your operating system release probably comes with a copy of *nslookup* (nameserver look-up). We will use *nslookup* for our testing:

```
$ nslookup
Default Server:  server
Address:  0.0.0.0

> server
Server:   server
Address:  0.0.0.0

Name:     server.gizniz.com
Address:  198.252.200.2
```

Start by typing **nslookup** at the shell prompt.† Upon start-up, *nslookup* will announce the nameserver's name and address. In this example, you can see 0.0.0.0 is returned. This is because our *resolv.conf* doesn't designate a name-server; the local nameserver is chosen by default. At the prompt, enter the name of the machine acting as your server. *nslookup* should return the address immediately. If you have a problem, double check to see that *named* is running, and that your zone files match mine in form.‡ If you configured "CNAME" records, as I did in the sample zone definitions, you should be able to test them now. Try entering **www**, for instance. *nslookup* should return the address of the server, as follows:

```
> www
Server:   server
Address:  0.0.0.0

Name:     server.gizniz.com
Address:  198.252.200.2
Aliases:  www.gizniz.com
```

---

* This can be a real pain. See *DNS & Bind*, published by O'Reilly & Associates.

† You might have to look around a little—it may be in */usr/etc*, for instance.

‡ To cause the daemon to reread your zone files, locate the process ID for *named* (type **ps aux | grep named**), and send the process a *HUP* signal: **kill -HUP <process-id>**. In some cases, *named* leaves its process ID behind in a file called */etc/named.pid*; you may be able to simply type: **kill -HUP 'cat /etc/named.pid'**.

Now we will check to see if MX records are set up properly. Within *nslookup*, set the *querytype* option to **MX**, then enter **gizniz.com**. You should see your MX host(s) listed, and perhaps the NS records for the domain.

```
> set querytype=MX
> gizniz.com.
Server:  server
Address:  0.0.0.0

gizniz.com       preference = 10, mail exchanger = server.gizniz.com
gizniz.com       nameserver = server.gizniz.com
gizniz.com       nameserver = server.provider.net.
server.gizniz.cominternet address = 198.252.200.2
server.provider.net       internet address = 192.65.177.3
```

Next, try a PTR look-up: set the querytype parameter to **PTR**, and enter an address from one of your *in-addr.arpa* zone definitions. I'm testing a reverse look-up for 198.252.200.3:

```
> set querytype=PTR
> 198.252.200.2
Server:  server
Address:  0.0.0.0

3.200.252.198.in-addr.arpa        name = server.gizniz.com
200.252.198.in-addr.arpa nameserver = server.gizniz.com
server.gizniz.cominternet address = 198.252.200.3
```

Finally, to make sure that you have contact with the rest of the DNS world, try looking up an address external to your own nameserver. Here, I chose *ruby.ora.com:*

```
> set querytype=any
> ruby.ora.com.
Server:  server.gizniz.com
Address:  0.0.0.0

Non-authoritative answer:
ruby.ora.com       internet address = 198.112.208.25

Authoritative answers can be found from:
ORA.COM nameserver = ruby.ora.com
ORA.COM nameserver = NIC.NEAR.NET
ORA.COM nameserver = NOC.CERF.NET
ruby.ora.com      internet address = 198.112.208.25
NIC.NEAR.NET      internet address = 192.52.71.4
NOC.CERF.NET      internet address = 192.153.156.22
```

The answers you get back from *nslookup* should look the same in spirit, though they won't match mine precisely. If you have a problem—if things look really wrong—check back through the zone definitions. It's very easy to forget a period or drop a line.

DNS Resolution for PCs and Macs

A nameserver running on a UNIX (or other) host can serve the whole community of IP clients, including personal computers; IP stacks for PCs and Macs are shipped with built-in DNS resolution capability. If you are connecting personal computers to the Internet, you will *really* want to use this. PC or Mac setup is analogous to configuration of *resolv.conf*. See Chapter 19 for more details.

Root Information for Isolated Networks

Up to this point, we have been configuring name service with the assumption that we have access to the Internet. However, there are situations where you might want to configure DNS for machines that don't have access. Perhaps the connection hasn't come in yet, though you would like to get a head start. Or maybe the nameserver is kept behind a nontransparent firewall, and will *never* have contact with the root nameservers. In either case, you can create a *faux* DNS hierarchy in which the nameserver thinks it is authoritative for every domain in the universe.

We can craft our ersatz universe using the configuration above as a starting point. The changes are straightforward: first, we replace the cache entry in *named.boot* with the following:

```
primary         .               db.root
```

This says that the local nameserver will be the primary nameserver for the DNS root. We also need a new zone definition file, *db.root*:

```
.       IN    SOA   server.gizniz.com. root.server.gizniz.com. (
                          1        ; Serial number
                          10800    ; Refresh every 3 hours
                          3600     ; Retry every hour
                          604800   ; Expire after a week
                          86400 )  ; Minimum ttl of 1 day
        IN    NS    server.gizniz.com.
```

Next, you should go back and remove any references to external nameservers, such as the record in *db.gizniz* that reads:

```
.....   IN    NS    server.provider.net.
```

Last, you may want to add some wildcard MX records to attract all mail towards an internal mail gateway (or perhaps a firewall), for ultimate delivery beyond the company walls. Logical equivalents of the following records could go into your version of *db.gizniz*:

```
server.gizniz.com.  IN    MX    10    server.gizniz.com.
gizniz.com.         IN    MX    10    server.gizniz.com.
```

```
*.com.    IN    MX    20    server.gizniz.com.
*.        IN    MX    20    server.gizniz.com.
```

Once everything is in place, you may want to run tests similar to those we ran earlier. Naturally, the results should differ: when you ask for resolution of an address other than those defined in your zone definition files, *nslookup* should immediately return with a message like "Non-existent host/domain." If the nameserver behaves otherwise—if *nslookup* takes a long time to come back to you—then you may have a problem with your root zone definition.

Of course, you don't *have* to use MX records on your internal network; PCs and Macs don't typically care about MX records. Likewise, you could manually channel UNIX mail to specific relay hosts—perhaps to the firewall. In fact, if your network is cut off from the Internet, you may not care to run a nameserver at all; host tables and hardwired mail routing tables may be all you need, particularly if you are behind a nontransparent firewall. The decision whether or not to run an internal nameserver often comes down to the complexity of your private network. Do you work for a large company? Are computers geographically distributed? Larger, more complicated IP networks may be better candidates for an internal DNS hierarchy than, say, a network built of PC LAN file systems.

If you choose to run an internal DNS hierarchy, it will cost you more time and a few confusing hours of setup. However, in your own microcosm, you will reap many of the same benefits the DNS provides to the Internet as a whole: Host and mail hub information will be administered from central locations, and replicated throughout the organization. Whenever an address changes or a new mail hub is introduced, all computers will learn about it at once.

DNS for Firewalled Networks

In Chapter 16, *Internet Security*, we discussed the need for a split DNS strategy in combination with a firewall built from the TIS toolkit. In some cases, as many as three separate nameservers were called for:

1. A nameserver that tells the outside world how to reach you. A minimal amount of information would be served, typically just an few MX records, a reverse (PTR) record for the firewall, and a few records to support information services (WWW, gopher, FTP, etc.).

2. A nameserver for the bastion host to use. The bastion host needs to be able to see hosts on the inside of the firewall *and* on the outside. The bastion host nameserver is for use by the bastion host alone.

3. An internal nameserver, for use by computers isolated behind the firewall.

We discussed configuration of the third nameserver a moment ago. In this section, I want to present you with formulas for the two remaining nameservers (the external and bastion host nameservers). Figure 17-3 shows this network configuration.

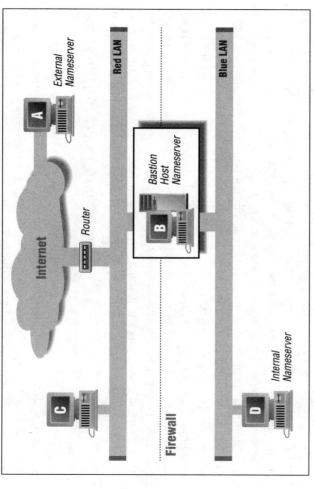

Figure 17–3: Nameservers for a firewalled network

What domain information should we provide to the outside world? We explored this in detail in Chapter 16, but for review, let's list the records that should be maintained on an external nameserver:

- MX records for the company (e.g., `*.gizniz.com`)
- A reverse (PTR) record for the bastion host
- Nameserver (NS) records
- A localhost record

Assuming that you are going to let the ISP manage the primary and secondary external nameservers for your domain, you can forget about NS and localhost records altogether. You only have to request that they maintain a small set of PTR, MX, CNAME, and A records, including the following:

```
firewall       IN     A       198.252.200.2
;
infoserver     IN     A       198.252.200.3
www            IN     CNAME   infoserver.gizniz.com.
gopher         IN     CNAME   infoserver.gizniz.com.
```

```
ftp                  IN  CNAME     infoserver.gizniz.com.
;
gizniz.com.          IN  MX    10  firewall.gizniz.com.
firewall.gizniz.com  IN  MX    10  firewall.gizniz.com.
```

These records assume that you have an external information server (host C in Figure 17-3) that is providing WWW, gopher, and FTP service. If, on the other hand, you are providing these services from the firewall itself, you should change the CNAME records to list the firewall's address.

Bastion Host DNS Configuration

If you have had a chance to look at Chapter 16, you may recall that the bastion host needs visibility into two worlds—the internal network and the great, wide Internet. This means that the DNS configuration serving the bastion host must be a hybrid, mixing private and public data together. We discussed two configurations for the bastion host's nameserver. One is protected by access lists: the bastion host directs requests for external domains through other nameservers via the named forwarders option. In the other configuration, we got to a point where we said "This is secure enough," and left the bastion host nameserver in charge of its own DNS look-ups. From a security point of view, the first option is better because it hides all details about the internal network from view, and makes the nameserver less susceptible to deliberate doping with bogus information. The downside is that DNS configuration and management become a little more convoluted.

The *named.boot* file shown above matches the simpler configuration. I have assumed that the "blue" LAN—the one inside the firewall—has an address of 192.168.0.* The visible, "red" LAN in this example has a 198.252.200 network address. The *gizniz.com* zone definition for these networks is shown below. It includes a mix of internal and external network host information:

```
; type
;
directory   /etc/named.data   ; running directory for named
;
; domain                        source file
;
primary     gizniz.com                   db.gizniz
primary     0.0.127.in-addr.arpa         db.127.0.0
primary     0.168.192.in-addr.arpa       db.192.168.0
primary     200.252.198.in-addr.arpa     db.198.252.200
cache       .                            db.cache
```

```
gizniz.com.  IN  SOA   firewall.gizniz.com. root.firewall.gizniz.com. (
                           1      ; Serial number
                           10800  ; Refresh every 3 hours
                           3600   ; Retry every hour
```

* As suggested by rfc1597.

```
                604800  ; Expire after a week
                86400 ) ; Minimum ttl of 1 day
                firewall.gizniz.com.
;
localhost       IN  NS
                IN  A      127.0.0.1
;
router          IN  A      198.252.200.1
firewall        IN  A      198.252.200.2    ; host 'B' from diagram
server          IN  A      198.252.200.3    ; host 'C' from diagram
www             IN  CNAME  server.gizniz.com.
gopher          IN  CNAME  server.gizniz.com.
ftp             IN  CNAME  server.gizniz.com.
;
; hosts on the inside
;
host1           IN  A      192.168.0.1      ; host 'D' from diagram
host2           IN  A      192.168.0.2
host3           IN  A      192.168.0.3
firewall-int    IN  A      192.168.0.254    ; internal firewall intfc
;
host1           IN  MX     10  host1        ; internal MX record
```

The reverse, in-addr.arpa zone definitions are analogous to the examples we reviewed previously; each host—both internal and external—for which you have an A record in *db.gizniz* (or whatever) should have a corresponding PTR record. This will assure that your log files contain host names for internal machines, rather than IP addresses. *

If you opt for the more secure configuration, your *named.boot* should look similar to the following:

```
;
; type       domain                   source file
;
directory    /etc/named.data  ; running directory for named
;
primary      gizniz.com               db.gizniz
primary      0.0.127.in-addr.arpa     db.127.0.0
primary      0.168.192.in-addr.arpa   db.192.168.0
primary      200.252.198.in-addr.arpa db.198.252.200
cache        .                        db.cache
forwarders   205.246.144.100
```

Everything is the same except that we have given the bastion host nameserver a forwarders reference to another nameserver that can help it out. Typically, this would be one of the ISP's public nameservers. The forwarders option works like this: When a DNS query comes in, the nameserver looks in its local cache. If the answer isn't found there, the nameserver sends the request to a forwarder. If the

* Note: you could clone the internal DNS information from an internal server by setting the bastion host up as a secondary nameserver.

forwarder doesn't have the answer (and we give the nameserver a hierarchy to search), the nameserver will—in a fit of self-reliance—exhaust any other search paths available.

Because forwarders traffic flows solely between the bastion host nameserver and the nameserver whose address is listed in the forwarders option, we can set up router filtering (Chapter 16) to keep others' queries out. If you wish, you can list multiple forwarders; this will provide some backup.

Other nameserver configurations

It may have occurred to you that there could be other ways to organize name-servers for a firewalled network. We could, for example, maintain private zone information on an internal nameserver, and configure the bastion host to be a sec-ondary. This would give us a single source for internal DNS information; the bas-tion host would clone the data from inside whenever an update occurred. Keeping external DNS data on your "red" LAN is another possibility: machine C, depicted in the network diagram a few pages back, would make a reasonable home for an external DNS server. Other permutations are possible too.

DNS for Transparent Firewalls

The firewalled nameserver configuration just described is most appropriate for use with a nontransparent firewall, such as you would create from the TIS toolkit. If you have a transparent firewall, such as *BorderWare*,[*] or *Gauntlet*—even if you have a simple router—then you might want to configure nameservers a little dif-ferently. For one thing, you will need to make external DNS information available to internal hosts; computers on the inside of transparent firewalls *can* use IP addresses for external destinations.

Figure 17-4 shows a simple layout for a network protected by a transparent fire-wall:

- Machine **B**, the firewall, needs visibility into the whole internal network, *plus* the whole Internet.

- Machine **E**, an internal PC, has to be able to see the whole internal network, and the whole Internet—just as the firewall does.

- Machine **A**, a random computer out on the Internet, should be able to find only limited information about the company's network—perhaps just an MX record, an in-addr.arpa address for the firewall, and the firewall's IP address.

---

[*] *BorderWare* runs two nameservers on one box: one for internal use, and another for external use. You don't even need to supply additional nameservers.

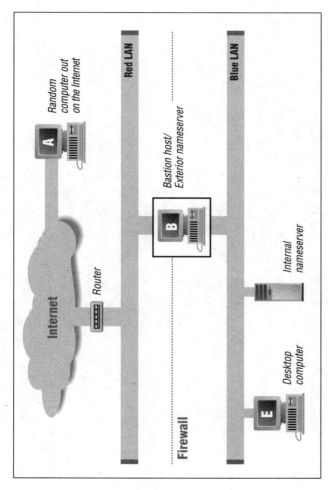

Figure 17-4: Nameservers for a network with a transparent firewall

There are several ways to skin this cat. Perhaps the most elegant configuration of nameservers (though certainly not the easiest to explain) would be one where the internal nameserver, **D** (of Figure 17-3), is authoritative for private information, and the firewall, **B**, serves up public DNS information. Here's where the confusion comes into play: though the firewall may be hosting a nameserver, it isn't required to *use* it. The firewall can resolve against any nameserver you choose. Since **D** will be maintaining private domain information—information that the firewall needs—it actually makes sense that the firewall should resolve against **D**'s nameserver—not its own. To throw an extra monkey wrench into the works, consider that in order for **D** to answer DNS requests for external addresses, it is going to need some kind of DNS window to the rest of the world. The problem is that many firewalls prohibit UDP traffic, which is at odds with DNS—but domain queries operate over UDP on port 53. How do we make this all work?

Configuring DNS for a Transparent Firewall

If you will allow me to borrow the renowned *GizNiz* name for a few more examples, I would like to demonstrate DNS configuration for transparent firewalls (and to some extent, router-protected networks) in detail. We will start with host **B**, the firewall/external nameserver in Figure 17-4.

External nameserver

We began this chapter with simple nameserver configuration, suitable for a company *without* a firewall. Configuration of an external nameserver for a firewalled network is nearly identical, except that we will leave out some details about internal hosts—information that people on the outside don't need to know. Here's what the *named.boot* for an external nameserver might look like:

```
; type      domain                    source file
;
directory   /etc/named.data  ; running directory for named
;
primary     gizniz.com                db.gizniz
primary     0.0.127.in-addr.arpa      db.127.0.0
primary     200.252.198.in-addr.arpa  db.198.252.200
cache       .                         db.cache
```

As before, the nameserver is acting as the primary for the *gizniz.com*, *0.0.127.in-addr.arpa*, and *200.252.198.in-addr.arpa* zones. Likewise, the cache has been seeded with information about root nameservers, as specified in the file *db.cache*. The difference between this and the first configuration is that the information kept within *db.gizniz* has been pared down:

```
gizniz.com.       IN  SOA  server.gizniz.com. root.server.gizniz.com. (
                               1       ; Serial number
                               10800   ; Refresh every 3 hours
                               3600    ; Retry every hour
                               604800  ; Expire after a week
                               86400 ) ; Minimum ttl of 1 day
                  IN  NS   server.gizniz.com.
                  IN  NS   server.provider.net.
;
localhost         IN  A    127.0.0.1
;
server            IN  A    198.252.200.2
;
ftp               IN  CNAME  server.gizniz.com.
;
gizniz.com.       IN  MX   10  server.gizniz.com.
server.gizniz.com IN  MX   10  server.gizniz.com.
```

As before, we have two nameserver (NS) records. The first nominates the firewall as a server for *gizniz.com* zone information; the second record says that your ISP (*provider.net*) will also be providing (secondary) service. Only one address (A) record—server.gizniz.com—appears within the zone. A CNAME gives server.gizniz.com a second identity—ftp.gizniz.com. Depending on your requirements, you may want to exclude this record, or add a few others like it, e.g., www.gizniz.com or gopher.gizniz.com.

Internal nameserver

The internal nameserver for the transparent firewall network (Figure 17-5) is going to be a bit trickier. As I mentioned a few moments ago, the internal nameserver needs a window to the outside world. However, the kind of traffic it would exchange with other nameservers—UDP traffic—won't pass through many kinds of firewalls. That means we need some other method for relaying outside DNS information through the firewall, and back to the internal nameserver.

Our secret weapon is the forwarders directive, described earlier. It will allow requests that cannot be resolved on the internal nameserver to be ferried off to the firewall. From there, the firewall can complete the requests, and send the results back to the internal nameserver:

```
;
; type       domain                         source file
;
directory    /etc/named.data  ; running directory for named
;
primary      gizniz.com                     db.gizniz
primary      0.0.127.in-addr.arpa           db.127.0.0
primary      0.168.192.in-addr.arpa         db.192.168.0
primary      200.252.198.in-addr.arpa       db.198.252.200
cache        .                              db.cache
forwarders   192.168.0.254
```

This copy of *named.boot*, taken from the internal nameserver, illustrates how the forwarders directive would be applied. Note that the firewall's *internal* interface (192.168.0.254) is specified; this is the interface closest to the internal nameserver.

The *gizniz.com*, *0.168.192.in-addr.arpa* and *200.252.198.in-addr.arpa* information kept on the internal server can be as complete and detailed as you like; the outside world will not be able to reach it.

```
gizniz.com.     IN   SOA  host1.gizniz.com. root.host1.gizniz.com. (
                               1    ; Serial number
                               10800  ; Refresh every 3 hours
                               3600   ; Retry every hour
                               604800 ; Expire after a week
                               86400 ) ; Minimum ttl of 1 day
                IN   NS   host1.gizniz.com.
;
localhost       IN   A    127.0.0.1
;
router          IN   A    198.252.200.1
firewall        IN   A    198.252.200.2   ; host 'B' from external intfc
                                          ; (Figure 17-5)
server          IN   A    198.252.200.3
www             IN   CNAME  server.gizniz.com.
gopher          IN   CNAME  server.gizniz.com.
```

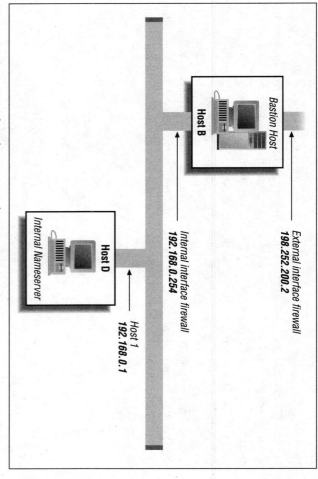

Figure 17–5: A network with an internal nameserver

```
ftp             IN   CNAME   server.gizniz.com.
;
; hosts on the inside
;
host1           IN   A       192.168.0.1   ; 'D', internal nameserver
                                           ; (Figure 17-5)
host2           IN   A       192.168.0.2
host3           IN   A       192.168.0.3
firewall-int    IN   A       192.168.0.254 ; 'B', internal firewall intfc
                                           ; (Figure 17-5)
;
gizniz.com.     IN   MX      10   firewall-int
```

The zone definition shown here mixes internal and external network addresses for the *gizniz.com* domain. Again, we can include the addresses for external *GizNiz* hosts because the firewall is transparent (in this case). Internal hosts can reach external hosts via their IP addresses.

Tying it all together

At this point, we have two nameservers—one internal and one external. How do we shuffle the appropriate communities to their respective nameservers? Remember: we want the bastion host firewall to use the internal nameserver, and we want the rest of the Internet community to use the firewall's nameserver. Somehow, we have to tell them.

Recall the discussion about resolvers—routines that perform DNS look-ups. The operation of the resolver is controlled by a file called *resolv.conf.* It specifies the domain suffix, and lists nameservers. *This* is where we make our choice; we will list the internal nameserver in the firewall's *resolv.conf.* This way—even though the firewall is running its own nameserver—it will consult the one inside.

The Internet community, on the other hand, will find its way to the external name-server via the NS records registered with the InterNIC. When somebody wants to locate a record from your site, their nameserver will wend its way around the Internet until it finally comes to the bastion host. The bastion host will tell them about computers on your site only to the extent that you have defined them in the bastion host's zone definition files.

How to Maintain Multiple DNS Domains

Organizations are sometimes interested in registering and maintaining multiple for-ward DNS domains on a single server. Many times, they are renting server space to, or reserving a domain name for, a partner organization. Really, there's not much to maintaining multiple domains; the process is identical to the one that went into setting up your first domain. I realize, however, that you may not have been involved in your own domain registration—the access provider may have done it for you. So, I thought I'd show you the ropes. To set up another domain, you need to:

1. Populate information for the new domain under DNS (on your nameserver).

2. Find another machine to act as a secondary nameserver.

3. Send a completed domain registration form to the InterNIC.

Step one means making another zone file like *db.gizniz,* described earlier, except that gizniz will be replaced everywhere by the name of the new domain. Gener-ally, everything else stays the same, including the addresses. Once the "db" file has been cloned, you need to make the nameserver aware of its existence by adding an entry to *named.boot.* This will look just like the gizniz.com entry that is there already:

```
primary     gizniz.com      db.gizniz
primary     zugzug.com      db.zugzug
```

Next, you have to find someone who is willing to provide a secondary nameserver for the new domain. Their server should be topologically distant from you (in Internet terms), if possible, so that both nameservers won't become inaccessible in the event that part of the network goes down. Assuming that you can convince a friend to provide secondary service, you will ask them to add an entry to their *named.boot* of the form:

```
secondary        zugzug.com        204.5.234.171        zugzug.zone
```

This will tell their nameserver to periodically clone DNS zone data for *zugzug.com* from your machine, and to be prepared to act as a nameserver for *zugzug.com* queries. *

Once the DNS files are set up, you can send your registration request to the Inter-NIC. Blank registration forms can be found in *ftp://rs.internic.net/templates*. You will find several types, corresponding to different flavors of domain registration; there are templates for com, edu, net, etc. domains, for the us domain, and for other country domains. Registration turnaround time can be many weeks, so plan early. Also, be aware that the InterNIC is now charging $50 a year for ".com" domains.

---

* Make sure that your router access lists allow them to make zone transfers: TCP/53.

18

Internet Mail

I guess we must be blessed: the computer industry has provided us with many electronic mail systems, particularly over the last few years. Some are end-user solutions; others have found roles as mail backbones. A few showed promising technical quality, and others were the product of successful marketing. The only thing that could improve the situation would be if there were fewer of them.

Interestingly, the late upturn in Internet activity is driving organizations toward something old and crusty—SMTP (*Simple Mail Transport Protocol*)—for their mail backbones. SMTP is not the most ornate or capable facility, but it *is* mature, it *works*, and it's extensible. I learned a few years ago that I could glue the worst collections of mail systems together with SMTP and still make it home in time for dinner.

Of course, you may have other plans for electronic mail that make SMTP impractical as an end-user solution (you may need *OLE* functionality, for instance). However, you are still going to need to connect your mail system to the Internet, and that's where you and I can get together. We need to create an SMTP mail hub: one machine that can be the central clearinghouse for all the mail coming into your organization via the Internet. This machine—the hub—will either know about every user on your network, or will know how to forward inbound mail to certain internal destinations (probably LAN gateways). Likewise, the hub will be able to deliver mail anywhere on the Internet. Figure 18-1 shows a mail hub.

Most likely, the SMTP hub will be a firewall or an Internet information server. To configure the hub, we are going to have to understand a little bit (or more) about *sendmail*, the most widely used SMTP mail transport agent. Part of the discussion will focus on configuration, and part will talk about managing *sendmail* mail IDs via *aliases*. After that, we will turn our attention toward marrying LAN-based email

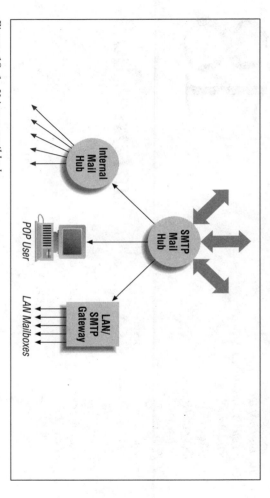

Figure 18-1: Using a mail hub

systems into the SMTP world. Next, we will talk a little bit about POP, an SMTP-flavored solution for personal computers. If you aren't operating a LAN email system already, then running POP may be able to save you a small fortune and a lot of heartache. Last, we will look at *sendmail* configuration in some detail.

A Few Words About sendmail

sendmail[*], called a *Mail Transport Agent* (MTA), is in charge of rewriting mail headers, rummaging through DNS for MX records, moving messages from place to place, managing the mail queue, and returning undeliverable messages. The jobs of presenting, organizing, filing, and deleting a user's mail, on the other hand, belong to a *Mail User Agent* (MUA) or mail client (e.g., *elm*, *pine*, or *Eudora*). Together, mail transfer agents and mail user agents make a complete electronic mail system. One handles mail trafficking and the other deals with the humans.

We care about *sendmail* because it natively speaks SMTP—the protocol by which hosts on the Internet trade mail. *sendmail* is not the only mail transport agent available. However, it is the most common; a copy of *sendmail* is shipped with practically every UNIX operating system.[†]

---

* For a comprehensive treatment of *sendmail*, see *sendmail*, by Costales, Allman, and Reickert, published by O'Reilly & Associates. You might also find *TCP/IP*, by Craig Hunt, useful—also from O'Reilly & Associates.

† *sendmail* has been ported to other operating systems, including Windows NT and OS/2. The discussion here applies to those environments, too. You might also look into *smail3* (not covered here) as an alternative to *sendmail*.

What is SMTP?

SMTP, defined by *rfc821*, is a simple dialog by which two computers may trade mail.

```
% telnet sparky.deadbeat.net 25
Trying 204.252.200.201
Connected to sparky.deadbeat.net
Escape character is '^]'.
220 sparky.deadbeat.net Sendmail SMI-8.6/SMI-SVR4-ATL ready
    at Sun, 4 Feb 1996 18:32:37 -0500
helo maddie.atlantic.com
250 sparky.deadbeat.net Hello maddie.atlantic.com [198.252.200.3],
    pleased to meet you
mail from:<dowd@atlantic.com>
250 <dowd@atlantic.com>... Sender ok
rcpt to:<dowd@deadbeat.net>
250 <dowd@deadbeat.net>... Recipient ok
data
354 Enter mail, end with "." on a line by itself
From: dowd@atlantic.com
Subject: Hello!

This is a test.

.
250 SAA01404 Message accepted for delivery
quit
221 sparky.deadbeat.net closing connection
```

The caller contacts the callee with a greeting—"HELO" [*sic*]. The callee responds with a numerical status (250)—the connection is accepted. The conversation continues; the callee transfers the sender's name (MAIL FROM:), list of recipients (RCPT TO:), and the message body (DATA). Each step of the way, the callee returns a numerical status indicating progress. The conversation concludes with "QUIT"—the message has been handed to the receiving MTA. *Headers*—fields in the body of the message—are defined apart from SMTP, in *rfc822*.

We looked at DNS in detail in the previous chapter. Hopefully it is becoming clear to you how *sendmail* and DNS might work together: the nameserver advertises MX records to attract mail messages to the server; *sendmail* receives the messages and attempts to direct them appropriately. For a user trying to send a piece of mail, the (hidden) objective is to pitch a message up to a mail transfer agent, and have it bounce its way around—from transfer agent to transfer agent—until it finally comes to rest on somebody's desktop (Figure 18-2).

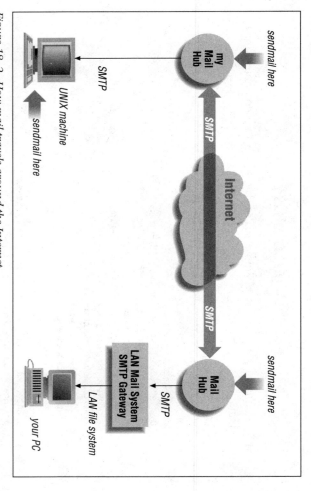

Figure 18–2: How mail travels around the Internet

The environment can be a hybrid—other, non-UNIX flavored mail systems may complete the picture. However, if mail crosses IP networks, chances are that one or several copies of *sendmail*—and several sets of MX records—will be involved.

Surveying Your sendmail Configuration

Like many UNIX-flavored facilities, the components of *sendmail* are scattered about the filesystem. The most important pieces for our discussion are:

sendmail

> *sendmail*, the mail transfer agent binary, runs both as a backend process for mail clients, and as a daemon for incoming (network) mail connections. Typical homes for *sendmail* are */etc*, */usr/lib*, and */usr/sbin*.

sendmail.cf

> The configuration file, *sendmail.cf*, tells the daemon how to rewrite addresses, how to deliver mail, how to handle errors, and so on. Typical homes for *sendmail.cf* are */etc*, */usr/lib*, and */var*.

aliases

> The aliases file lists alternate mail IDs. Once *sendmail* has determined that a message is for local delivery, it consults these aliases for forwarding addresses. *Aliases* may be found in */etc* or */usr/lib*.

newaliases

This is a facility for preprocessing information in the *aliases* file for fast retrieval by *sendmail*. Typically, *newaliases* is a link to the *sendmail* binary.

The *sendmail* distribution on your computer could be any vintage; *sendmail* has been in widespread use for over 10 years. For our purposes, the later the release, the better. Newer editions of *sendmail* are more flexible and secure, and, perhaps most importantly, they will be easier to configure. Accordingly, let's start by checking the revision level. From the command line prompt on your mail hub, type:

```
telnet localhost 25
220-maddie.atlantic.com Sendmail 8.6.12/8.6.10 ready at Thu, 11 May
   1995 14:31:37 -0400
220 ESMTP spoken here
quit
```

You should get a banner, as here. If *sendmail* doesn't respond, it probably means that mail handling hasn't been enabled; you may need to go back and enable *sendmail* within your start-up (*rc*) files.* For the time being, you can run the daemon from standard input:

```
/usr/lib/sendmail -bs
220-maddie.atlantic.com Sendmail 8.6.12/8.6.10 ready at Thu, 11 May
   1995 14:32:39 -0400
220 ESMTP spoken here
quit
```

The greeting above tells us that we are running version 8.6.12 of the daemon, with an 8.6.10 revision of the *sendmail.cf* configuration file. Something more like 8.7.6 would be a good sign; late revisions are sufficiently modern, and sufficiently secure. If you need an update, the best (easiest) source would be your system vendor, or a third party compilation of system utilities. If an update is impractical, you can find configuration help later in this chapter, and in the references mentioned at the beginning of the chapter.†

We are also going to need a *sendmail.cf* that is "close"—one that we can tweak to match our requirements. In the event that you have an operating system release with a late version of *sendmail*, the associated *sendmail.cf* will probably be perfect. In a pinch, the *sendmail* source code distribution also comes with templates for a variety of host types and configurations, which would be a good place to start if you are unsure of what you have. What we need is a fairly vanilla setup:

---

* A typical invocation of *sendmail* would be: /usr/lib/sendmail -bd -q15m.
† You could build *sendmail* from source, too: see *ftp://ftp.cs.berkeley.edu/ucb/sendmail*. You will probably also want to use the Berkeley DB software in conjunction with the new *sendmail—ftp://ftp.cs.berkeley.edu/ucb/4bsd/db.tar.Z*. A copy of *mail.local* from the contributed software collection might be necessary, too.

SMTP mail via a network, plus local delivery ("smtp" and "local," in the distribution's ".mc" files).

Typically, we need to make just one change to nominate a server as the mail hub for the organization:

```
Cwlocalhost gizniz.com
```

The line above defines a *sendmail class* (the "w" class). *sendmail* checks mail destinations against the members of this class (and against the actual host name) to determine whether the mail should be delivered locally. Assuming that we are part of the *GizNiz* corporation, and that our domain is *gizniz.com*, the above addition of "gizniz.com" to the Cw class will do the trick. If another host contacts the *sendmail* daemon and requests message forwarding to *gizniz.com*, *sendmail* will recognize itself as the recipient and attempt to deliver the message locally.

Aliases

The *sendmail aliases* facility provides alternate mail IDs for local mail recipients. You might use an alias to identify a local user (somebody with an entry in the password file) by a second name. Or, an alias might forward mail to another mail hub, in another domain. Likewise, aliases can also be used to make primitive mailing lists; everyone listed in a multiple-user alias will receive copies whenever the alias gets mail. You can do other things with aliases as well.

```
fredsmith: fred
smith: fred

jones: jones@server.deadbeat.net

users: fred,jones
```

For our purposes, aliases are important because they give us a basic building block for our mail infrastructure: we can maintain a single mail hub for the whole organization, regardless of where its members are actually located. Consider that it doesn't really matter where Fred Smith picks up his mail (he could be an AOL or CompuServe user). As long as we maintain an alias, he will have an address bearing our domain name (e.g., *fred@gizniz.com*).

```
fredsmith: fred
smith: fred
fred: fredxx99@aol.com
```

By the same token, aliases give us a mechanism to hide the complexity of the in-house mail infrastructure. Though we may have some users who receive mail via

---

* Remember, it is DNS's job to attract the mail....

POP, others who use a LAN mail system (like cc:mail or Microsoft Mail), and others with UNIX workstations, they can all have addresses of the same form soandso@gizniz.com. Furthermore, users can switch platforms without ruining their business cards; someone who receives mail under UNIX today can keep the same address, even if they switch to cc:mail tomorrow.

Alias Maintenance

File *aliases*, the mail alias list that *sendmail* consults, can be found in either */etc* or in */usr/lib*. You can edit it with a text editor, making updates of the sort we discussed earlier. Once you have finished, you will "compile" *aliases* into an internal, database format for use by *sendmail*, via the *newaliases* command:*

```
# newaliases
/etc/aliases: 60 aliases, longest 372 bytes, 2315 bytes total
```

Upon completion, *newaliases* will return an alias count, as shown here.

LAN/SMTP Mail Gateways

At this point, we have a way to bring SMTP mail into the organization. The trouble is that everything so far has been SMTP-based. Perhaps your organization has a mail infrastructure based on something else, say a PC LAN mail system, such as *cc:mail* or *Microsoft Mail*. It probably took a long time to set up, and people are probably fond of swearing at it. The question is: How do we integrate the existing PC mail system with Internet SMTP mail? The quick answer is that we need an SMTP mail gateway (Figure 18-3).

An SMTP gateway has to be bilingual; it must speak both the local LAN protocol (NetBEUI, Novell IPX, whatever) and IP. On the LAN, the gateway appears to be a post office. On the IP side, it looks like an SMTP mail hub.

A Few Possibilities

Some SMTP/LAN Mail gateways are dumb—they require the services of an intelligent SMTP mail hub (such as the server in Figure 18-3). Others are capable of delivering their own mail, directly to Internet destinations. Some are DOS-based; others run in the Mac environment; some run on top of OS/2; some run as NT services.

If you are running *cc:mail*, you have several choices, including Lotus's own cc:mail/SMTP gateway. This installs relatively smoothly. The gateway cycles,

---

* In *sendmail.cf*, you will find an OD option for selecting automatic aliases compilation. If this is set to "true," *aliases* will be recompiled automatically.

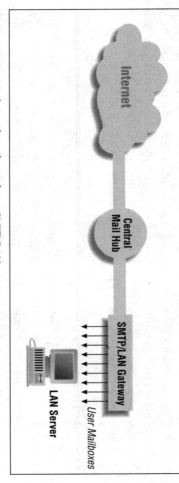

Figure 18–3: Mail traveling through an SMTP/LAN gateway

accepting mail at 5-minute intervals. For outgoing mail, it depends (like many PC LAN mail gateways) on a smart host to forward mail to the Internet. Attachments are uuencoded. Uuencoding is inferior to the preferred alternative—MIME encoding—but it works.*

Another, more featureful alternative for cc:mail users is *Internet Exchange*, from International Messaging Associates, Ltd (IMA). It comes with built-in MIME support and the intelligence to deliver its own mail; you could theoretically operate an IMA cc:mail/SMTP gateway without a UNIX mail hub *(http://www.ima.com/)*. Other possibilities include ThingNet-Mail Gateway *(http://www.thinque.com/)*, and *PostalUnion*, described later.

Microsoft Mail users, likewise, have a number of choices in SMTP gateways. For starters, there's Microsoft's own DOS-based Microsoft Mail gateway. It behaves very much like Lotus's cc:mail gateway—runs on a dedicated PC, depends on a smart host for SMTP delivery, and prepares attachments by uuencoding. Microsoft also has a relatively new, all-purpose gateway solution for NT-based Microsoft Mail environments, called *Exchange* (the mail package that comes with Windows 95 is also called Exchange; it is the client piece). Exchange is bigger than a gateway—it is designed for groupware functionality. SMTP interconnectivity is just a portion of the whole package. Exchange works, although it requires a great deal of machine resources—disk and memory.

NT-based Microsoft Mail can also be gatewayed via third-party alternatives. Information Electronics *(http://www.ie.com/)* has a modular, NT-based product called *PostalUnion*. You pair the protocols you need, including SMTP mail (with MIME attachments), Microsoft Mail, Notes Mail, and cc:Mail. Each module runs as an NT

* *Uuencoding:* Files are translated into a block of ASCII characters for transport via the mail. Multipurpose Internet Mail Extensions (*MIME*) is a comprehensive suite of recommendations for transporting text and nontext information via electronic mail, in which uuencoding may play a part. See rfc1341.

service, with its own control panel and logging. Other possible Microsoft Mail/SMTP gateway solutions include *NetGain Mimetic SMTP gate* (*http://www.netgain.se/*), *SpikeMail* (*http://www.bitools.com/*) (inexpensive), *MailNet* (*http://www.consensys.com/samples/mailnet/mailnet.htm*), *NetConnex* (*http://www.worldtalk.com/*), and S-Bridge NT (*http://www.compumail.com/ sbntmsml.htm*).

My favorite NT-based Microsoft Mail gateway is *smtpgate* (favorite because it is available at no charge). You can find it buried in Microsoft's FTP server, or try *ftp://ftp.winsite.com/pub/pc/winnt/misc/smtpgate.zip*. It isn't as glitzy as some of the other alternatives, but it sets up very quickly, and (in my experience) works quite reliably (though it does need a restart once a day . . .). *smtpgate*'s biggest fault is that it doesn't have MIME support, although it can uuencode attachments. To use *smtpgate*, and some of the other packages mentioned, you will need the full NT Microsoft post office—not the workgroup post office—with extensions for AT&T mail. This post office upgrade is available from Microsoft as an upgrade to Windows NT.

Lotus Notes users have a couple of options: Lotus sells an OS/2-based SMTP gateway. The heart of the SMTP connectivity is supplied by *sendmail. PostalUnion*, mentioned earlier, also has a module for Notes/SMTP connectivity.

Mac users might take a look at Starnine's offerings (*http://www.starnine.com*). Starnine produces good products, including SMTP gateways for Apple-based Quarterdeck Mail (formerly Microsoft Mail),* Quickmail, and MHS. MHS users might also check out *Charon* (*ftp://omnigate.clarkson.edu/*), and *Mercury* (*ftp://risc.ua.edu/*).

As you can see, there is a variety of mail gateway products to choose from—a separate book's worth. However, stepping back just a short distance, we will find that the integration process is generally the same for all of them:

1. Install the SMTP gateway on the PC LAN.

2. Make the organization's SMTP mail hub and SMTP/LAN gateway talk to each other.

Mail flowing into the company will make a first stop on the mail hub, and then be forwarded to the LAN SMTP gateway. Outbound mail may or may not go through the mail hub—depending on how you configure your mail environment. We will talk about several LAN/SMTP scenarios later. For now, I'd like to make a case for a central, incoming mail hub.

---

* Macintosh users have two varieties of Microsoft Mail: AppleTalk-based Microsoft Mail and PC-LAN-based Microsoft Mail.

Arguments for a sendmail-based Mail Hub

You may prefer to forget about *sendmail* altogether, and use a LAN SMTP gateway—the middle box in the picture a few pages back—as the central mail hub for your organization. This will be particularly attractive for folks who aren't comfortable with either UNIX or the *sendmail* environment. However, I would like to offer my arguments *against* using a PC LAN SMTP gateway as the main mail hub—even if *all* you have is a PC LAN SMTP mail system.

First, the DOS-based PC LAN SMTP gateways are not always available to accept SMTP connections. If, to take a few examples, a DOS-based cc:mail gateway is cycling through its queue, or if a Microsoft gateway is currently conducting an SMTP discussion with another computer, no processes will be listening on port 25/TCP to answer new SMTP connection requests that come in. The DOS gateways can do just one thing a time. This might not be a huge problem; mail will (probably) be queued on the sender's machine, and retried for several days (!), if necessary. On the other hand, you (the mail administrator/architect) can proactively attract Internet mail for the PC LAN Mail gateway to the UNIX server via MX records. That way, delayed messages will queue up on *your* computer, rather than all across the Internet. You will have more control; the process will be more secure, and it will reduce the likelihood of lost mail.

The second reason for choosing a capable server as your mail hub is that *sendmail* has rich store and forward capabilities. One day, someone from the company will want to have their mail forwarded to their CompuServe account (or the like), while they are on the road. Aliases make this a simple procedure; you edit the *aliases* file, run *newaliases*, and you're done. You can even have *sendmail* send carbon copies to the user's regular, in-house mailbox. It can be very difficult, on the other hand, to bounce Internet mail back out of the PC LAN mail system once it has reached the desktop. Most likely, the traveler's embattled secretary will have to forward the messages by hand.[*]

The third reason for making a *sendmail*-based machine play the role of mail hub is that there are other kinds of things you may wish to do with electronic mail—mailing lists, automatic mail transponders—which may be difficult or impossible from the LAN mail system. The UNIX server, on the other hand, can channel mail into processes (such as mailing list servers) very easily, again via *sendmail* aliases.

Okay, so now I agree with myself: I think we should make *sendmail* act as the server for inbound SMTP mail. Should we make the UNIX machine an exit stop for outbound mail as well? The answer, in many cases, is that we *have to*; some of the

---

[*] Actually, there is *some* hope: check out a product called *MAPIPOP* from Optimedia Ltd. (*http://www.optimedia.co.il/mapipop/*). This will allow dial-up users to retrieve the Microsoft Mail via a POP client, such as Eudora.

gateways depend on a smart mail hub for final delivery, out to the Internet. What if the mail gateway can fend for itself on outbound delivery? Then the decision is up to you, though you may still want to channel mail through the UNIX mail hub. This would give you an extra ability to rewrite addresses (in case you want to hide site details), and allow you to keep all of your SMTP logging in one spot. Of course, if you are behind a firewall, you may be forced to send your mail through the server. In any case, we have some work ahead of us yet; there are choices to make about how the LAN SMTP gateway should be integrated with the *sendmail* (and prehaps UNIX) mail hub.

Inbound Mail for LAN Mail Users

We will start with inbound mail. Figure 18–4 shows how incoming mail is handled. Presumably, mail will be coming into your organization with an MX domain similar to *gizniz.com*. This mail, as we discussed earlier, will be directed to the organization's main mail hub, and distributed via *sendmail* aliases.*

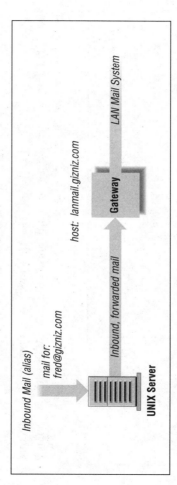

Figure 18–4: Inbound LAN mail

Say that your LAN mail system SMTP gateway is called *lanmail.gizniz.com*, and that Fred Smith is a Microsoft Mail user with an ID of "smith." Appropriate UNIX aliases for Fred might be:

```
fred:           smith
fred.smith:     smith
smith:          smith@lanmail.gizniz.com
```

This will give Fred three different mail IDs—`fred`, `fred.smith`, and `smith`. Chances are that he will use just one (say, "smith"). However, he will still be identified by several names. So even if a user on the outside takes a wild guess ("fred"

---

* It may occur to you, especially if you work for a large organization, that maintaining a central list of aliases could be an administrative burden. For this reason, some sites forward otherwise unqualified addresses directly to internal, LAN-based mail hubs, and let mail be distributed from there. We cover this at the end of the chapter.

would count as a wild guess), mail will still reach him. A similar pattern of aliases could be applied to others in the organization. Aliases can get more cryptic than this, of course. Here's a possible cc:mail alias:

```
bill:  smtplink&bill_at_mailhub@alarmail.gizniz.com
```

With a centrally maintained alias, all Bill has to tell people is *"bill@gizniz.com."* Clearly, *bill@gizniz.com* is going to be a lot easier to fit on a business card.

Once the aliases are in place, the gateway is working, and the UNIX server can find it (via aliases and DNS or hosts), you should be ready to accept inbound mail traffic to human-friendly addresses. There's a good chance that outbound mail will work too, without modifications (and it may even be replyable). Let's give it a little thought, though; you might care to sculpt your mail infrastructure differently from what you get "out of the box." We'll talk about three *outbound* mail scenarios.

Outbound LAN Mail, Scenario #1

Figure 18-5, which I will call *scenario #1*, shows what your mail architecture is probably going to look like if you simply install the LAN SMTP gateway, point it at the server, and go home.

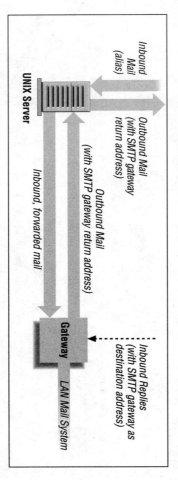

Figure 18–5: Outbound LAN mail, scenario 1

Inbound SMTP mail will come through the mail hub, be resolved against an alias, and be forwarded to the LAN Mail SMTP gateway. Going the other direction, outbound mail will be sent to the UNIX server for Internet delivery, but will retain a return address for the gateway. Note what happens next: If a user on the Internet replies to a message that originates *from* the LAN, the return path won't be written in terms of the user's UNIX alias. Instead, it will specify the user's mail ID on the SMTP gateway. That is, mail will bypass the UNIX server and go directly to the gateway. This may work OK, as long as the gateway is reachable from the outside. However, I ask that you consider my litany of reasons a few sections back for not making the LAN SMTP gateway be the first stop for incoming mail. You may want to tweak the environment to make it look like *scenario #2*, described next.

By the way, you can sometimes instruct the LAN SMTP gateway (depending on the brand) to tack a specific domain name on the end of the return address, giving you the option of rewriting outgoing mail headers to refer back to the mail hub. This would be a big improvement; when a user replies, the mail goes to the UNIX machine. You would just need to make doubly sure that the user's mail ID for the LAN is included in the UNIX machine's alias list, so that replies can be forwarded correctly.

Outbound LAN Mail, Scenario #2

Scenario #2, shown in Figure 18-6, is very much like the first scenario: outbound mail retains the address of the LAN SMTP gateway. Only this time, we arrange for DNS and *sendmail* to hijack inbound mail addressed to the SMTP gateway (replies, typically), and send it to the UNIX server. (Again, the reasons why we don't want the mail to go directly to the SMTP gateway were explained earlier.)

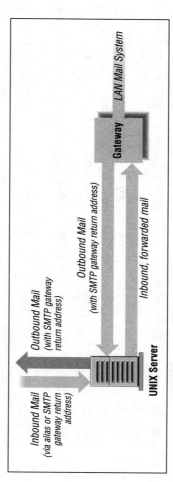

Figure 18–6: Outbound LAN mail, scenario 2

Once the mail arrives, we can either resolve the user's mail ID against an alias (by claiming in the Cw class that the UNIX server *is* the LAN SMTP gateway), or forward the mail to the LAN SMTP gateway without messing with the user ID. I'm going to choose the second method, blindly forwarding the mail from the UNIX server to the SMTP gateway. Presumably this will be OK, since the mail is a reply to a previous message, and the return address was originally created on the SMTP gateway.

Here are the MX records that will hijack mail addressed to the SMTP gateway over to the UNIX server:

```
; ...other MX records
gizniz.com.          IN  MX  10   server.gizniz.com.
lanmail.gizniz.com.  IN  MX  10   server.gizniz.com.
lanmail.gizniz.com.  IN  MX  20   lanmail.gizniz.com.
```

This probably looks peculiar, because we have two MX records for *lanmail*, the LAN SMTP gateway. The first attracts mail to the UNIX server; the second sends it off to the gateway. Here's the reasoning: The lower-valued (10) MX record is going to take precedence; the mail will go to the UNIX machine. Once *sendmail* receives a message for "*soandso@lanmail.gizniz.com*," and recognizes that the mail isn't for local delivery (that is, once *sendmail* recognizes that the *Cw* macro doesn't list "lanmail" as one of its alter egos), it is going to attempt to forward the message.

The next step involves a process we haven't discussed yet. *sendmail* is going to toss its own host MX record off the list, plus any records of equal or lower priority, and go with whatever is left over. If there are no more MX records to pursue, *send-mail* will fall back on an address (WA) record.* This works great: based on an address record, the server will then hold an SMTP discussion with *lanmail*, to complete the last leg of the journey.†

Outbound LAN Mail, Scenario #3

Let's look at one final scenario—*scenario #3* (Figure 18-7). All outgoing mail will be directed through the UNIX mail hub, as in the previous configurations. This time, however, we will ask *sendmail* to strip remnants of the LAN SMTP gateway's return address from the outbound mail (the procedure was described earlier). For example, *smith@lanmail.gizniz.com* will become *smith@gizniz.com*. Accordingly, *scenario #3* may be of interest to you if you are constructing a firewall.

When someone from the outside replies, the mail will go back to the UNIX mail hub, and again be distributed via aliases. Note that there's one danger here: If the UNIX server doesn't have aliases that speak for each user's ID on the LAN mail system, then some inbound mail may be undeliverable—we may have no way to return an incoming reply to a LAN mail system user. The cure is simple: spend more time maintaining *sendmail* aliases; each user will need to have an alias that is identical to their user ID on the LAN mail system.

* Assuming Version 8 *sendmail*, you must specify *sendmail.cf* option O TryNullMXList or set the Cw option to TRUE, depending upon the *sendmail* revision.

† Why bother with the second, priority 20 MX record? If the server is down for some reason, mail delivery will fall over to the second, priority 20 MX record? If the server is down for some reason, mail delivery will fall over to *lanmail*, which puts us back in *scenario #1*. Of course, server *lanmail.gizniz.com* has to be reachable, for this to work.

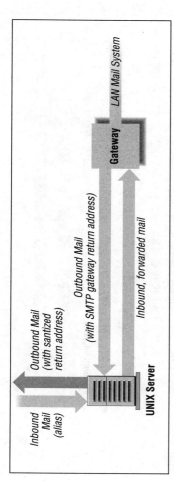

Figure 18-7: Outbound LAN mail, scenario 3

POP

I regret having been too soft-spoken in the past regarding SMTP-based mail systems, when asked my opinion by organizations that did not yet have a mail strategy. There are wonderful SMTP-based desktop mail tools—particularly POP-based systems. Clients support multimedia extensions; you can use *POP* (Post Office Protocol) and SMTP to move spreadsheets around the company, for instance. And it's robust. I'd think twice before implementing a LAN-based mail system if you don't already have one installed. POP can do the job.

Like most personal computer mail systems, POP requires a server. That's a simple requirement in our case; the server can be the SMTP mail hub/firewall/DNS server. The POP clients run natively, on the desktop computers. The exchange between the POP server and the POP client is asymmetric, depending on whether mail is being sent or received. For outbound mail, the client initiates a terse SMTP conversation with the server, expecting that the server will forward the message to its ultimate destination. Note that SMTP is (probably) the same transport mechanism that the server is going to use for final delivery. The difference is that the server can hold an SMTP conversation with any computer it pleases. The POP client, on the other hand, knows only about the server.

Mail retrieval works by a completely different mechanism. Periodically, the POP client checks with a POP daemon on the server to see if new mail has arrived. If it has, the client copies the messages down to the desktop, and (typically) cleans out the mailbox.

`fred:ZzecBSajHDBHo:150:100:Fred Smith:/home/fred:/bin/false`

From the server's point of view, people who retrieve mail using POP are the same as login users: they must have accounts. They don't have to have login accounts *exactly*; you can provide POP users with a shell of */bin/false* if you wish to keep them off the server. Even so, each user needs a password file entry, and will

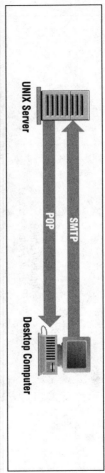

Figure 18-8. Using POP for desktop email

consume some space in the spool directory. A real home directory (as opposed to, say, */tmp*) is a good idea too; late versions of POP tools provide extra per-user functions (such as information bulletins), which are tracked by files kept in home directories.

The POP Server

Your UNIX distribution may or may not have come with POP support; you might have to build and install a POP server yourself. Two common servers are *pop3d*, available from the University of California at Davis (*ftp.ucdavis.edu:/unix-public/pop3d.tar*), and *qpopper*, originally from Berkeley, but now maintained by Qualcomm (*ftp.qualcomm.com://quest/unix/servers/popper*). *qpopper* is very capable, so I'd start there.* The package comes with makefiles for a number of architectures; pick the one that is closest, and compile. Installation is straightforward: You need to copy the binary to a reasonable system directory, and add a line to each of */etc/services* and */etc/inetd.conf:*

```
/etc/services:
pop-3        110/tcp

/etc/inetd.conf:
pop-3   stream tcp   nowait root   /usr/sbin/popper popper -s
```

Typical additions are shown above. It would probably be a good idea to run the daemon under a service wrapper too (such as *TCP Wrapper*, described in Chapter 16), to give you access lists and additional logging capability. Don't forget to send inetd a "HUP" signal to tell inetd to reread *inetd.conf.*

POP and Passwords

There's one extra administrative problem that we haven't addressed: How do POP users change their passwords, particularly if we don't let them log into the server? Certain POP clients, particularly copies of Eudora, *do* have a "change password" option built into them. This might lead you to believe that password update is part

---

* Qualcomm is also the home of the popular POP client, *Eudora*.

of the POP protocol suite. It isn't. Rather, this "change password" option is a hook for a separate TCP service that executes the *passwd* command on behalf of the user. If we are going to allow users to change their own passwords, then, we are going to have to come up with another daemon.

Returning to Qualcomm's FTP site again,* you will find a small collection of contributed POP password daemons. My favorite of the group is *poppassd*, though it is not without problems (I'll explain later). *poppassd* listens on port 106/TCP for connections from the POP client, willing to engage in a short password-changing conversation. On the back end, the *poppassd* daemon forks a copy of the UNIX *passwd* command, and stuffs the appropriate responses down a pipe.

Consider what you would see if you entered the password command from the shell prompt:

```
# passwd smith
Changing password for smith.
Enter new password: new password
Re-type new password: new password
Password changed.
```

There's nothing special going on. The computer types something, then you type something, and so on. The trick to automating this conversation in *poppassd* is to build a table of expected prompts and the appropriate responses. However, trouble occurs when the *passwd* command returns a response that the password daemon doesn't expect. This might occur if, say, a user selects a password that doesn't fit an administrative criterion (say, "Password too short"). Suddenly, the conversation becomes unscripted, and the user is left wondering what happened.[†]

The second problem is generic, and extends not only to password changes, but to POP logins as well (and telnet sessions, and FTP sessions . . .). In each case, clear-text passwords are being sent over the local area network. These could, in theory, be intercepted. There is some hope: the POP-3 protocol supplements a simple PASSWORD sequence with another primitive, APOP, that masks passwords when making a connection. Naturally, POP clients have to be written so as to make use of the primitive; not all are.

---

* *ftp://ftp.qualcomm.com/quest/unix/servers/passwd*

† What we really need is a program that knows how to update the password file without going through the *passwd* command.

sendmail Configuration in More Detail

Of course, *sendmail* configuration can be more complicated than just changing a single line, as we did at the beginning of the chapter. Perhaps you need to apply some special-case handling to a few mail addresses. Maybe you would like to remove host names' return addresses as mail passes to the outside. Or perhaps you have an old version of *sendmail*—you're stuck with it—yet you still need to get it working. Whatever the reason for that thorn in your side, you are going to need to know more about *sendmail* configuration to get the job done.

sendmail.cf

As we saw earlier, the behavior of *sendmail* is controlled by its configuration file, *sendmail.cf.* The file is typically divided into two sections. Macro definitions, class definitions, options, and other global settings appear near the top. The lower portion of *sendmail.cf* is devoted to address rewrite rules and delivery agent definitions. Let's look at some of *sendmail's* components now. We will return to the big picture in a little while.

Macros and classes

A *macro* gives us a way to equate a string with a label, and the ability to reference it elsewhere within the body of *sendmail.cf.* We might use this to set the name of a mail relay, for example, near the top of the configuration file:

```
DRmailhub.deadbeat.net
```

Elsewhere within *sendmail.cf,* we may refer back to this definition by giving its label following the "$" character, e.g. "$R." Typically, we use macros within rules—either in comparisons, or in substitutions.

Class definitions give us the ability to define *multiple* values, and to associate them with a single label. A few sections back, we used Cw class definition to list an array of possible mail addresses that *sendmail* should consider to be local. We can similarly use classes to test for any kind of group membership. We could, for instance, create an exclusive class of machines—say, internal mail hubs—whose addresses need special treatment. By testing for class membership, we can change the normal course of *sendmail* address processing.

```
DKcom edu org
```

The line above shows a class definition. We will learn how to make use of the definition, shortly.

The Anatomy of a Mail Message

Body

The *body* is the text of the message.

Header

The *header* is the section you see at the top of a message. It contains information about the sender, the recipient, and other, optional information, such as the message subject, the type of mail system the sender has, etc.

Envelope

The *envelope* is a hidden portion of the message delivery process; you don't see it. It is passed in the private conversation that takes place between two MTAs, as they exchange mail. MTA #1 may contact MTA #2, for instance, and say, "This message is for so-and-so, please deliver it." Note that the header and the envelope may not agree about the number of recipients, or who they are. For example, I might receive a blind carbon copy of a letter from you to somebody else. My name won't appear in the header, but I will be nominated as a recipient in the envelope's accompanying MTA transports from your site to mine.

The distinction between the header and the envelope can be important—particularly when one is configuring *sendmail* to rewrite addresses. In some cases, header and envelope addresses will be rewritten together. In others, they will be treated separately.

Rules

The actions of *sendmail* are directed by a collection of *rules* that test for patterns in mail headers (and envelopes), and take some actions when the tests are successful. Often, matching text is rewritten. Sometimes, a match changes the flow of control through the rules. At some point, pattern matching will identify a method for the next step in the delivery process (called a *delivery agent*).

Individual rules are organized as pattern/action pairs. Pattern templates appear on the left side; actions and rewrites appear on the right. Comments are optional, and may appear on the far right. Each field is separated from its neighbor by tab characters. Here's a sample rule for illustration:

```
R$* < @ $- . gizmiz . com > $*    $1 < @ gizmiz . com > $3    comment here
```

The R in the leftmost column marks the start of a rule. The elements of the rules may be literals (such as gizmiz and <), regular expressions (such as $* and $+), operators (such as $3), macro references, or separators (.:%@!^/[] (typically)).

We call each individual component of a pattern a *token*. The rule above would match patterns of the form:

```
any_number_of_tokens < @ one_token . gizniz . com > any_number_of_tokens
```

We might use this rule to perform site-hiding; it could translate an address such as fred<@xxx.gizniz.com> into fred<@gizniz.com>, eliminating a portion of the domain information.*

The left-hand side and right-hand side of rules are restricted to different kinds of rule elements. This makes sense. On the left we are trying to find a match for a pattern—the elements of the left-hand side have to include various forms of wild-cards. The right side, on the other hand, contains elements whose values are defined, and may be used in substitutions.

The Left-hand-side

A limited set of regular expressions perform pattern "wildcarding" on the left. The expressions may be one of the forms shown in Table 18-1.

Table 18-1: Left-hand-Side Expressions

Expression	Pattern
$@	Matches zero tokens
$-	Matches one token
$+	Matches one or more tokens
$*	Matches zero or more tokens
$=X	Matches a token from a class X
$~X	Matches a token not in X

We used $* in the "giziniz.com" example, earlier, to match all tokens preceding the "<.". The user name could have been almost anything—fred, fred.smith, fred_smith—the rule would have matched. If we had placed $- in the rule, on the other hand, then fred would have matched, but fred.smith wouldn't have. The difference is that the first example contains a single token; the latter contains three tokens: fred, smith, and a separator, ".".

The two expressions at the end of Table 18-1 test for class membership. Earlier, we saw how classes are defined. Now we can use them in the left-hand-side expressions to match patterns containing a limited selection of distinct possibilities.

DUdeadbeat
DIcom edu org

---

* The <'s and >'s are added by earlier rules within *sendmail.cf*, in order to separate the user's mail ID from the domain.

Given the above macro and class definitions, for example, we can construct a left-hand-side subpattern—"$U.$=k"—that would match deadbeat.com, dead-beat.edu, or deadbeat.org.

Complete left-hand-side expressions can be any combination of literals, macros, regular expressions, and separators. Here are some possible left-hand-side expressions:

$*<@$*>$*

This matches any number of tokens, followed by "<@", any number of tokens, another literal—">"—and any number of tokens. Addresses that will satisfy this left-hand-side include fred<@deadbeat>, <@>, fred<@gizniz.com>, and fred<@gizniz.com>trailing_stuff.

$*<@$*.$~k>$*

Matches any number of tokens, the literal "<@", another stretch of any number of tokens, the character ".", followed by anything *not* in the **k** class, ">", and any number of tokens. Assuming that the **k** class is defined as it was earlier, this pattern will match almost any fully qualified domain address. Exclusions are those that end with com, org, or edu.

$U<@$+.com>$*

Using the "$U deadbeat" macro definition given earlier, this example will match any address with a mail ID of deadbeat, in any com domain.

The Right-hand-side

Again, the right-hand-side tells *sendmail* what to do when an address matches a left-hand-side pattern. We might rewrite the matching address, for instance, or change the flow of control within the *sendmail* rule collection.

The right-hand and left-hand sides share some elements. We can reference literals and macros on either side, for instance. We cannot, however, include regular expressions on the right side (it wouldn't make sense—the pattern match has already occurred by the time we get to the right-hand side). Similarly, we can use some operators on the right-hand side that are illegal on the left. One of these operators is a numbered reference (actually, it's a copy). We saw a use for it in our first example:

```
R$* < @ $~ . gizniz . com > $*      $1 < @ gizniz . com > $3      comment here
```

In the rule above, for example, $1 appearing on the right is a reference to any and all tokens that match the first regular expression—"$*"—on the left. Likewise, $3 references the contents of the second $*. Note that we don't have to reference everything; the matching $~ expression is not used anywhere on the right; had it been, it would have been copied as $2. To take a specific example, an address of the form `fred<@xxx.gizniz.com>` would match. `$1` would be set to `fred`; `$2` would be set to `xxx`; `$3` would match anything trailing the closing ">."

Notice that the address *fred<@xxx.gizniz.com>* will match just once; the rewritten text—`fred<@gizniz.com>`—will not be a candidate for the expression `R$*<@$- .gizniz.com>$*`. This is important because, unless otherwise instructed, *sendmail* will attempt to apply a rule over and over—repeatedly rewriting the input—until the left-hand-side pattern no longer matches. Control then passes to the next rule.

Repeated rule application can be a convenience. You may, for instance, be stripping an address of redundant outer layers. However, sometimes you need rule application to behave differently. For these cases, *sendmail* supports a few special right-hand-side operators (Table 18-2), including:

Table 18-2: Right-hand-side Operators

Operator	Action
$:	Apply this rule one time.
$@	Apply this rule and terminate ruleset.
$>*n*	Pass control temporarily to ruleset *n*.
$#*agent*	Invoke a delivery agent.

Below, we see how the $: operator might be used in a rule that applies a suffix, $M, to an address:

```
R$* < @ $* > $*     $: $1 < @ $2 . $M > $3
```

Say that $M is set to a domain name—"gizniz.com." An address like *fred<@foo.bar>*, then, will be rewritten as `fred<@foo.bar.gizniz.com>`. Note that without the $:, the rule would be applied repeatedly:

```
fred<@foo.bar.gizniz.com>                        -->
fred<@foo.bar.gizniz.com.gizniz.com>             -->
fred<@foo.bar.gizniz.com.gizniz.com.gizniz.com>  -->
```

and so on, *ad infinitum*—probably not what we want. The $: operator terminates current rule processing after one pass through.

The second operator in the list, $@, terminates more than just a rule—it terminates a *ruleset*. Rulesets are sequential collections of rules, identified along the left-hand column of *sendmail.cf* by strings of the form S##, where ## is the ruleset number. A ruleset ends where a new one begins.

```
S12
R$* < @ $* . > $*       $1 < @ $2 >     strip trailing dots
R$* < @ $=w >           $1              strip local name
R<@ $- . UUCP > : $+    $1 ! $2         convert to UUCP format
R<@ $+ > : $+           $1 ! $2         convert to UUCP format
```

```
RS* < @ $-. UUCP >           $2 ! $1              convert to UUCP format
RS* < @ $+ >                 $2 ! $1              convert to UUCP format
RS$h ! $+ ! $+               $@ $1 ! $2           $h!...!user => ...!user
RS$h ! $+                    $@ $&h ! $1          $h!user => $h!user
RS$+                         $: $U ! $1           prepend our name
R$! $+                       $: $k ! $1           in case $U undefined
```

Ruleset 12 from the Berkeley sendmail.cf distribution files

Typically, the contents of a ruleset are cobbled together with a common purpose. A ruleset might parse UUCP addresses, for instance, or rewrite mail headers on outbound messages. At run-time, control flows from top to bottom until an exception occurs—either we reach the end, or a right-hand-side operator terminates ruleset processing early.

```
RS* < @ $* . foo > $*        $@ $1 < @ $M > $3
```

The rule above shows an example of the right-hand-side $@ operator. It says that an address match of the form *soandso<@something.foo>trailing_stuff* should be rewritten according to the right-hand side, and that this will terminate processing of the ruleset; control will pass back from callee to caller. Assuming again that $M is set to "gizmiz.com," invoking the previous rule with fred<@bar.foo> would cause a rewrite in the form of fred<@gizmiz.com>, and terminate the ruleset. We might use the $@ operator when we have found the desired pattern, and therefore have no need to test the remaining rules within the ruleset.

The third operator in the table, $>*n*, invokes other rulesets, such as procedure calls.

```
RS+                          $: $>20 $1
```

The rule above, for example, says that when matching any address with at least one token ($+), pass the pattern ($1) and control of processing to rule 20 ($>20), and do it just once ($:). Again, we might pass control to another ruleset if we were looking for some specific patterns, or performing some special address rewriting.

The most deliberate right-hand-side operator in the list is the last one—"$#". It selects a delivery agent—a method for forwarding the mail on to its final destination.

```
RS* < @$* > $*               $#smtp $@ $2 $: $1 < @ $2 > $3
```

This rule shows an example of the $# operator. A match on the left prompts the action on the right; *sendmail* invokes a delivery agent labeled smtp. Notice that there are $@ and $: operators intermixed with the numbered operators and literals on the right-hand side. These have different meanings within the $# operation than they do when they appear alone. The $2 pattern that follows $@ is taken to be the name of the downstream mail host that will receive the forwarded SMTP mail. The $1<@$2>$3 pattern following $: is taken to be the address of the remote mail recipient. If, for example, we matched this rule with the pattern fred<@gizniz.com>, the resulting substitutions would be:

```
$#smtp $@ gizniz.com $: fred < @ gizniz.com >
```

Mail (MX) host gizniz.com would receive the mail; fred@gizniz.com would be the recipient. Notice that this would be a convenient place to nominate a second host—a hub—to handle mail forwarding to gizniz.com, or for any destination. We will talk about modifying sendmail.cf to direct mail to central mail hubs in more detail, later.

Delivery agents

SMTP delivery is not the only possibility; delivery agents can copy mail into local mailboxes, invoke UUCP, send mail to non-SMTP MTAs, even execute programs. Accordingly, you will find that your sendmail.cf contains a variety of rules containing $# operations. In most cases, the label in the $# rule (such as smtp, above) refers to a delivery agent definition found elsewhere within your sendmail.cf.

```
Msmtp,      P=[IPC], F=mDFMuX, S=11/31, R=21, E=\r\n, L=990, A=IPC $h
```

This line shows what an SMTP delivery agent declaration looks like. It starts with "Msmtp"—the same label used when invoked by the $# right-hand-side operator. There can be a number of parameter fields—two are required (P= and A=). Others may or may not be present, depending upon the delivery agent.

The P= field, shown in this example, gives the path to the program or service that is responsible for actual delivery or forwarding. In this case, we are using built-in SMTP (interprocess communication, [IPC]). Compare this to the local delivery agent that follows, which uses program /bin/mail.local.

The F= parameter tells sendmail a thing or two about the delivery program. It is unlikely that you will have to fiddle with these flags, but, in case you do, Table 18-3 lists a subset so that you can get a feel for the kinds of effects they have:

Table 18–3. Delivery-Agent Flags

Flag	Effect
a	Run extended SMTP (ESMTP).
C	Add a domain name to recipient if not qualified.
D	Delivery agent needs a Date: line in the header.
E	Change From in text to >From (to hide it from MUAs).
L	Limit line lengths.
l	This is a local mailer—will not be forwarding.
M	Delivery agent needs a Message-Id: in header.

Table 18-3: Delivery Agent Flags (continued)

Flag	Effect
m	The delivery agent can handle multiple recipients.
n	Don't insert a From: line.
P	The delivery agent wants a Return-Path: header.
s	Strip quotes from addresses before calling the delivery agent.
U	Mailer wants From: lines.
u	Preserve case in user names.

S=... and R=... parameters nominate rules for last-minute rewriting of sender and recipient addresses, respectively. On later versions of *sendmail*, each parameter can name two rules (R1/R2): the first applies to the header, and the second applies to the envelope.

```
Mlocal,    P=/bin/mail.local, F=lsDFMrmn, S=10, R=20/40, A=mail -d $u
```

The E= line (if present) describes the end-of-line characters. L= sets the maximum line length. Lastly, the A= parameter passes arguments to the delivery process. Other flags may be present as well.

The Big Picture

Now we get to the point where we can talk about what happens when you turn the crank. The second half of your *sendmail.cf* probably lists rulesets in a succession that reveals little about the order of rule processing. As I said earlier, the flow of control can vary as a function of the input. However, the basic scheme is always the same: we start by preprocessing the addresses—sender and recipient—in ruleset 3. This strips the users' personal information, if present, and places the addresses in a focused form (domains between the <>'s).

Next, ruleset 0, and all of the rulesets it calls, choose the delivery agent that will forward mail toward its final destination (e.g., smtp, local, etc.). Rulesets 1 and 2, if present, perform generic sender and recipient address rewriting. Figure 18-9 shows this process.

The next steps are specific to the delivery agent chosen. As we saw above, the delivery agent's S= and R= parameters specify custom rules for sender and recipient address rewriting. Upon exiting from rule 0, we will have already chosen a delivery agent, and therefore know which rules these are to be. For instance, in the smtp delivery agent definition, above, the sender rules are 11 and 31, and the recipient rule is 21. If smtp was chosen as a delivery agent, then control of sender and recipient address rewriting would pass from rules 1 and 2 to 11/31 and 21, respectively.

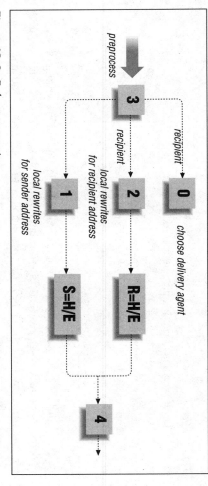

Figure 18–9: Ruleset processing

Ruleset 4 performs final rewriting of all addresses. Other rules within your *sendmail.cf* may be called as helpers, or may perform delivery-agent-specific address rewriting. However, Figure 18-9 captures the basic flow.

At this point, we know enough to make a stab at *sendmail* changes. For instance, if we needed to recognize an address requiring special mail handling, we could craft a rule for it within ruleset 0. Upon a match, we could either perform a custom rewrite, invoke another ruleset, or call up a delivery agent. Similarly, it should be apparent where one might place rules to rewrite return or outbound addresses—in the R= and S= rules specified by the delivery agent definition. You aren't restricted to the structure you found when you arrived, by the way; if you need to, you can make up your own rulesets and define delivery agents to suit your needs.

Testing

sendmail has a test mode that you can use to check rule additions or changes. Of course, you might want to make your changes in a copy of *sendmail.cf* before inflicting them on the world. Assuming, then, that you are modifying a separate copy of *sendmail.cf*, called *sendmail.cf.new*, this is how you would run your tests:

```
% /usr/lib/sendmail -bt -C./sendmail.cf.new
ADDRESS TEST MODE (ruleset 3 NOT automatically invoked)
Enter <ruleset> <address>
>
```

You can exit *sendmail*'s address test mode by entering a ^D.

The prompt shown above is asking you to enter a rule number, followed by an address. Recall that for all but the very first ruleset (ruleset 3), addresses are being handled in a focused form, à la *fred<@deadbeat.net>*. Accordingly, you will need to enter addresses in focused form for all rulesets other than ruleset 3. In the following example, I am testing ruleset 0 to see which delivery agent will be chosen when I ask the system to send mail to *fred<@deadbeat.net>*:

```
> 0 fred<@deadbeat.net>
rewrite: ruleset  0  input: fred < @ deadbeat . net >
rewrite: ruleset 98  input: fred < @ deadbeat . net >
rewrite: ruleset 98 returns: fred < @ deadbeat . net >
rewrite: ruleset  0 returns: $# smtp $@ deadbeat . net $: fred < @ deadbeat . net >
>
```

As you can see, delivery agent smtp was chosen. Notice too that the auxiliary fields—the next mail host in the chain ($@), and the user's address($:)—appear in the result.

In the next example, I am checking to see that ruleset 3 correctly strips user information and focuses an address of fred@gizniz.com (which it does):

```
> 3 Fred Smith <fred@gizniz.com>
rewrite: ruleset  3  input: Fred Smith < fred @ gizniz . com >
rewrite: ruleset 96  input: fred < @ gizniz . com >
rewrite: ruleset 96 returns: fred < @ gizniz . com >
rewrite: ruleset  3 returns: fred < @ gizniz . com >
>
```

Granted, these aren't terribly interesting examples. However, this *sendmail* test mode starts to become very useful when you are crafting custom rules for jobs like site-hiding, mail hub selection, or special delivery agents. You can see in advance what form rewritten addresses will take.

Of course, the real success comes when a message is delivered. *sendmail* address processing tests can't anticipate all of the potential problems. You might have DNS difficulties, for instance, which won't show up in test mode. Once I am satisfied with *sendmail.cf* rule modifications, I typically execute *sendmail* in verbose (-v) mode to watch how a message will be dispatched:

```
% /usr/lib/sendmail -v dowd@spike.deadbeat.net
From: dowd@atlantic.com
Subject: Bang!

I broke your mail.
.
dowd@spike.deadbeat.net... Connecting to spike.deadbeat.net. (smtp)...
220-spike.deadbeat.net Sendmail 8.6.12/8.6.12 ready at Sun, 28 Jan 1996 11:37:37 -0500
220 ESMTP spoken here
>>> EHLO maddie.atlantic.com
250-spike.deadbeat.net Hello maddie.atlantic.com [198.252.200.3], pleased to meet you
250-EXPN
250-SIZE
250 HELP
```

```
>>> MAIL From:<dowd@maddie.atlantic.com> SIZE=57
250 <dowd@maddie.atlantic.com>... Sender ok
>>> RCPT To:<dowd@spike.deadbeat.net>
250 <dowd@spike.deadbeat.net>... Recipient ok
>>> DATA
354 Enter mail, end with "." on a line by itself
>>> .
250 LAA12149 Message accepted for delivery
dowd@spike.deadbeat.net... Sent (LAA12149 Message accepted for delivery)
Closing connection to spike.deadbeat.net.
>>> QUIT
221 spike.deadbeat.net closing connection
```

The text above is a transcript of *sendmail*'s successful delivery. I nominated dowd@spike.deadbeat.net as the recipient on the command line, and I also hand-typed a "From:" line directly into *sendmail*. This is because I wanted to see how both parts—the envelope and header would be treated. If I'm in a hurry, I might shorten the test like so:

```
% /usr/lib/sendmail -v < /dev/null fred@deadbeat.net
```

The message should be delivered just the same, though I won't see specific header modifications.

Site-Hiding

Often, sites wish to hide the details of their internal mail system. Earlier, we saw a LAN mail scenario where this makes great sense. It is also important if you are erecting a firewall; typically, mail can only be directed to the firewall, and therefore return addresses shouldn't bear any extraneous host-specific domain information. *

Now that we have had a look at the workings of *sendmail*, you can imagine how we might go about stripping extra domain information from outbound mail. Again, a message's mail headers (and envelope) may be rewritten many times before a delivery agent is selected. And even after that, some more mail header and envelope rewriting occurs. *This* is where we want to place our changes; in the *sendmail* rules that rewrite "sender" addresses just before mail goes out the door. The first thing you have to do is identify the delivery agent definition that is responsible for passing your mail to the Internet.

---

* By the way, removing return address information doesn't imply removing the *Received* headers in a mail message. These provide an audit trail—a record of the agents that have handled the letter. You might think that you would want to remove them because they reveal some private details about your internal mail handling. However, the *Received* headers also give *sendmail* a mechanism for detecting mail loops; removing them can cause problems.

```
% /usr/lib/sendmail -v < /dev/null dowd@foo.deadbeat.net
dowd@deadbeat.net... Connecting to spike.deadbeat.net. (smtp)...

(other stuff)
```

You can see how I would discover the delivery agent, in this example: I send a blank mail message to someone, and note the name of the agent (smtp), given in parentheses. I expect to be able to find this label at the start of a delivery agent definition within *sendmail.cf* (which I did):

```
Msmtp,     P=[IPC], F=mDFMuX, S=11/31, R=21, E=\r\n, L=990, A=IPC $h
```

As I explained earlier, the S= parameter nominates rulesets that will perform delivery-agent-specific header and envelope rewriting for sender addresses. Rulesets 11 and 31 get the job. Here are rulesets 11 and 31, taken from my copy of *sendmail.cf*:

```
S11
R$+                 $: $>51 $1             sender/recipient common
R$* :; <@>          $@ $1 :;               list:; special case
R$*                 $@ $>61 $1             qualify unqual'ed names

S31
R$+                 $: $>51 $1             sender/recipient common
R$* :; <@>          $@ $1 :;               list:; special case
# do special header rewriting
R$* <@> $*          $@ $1 <@> $2           pass null host through
R< @ $* > $*        $@ < @ $1 > $2         pass route-addr through
R$=E < @ $=w . >    $@ $1 < @ $2 >         exposed user as is
R$* < @ $=w . >     $: $1 < @ $M >         masquerade as domain
R$* < @ >           $: $1 < @ $j >         in case $M undefined
R$*                 $@ $>61 $1             qualify unqual'ed names
```

Note that within both the header and envelope rulesets (11 and 31), control is temporarily passed to ruleset 61. In order to kill two birds with one stone, this is where I chose to add a rule that says "replace host+domain in the return address (e.g., fred@larmail.gizniz.com) with the domain name alone (e.g., fred@gizniz.com)".

```
DUgizniz.com

...intervening lines

R$+ <@ $+ . $U> $*     $: $1 < @ $U > $2              Remove host name
```

This rule, placed at the top of ruleset 61, does the trick. The pattern on the left-hand side tells *sendmail* to match addresses of the form:

one_or_more_tokens < @ one_or_more_tokens .gizniz.com > any_number_of_tokens

Matching addresses will be replaced with a simpler form containing the shortened domain name, "gizniz.com". Of course, this isn't the only way to go about rewriting return addresses; *sendmail* provides lots of opportunities for customization. But this should give you a feel for the possibilities.

Once the changes are complete (save a copy of your old *sendmail.cf*), you will need to kill and restart *sendmail*:

```
# ps aux | grep sendmail
<...process list comes back...>
# kill <pid>
# /usr/lib/sendmail -bd -q15m &
#
```

Note that if you are running *sendmail* from inetd, or if SMAPD is running it for you (see Chapter 16), then restarting the daemon will not be necessary (or even the right thing to do).

Passing Mail to a Relay Host

In some cases, you may wish to have *sendmail* pass all mail of a certain type to a second host for further processing. Perhaps you are behind a firewall, and need to forward outgoing mail to the bastion host for external delivery. Or maybe you wish to forward all incoming LAN mail traffic to a LAN/SMTP gateway, rather than going through the bother of maintaining *sendmail* aliases for everyone in the company. For illustration, I am going to take the last case, since it comes up occasionally (Figure 18-10).

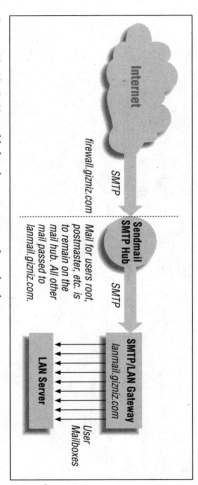

Figure 18-10: LAN mail behind a gateway and a relay host

Internet

firewall.gizniz.com
SMTP

Sendmail
SMTP Hub
SMTP

Mail for users root, postmaster, etc. is to remain on the mail hub. All other mail passed to lanmail.gizniz.com.

SMTP/LAN Gateway
lanmail.gizniz.com

LAN Server

User Mailboxes

First, let's elaborate on our plans a little. Let's say that we want *all* incoming mail to *whomever@gizniz.com* to be forwarded to the LAN/SMTP mail gateway, *lanmail.gizniz.com*, with just a few exceptions: mail for root, postmaster, daemon, uucp, mailer-daemon, and fred is to remain on the *sendmail*-based (UNIX) mail hub. Most goes, but some stays. How do we approach this? Remember, ruleset 0 decides how mail is to be dispatched, and is therefore the right place to apply our changes.

```
Cwlocalhost gizniz.com
Ckroot postmaster daemon uucp postmaster daemon uucp mailer-daemon fred
DNlanmail.gizniz.com

...<intervening lines>...

S0

...<intervening lines>...

R$=k < @ $=w > $*            $#local $: $1
R$* < @ $=w > $*             $#smtp $@ $N $: $1 <@ $N > $@
```

This is how *I* worked it: First, I chose to create a new class, **k**, and a new macro, **N**, that I could use in my new rules. **N** is set to the name of the LAN/SMTP gateway. Class **k** lists all the special-case users (root, postmaster, etc.). The left-hand-side pattern of the first new rule (R$=k<@$=w>$*) matches any of these users whenever the accompanying domain is either of localhost, gizniz.com, or firewall.gizniz.com.* Upon a match, the mail is handed off to the local delivery agent, to be deposited in the user's mailbox. Mail for any other recipients with domains in the "w" class is automatically forwarded to lanmail.gizniz.com, as specified by the $N macro. That's all there is to it!

Where would you place these rules? They should go far enough into ruleset 0 to avoid initial error processing, but not so far down that other rules' patterns have a chance to match first.

---

* The host's real name—in this case firewall.gizniz.com—is automatically included in the "w" class.

19

IP on the Desktop

Up until this point, we have looked at the infrastructure underlying a working Internet connection. There is a fair amount to think about. The trouble is that you may be the only one in your organization who really appreciates the number of technical topics you have to juggle. When you emerge from the wiring closet, thumbs in your suspenders, and announce, "it's all set!" is anyone really going to understand what has been accomplished? To date, it looks as if you have spent a lot of time and money doting over a computer and some data communications equipment, off in a corner. Eventually, you will have to deliver the goods to the desktop; you will have to get the rest of the company hooked into the Internet. This means crafting a strategy for desktop IP connectivity and providing Internet clients, or browsers.

In this chapter, we are going to concentrate on Macintoshes and PCs. The basic plan is to make each computer on the LAN bilingual; in addition to the normal LAN-based protocols (i.e., Novell, LAN Manager, AppleTalk), every client will speak IP as well. In some cases we can hide IP within an existing protocol. Where there is no LAN, we will introduce IP as the first network protocol.

Anyway, there's a lot to cover. We will begin with MS DOS, Microsoft Windows, and Windows 95, look briefly at OS/2, and then cover the Macintosh. When we have finished with basic networking, we will talk a little about dynamic address assignment, and then touch on encapsulated IP. We *won't* talk about applications, however. All the tools you may want to run—*Netscape, Mosaic, Eudora*, etc., will drop easily on top of the networking we have configured. However, choosing and configuring browsers is up to you.

IP Networking on the PC

In 1980, MS DOS was released in tandem with the IBM personal computer. Microsoft Windows appeared in the middle 1980s, becoming terrifically popular with the release of Windows 3.1 in 1992. Naturally, if you were designing networking applications for PCs today, you would target the Windows/Windows 95 world. By the same token, a designer crafting a solution to PC networking in the mid-1980s would focus on the MS DOS environment. IP networking solutions in circulation today come from both eras. Evidence of their lineage is often buried in the software like fossilized remains.

There have been two historical problems in PC networking. The first involves memory: because of some early IBM design decisions, DOS memory is limited to 640 kilobytes. Applications must contend with other components—drivers, TSRs, and shared buffers—for a chunk of the 640 Kb; it can be a battle to free up enough memory to allow applications to run. You can play a few tricks, and use space above 640 Kb for certain things; however, memory problems still plague owners of DOS-based PCs, even in the mid-1990s.

In the same vein, networking software suites that were written for the DOS world typically require more DOS memory than later implementations, written for the Windows world. Earlier packages load vital pieces and run applications in DOS memory—even when Windows is loaded. Later packages take advantage of Windows memory (of which there is "more"), by placing as much of the networking software as possible into Dynamic Link Libraries (DLLs), or, lately, into virtual device drivers (VxDs).

The second networking challenge involves drivers. A driver is a piece of software that interacts with a piece of hardware to provide an interface for programs. A program that wishes to use the device fashions an appropriate request, and hands it to the driver. Some action occurs—a disk seeks or a tape spins—and data is transferred. The danger is that if the driver interface is too specific, or too proprietary, then some applications won't be able to use it—they will not have been crafted with the interface in mind. In other words, two programs, each with its own idea of what a driver interface should look like, can't cooperate on the same computer. One gets to use the device, and the other doesn't.

When booted, MS DOS loads drivers as instructed in *config.sys* or *autoexec.bat*, and typically keeps them loaded until the next boot. This once constrained people trying to network PCs; it could be a challenge to find a set of applications (or, more precisely, protocol stacks) that could all share the same network driver interface.

Drivers

The sad fact is that drivers didn't have to be so proprietary. Wouldn't it be better, for instance, if drivers *abstracted* the hardware into a common interface format? That way, an application would talk to the network by a single method, regardless of the personalities of a particular network card. Moreover, wouldn't it be nice if the interface were published, so that other applications could be tailored for it? If the standard was good, it would continue to live on as new programs were written and new network hardware was designed.

Fortunately, there has been a good deal of progress in these directions. Today, published standards, or APIs (*Application Program Interfaces*), can be found at all levels in PC networks. Of course, a *single* standard would be unheard of; today, there are several PC network driver APIs in common use. They're not all identical in function—different standards operate with different features. However, the benefits are the same: APIs provide a base upon which to build plug-compatible network applications.

Packet drivers

One of the most important contributions to PC networking has been a collection of contributed interfaces called the *Clarkson Packet Drivers*, written to a specification published by FTP Software.[*] Crafted for many brands of Ethernet cards (and other devices), each packet driver provides an identical interface to the lowest network layers. Once the driver is loaded, the remainder of the software can be blissfully ignorant of everything that lies below. Furthermore, the interface can be shared; multiple protocol stacks can be assembled on top of a single packet driver (Figure 19-1).

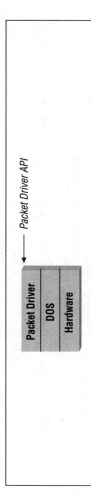

Figure 19–1: Packet driver API

Because the packet driver specification was readily available, and because the packet drivers were distributed at no charge, they became a popular standard upon which to build IP networking. These days, Ethernet card vendors regularly ship packet drivers with their products.

---

[*] The Clarkson Packet Drivers, or just "Packet Drivers" for short, are now maintained by Russ Nelson of Crynwr Software.

Open datalink interface

ODI (Open Datalink Interface) is another driver API. Like the packet drivers, ODI drivers provide a standard upon which to base higher-level networking protocols. Novell and Apple Computer collaborated on ODI, and published the specification in 1989. Novell had long been shipping networking software, of course. Netware IPX clients included all networking layers in monolithic, dedicated drivers. This made it difficult to support multiple protocols; essentially, you needed another network interface for every new protocol. The move towards API-based network drivers gave IPX LAN software developers a clean platform from which multiple networking protocols could run.

Today, Novell LANs can be a mix of dedicated IPX and ODI-based protocol stacks. If you are running the dedicated drivers, it's time to replace them so that you can also run IP from the same Ethernet card (or other interface). It's not too difficult to do; I'll show you how a little later.

Network driver interface specification

NDIS (*Network Driver Interface Specification*) is the creation of a collaboration between 3Com and Microsoft. Like the packet drivers and ODI, NDIS provides a network API upon which to load different protocol stacks. Again, applications don't speak directly with the network interface. Rather, networking software "binds" itself (to borrow NDIS parlance) at the NDIS API, and thereby shares access to the hardware.

Shims

It's nice to have a choice. However, with three interface APIs, you might guess that there are cases where a protocol stack crafted for one API has to be used with another.

Sometimes—not always—you can find *shims* to adapt between APIs. A shim is a program whose whole role is to transcribe requests between formats. Figure 19-2 illustrates how a shim could be placed above ODI to provide a packet driver

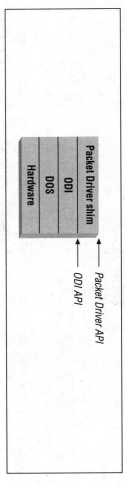

Figure 19–2. Using a shim on top of ODI

interface. Below we will look at situations where two APIs are in use at the same time, and where a shim plays an important part. Shims, like the drivers themselves, are available from various sources, and for various combinations of APIs.

Stacks

Without defining terms, we have already begun to approach PC networking protocols by talking about a "stack." You have probably seen protocol stacks used to explain networking concepts before. General discussions often begin with a description of the OSI seven-layer model: the lowest level addresses the network medium, and is followed by a method for modulating a signal onto a wire, and so on, all the way up to network applications. The idea is that the layers have analogs on all machines, and that the interface between layers is clearly delineated. A process speaking at a particular layer on one machine will have a peer speaking the same language on another; neither needs to know anything about the layers below.*

In the PC world, the term "protocol stack" is often used more narrowly to describe the portion of the layers that makes up the network (and transport) protocols—SPX/IPX TCP/IP, NetBEUI, etc. In terms of our diagrams, this is the piece that sits just above the drivers or shims. To be really precise, the networking hardware and the functions the driver performs should be considered as part of the "stack" as well. However, because of the way the PC networking software is assembled—in modules—the middle layers have come to be called the "protocol stacks," to the exclusion of the rest.

Of course, protocol stacks differ, not only in their interfaces, but in their function. Depending on what you ultimately plan to do with your network, you might choose one combination of modules over another. For instance, if you need to run both IP and IPX on the same client, you will be looking for a way to assemble pieces to make both protocol stacks available at the same time.

Figure 19-3 depicts a configuration running both IPX (for Netware), and IP for Internet applications, above an ODI driver. This looks a lot like Novell's LAN Workplace for DOS in combination with a Netware client.† Often, protocol stacks come bundled with other software (as in the case of Windows for Workgroups LAN Manager clients, or Netware). Some applications have their own protocol stacks built in.

---

* A little nitpicking here: The seven layer model is just that—a model. Most networking protocols, IP included, are less religious in their segregation of layers. See Chapter 6, *OSI Networking Layers and IP*.

† Just in case you missed it: the diagrams we are using are *not* representations of "protocol stacks," nor do they express the order in which the components are loaded. Instead, the diagrams show how the modules—hardware, drivers, shims, stacks, and applications—fit together. "Protocol stack" is the name given to the middle network layers—IP, IPX, NetBEUI, etc.

cations.

As we saw before, driver APIs simplified the problem of running multiple protocol stacks. However, the same kinds of challenges appear elsewhere. Now, focusing a level or two above the driver, we can again ask how we might run multiple applications.

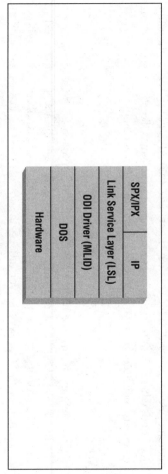

SPX/IPX	IP
Link Service Layer (LSL)	
ODI Driver (MLID)	
DOS	
Hardware	

Figure 19-3: Dual stacks on one machine

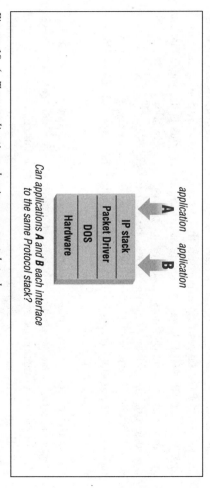

application   application

| IP stack |
| Packet Driver |
| DOS |
| Hardware |

Can applications A and B each interface to the same Protocol stack?

Figure 19-4: Two applications sharing one protol stack

Consider that two IP network applications might be written assuming different protocol stack interfaces (as in Figure 19-4). This could cause a problem. If application A cannot share an interface with application B, then we might be forced to switch stacks in midstream.[*] The question is more than academic; such problems actually have plagued the DOS world. Fortunately, standards efforts in the Windows world have overtaken the Tower of Babel phenomenon. All new IP applications are being written to a standard called *Winsock*.

---

[*] It *is* possible to load multiple protocol stacks of the same type. You could, for instance, have two different implementations of TCP/IP running to accommodate different IP applications.

Winsock

The Winsock (1.1) specification grew out of a collaboration between members of a Birds of a Feather session at Interop, 1991. The first draft was issued in December 1991. As with the other APIs we have looked at, Winsock provides a standard interface that application developers can write to. The specification is rich, and not limited to IP networking, although at this time, activity is centered around IP applications running under Windows.

From a programmer's point of view, the Winsock specification looks very much like the Berkeley socket abstraction—the favored interface for IP communications under UNIX—with some enhancements. Because the specification is open, anyone can take a shot at writing their own Winsock networking layer. Many implementations have sprung up—some commercial and some shareware. In the last few years, Winsock's overwhelming endorsement has had a tremendous effect on IP networking for PCs: programs no longer have to be written for compatibility with four or five networking interfaces. Instead, every new Windows application can be crafted with Winsock as the target.

Winsock development continues. Winsock version 2 was in beta at the beginning of 1996. For more information about Winsock, see *http://www.stardust.com/*.

IP on a PC

Because most of the applications we are interested in run under Windows, that's where we will focus our efforts. The trick for us is to choose building blocks that extend from the network card on the bottom to a Winsock layer on the top. Certainly, a lot of combinations are possible. In this section, we will look at a few common configurations, to see if we can find one that suits you. Even if we don't, at least you will get an idea of how these components are assembled, and you can proceed from there.

Packet-Driver-based Stacks

If you aren't running any networking software at all (no Netware or LAN Manager, for instance), then the packet drivers are a possible starting point. A complete kit of drivers—one for almost every common network interface card—can be obtained in *zip* format directly from the site where the software is maintained, (*ftp://ftp.crynwr.edu/drivers*), or from any number of FTP servers and bulletin boards. Packet driver shims, and drivers for less common interfaces, are scattered about other sites as well. The packet driver documentation will give you leads for these. Note too that Ethernet card manufacturers often ship a commercially-supported packet driver along with their boards.

Anyway, we're getting a little ahead of ourselves. Before selecting a packet driver, we have to choose a network interface (Ethernet card, SLIP, etc.). For illustration, say that we have an Elite-16 Combo, manufactured by SMC. This card, like many others, is configured by setting three parameters: an interrupt (IRQ), an I/O base address, and a shared memory address.

Briefly, the IRQ specifies a *hardware interrupt* associated with the Ethernet card. Via the interrupt, the card will asynchronously signal the operating system that it needs attention when some significant change has taken place—I/O has been completed, an error has occurred, etc. Because each IRQ is identified with a specific device, IRQs cannot be shared; you must install the Ethernet card to work with a free interrupt.

Likewise, each hardware interface has some addresses reserved for control functions. Hardware devices in PCs are *memory-mapped*, meaning that their actions are controlled by writing to and reading from registers that appear to be part of the computer's memory address space. To talk to the device, the driver issues a memory *store* instruction. To inquire about the device's status, or perhaps to retrieve some data, the driver performs a memory *load*. As part of boot-time configuration, one has to tell the driver (or it has to discover by some other means) the address where it can find the device's I/O control registers.

Last, certain devices need scratch areas for data buffering. An application might write data into the scratch area, eventually to be transferred directly by the controller to the device (DMA). Data returning from the device could also use the same buffers. Because these buffers are available to the controller, driver, and some applications, the associated memory is said to be *shared*.

The trick is to find a range of addresses and an interrupt that is not already in use by some other card, and then assign them to the network device. These same settings have to be passed along to the driver so that it knows how to talk to the card (they must match). As an example, the line below tells DOS to load the packet driver for the SMC Elite 16 Combo on interrupt 10, I/O address 300 (hexadecimal), with shared memory buffers located at cc00 (hexadecimal).

8003pkdr /e:62 /i:10 /b:300 /r:cc00

This line would be included in *autoexec.bat*, to be executed upon DOS boot. Naturally, somewhere in its path, DOS would have to be able to locate the module *8003pkdr.com*.

For comparison, here is the line used to load the packet driver for the Intel Ether-Express Ethernet controller:

```
exp16 -w 0x62
```

Notice that many of the parameters we used for the SMC card are missing (except for the mysterious "62," which I haven't explained yet). In this case, the driver searches for the controller and, upon finding it, configures itself. The parameters—interrupt, I/O address, and shared memory address—have to have been chosen on the card, in advance. I could keep listing possibilities, but the documentation with the packet driver kit is good. Each card is described with a list of configuration parameters and any special notes that might apply.

The "62" (hexadecimal) that appears in both the Intel and SMC configuration examples describes a *software interrupt*, to be associated with the next layer of the stack. As you know, the controller uses a hardware interrupt to tell the operating system (and driver) that something has happened, and that it needs attention. Likewise, the packet driver needs a mechanism to signal the next layer of the protocol stack that data is ready, or that an important event has happened; this is the software interrupt's function. The selection of "62" was arbitrary. Any software interrupt between hexadecimal 60 and 80 would have been OK, provided it wasn't already in use by another application or driver.

Trumpet Winsock

Once we have successfully installed the packet driver, protocol stacks written for the API can register themselves with the driver, and share access to the network. Ultimately, we want to add more building blocks so that we can provide Windows Internet client applications with a Winsock interface. As I mentioned before, we have a number of "Winsocks" to choose from. Many contain the IP protocol stack within them, so little else is needed.

One of the most popular Winsock implementations is *Trumpet Winsock*, created by Peter R. Tattum. Trumpet Winsock can be found on numerous FTP sites and bulletin boards, or you can get it from its home site (*ftp://ftp.trumpet.com.au/*). Registration fees are low. Along with some very good documentation, the Trumpet Winsock "zip" file contains the following pieces:*

winsock.dll
    Windows Sockets IP interface

tcpman.exe
    An interface program for Winsock management

---

* Unpack with *pkunzip*.

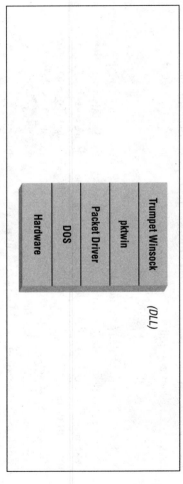

Trumpet Winsock	(DLL)
pktwin	
Packet Driver	
DOS	
Hardware	

Figure 19–5: Trumpet Winsock layer

winpkt.com

    Virtual packet driver interface for Windows

hosts

    An IP host table

services

    A table of IP services in the form of */etc/services*

protocol

    A table of IP protocols

The Winsock interface is implemented as a dynamic link library (DLL), *winsock.dll*. On the bottom, Trumpet Winsock expects to interface with the packet drivers (though it can be used with other network stacks, such as ODI and NDIS, via shims) (see Figure 19-5). The bridge between DOS and Windows is made with a small program called *winpkt.com*, which extends a virtual packet driver interface into the Windows environment, for Winsock to use (Figure 19-6).

Under the interface management program, *tcpman.exe*, IP networking parameters (such as IP address, default route, nameserver) can be set interactively. Let's go over setup, briefly.

Installing Trumpet Winsock

To install Trumpet Winsock, make sure that DOS has a path to the directory where you have unpacked the "zip" file. Add a line like the following to *autoexec.bat*, just below the line where we set the parameters for the packet driver:

```
8003pkdr /e:62 /i:10 /b:300 /r:cc00
winpkt 0x62
```

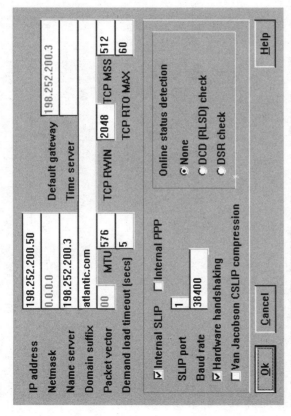

Figure 19–6: tcpman configuration screen

Notice that the software interrupt specification appears here. This will tie the actual packet driver into the virtual packet driver interface. Naturally, you will replace the "62" with whatever software vector you have chosen.

Reboot your computer. You should see the packet driver announce itself, followed by successful installation of *winpkt*. If everything looks OK (no error messages), bring up Windows. From within the File Manager, start the program *tcpman.exe*. The first time it runs (before an ".ini" file exists), *tcpman* will present you with a configuration screen. This is the point at which you would enter the usual IP parameters for the computer—IP address, netmask, default gateway, nameserver, etc. That's all there is to it! Because Winsock is implemented as a DLL, IP networking initiates on demand—as soon as the user brings up an IP application.

ODI-Based Stacks

Because many office environments use Novell Netware for their PC LAN connectivity, IP configurations that are compatible with Netware may be important to you. As you might guess, there are a number of ways to go about combining IP and Netware. For example, we could start with ODI and build our way back up to Trumpet Winsock, if we liked (we will look at this possibility). However, a common solution within the Netware environment is to use Novell's own IP and Winsock implementation, bundled as part of LAN Workplace for DOS (LWP). LAN Workplace installs easily over Netware, and comes with a complete set of tools. The stack is available by itself, as well.

To start, let's look a little more closely at how ODI-based stacks are assembled. The central component is a program known as the *Link Support Layer* (*LSL*), *lsl.com*—part of the Novell ODI driver kit. LSL acts as a go-between for the LAN drivers and the protocol stacks. On the top, LSL provides the ODI interface. Below, it talks to the hardware driver(s) (called *MLID*s in Novell parlance). See Figure 19-7.

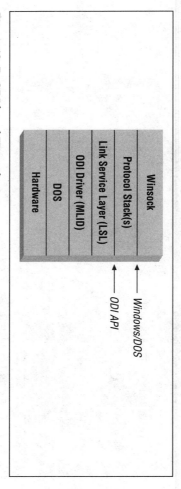

Figure 19-7: ODI-based Winsock

Once LSL has set up shop, the hardware interface driver(s) can be loaded. These remain resident for the life of the DOS session. Last, the protocol stacks are loaded on top of LSL and configured.

Central to MLID, LSL, and protocol stack configuration is a file called *net.cfg*. Similar to a Windows ".ini" file, *net.cfg* is marked off into sections—each dealing with a particular portion of the network configuration. One section might deal with the MLID parameters (device interrupt, address). Another might tell how Netware should be configured. We will look at specific examples shortly.

Installing an IP-only ODI stack

If you are reading this section at all, it probably means that you already have ODI drivers loaded for Netware, in which case IP would be an add-on to your current configuration. For illustration, however, I'm going to approach things a little differently, and *start* with IP and Winsock. From there, we'll take a look at a dual IP and Netware configuration. This way, we can clearly see which pieces provide IP connectivity.

Novell's Netware clients and IP stack are licensed products, so you should be sure that you have the right to use them. Some of the components you need will come with your Netware client kit, so you should already have a start. However, I will tell you where they can be located, in case you need updated copies. From *ftp.novell.com*, you need a copy of *lsl.com*. This can be found in a self-extracting archive, *vlm.exe* (containing Netware *virtual loadable modules*). The exact path may change, so I'll avoid giving it here. Also from Novell's FTP server, obtain a copy of lwpxxx.exe. Be careful: all LWP updates are numbered using the same convention—you should look at the *README* files to be sure that you are getting the IP protocol stack. Last, you need an ODI driver. Typically, manufacturers ship ODI drivers with their network interfaces. If you need a driver for a Novell (NE2000) card, you can find it on Novell's FTP server as well.

As with the packet drivers and Trumpet Winsock, we will load driver software at boot time, within *autoexec.bat*. To begin, we start a copy of LSL, followed by an ODI driver (an *MLID*). Make sure that DOS has a path to each of the programs:

```
LSL.COM
NE2000.COM
```

In this example, I have chosen an NE2000 (Novell) Ethernet card. As with other cards, this one requires I/O addresses and an interrupt assignment. The parameters don't appear here on the command line, however. Instead, the device specifics are given in a file called *net.cfg*, along with configuration parameters for the protocol stack(s):

```
Link Support
     Buffers  8 1500
     MemPool 4096

Link Driver NE2000
     PORT 300
     INT 2
     FRAME Ethernet_II

Protocol TCPIP
     PATH TCP_CFG    D:\NOVELL\TCPIP
     bind            NE2000
     ip_address      198.252.200.2
     ip_router       198.252.200.1
     ip_netmask      255.255.255.0
     tcp_sockets     8
     udp_sockets     8
     raw_sockets     1
     no_bootp
```

Briefly, this copy of *net.cfg* specifies our networking configuration at three levels: hardware (and driver), ODI interface, and protocol stack. The *Link Support* section configures LSL. Here, we choose the amount of memory and buffer to reserve. The *Link Driver* section tells the ODI driver how the Ethernet card has been configured—interrupt 2, with I/O addresses starting at 0x300. You would, of course, choose parameters that match your own configuration. Note too that the Link Driver section also specifies an Ethernet packet (framing) standard; more than one frame type is possible.* The last section is for IP configuration parameters, including IP address, (default) router, and netmask. You can omit the IP parameters, and remove the no_bootp statement if you prefer to use the remote BOOTP configuration, described later. Like LSL and the ODI driver, *net.config* should be located within the DOS path.

If you haven't done so already, explode the *lupxxx.exe* in a directory by itself. A number of files will be produced, including the following:

tcpip.exe

    Novell IP protocol stack

winsock.dll

    Novell Winsock Interface

wlibsock.dll

    Supporting DLL for Winsock

novasyc.exe

    Supporting application for Winsock

You will need a path to the directory, so modify your *autoexec.bat* if necessary. While you are at it, add the two lines mentioned above, plus this one to load the Novell IP protocol stack:

You will need a path to the directory, so modify your *autoexec.bat* if necessary. While you are at it, add the two lines mentioned above, plus this one to load the Novell IP protocol stack:

In addition to the networking components, the IP stack needs a few configuration files. Note the PATH TCP_CFG specification in the *net.cfg* file. This tells TCPIP where the configuration files can be found. The most important of these is *resolv.cfg*, the nameserver specification:

```
domain atlantic.com
nameserver 198.252.200.3
```

That's it! You should be able to run IP applications. Winsock will load automatically when a program calls for it.

Installing IP and netware together

I'll be the first to suggest (and plead) that Netware configuration is outside the scope of our discussion, so let me just show you how *net.cfg* might look when customized for Netware and IP at the same time:

```
LSL.COM
NE2000.COM        ...choose an appropriate driver
TCPIP.EXE
```

* *Ethernet II* is the "old" Ethernet standard. IEEE 802.3 is a later standard, adopted by Novell for Netware (IPX), but largely rejected by the IP community.

```
Link Support
     Buffers      8 1500
     MemPool      4096

Link Driver EXP16ODI
     PORT 300
     FRAME Ethernet_II
     FRAME Ethernet_802.2        (order counts)
     INT 10

NetWare DOS Requester
     FIRST NETWORK DRIVE = F
     NETWARE PROTOCOL = NDS BIND
     PB BUFFER=3
     NAME CONTEXT="OU=LABS.O=ATLANTIC"

Protocol TCPIP
     PATH TCP_CFG     C:\NWCLIENT\TCPIP
     bind             EXP16ODI
     ip_address       198.252.200.22
     ip_router        198.252.200.100
     ip_netmask       255.255.255.0
     tcp_sockets      8
     udp_sockets      8
     raw_sockets      1
     no_bootp
```

In this case, we are using an EtherExpress card, configured at address 0x30fR, interrupt 10. A second protocol stack is represented by the DOS Requester section, and *ipxodi.com*, loaded at boot time. Notice that the IP configuration parameters don't change; IP shares the connection through LSL with Netware, without modification.

Trumpet Winsock and ODI

Remember I mentioned "shims"? Now we get to try one out. Let's say that we want to run ODI and Trumpet Winsock together. Here's the challenge: LSL provides us with an ODI interface, but Trumpet Winsock has been written for packet drivers. A shim called *odipkt.com** is going to act as a go-between for us, translating between the two APIs. That will give us the option of purchasing Trumpet Winsock and running it on top of ODI, in lieu of Novell's Winsock (Figure 19-8) (We'll save some memory too.)

Again, you will need a copy of Trumpet Winsock and the appropriate ODI components, as discussed before. Make sure the programs can be located along a DOS path. In *autoexec.bat*, the commands to load the drivers look like this:

---

* *odipkt* was written by Dan Lanciani, of Gloucester, MA. Pointers to it can be found with the Packet Driver documentation.

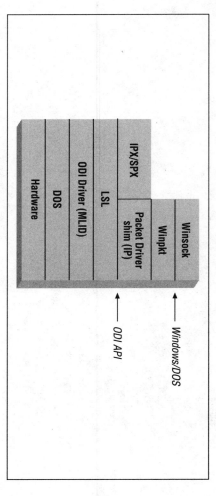

Figure 19-8. Trumpet Winsock on top of ODI

As before, LSL is loaded first, followed by an ODI driver. In this example, the Novel DOS requester starts next, followed by the packet driver shim. Perhaps you remember *winpkt.com* from the previous discussion about Packet Drivers and Trumpet Winsock. Then, we chose a software interrupt of 0x6. Why did I pick 0x69 here? Again, the choice is arbitrary (within bounds), though in this case, *odipkt.com* selects 0x69 by default.

Now let's take a look at *net.cfg*:

```
Link Support
    Buffers    8 1500
    MemPool    4096

Link Driver NE2000
    PORT 300
    INT 2
    FRAME Ethernet_802.2
    FRAME Ethernet_II

NetWare DOS Requester
    FIRST NETWORK DRIVE = F
    NETWARE PROTOCOL = NDS BIND
    PB BUFFER=3
    NAME CONTEXT="OU=LABS.O=ATLANTIC"
```

As before, we chose two frame types—one in support of IPX and another in support of IP. But something is missing: Where is the TCP/IP configuration section? It

```
lsl.com          <--- Novell's Link Support Layer
ne2000.com       <--- choose an appropriate driver
ipxodi.com       <--- Netware DOS requester
odipkt.com       <--- Packet Driver shim
winpkt 0x69      <--- Virtual Packet Driver for Windows
```

doesn't appear in *net.cg* because we aren't using a Novell protocol stack. Rather, the Trumpet Winsock stack is configured via *tcpman.exe*, as described earlier.

NDIS-Based IP Stacks

NDIS is the foundation for Microsoft networking products, including the NetBEUI-based LAN Manager suite that comes with Windows for Workgroups. Microsoft provides products for IPX and IP over NDIS as well. In fact, if you are running Windows for Workgroups (3.11), you can get a complete IP stack for NDIS(3) directly from Microsoft. It installs cleanly via the network setup program, giving you a memory-friendly VxD-based Winsock IP stack (which follows).

Microsoft's plans for IP and Internet connectivity go beyond add-on products. IP—along with IPX and NetBEUI—comes standard within *Windows 95*. And IP is available as a transport, not only for traditional Internet applications, but for LAN (NetBIOS) functions too—file sharing, printing, etc. I could just stop talking about shims and protocol stacks, I suppose, and just talk about menus under Windows 95. However, many companies are still holding back on Windows 95, partly because of the training investments involved in migration, and partly because of the computer resources required. Accordingly, there is still plenty of room for discussion of hand-assembled IP over NDIS.

NDIS-based stacks are constructed in pieces, just like the other configurations we have seen.

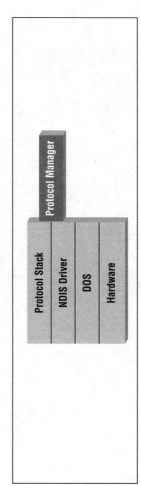

Figure 19-9: NDIS and protocol manager

On the bottom, we have a network interface and an operating system. Above that, we load an NDIS driver, then make one or more NDIS compatible protocol stacks available. A separate program—*Protocol Manager*—oversees the interface of the drivers with the protocol stacks (Figure 19-9). Upon initialization, drivers and protocol stacks are said to *bind*. That is, they trade information about their interfaces so that they can work together. Protocol Manager's initialization file, *protman.ini*, specifies how the binding should take place.

NDIS and Trumpet Winsock

As with ODI, we can adapt an NDIS interface to a packet driver interface via a shim, and add Packet Driver-based stacks above. This is how we would go about adding Trumpet Winsock to a a LAN Manager NetBEUI configuration, for instance. Start with a working NetBEUI installation. I assume that you have the correct NDIS driver installed, and that the network has been tested. From there, we will go about changing a few configuration files, and adding a few pieces.

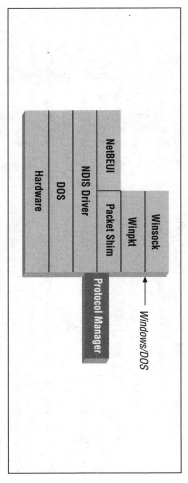

Figure 19-10: Trumpet on NDIS

To begin, we need to locate a shim to bridge the gap between an NDIS API and a Packet Driver API (see Figure 19-10). *DIS_PKT9*, written by Joe R. Doupnik, fits the bill perfectly. And for this particular example, we also need the pieces for Trumpet Winsock, as detailed earlier.* Unzip *dis_pkt9.zip*, and move a copy of *dis_pkt9.dos* into the *Windows* directory. Edit your *autoexec.bat*, adding a couple of lines after the point where the networking software is booted:

```
NET START
NET START NETBIND      <--bind multiple stacks
WINPKT 0x62            <--provide packet driver intfc to Windows
```

Next, edit *system.ini*, found in the *windows* directory, adding "dis_pkt9.dos" to the transports specified on the "[network drivers]" section:

```
transport:...,dis_pkt9.dos
```

Edit *protocol.ini*, also in the *windows* directory, adding a few lines to the "[network setup]" section. In the example that follows, I am using an NDIS driver identified with an NE2000 Ethernet interface "clone" (hence the name

---

* You can find *dis_pkt9.zip* on a number of sites, including *ftp.cdrom.com*.

ms$ne2clone). Enter a substitute for the NDIS driver you are using. The name should be clear from the NetBEUI declaration nearby:

```
[network.setup]
version=0x3110
netcard=ms$ne2clone,1,MS$NE2CLONE,3
transport=ms$nwlinkmb,MS$NWLINK
transport=ms$ndishlp,MS$NDISHLP
transport=ms$netbeui,NETBEUI
transport=pktdrv,PKTDRV              <-- add this
lana0=ms$ne2clone,1,ms$nwlinkmb
lana1=ms$ne2clone,1,ms$ndishlp
lana2=ms$ne2clone,1,ms$netbeui
lana3=ms$ne2clone,1,pktdrv          <-- add this
```

Below that, add a whole "[PKTDRV]" section to *protocol.ini*:

```
[PKTDRV]
drivername=pktdrv$
bindings=MS$NE2CLONE
intvec=0x62
novell=n
LANABASE=0
```

Within the Windows Network Setup section, be sure you have chosen the "RealMode and Extended Mode NDIS driver" for your card. Last, see that your *config.sys* loads *ifshlp.sys*. For instance:

```
DEVICEHIGH=C:\WINDOWS\IFSHLP.SYS
```

We are now ready to configure Trumpet Winsock. The rest of the setup is exactly the same as described in the section on packet driver-based stacks, discussed earlier: unpack Winsock along a path accessible via the DOS path, and set the network parameters within *tcpman.exe*.

Microsoft's IP stack

As I mentioned earlier, Microsoft has a 32-bit IP stack, Winsock, and a few IP applications available as a free upgrade for users of Windows for Workgroups. The software has built-in support for NetBIOS over IP, including client support for *Windows Internet Name Service* (WINS). Via WINS, computers register themselves with a NetBIOS Name Server (if one exists) as they become available on the network. Naming is dynamic—machines may come and go, claiming names dynamically.

Also included in the software is support for the *Dynamic Host Configuration Protocol* (DHCP). DHCP provides a facility a computer can use to discover its environment—netmask, default router, etc.— at boot time. This will allow machines to move from network to network, without IP parameter reconfiguration. We will talk about this a little bit more later.

Of course, to support NetBIOS Name Services, or to supply host configuration information, you will need servers on the network. As you might expect, such services are available on Windows for Workgroups and Windows NT servers. They're available other places too. You might take a look at Samba, and UNIX-based SMB server and client suite for LAN Manager. Samba will allow you to mix UNIX resources and Lan Manager resources over IP. We will talk about UNIX-based DHCP in a little while.*

Installing Microsoft's 32-bit IP stack

Configuration of Microsoft's WFW IP stack is straightforward, provided Windows for Workgroups 3.11 is already loaded. If you have somebody else's IP stack and Winsock on the machine, you should unconfigure them before you begin, and change the DOS path so that the former components (particularly *winsock.dll*) are not mistakenly activated.

Begin installation by retrieving a copy of self-extracting archive *wfwt32.exe* from *ftp.microsoft.com*. Explode the archive in a directory by itself. I could go over the steps in long-winded detail, but perhaps it would be more efficient if I just mentioned that you will find a complete set of instructions for installing the IP stack in the Windows help file *mtcpip32.hlp*. Be sure not to specify DHCP IP configuration unless you have a DHCP running on the network. Otherwise, choose IP address, default router, etc., as appropriate.

IP on Windows 95

Windows 95 ships with a Winsock IP stack. Before you can configure the stack, you will need to add a driver for your network card, and you will need to bind the IP protocol stack to the driver. Windows 95 may offer you configuration menus the first time it encounters your network interface. You can also go back later, to perform configuration by hand: start by going into the *Control Panel*. Choose the *Network* icon (Figure 19-11).

Under the configuration menu, see if your network card is listed. If it isn't, press the *Add* button, and then choose *Adapter*. Your network card should appear as one of the choices in the list. In a similar fashion, add IP (*TCP/IP*) from the *Protocol* list. Last, go back to the adapter selection and "bind" TCP/IP to the card (Figure 19-12).

Once the adapter and protocol stack are installed, you will need to enter the usual assortment of parameters: IP address, default gateway, domain, and nameserver.

* Retrieve Samba from *ftp://nimbus.anu.edu.au/pub/tridge/samba*.

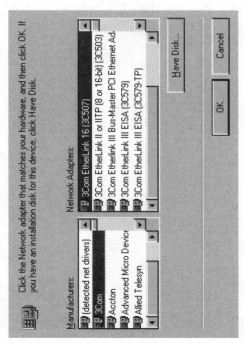

Figure 19–11: Add screen

Spots for these can be found under *Properties*, within the TCP/IP setup area. Alternatively, the machine can learn its configuration from DHCP, discussed later.*

IP Under OS/2

Like Microsoft, IBM is making "networking out of the box" a central part of their strategy for new and upcoming OS/2 releases. A solid IP stack has long been available separately for OS/2 2.1. The newer *WARP* release of OS/2 (Version 3) comes with an IP stack as part of its standard fare.

The assembly of IBM's networking software is similar to some of the configurations we examined earlier. At the bottom, we have network interfaces coupled into drivers that provide a NDIS API for the protocol stacks loaded above them (see Figure 19-13).† In the case of IP, the higher level networking functions—sockets, name services, application support—are supported by a set of Dynamic Link Libraries (DLLs), kept in a subdirectory *\TCPIP\DLL*:

so32dll.dll
    32-bit socket services

tcp32dll.dll
    32-bit name services, and miscellaneous functions

---

* If you need more help, an excellent resource for Windows 95 configuration information is *http://www.windows95.com.*

† Or it could be ODI, for Netware.

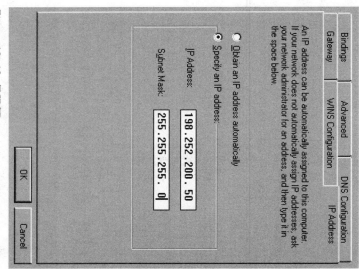

Figure 19-12: TCP/IP setup

`tcpipdll.dll`
16-bit IP support for older applications

`ftpapi.dll`
Special support for FTP

A *winsock.dll* is present too, allowing most Windows Internet browsers to run directly under OS/2. Support for some networking protocols, such as NetBEUI, depends upon having Windows loaded in addition to OS/2.*

IP on the Macintosh

As with PC networking, there is a world of possibilities for networking the Macintosh. The good news is that basic pieces—the IP networking layers—are ably handled by just one package: *MacTCP*, available from Apple Computer.

MacTCP used to be freely bundled with networking applications. At the time of the release of System 7.1, MacTCP became a product for sale. Now, with the

---

* For a comprehensive (and refreshing) discussion of IP networking under OS/2, visit the Web site "PC Lube and Tune" (*http://pclt.cis.yale.edu/pclt/default.html*), maintained by Howard Gilbert.

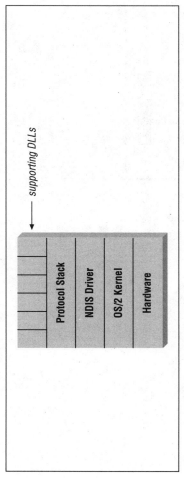

Figure 19-13: NDIS on OS/2

release of System 7.5, it is shipped with operating system software. Depending on the operating system release you are running, you may need to purchase MacTCP (or you may want to upgrade to System 7.5). A single user MacTCP license is priced in the neighborhood of $50.

Of course, a network interface is necessary. The new Power Macintoshes are being shipped with Ethernet interfaces already installed. To connect to a local area network, you will have to buy an adapter (a pig-tail) from Apple. Older Macintoshes and Powerbooks may not have a network interface, in which case you will have to purchase one. Depending on the model, a SCSI-based Ethernet may do the trick, or you may need to install an Ethernet card directly into the machine.

MacTCP Installation

MacTCP comes on a single floppy, which includes components above and beyond the basic networking software. For example, there is a network monitoring agent (SNMP), as well as network support tools. For our purposes, MacTCP is all we need, although installation of the other pieces will do us no harm.

Insert the disk in your floppy drive, open the associated folder, and double-click the installer icon. Choose *install* from the options available (Figure 19-14). (If some portion of the installation gives you trouble, you may go into the *custom* configuration submenu and choose to install MacTCP alone.) Reboot.

When the machine comes back up, select the *Control Panels* under the Apple menu and double-click the icon for MacTCP. You will be presented with a panel that shows a (zeroed) network address, and a *More . . .* button. At the top, you will see icons for each of the interfaces MacTCP can choose from (typically two—Localtalk and Ethernet). Choose an appropriate interface (probably Ethernet). When done, select the "more" button at the bottom to get to the IP configuration menu.

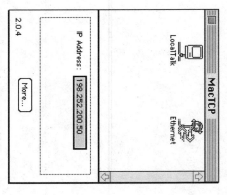

Figure 19–14: First MacTCP screen

There are a number of choices to make, but most of them will be clear to you (now that you've gotten this far into the book). For review, however, let's talk about the most important items. In the upper left-hand corner, you may choose how your Macintosh will learn of its network address; the choices are "dynamically," "from the server," or "manually" (you type it in). Let's assume that you know the address, and are going to type it in by hand. Select *manually* from the list of options.

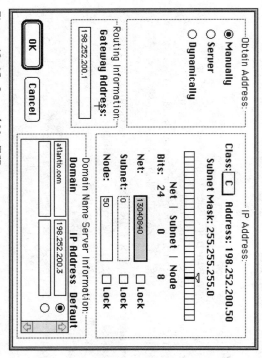

Figure 19–15: Second MacTCP screen

In the upper right, choose your network class (A, B, or C) (see Figure 19-15). The slider-bar associated with the network mask will move into its default position.

Move the slider, if necessary, to accommodate a subnetworked environment. In the lower left, choose a default gateway. This is the router or host that knows how to move traffic beyond your local area network to the rest of the world.

On the right, choose a nameserver or nameservers for your organization. If you are behind a firewall, be sure to choose a nameserver that serves local address information, rather than one that serves addresses back out to the Internet. Don't forget to *check* the radio button next to the nameserver selection in order to enable it.

When you have finished, select *OK* from the panel options. You will be returned to the first panel you saw when you invoked MacTCP from the *Control Panels*. At this time, you can fill in your IP address in the box provided (if you checked manual addressing). Close the window, and you're done.

Dynamic Address Assignment

Sometimes, network administrators would prefer to mete out addresses from a central location, rather than visit each desktop. This makes sense: after all, you can distribute the IP protocol stack via a LAN file system. It would be a shame to have to then go to each PC and fool with the configuration files.

In the IP world, there have been two common mechanisms for assigning addresses from central locations. The first, *Reverse ARP* (RARP), operates upon MAC-level broadcasts. A booting computer knows its own low-level MAC address, but may need to discover its IP address. The client boots up, broadcasts a RARP request, which is (hopefully) answered by a server. Having learned its IP address, the client may then interact at the IP level to gather the other things it needs—a default gateway setting, a domain name, or even an operating system image. RARP isn't used much anymore; it has been superseded by configuration discovery protocols, like BOOTP, that work at the IP level.

BOOTP (Bootstrap Protocol),* solves the same basic problem as RARP: it gives a client a mechanism for discovering its own identity. The client comes up and broadcasts a BOOTP request, hoping that a BOOTP *server* will answer (Figure 19-16). When a response *does* come back, it may include multiple configuration parameters—an IP address, nameserver address, domain name, and more.

The BOOTP conversation begins with an IP broadcast; the client issues a scatter-shot message that says: "I'm here. Someone send me my configuration." Depending on the circumstances, the client may already know a little bit about itself. It may already know its own IP address, for instance, but may be in need of other

---

* rfc951

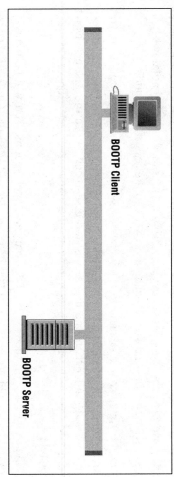

Figure 19-16: BOOTP client and server

settings, such as a default gateway. In other cases, the client knows nothing. Multiple BOOTP servers may be listening to the broadcast, and multiple servers may answer the call. A server can respond by one of two methods; it can return the configuration data to the MAC address of the requesting client (perhaps by merely sending an IP datagram), or it can broadcast the results onto the network segment on which the client resides.

Of course, your environment may be larger than a single network. Out of the box, this could cause a problem for BOOTP: *broadcasts* cannot be replicated across routers (without the risk of flooding every segment on the planet). To get around the problem, BOOTP supports the notion of a BOOTP *forwarder*—a facility that will enable a router to forward the BOOTP requests it hears on one interface over to a second interface (Figure 19-17). When the BOOTP server responds, it will do so with a routable address; broadcasts are not needed in the reverse direction.

How does the server know what address to assign to the client making the request? With BOOTP, a central table (typically */etc/bootptab*) maps low-level MAC addresses to IP addresses and other IP parameters. An administrator, then, has to gather MAC addresses for all of the PCs on the network and assign each a space in the table.

```
generic:hd=/tmp:bf=null:\
        :ds=198.252.200.3:\
        :sm=255.255.255.0:\
        :gw=198.252.200.1:\

# Define all individual entries.
pc1:ht=1:ha=08002b2a5ec2:ip=198.252.200.11:tc=generic:
pc2:ht=1:ha=0020af37dbbe:ip=198.252.200.12:tc=generic:
pc3:ht=1:ha=00aa0061aa62:ip=198.252.200.13:tc=generic:
pc4:ht=1:ha=0020afe518eb:ip=198.252.200.14:tc=generic:
pc5:ht=1:ha=0020af385650:ip=198.252.200.15:tc=generic:
```

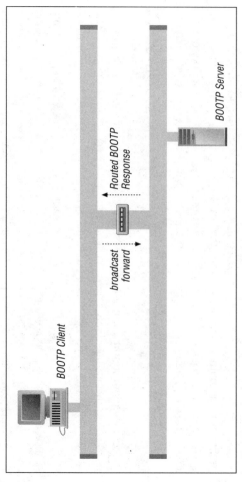

Figure 19–17: BOOTP forwarding

This clipping shows how *bootptab* might look. Some generic settings—the domain name server (ds), subnet mask (sm), and default gateway (gw) are grouped under the label generic. Following that, five PCs are listed: the hardware type (ht) specifies Ethernet; the hardware address (ha) gives the PC's MAC address; the IP address is assigned from the ip field. Many other fields are possible (see references later in this chapter).

At one time, BOOTP was used extensively as a stepping stone to booting diskless workstations and X terminals from remote hosts. BOOTP could return the name of a TFTP (Trivial File Transfer Protocol) server and the name of an appropriate operating system image. The client would subsequently download and boot the image. Costs of computing have changed, of course: one and a half gigabytes of disk is about the same price as eight megabytes of memory, and diskless workstations have become an antique notion. For this reason, BOOTP is now more likely to be used for configuration discovery than as an avenue for remote booting.

DHCP

Dynamic Host Configuration Protocol (DHCP)* is a newer protocol that extends BOOTP to provide more flexible address allocation capabilities, and to give clients the ability to entertain responses from multiple servers. Notice that with BOOTP, we statically map MAC addresses to IP addresses, via a table. With DHCP, we can allow the servers to pull addresses from a pool and even assign them on a temporary basis. This becomes important when the number of available addresses is

---

* rfc1541

smaller than the client community, or in cases where the client community is on the move. Consider that if a PC is plugged into one network today and another tomorrow, it will have to change IP addresses, DHCP provides automatic reconfiguration without system administration.

DHCP is backwards compatible with BOOTP. This means that a DHCP server can provide IP information to DHCP and BOOTP clients alike. Furthermore, BOOTP forwarders can pass along DHCP requests and responses, without modification.

DHCP/BOOTP Servers

You can find BOOTP and DHCP servers in multiple environments. A DHCP server is included with Windows NT. Microsoft IP stacks support DHCP natively, so if you already have a Windows for Workgroups environment then distributing IP configurations via DHCP will be straightforward.

UNIX implementations of BOOTP and DHCP servers are available from several sources. All of these started from the same Stanford/CMU BOOTP source, with improvements and DHCP functionality added incrementally. Up-to-date BOOTP code is available from *ftp://ftp.mc.com/pub/bootp-2.4.3.tar.Z*. Code with DHCP additions, including dynamic address assignment, can be found at *ftp://ftp.ntplx.net/pub/networking/bootp/bootp-DD2.4.3.tar.gz*.

IP over IPX

You can realize the goal of assigning IP addresses from a central location by means other than BOOTP and DHCP. There are a few products that go about the IP-to-the-desktop problem differently than those we have considered so far—particularly in the Novell world.

Instead of providing each desktop client with its own IP protocol stack, these "gateways" package IP transport traffic (TCP, UDP, ICMP) into IPX, direct the traffic to a central server, and then convert it to full IP from there. The gateway may either be an NLM running on a Netware Server or it may be a separate IPX/IP-based host. Applications making use of the IPX/IP conversion don't know that they aren't speaking IP directly, because the API is exactly the same. As with the IP protocol stacks we looked at before, IPX/IP clients are supplied with a Winsock layer. Underneath, however, the IP transport-layer traffic is absconded with by IPX, sent to the gateway, and repackaged into IP (Figure 19-18).

At this point, you may be wondering what any of this has to do with IP address management. It looks as if the real story is that you can distribute IP connectivity to the desktop without actually distributing IP. That in itself is important, but I bring the subject up in this section because one of the biggest side benefits of encapsulated IP over IPX is that address management (actually, user management)

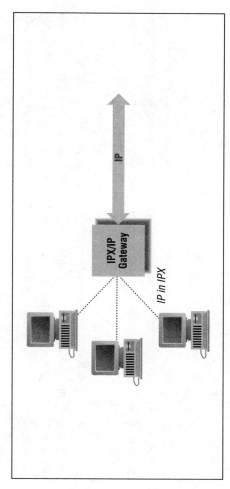

Figure 19–18: IP encapsulated under IPX

is centralized. From the IPX/IP gateway, the administrator can assign connectivity privileges to individual IPX clients—as with BOOTP and DHCP. But here's the important difference: connectivity is managed on a *user* basis, not as a function of the MAC address. That means I can sit at my desk today and at your desk tomorrow, but still be known to the IPX/IP gateway as the same user. Consider that when using MAC addresses, as with BOOTP, DHCP, or hand-configuration, the (IP) identity of the user is tied to the PC. If I send the secret sauce recipe out from your computer, people may accuse you.

IP/IPX gateways provide a single conduit to the rest of the Internet. From outside the IP/IPX gateway, traffic emanates from one, several, or many IP addresses—depending on the brand and the way the administrator has chosen to configure it. This gives the gateway some of the same qualities as a proxy firewall (see Chapter 16, *Network Security*): it hides the network usage patterns of individual IPX/IP clients; it relieves the administrator from having to provide registered IP addresses; and it provides a central point of logging and access control. IPX/IP gateway products include *NOV*IX*, from Firefox Communications (*http://www.firefox.com/product/novix.htm*), and *IWare Connect*, from Quarterdeck Corporation, Inc. (*http://www.qdeck.com/qdeck/products/iware_connect/*).

Dynamic Address Management Trade-Offs

There are clear benefits to doling out IP addresses dynamically—via BOOTP or DHCP, for instance—or to hiding multiple clients behind a single address—as with an IP/IPX gateway. One benefit is that a smaller number of IP resources can be spread out more efficiently. This may be important if IP addresses are in short supply. Furthermore, dynamic address assignment, or IP encapsulation, allows the user community to be more mobile; computers can reconfigure themselves.

There can be downsides too, however—particularly with respect to network management and security. It all boils down to being able to see who-is-doing-what. An application proxy firewall, for instance, typically implements access policies based upon IP addresses. If (as is the case with dynamic address allocation) users' addresses change arbitrarily, or if a single address represents multiple users, it can be difficult to log and filter traffic with any degree of certainty. Furthermore, network management tools will only be partially helpful in isolating problems if the network is allowed to spontaneously re-map hosts. Neither of these reasons should be strong enough to dissuade you from a dynamic address policy or IP/IPX gateway, if it otherwise makes sense to you. However, you should factor them into your decision.

A

Access Lists

Here are three separate sets of access lists, for three separate routers. All do essentially the same thing:

• Deny spoofed inbound connections (to 198.252.200.0 and 127.0)

• Allow inbound ICMP (all types)

• Permit connections from a specific NNTP server network (192.48.96.0) to a specific server (198.252.200.3)

• Permit mail, WWW, and FTP connections to one particular server (198.252.200.3)

• Allow DNS zone transfers from a specific host (198.252.200.3) to a specific host (192.65.177.3)

• Allow inbound UDP and TCP traffic above ports 1023

These samples accompany the discussion in Chapter 16, *Network Security*. Note that they are *not* as rigorous as some access list configurations you might come up with. Nor do they illustrate the range of possibilities for any of these routers. Accordingly, you should read Chapter 16, and your router documentation, to determine what *your* lists should look like. In particular, note that I left a huge UDP hole above 1023, and that I allow all ICMP through (just to make sure that you don't copy the samples verbatim). For many sites, this would be unacceptable.

cisco

The first set applies to a cisco router with inbound traffic through the serial interface. List application takes place in two steps: you assemble the list, then apply it to the interface:

```
Router> en
Router# conf t
Enter configuration commands, one per line.  End with CNTL/Z.

<access lists commands shown below>

Router(config)# int s 0
Router(config-if)# ip access-group 101 in
Router(config-if)#ex
Router(config)#ex
Router#ex
```

Be sure to test the configuration before committing it to flash memory.

```
!
no ip source-route
!
! Prevent spoofing:
!
access-list 101 deny ip 127.0.0.1 0.0.0.0 0.0.0.0 255.255.255.255
access-list 101 deny ip 198.252.200.0 0.0.0.255 0.0.0.0 255.255.255.255
!
! Allow ping, etc.
!
access-list 101 permit icmp 0.0.0.0 255.255.255.255 0.0.0.0 255.255.255.255
!
! Permit a newsfeed from 192.48.96.0:
!
access-list 101 permit tcp 192.48.96.0 0.0.0.255 198.252.200.3 0.0.0.0 eq 119
!
! Allow SMTP, WWW, FTP access from outside:
!
access-list 101 permit tcp 0.0.0.0 255.255.255.255 198.252.200.3 0.0.0.0 eq 25
access-list 101 permit tcp 0.0.0.0 255.255.255.255 198.252.200.3 0.0.0.0 eq 80
access-list 101 permit tcp 0.0.0.0 255.255.255.255 198.252.200.3 0.0.0.0 eq 21
!
! Allow Zone Transfers from secondary server:
!
access-list 101 permit tcp 192.65.177.3 0.0.0.0 198.252.200.3 0.0.0.0 eq 53
!
! Let DNS Queries Through
!
access-list 101 permit udp 0.0.0.0 255.255.255.255 198.252.200.3 0.0.0.0 eq 53
!
! Enable Return traffic
!
access-list 101 permit tcp 0.0.0.0 255.255.255.255 198.252.200.0 0.0.0.255 gt 1023
access-list 101 permit udp 0.0.0.0 255.255.255.255 198.252.200.0 0.0.0.255 gt 1023
```

Morning Star

In this case, the access lists are being applied to all traffic coming in through the serial interface of a Morning Star router. Again, you may desire a more ornate set of access lists, particularly if you have a firewall router with multiple LAN ports.

```
default
#
# Prohibit source routing
#
        pass    !ip-opt=srcrt/unreach=srcfail
#
# Allow ICMP
#
        icmp
#
# Allow NNTP access from news feed:
#
        nntp/recv/syn/192.48.96.0
#
# Allow SMTP, WWW, FTP access from outside:
#
        smtp/recv/syn/198.252.200.3
        www/recv/syn/198.252.200.3
        ftp/recv/syn/198.252.200.3
#
# Allow ftp-data (return connections)
#
        ftp-data/syn/recv/198.252.200.3
#
# Allow Zone Transfers from secondary server:
#
        domain/tcp/syn/recv/192.65.177.3
#
# let DNS queries through
#
        domain/udp
#
# Enable Return Traffic
#
        !1-1023/tcp/syn/recv/unreach=host
        1024-65535/udp
        !1-1023/udp/recv/unreach=port
```

This access list is applied to the router by copying the rules into a file named *Filter*, and then sending a **kill -ALRM** to the *pppd* or *frd* running on the router:

```
% ps aux
<process list is returned; find PID for pppd or frd>
% kill -ALRM <pid>
```

If you make a mistake, you can reboot the router; access list configuration won't be saved until you issue a **save Filter** command.

Livingston

This is a set of lists for a Livingston IRX router. Access list rules are applied to a single LAN port; however, as with the Morning Star router, you may actually have two. Note too that no rules protect the serial port in this case.

```
#
# ------------ from ------------|------------ to ------
#
add filter port1.out
#
# These rules disallow address spoofing:
#
set filter port1.out 1 deny   198.252.200.0/24 0.0.0.0/0
set filter port1.out 2 deny   127.0.0.1/32 0.0.0.0/0
#
# Permit newsfeed from 192.48.96.0
#
set filter port1.out 3 permit  192.48.96.0/24 198.252.200.3/32 tcp dst eq 119
#
# Allow SMTP, WWW, FTP access from outside:
#
set filter port1.out 4 permit  0.0.0.0/0 198.252.200.3/32 tcp dst eq 25
set filter port1.out 5 permit  0.0.0.0/0 198.252.200.3/32 tcp dst eq 80
set filter port1.out 6 permit  0.0.0.0/0 198.252.200.3/32 tcp dst eq 21
#
# Allow Zone Transfers from secondary server:
#
set filter port1.out 7 permit  192.65.177.3/32 198.252.200.3/32 tcp dst eq 53
#
# Let DNS Queries Through
#
set filter port1.out 8 permit  0.0.0.0/0 198.252.200.3/32 udp dst eq 53
#
# Enable Return Traffic
#
set filter port1.out 9 permit  0.0.0.0/0 198.252.200.3/32 tcp established
#
# Allow inbound ftp
#
set filter port1.out 10 permit  0.0.0.0/0 198.252.200.3/32 tcp dst eq 21
#
# Allow return ftp connections
#
set filter port1.out 11 permit  0.0.0.0/0 198.252.200.3/32 tcp src eq 20 dst gt 1023
#
# Open a wide whole for UDP above 1023.
#
set filter port1.out 12 permit  0.0.0.0/0 198.252.200.3/32 udp dst gt 1023
#
# Allow ICMP
#
set filter port1.out 13 permit  0.0.0.0/0 0.0.0.0/0 icmp
```

```
#
# Do it.
#
```

set ether1 ofilter port1.out

This set of lists has a couple of extra twists to it. In particular, note that we allow inbound TCP traffic to *any* port, as long as the connection is already established; no SYN packets are allowed in. In tandem, FTP return connections (port 20) are allowed to ports above 1023. After testing, you save this configuration by issuing a **save all** command.

B

Calculating Your Bandwidth Requirements

This appendix is a supplement to Chapter 2, *Service Options*. The goal is to develop a bandwidth requirement estimate based upon an anticipated mix of interactive and batched Internet traffic. If you asked me whether everyone who gets an Internet connection goes through this kind of analysis, I'd have to say no. Furthermore, I'd be reluctant to label the analysis pure science. However, it can help you identify where and when you will need bandwidth to the Internet. See Chapter 2 for more details.

Bandwidth Requirements Worksheet

```
1)  News distribution totals            _____
2)  Personal electronic mail traffic    _____
3)  Mailing lists                        _____
4)  Other background traffic             _____
5)  Batch total                       + _____

6)  Incoming FTP                        _____ a _____ b
7)  Outgoing FTP                        _____ a _____ b
8)  Inbound Web/Gopher                   _____ a _____ b
9)  Outbound browser traffic             _____ a _____ b
10) Other interactive traffic            _____ a _____ b
11) Interactive total                 + _____ a _____ b

12) Acceptable transfer rate (14.4 Kbs?)  _____
13) Batch traffic demand (choose hour)    _____

14) Transfer time                         _____
15) Expected hits (hour)                  _____
16) Transfer fraction                     _____
17) Concurrent hits (hour)                _____
18) Interactive traffic demand (hour)   + _____

19) Total traffic demand (hour)           _____
```

Line 1—News

Are you planning to have a USENET newsfeed? A full feed runs nearly 600 Mbytes per day. Partial distributions are approximately as shown in Table B-1.

Table B-1: Usenet News Daily Transfers

Hierarchy	Size (Daily Mb)
alt	370
rec	45
comp	25
soc	16
misc	10
sci	5
talk	3
news	1

Accumulate the news distribution totals that apply to you, and record that figure as your background load, then enter it on line 1. We'll add more to it soon. Assume that any unlisted news hierarchies amount to a couple hundred kilobytes per day.

Line 2—Personal Electronic Mail Traffic

Unless part of your business is predicated upon electronic mail, you can probably leave personal email loading out of the calculations. Though you may feel that a lot of electronic mail is being generated and received, the amount of mail each person can create and consume in a single day is actually fairly limited. The exception would be where a few members of your group subscribe to a large number of mailing lists—far more than they can digest. In that case, a personal mailbox can accumulate from one to five megabytes each day.

If you believe that a large amount of personal mail will be exchanged, estimate the number of megabytes generated and received during the day, and enter that figure on line 2.

Line 3—Mailing Lists

If you are planning to run a mailing list server, go through the following procedure for each list being sponsored. Estimate the total number of subscribers you expect, and the number of these who you expect will post something on a given day (assume 2 percent if you don't know). Also, estimate average size of each message posted (assume 2000 bytes if you are unsure). From these numbers, calculate the load contribution from each list:

```
list_contribution = posting_size * number_subscribers * number_postings
```

Tally the contributions of the mailing lists together, and enter the result on line 3. Add this to the background load.

Line 4 — Other Background Traffic

If your organization will be making other kinds of significant batch exchanges, enter the total estimated daily size on line 4. Examples of such traffic might be automated file transfers, database synchronization, or remote data exchange.

Line 5 — Batch Total

Add the amounts recorded on lines 1 through 4, and enter the result on line 5.

Line 6 — Incoming FTP

We are now starting to consider traffic that falls into the interactive category. As with other information offerings, it can be a little tricky to estimate the load attributable to (anonymous) FTP transfers; you can't know in advance how popular your site will be. A few questions are in order. How specialized are the programs or files you will be offering? Do they interest a very small community, or will they be something that the whole world wants? For specialized materials, assume a handful of transfers per day. If you are making pictures of naked humans available, assume a tremendous number of hits daily (perhaps thousands). Multiply the expected number of FTP "hits" by the size of the files, to come up with an initial interactive load.* Enter this total on line **6a**. Record the estimated number of hits on line **6b**.

Line 7 — Outgoing FTP

Of course, anonymous file transfer is a two-way street. There are probably a number of people within your organization who will be using FTP to retrieve programs and documents from other Internet sites. Guess the number of active Internet users, and figure that they will account for an additional 200 kilobytes of file transfer per day, per person (average). Multiply the number or users by the estimated transfer size, and enter the result on line **7a**. Record the estimated number of hits on line **7b**.

Line 8 — Inbound Web/Gopher

As with anonymous FTP, the volume of Web or gopher traffic is related to a couple of parameters, namely the number of pointers sprinkled about the net and the appeal of the information that you have to offer. A site selling computer-related items, such as books or software, for example, can expect to receive a couple hundred hits a day. Servers with public service information may receive from fifty hits to many thousands of hits a day, depending on how broadly useful the documents are.

---

* A "hit" means a page request. One person browsing may account for several hits.

Multiply the estimated number of hits by the average size of the pages being offered. You can assume 2 kilobytes for text, plus 20 kilobytes per graphic. MPEG movies or .WAV files can amount to megabytes. Enter the transfer totals (size times number of hits) result on line **8a**. Record the number of hits on line **8b**.

Line 9—Outbound Browser Traffic

Again, as mentioned before, we have to also consider the people on the inside of your organization who will be pulling Web documents in from the outside. Assume that an active Web user's browsing takes him or her to about thirty pages a day (average). This will add an interactive load of perhaps one megabyte per day per user. Enter the estimated number of hits (number of people times number of pages) on line **9b**. Record the transfer total (size times number of hits) on line **9a**.

Line 10—Things Unaccounted For

Other activities consume network bandwidth as well. Some are related to the interactive and batched applications we've considered already (all network transactions include some overhead). There are some applications we haven't accounted for at all (such as DNS traffic, telnet sessions). Consider whether any unnamed interactive activities are significant. Record traffic totals and number of hits on lines **10a** and **10b**.

Line 11—Interactive Total

Add the amounts recorded on lines **6a** through **10a**, and enter the result on line **11a**. Likewise, accumulate the total of lines **6b** through **10b** onto line **11b**. This gives us a figure for the total expected interactive demand, and a total hit count for interactive transfers.

Line 12—Eye of Newt

Now we will take the interactive and batched traffic estimates and apply them to a template. This should help us determine the amount of bandwidth necessary for your connection. We have to pull a couple of numbers from thin air, though. One is a subjective measure of what constitutes "acceptable" interactive speed. I suggest that 14.4 Kbit/s (the speed of a V.32bis modem) is a reasonable standard for bearable interactive transfer—by today's reckoning, anyway. It's true that many people have higher speed connections, and that for some applications 14.4 Kbs would be far too restrictive. However, for communications with the generic Web site, this will do. Adjust the number as you like, and enter it on line **12**.

Line 13—Hourly Background Contribution

As I mentioned earlier, the traffic curve for Internet activity (within the continental United States) mounds up in the middle of the day. For planning purposes, we will assume that your background traffic will follow a similar curve, as depicted in Figure B-1.

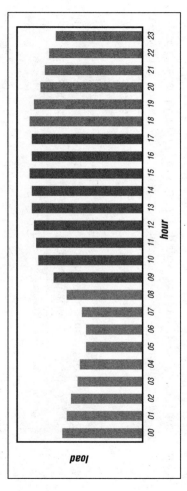

Figure B-1: Daily activity

The X-axis represents time. The Y-axis shows bits per second (bandwidth). The area under the curve tells us how many bits are being moved. If we take the daily traffic load, divide by 24 hours, scale, and multiply by your background traffic demand, we come up with a picture of your own organization's batch requirements.

Table B-2: Scale Factors by Hour (scale_factor(hour)) (EST)

Hour	Factor	Hour	Factor
00	.037	12	.050
01	.035	13	.051
02	.033	14	.051
03	.030	15	.052
04	.029	16	.051
05	.026	17	.051
06	.026	18	.052
07	.028	19	.050
08	.035	20	.047
09	.041	21	.045
10	.048	22	.043
11	.049	23	.040

It might be a bit of overkill for us to generate an array of 24 load figures, and carry them through the rest of this template. Usually you will be interested in a particular hour of the day anyway—often the peak hour, 10:00 a.m. In the interest of expediency, let's skinny our calculations down to consider just one particular hour. You pick the hour. Of course, if you would like the complete curve, you will have to run through the following exercise for each of the 24 hours of the day.

To create the target hour's contribution to the background load, multiply the number of bytes of batched traffic already calculated (line **5**) by eight (8) to get kilobits. Multiply this figure by the appropriate scaling factor (these are for the eastern U.S.) from Table B-2, and divide by 3600 seconds (1 hour).

```
batched_demand(hour) = 8 * total_batch_loading * scale_factor(hour) / 3600
```

Enter the result on line **13**. This is our adjusted background load for each hour of the day. If you plan to shift some of the batch processing off to the evening hours, you may adjust the shape of the curve and scaling appropriately.

Line 14—Interactive Loading

As with batched transfers, interactive transfers also mound up in the late morning. The difference (if any) is that the hump may be more pronounced, particularly if people within your organization are doing some Internet browsing of their own at the same hours that people are visiting your site from the outside world.

We could just tally the daily network demand for interactive traffic and multiply by scale factors, as we did a moment ago for batched traffic, but this won't tell us exactly what we want to know. Remember, we are trying to provide each user with at least 14.4 Kbit/s (or whatever you entered on line **12**) of bandwidth. This means that if two people are likely to be transferring data at the same time, then we will want to have 28.8 Kbit/s of headroom at our disposal. (Of course, there's no good way to make sure it is distributed evenly between them . . .). We need a way to estimate the spare bandwidth necessary to accommodate multiple concurrent hits.

To begin, let's make a pessimistic estimate of the amount of time each interactive hit is going to take. You can arrive at this by summing the total number of bytes tallied for interactive transfers (line 11a), then dividing by the total number of "hits" (line 11b) expected. This will give us the number of bytes per hit.

```
bytes_per_hit = total_interactive_loading / total_estimated_hit_count
```

Multiply this by eight (8) to get kilobits, then divide that figure by 14,400 (or whatever rate you chose) to give us the amount of time (*transfer_time*) it will take to make the transfer.

Enter the transfer time on line **14**.

In Table B-2, each hour has a scale factor associated with it. If you multiply the total number of hits expected during a 1-day period (line **11**) by one of the hourly

```
transfer_time = bytes_per_hit * 8 / 14,400
```

scale factors (say 10:00 a.m.), you obtain a figure for the number of hits expected during that hour.

```
expected_hits(hour) = scale_factor(hour) * total_estimated_hit_count
```

Record the result on line **15**. We would like to use this figure to derive an estimate for the number of hits that are likely to occur on top of one another, so that we can plan how many multiples of 14.4 Kbit/s we will have to make available.

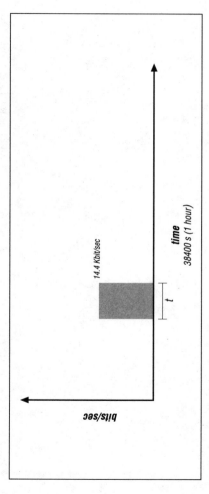

Figure B–2: Size of a bit

One crude way to estimate the size of a hit is to calculate the "width" (in time) of the transfer associated with each hit, and then calculate how many total hits are likely to occur during one such period. To do this, calculate the fraction of an hour each transfer represents, by dividing the transfer time (line **14**) by 3600:

```
transfer_fraction = transfer_time / 3600
```

Record the transfer fraction value on line **16**. Now multiply this figure by the number of hits expected in the hour (line **15**) to arrive at an estimate of the number of hits that are likely to come in concurrently during that hour.

```
concurrent_hits(hour) = transfer_fraction * expected_hits(hour)
```

Round this value up to the nearest whole number and record it on line **17**.

Line 18—Interactive Traffic Demand

Multiply the number on line **17** by the number on line **12** to get an estimate of the interactive bandwidth requirement for the hour in question, and record the result on line **18**.

```
interactive_demand(hour) = concurrent_hits(hour) * 14,400
```

Line 19—Hourly Total Traffic Demand

Sum the values in lines **13** and **18** to obtain a total traffic demand figure, in kilobits per second, for the hour in question.

```
total_demand(hour)        = interactive_demand(hour) + batched_demand(hour)
```

Again, you can rerun the calculations for any hour of the day that is important to you. To give yourself some headroom, you might consider adding another multiple of line **12** to the figure in line **19**.

World Wide Web Server

My guess is that if you are connecting to the Internet, you are probably planning a Web server. I also assume that you are planning a full-time connection of your own, as opposed to renting space from someone else. (Otherwise, you wouldn't be reading this book.) You could, of course, rent space on a third party's server. This may be a good idea if you are only interested in a Web presence; you can avoid the hassles of maintaining your own site, *and* get behind a faster Internet connection, for less money. Of course, you lose some control, updates become a little more cumbersome, and you don't benefit from having your whole organization networked.

Anyway, if you *do* plan to host a Web server at your site, you have several hurdles to jump:

- You need to select Web server software. A short list of possibilities includes The *National Center for Supercomputing Application's (NCSA) http daemon*, the *CERN http daemon*, *Website* from O'Reilly & Associates (NT-based), and *Netsite* from Netscape Communications. You might even decide to base your server on a MAC or DOS-based PC.

- You need to install and configure the software. Depending on your choice, there may be some compilation involved.

- You need to pull a Web (HTML) document collection together.

Managing Internet Information Services, published by O'Reilly & Associates, provides good, detailed overviews of all parts of the process—installation, configuration, document creation, scripts, and logging. You should obtain a copy if you plan to host a serious Web site. To get you bootstrapped, however, I'm going to describe a minimal server setup, using NCSA's *http daemon*, and a skeleton document collection. A few modifications, and you will be on the air.

Configuring NCSA's httpd

NCSA's httpd (*hypertext transfer protocol daemon*) is available free of charge from:

```
ftp://ftp.ncsa.uiuc.edu/Web/httpd/Unix/ncsa-httpd/current
```

As of this writing, *httpd* is in revision 1.5. You will find the software available, both in source and binary form, for a number of platforms. I suggest that you fetch a binary, if one is available for your computer. Otherwise, you will have to get the source code and compile it yourself. I'm going to pretend that this isn't a problem—that you can come up with a binary for the daemon, and that we can proceed.

For purposes of discussion, let's say that you have installed the distribution under */usr/local/etc/httpd*.* You will have, among other things, subdirectories named *cgi-bin*, *cgi-src*, and *conf*. Create *htdocs* and *logs* directories as well:

```
$ cd /usr/local/etc/httpd
$ mkdir htdocs logs
```

Figure C-1 shows the result of your handiwork. Now let's visit each directory in turn, sprinkling configuration around. Then we'll start the daemon. When we are finished, we will have a small, working Web server.

conf

Our story begins in the *conf* directory, where we find configuration files for the daemon. File *access.conf* lists some global settings. Provided that you have installed everything along the path */usr/local/etc/httpd*, you can simply rename the prototype—*access.conf-dist*—as *access.conf*, and then continue; no changes will be necessary. The same is true for *srm.conf*, the file that describes where HTML documents will be stored: rename *srm.conf-dist* as *srm.conf*, then continue.

Turning our attention to the daemon configuration file, *httpd.conf*, we again move a prototype in place: rename *httpd.conf-dist* as *httpd.conf*. This time, however, we have to make a few modifications. Look for the line that starts with ServerAdmin, and change it so that it names the person responsible for your Web server.

```
ServerAdmin webmaster@gizniz.com
```

Typically, this person is called *webmaster*. Their true identity will be hidden behind a *sendmail* alias.

You will also have to specify the name of your Web server. Again, editing *httpd.conf*, you *could* choose the actual host name—e.g. *server.gizniz.com*. However, you might want to use the canonical name we set up when we configured DNS in Chapter 17, *Domain Name Service*.

* Everything "untars" under *httpd_<version number>*. You can either *mv* this to *httpd* or create a link.

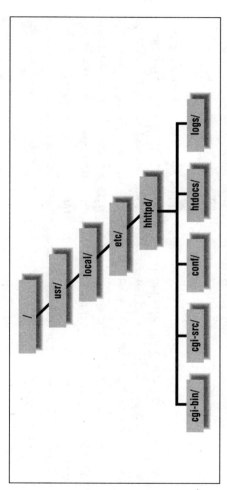

Figure C–1: Web server directory structure

ServerName www.gizniz.com

This will complement people's notion of what your server should be named (*www.something.something*). Furthermore, the use of a CNAME will give you the ability to migrate the server to another host later, if necessary.

File *mime.types* lists file types and the extensions associated with each. Through *mime.types*, for instance, a plain text file (type *text/plain*) will be associated with the filename extension of .txt. An MPEG video, to take another example, is listed as type video/mpeg, and associated with any of the extensions .mpeg, .mpg, or .mpe.*

```
...
text/html                    html
text/plain                   txt
...
video/mpeg                   mpeg mpg mpe
video/quicktime              qt mov
video/x-msvideo              avi
...
```

You don't generally have to change *mime.types*. A possible exception may occur if you need to add another file extension to the list. For example, you might want to serve HTML markup that has been generated on a PC. Peering suspiciously at DOS's 3 character extension (.htm), the daemon won't recognize the files you ship over as being HTML. Adding the shorter .htm extension to the list expands the text/html MIME type and causes the daemon to serve the DOS-born HTML files correctly.

---

* For more information about *Multipurpose Internet Mail Extensions* (MIME), and MIME types, see rfc1341.

logs

The *logs* subdirectory collects information from the daemon as it runs. Errors go to *error_log*; configuration errors and daemon startup and shutdown events are recorded. You will also see an entry for each time somebody requests a document that doesn't exist. Aside from that, *error_log* should be pretty quiet. You can probably let messages accumulate for a year without experiencing any discomfort.

File *access_log* lists every "hit" you have received—one hit per line. You can tell what document (or graphic, etc.) people looked at, when they looked at it, and where they came from. You generally can't tell who they are; unless you have enabled authentication, they will be nameless.

```
137.99.23.77 - - [05/Jun/1995:15:37:32 -0400] \
  "GET /ctguide/news/courant/graphics/team2.gif HTTP/1.0" 200 25010
ccsua.ctstateu.edu - - [05/Jun/1995:15:37:52 -0400] \
  "GET /ctguide/news/courant/news.html HTTP/1.0" 200 10327
crl3.crl.com - - [05/Jun/1995:15:39:34 -0400] \
  "GET /ct/intro.html HTTP/1.0" 200 1194
scs-mac-30.wustl.edu - - [05/Jun/1995:15:39:46 -0400] \
  "GET /atlantic/dowd/hotfish.html HTTP/1.0" 200 2043
scs-mac-30.wustl.edu - - [05/Jun/1995:15:39:48 -0400] \
  "GET /atlantic/dowd/graphics/hotfish.gif HTTP/1.0" 200 1846 \
scs-mac-30.wustl.edu - - [05/Jun/1995:15:40:00 -0400] \
  "GET /atlantic/dowd/ HTTP/1.0" 200 721
```

Here, you can see a snippet from an *access_log* file, folded so that it will fit on a printed page. The leftmost field lists where each hit came from. Typically, this will be a domain name, though in some cases you will see an IP address—it depends on whether your visitor has a reverse domain address.

The second two fields (shown as "- -") contain user information obtained from the remote host via *IDENT*, if configured, and via one of several other authentication methods (*PEM, PGP*, or a password), if configured. By default, no user information or authentication is processed.

The next field records the time of day, including the correction from GMT. Next we see a record of the requests made by remote browsers.[†] The last two numbers are the status of the request (200 is "good"), and the number of bytes transferred.

It is interesting to look through the logs to see what documents people are browsing. You could, in fact, lose a good hour in the logs, grepping and counting. There are, however, some very good data reduction tools available. In many cases, these will generate graphics and HTML output; you can browse the statistics with your Web client. For starters, take a look at *getstats* (*http://www.eit.com/software/getstat/getstat.html*), *wwwstat* (*http://www.ics.uci.edu/WebSoft/wwwstat/*), or

---

* See rfc931.

† I am pleased to announce that there were 1807 requests for my Hot Fish Oil recipe in the month of May.

wwsage (http://siva.csbl.org/wwsage.html). Note that the *access_log* file can grow very quickly. You will probably need to stop the daemon, move (or delete) the log, and restart the daemon from time to time. Our site (relatively quiet) grows 15 megabytes of log data per month.

Starting the HTTPD daemon

You have the option of running the NCSA *httpd* in one of two fashions: stand-alone, or under control of *inetd* (or some other daemon). Typically, sites let the daemon run stand-alone; incoming connections fork off copies of the daemon (or hand the processing to preforked threads). This is more efficient; fewer processes are created, and there is less overhead. If you prefer to run the daemon under control of *inetd*, you will have to go back and edit *httpd.conf*, then change the ServerType parameter to specify *inetd*, and make appropriate changes to *inetd.conf.*

Start the daemon with the following incantation (as root):

```
# /usr/local/etc/httpd/httpd
#
```

Your prompt will come back. You can check to see that the daemon is running by doing a *ps*, or by "Telnetting" into TCP port 80:

```
$ telnet localhost 80
Trying 127.0.0.1...
Connected to localhost.
Escape character is '^]'.
GET / HTTP/1.0

HTTP/1.0 200 OK
Date: Tuesday, 06-Jun-95 18:58:21 GMT
Server: NCSA/1.3
MIME-version: 1.0
Content-type: text/html
Last-modified: Tuesday, 16-May-95 10:32:55 GMT
Content-length: 962

...<other stuff, possibly>....
```

The daemon will return revision information, and either the contents of file */usr/local/etc/httpd/htdocs/index.html* (if it exists), or a listing of the */usr/local/etc/httpd/htdocs* directory. Presumably, the directory will be empty, since we have just created it. Now let's take some time to populate the server with HTML documents.

A Skeleton HTML Collection

I'm going to suggest a very small collection of HTML documents—just enough to put you on the air. To start, we will have:

- A home page
- A second-level informational page
- A fill-in form

You can use these as templates for your own site, though you will probably find that you have outgrown them in an hour or so. HTML markup is addictingly fun to experiment with, and straightforward to create. Ours will be simple, and easy to copy—something to clone. I have used graphics in a few spots, but unfortunately I can't supply these; you will have to come up with your own *GIF** images. Anything will do, although you will probably want to get your organization's logo into GIF format as soon as you can.

Top level: home page

A simple home page might look like the following: we have a banner graphic, a helper graphic thrown in for good measure, and a couple of links. You should name the document *index.html*, and store it in the */usr/local/etc/httpd/htdocs* directory.

```
<HTML>
<HEAD>
<TITLE>GizNiz Home Page</TITLE>
</HEAD>
<BODY>
<P>
<CENTER>
<H1><IMG ALT="GizNiz Corporation" SRC="/graphics/gizniz.gif">
Widgets are our business!
</H1>
</CENTER>
<HR>
<H2>
<P><IMAGE ALIGN=LEFT src="/graphics/look.gif">
Widgets On-line!
</H2>
<HR>
<H1>Welcome to GizNiz Corporation!</H1>
Select from the following:
<UL>
<LI><A HREF="about.html">About</A> GizNiz Corporation.
<LI><A HREF="http://www.w3.org/hypertext/WWW/MarkUp/MarkUp.html">
All about HTML</A>
```

* *Graphics Image Format*—popularized by CompuServe, GIF is in wide use around the Internet.

```
</UL>
<A HREF="form.html">Leave</A> us a comment using our on-line form.
<HR>
<ADDRESS>info@gizniz.com</ADDRESS>
</BODY>
</HTML>
```

Sprinkled through the document you see markup tags, delimited by the < and > characters. Some appear in pairs (such as <CENTER> and </CENTER>). Others stand alone (such as <P>). A quick tour of the tags used in our example includes:

`<HTML>, </HTML>`

These tags identify the text between them as *Hypertext Markup Language* (HTML). Not all HTML documents contain them; the MIME type of the document (text/html) is often sufficient to tell what the contents are.

`<HEAD>, </HEAD>`

The head of the document is marked by these tags, and is meant to contain information about the HTML document, but none of the document text. The document head may be missing.

`<TITLE>, </TITLE>`

The document title appears in the head of the document, enclosed in these two tags.

`<BODY>, </BODY>`

The "body" tags demark the start and finish of the HTML text. These may be missing.

`<P>`

This is a paragraph break.

`<CENTER>, </CENTER>`

The "center" tags indicate that the text and images between them should be centered within the display.

`<H1>, </H1>`

H1, H2, H3, H4, H5, and H6 are headings tags; they (among others) are used to control the appearance of document text, particularly its size. Typically, H1 picks the largest font, and H6 picks the smallest, though the owner of the browser has the option of mapping headings to fonts as desired. Heading selections are generally terminated by a mate, as in <H1>Hello!</H1>.

`<IMG ...>`

This tag indicates that an inline image is to be presented. In this case, the source for the image is given by the (brief) URL */graphics/gizniz.gif* (explained later). Browsers without the ability to display inline images will display the contents of the ALT attribute. The ALIGN attribute gives you some control ({TOP, MIDDLE, BOTTOM, LEFT, RIGHT}) over image placement.

`<UL>,<LI>,<LI>,...</UL>`

These tags mark the start and finish of an unordered (unnumbered) list, and the items to be inserted into the list.

`<A HREF=...>...</A>`

This is an anchor tag pair, marking a hypertext link. The HREF attribute is followed by a *URL*, which describes where the link will take you.

`<HR>`

The HR tag draws a horizontal rule within the body of the document.

One of a number of rendering element types, ADDRESS chooses a font—typically italic—for emphasis.

`<ADDRESS>,</ADDRESS>`

Again, this isn't a comprehensive glossary; you can find complete information both in printed form and on the Web.[*] Apologies aside, the results are shown in Figure C-2.

By the way, if you see another home page that you like better, you can always clone *that* instead. How? Most browsers have a "show source" option, which will display the HTML markup for the page you are currently viewing. Beyond that, you already know how to Telnet into the server and dump a document (perhaps to a cut-and-paste buffer). If you see it, you can get a copy of it.[†]

Second level: informational page

Our second-level page, *about.html*, isn't going to be quite so elaborate. You will see many of the same components we used on the home page; the only addition is the `<I>`, `</I>` pair (italics).

```
<HTML>
<HEAD>
<TITLE>About GizNiz Corporation</TITLE>
</HEAD>
<BODY>
<H1>About GizNiz Corporation...</H1>
We make <I>things</I>.  Widgets, mostly.
<P>
<A HREF="index.html">Return</A> to home page.
<HR>
<ADDRESS>info@gizniz.com</ADDRESS>
</BODY>
</HTML>
```

Note that we have a link here, too (`<A HREF...>`), except that instead of taking us away from the home page, this one brings us back.

---

[*] *http://www.w3.org/hypertext/WWW/MarkUp/MarkUp.html* is probably the best online source for information about HTML.

[†] To steal graphics, try clicking your right mouse button on top of the desired image.

Figure C–2. Top-level page

HTML forms

One of the features that makes the Web so attractive is the ability to elicit input from the reader. This is so unlike printed documents, there's no comparison; you can't scratch something into a magazine, for instance, and have your remarks appear someplace else. Of course, if you ask for input, you have to be prepared to do something with it when it comes in; someone must be waiting to collect and process the information. In our example, we are going to have the input mailed to a user account. Someone fills out a form—someone else receives a mail message.

Here's the HTML that we need for our form. Again, this shouldn't pass for a complete treatment of the subject; there are more element types and methods than I will present here. However, this should get you started:

```
<HEAD><TITLE>More Info Please</TITLE></HEAD>
<BODY>
<FORM METHOD=POST ACTION="mailto:fred@gizniz.com">
<P>
<H1>Thank you...</H1>
<H2>for your interest in GizNiz Corporation</H2>
We would be pleased to provide you with more information.
```

```
<HR>
<P>
<DL>
<DT><I>Please...</I>
<DD><INPUT TYPE="radio" NAME="respond" VALUE="call" CHECKED >
    Have someone call me at the number below.
<DD><INPUT TYPE="radio" NAME="respond" VALUE="send-literature">
    Send me paper literature.
<DD><INPUT TYPE="radio" NAME="respond" VALUE="send-email">
    Send information via email.
<P>
<DT><I>I am interested in...</I>
<DD>(check all that apply)
<DD><INPUT TYPE="checkbox" NAME="interest" VALUE="widgets">
    Widgets.
<DD><INPUT TYPE="checkbox" NAME="interest" VALUE="hammer">
    having a hammer dropped on my foot.
<DD><INPUT TYPE="checkbox" NAME="interest" VALUE="job">
    a job with GizNiz Corporation.
<DD><INPUT TYPE="checkbox" NAME="interest" VALUE="other">
    Other.
<P>
<DT><I>Your name?</I>
<DD><INPUT TYPE="text" NAME="name">
<P>
<DT><I>Address?</I>
</TEXTAREA>
<DD><TEXTAREA COLS=60 ROWS=5 NAME="address">
<P>
<DT><I>Email?</I>
<DD><INPUT TYPE="text" SIZE=60 NAME="email">
<P>
<DT><I>Telephone?</I>
<DD><INPUT TYPE="text" SIZE=60 NAME="phone">
</DL>
<P>
<INPUT VALUE="Send Request" TYPE=submit> We will get back to you right away.
</FORM>
<HR>
<ADDRESS>info@gizniz.com</ADDRESS>
</BODY>
```

A quick explanation of the HTML elements shown above is in order. I'll skip the ones we have discussed already. See Figure C-3 for a picture of the form.

`<FORM>, </FORM>`

These tags identify the text between them as part of an HTML form. ACTION gives the URL to be invoked when the form is completed. I chose to use a *mailto* URL; the form data will be forwarded via email.

`<DL><DT><DD><DT><DD> . . . . </DL>`

These tags make up a definition list. They're not form elements at all—we just haven't seen them before. They make the form more attractive.

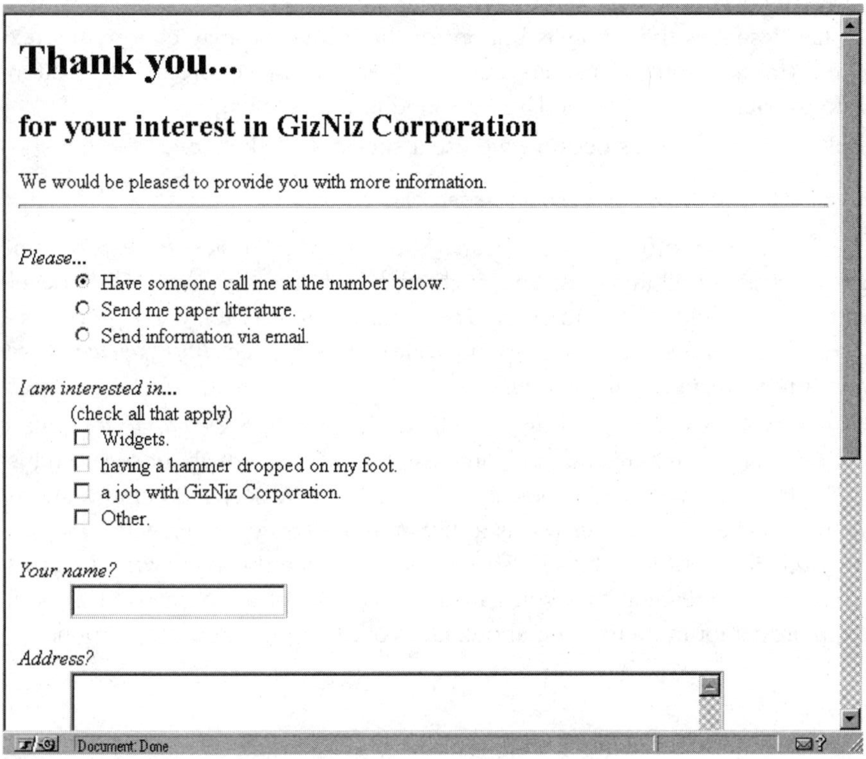

Thank you...

for your interest in GizNiz Corporation

We would be pleased to provide you with more information.

Please...

- ⊙ Have someone call me at the number below.
- ○ Send me paper literature.
- ○ Send information via email.

I am interested in...
(check all that apply)
- ☐ Widgets.
- ☐ having a hammer dropped on my foot.
- ☐ a job with GizNiz Corporation.
- ☐ Other.

Your name?

Address?

Figure C–3: Interactive form

`<INPUT TYPE=radio ... >`

The INPUT tag says that this is an input field. NAME sets a class for the field; you will notice that other input fields share the same setting. TYPE="radio" says that the field will mimic "radio buttons"—if the user punches one button in, another pops back out. The VALUE field shows the keyword that will be returned if the button is selected. Notice that one of the options is "checked" in advance.

`<INPUT TYPE=checkbox ... >`

This input field is similar to the radio buttons, except that the user may pick all or none of the choices.

`<INPUT TYPE=text ... >`

Text-type input fields accept character input. You can see that some of the text fields have a SIZE parameter; this sets the desired width of the text input field.

`<TEXTAREA ... >`

The TEXTAREA tag declares a rectangular input block for text. You can pass the desired number of rows and columns as parameters.

```
<INPUT TYPE=submit ...>
```

This tag describes the "submit" button for the form. You may choose any text desired (in fact, you can use an image). When the user depresses the button, the form data is passed to the URL specified in the FORM tag.

The results come back to us because we use a special URL, known as *mailto*:

```
<FORM METHOD=POST ACTION="mailto:webmaster@gizniz.com">
```

This should get you off to a good start. You have the basics: a server, some markup, images, and fill-in forms. You might also look into the many HTML development tools available on the Internet. There are macro kits for word processors, HTML sensitive editors, and markup translators (again, see *http://www.w3.org/hypertext/WWW/MarkUp/MarkUp.html*).

Perhaps you will also want to shop around for servers. NCSA's *httpd* works very well, but others have features that may interest you. If you care about secure transactions, you might look into *Netsite* from Netscape Communications. *Website*, from O'Reilly & Associates, is a *Windows NT*-based server with CGI support in *Visual Basic*. CERN's httpd also makes an excellent choice, *and* it can act as a proxy server, meaning that you can use it as part of a UNIX-based firewall.[*] Anyway, there's a lot more to think about. Get your bearings, and shop around.

---

[*] You can get a computer to recognize itself as having multiple IP addresses by configuring multiple IP interfaces. For instance, you can *ifconfig* a SLIP interface in addition to your regular network interface; this will give the machine two identities. Usually (not always) computers with multiple addresses will recognize packets for either, regardless of the interface the packets arrive on.

Anonymous FTP

File Transfer Protocol, or FTP, is one of the original TCP/IP services commissioned by DARPA in the late 1960s; it has been around a long time. Even so, it is still one of the most heavily used Internet applications. FTP is a terrific way to distribute information, software, or software updates. Accordingly, you may want to make it part of your Internet information services strategy.

FTP is really two programs—a client and a server (daemon). An FTP client (initiated by the user) contacts a server on a remote machine, establishes a connection under a user name and password, and requests directory listings or files. FTP file access permissions are limited to those of the user account on the server.

Anonymous FTP is a special case FTP server configuration. Guests who identify themselves by the login *anonymous* are given rummage rights to a public file collection. The password they supply is typically unrestricted; by convention, people leave an email address.

```
% ftp wisper.atlantic.com
Connected to wisper.atlantic.com.
220 wisper FTP server (Version 4.1 2/8/90) ready.
Name (wisper:dowd): anonymous
331 Guest login ok, provide ident as password.
    Password: dowd@atlantic.com          <invisible>
230 User anonymous logged in.
ftp>
ftp> get README
local: README remote: README
200 PORT command successful.
150 Opening ASCII mode data connection for README (670 bytes).
226 Transfer complete.
688 bytes received in 0 seconds (0.67 Kbytes/s)
ftp>
ftp> bye
221 Goodbye.
```

As ever, there is more than one path you can take: you can configure the FTP server software that came with your UNIX machine, or you can get a copy of a third-party server. The most popular server, by far, is the Washington University FTP server, *wu-ftpd* (*ftp://unarchive.wustl.edu/packages/wuarchive-ftpd/*), version 2.4. Again, I refer you to *Managing Internet Information Services* for a more detailed discussion of *wu-ftpd* and FTP in general. At the same time, I promise we'll cover enough here to get you bootstrapped.

chroot

One of the biggest questions people have about anonymous FTP is, "Is it safe?" The answer is "yes." An anonymous user has a very restricted view of your computer's file system. There *are* some things you have to be careful about when setting the server up—we'll cover these below. But, in general, FTP is safe.

Here's why: The UNIX kernel has a primitive called *chroot()*, or "change root." When a program calls *chroot()*, it irrevocably curtails its notion of where the top of the file hierarchy begins. If I execute a program that executes the following instruction, for instance, my program's view of the UNIX filesystem will be limited to */tmp* for the rest of its life:

```
...
chroot ("/tmp");
...
```

In the same fashion, the FTP daemon uses *chroot()* to restrict an anonymous user's view of the filesystem; you can sculpt their world as you see fit. Again, there are some things that you need to be careful about *within* the anonymous FTP directory.

Enabling Anonymous FTP

To begin, we have to create a special *ftp* user. On many systems, we can simply add this user to the */etc/passwd* file. On your system, however, you may be running with shadow passwords, or some other security feature. In that case, you will want to add the *ftp* user with the administration tools you normally use, and then go back and modify the password or shadow password files to restrict access.

In this example, you can see how the password file entry should look. User *ftp*'s logins are disabled (via the * in the password field). The user ID is arbitrary; "500" bears no special significance—choose whatever you like. We have set the shell to */bin/false*—no logins enabled. And we have specified a home directory: */usr/ftp*. This is where we set up the *chroot*-protected anonymous FTP files.

```
ftp:*:500:20:anonymous ftp:/usr/ftp:/bin/false
```

As root, create a */usr/ftp* directory. Since this is going to be the anonymous user's whole universe, we will have to fit the directory with those subdirectories and system files we need to mimic the filesystem root. As a minimum, this includes subdirectories */bin*, */etc*, */tmp*, and probably */lib*. Depending on the system you are using, you might also need */usr/lib* or */dev* directories (more in a moment).

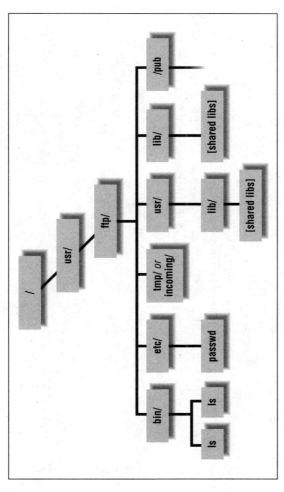

Figure D-1: Anonymous FTP directories

Working from left to right in Figure D-1, create a */usr/ftp/bin* directory. Copy binaries *ls* and *sh* from the real */bin/* directory into the new directory:

```
# mkdir /usr/ftp
# mkdir /usr/ftp/bin
# cp /bin/ls /bin/sh /usr/ftp/bin
```

Next, create an *etc/* subdirectory:

```
# mkdir /usr/ftp/etc
```

We will populate the directory with a *passwd* file containing the minimum number of entries we can get away with. *Don't* copy your real *passwd* file. This would make it available for mischievous folks who want to run password crackers against it. Here's a sample you can copy:

```
root:*:0:0:root:/:
bin:*:1:1:bin:/:
ftp:*:500:20:anonymous ftp:/:
```

You may also want a generally readable/writable *tmp* directory. This will be a convenient place for people to drop files off and pick them up. Be careful though: there have been cases where people used anonymous */tmp* directories as swap points for inappropriate materials. If you have a *tmp* directory, be sure to keep an eye on it.

```
# mkdir /usr/ftp/tmp
# chmod 777 /usr/ftp/tmp
```

As an alternative, you could create an *incoming* directory with write and execute permissions, but no read permission. This will make it nearly impossible for people to grope your drop-off point for interesting files:

```
# mkdir /usr/ftp/incoming
# chmod 733 /usr/ftp/incoming
```

At the same time, people who *know* the names of files within the *incoming* directory will be able to "get" them—even though they cannot list the directory. Now we get to a trickier part. In order to run the binaries in */usr/ftp/bin*, you will probably need to have some shared object libraries present, in their appropriate places, under the */usr/ftp* directory. On some machines, this will be *lib*; on others, *usr/lib* is the right spot. In most cases, you can check by running a program called *ldd* against the binary; this will report dynamic dependencies:

```
# ldd /bin/sh
<libraries listed>
# ldd /bin/ls
<libraries listed>
```

Once you have determined the shared libraries that you need, you can create a matching *lib* or *usr/lib* directory under */usr/ftp*, and then copy the libraries down. You will also need to copy the shared library loader, *ld.so*, into the directory where the shared libraries are kept.*

```
# cp /lib/libc.so... /usr/ftp/lib     <for example>
# cp /lib/ld.so... /usr/ftp/lib       <for example>
```

CAUTION

Please be careful here! Don't inadvertently copy over your working shared libraries, or otherwise destroy a system binary.

---

* If you are running on a Sun, you will also need to create a *dev/* directory, and make a *zero* device:
mknod /usr/ftp/dev/zero c 3 12.

The last directory we need is *pub/*. By convention, this is where users will expect to find files that you offer for general consumption:

```
# mkdir /usr/ftp/pub
# cat > /usr/ftp/pub/README
Hello!
^D
#
```

We're almost done. Let's take one quick pass through to make sure that file permissions are correct. First, check to be sure that all files, starting with */usr/ftp* and below, are owned by *root*. Next, make sure that root is the only one with write access to all but your *tmp* or *incoming* directories. Be sure that *ls*, *sb*, and *ld.so* are executable. That's it! You can test your server by FTPing in as anonymous and grabbing a file.

Mail Transponders

For lack of a better alternative, I often use the term *mail transponder* to describe tools that provide canned responses to electronic mail. You have probably communicated with a mail transponder before: you send an empty message to *info@soandso.com*, and information about the Soandso Corporation shows up in your mailbox a few minutes later. I admit that I am probably alone in my use of the term. Other labels—"email file server" or "email librarian"—describe programs that manipulate file archives through electronic mail and can easily act as transponders. A mailing list server (if you are running one) will often do double duty—both managing communities of list subscribers, and acting as a mail transponder. In fact, some mailing list servers come with powerful features—automatic uuencoding, header parsing—that also make them good archive servers.

Anyway, here's my self-appointed challenge: I need to cut a swath through the many tools that can double as mail transponders, and concentrate solely on providing automated mail responses to things like "info" requests. If you have a similar singular requirement—to make information about your company, products, or services available via electronic mail—then this section should be useful to you. If, on the other hand, your primary need is to operate mailing lists or mail archives, you might look into other tools, such as *Majordomo, ListProcessor,* or *Procmail*. (See *Managing Internet Information Services* for a good discussion of mailing list servers.) Of course, you can mix and match tools, too; mailing lists can be maintained with one set of functions, and transponders can be maintained with another. How much time do you have?

A Simple Mail Transponder

Managing Internet Information Services, from O'Reilly & Associates, describes a nifty little PERL program called *canned_reply*, written by Jerry Peek. *canned_reply* executes via a sendmail alias, returning a file to the person who sent the request.

```
info: "|/usr/local/etc/canned_reply nobody@gizniz.com
       /usr/local/etc/info.txt postmaster"
```

Here, you can see the alias that invokes *canned_reply*, and the arguments passed when it is called. The first is the "from" address that will be placed on the mail sent back to the sender. In this case, the response will appear to have come from a user named *nobody@gizniz.com*. The second argument gives the name of the file to be sent in response to mail that "info" receives. The third argument gives the name of the user to receive error reports if the canned response is undeliverable.

To use *canned_reply*, you will need to create an alias in */etc/aliases*, like the one shown above. Don't forget to run *newaliases* once you have made the update. And, of course, you need a copy of *canned_reply*. It is available in the collection at *ftp://ftp.ora.com/pub/examples/nutshell/miis*.

Mailagent

canned_reply's selling point—simplicity—also happens to be its fault. It is very easy to use; you can have *info@gizniz.com* working in a couple of minutes. However, *canned_reply*'s functionality is limited. Unless you know how to modify the code, you may find yourself wishing *canned_reply* could do more.

When would a more sophisticated mail transponder be important? Perhaps you are managing multiple domains from a single mail hub. In that case, the mail transponder should know how to differentiate between info requests for different companies—*info@gizniz.com* versus *info@zugzug.com*, for example. Or perhaps you want your responses to be sensitive to the text in the "subject" line. This could, for example, give remote users a way to navigate through an information tree and receive tailored replies.

Again, there are many packages available for serving files via electronic mail (see mail-archive and filtering-mail FAQs that appear in *comp.mail.misc* periodically). In the interest of getting you up and running, however, I will focus on just one, the one we use most often: *mailagent*, written by Raphael Manfredi. *Mailagent* is a mail-processing package with a rich set of pattern matching primitives for parsing mail headers.* You can have it return (customized) canned responses, sort mail into folders, deliver vacation messages, post to USENET news, or even execute a command. I am going to show you how to configure *mailagent* to provide the same kind of functionality as *canned_reply*, though with a bit more embellishment. If you choose to run *mailagent*, you will probably want to explore its other abilities too; it is very capable.

Configuring Mailagent

As with almost every other tool we have looked at, getting *mailagent* up and running is a two-part process: first we have to build and install the code, and then we have to configure it. You will need a C compiler and PERL. Fortunately, *mailagent* builds pretty easily; a "Configure" script generates a custom makefile, which, in turn, builds and installs the necessary binaries on your machine. Accordingly, I am going to assume that you can get through installation without my help, and are now ready to customize the package.

To start, we need to nominate somebody as the owner and author of the canned replies. I propose that we choose "nobody." When you receive mail from "nobody," you don't expect too much. If, on the other hand, the canned responses came from (say) "smith," the user might mistake "smith" for a human, and be insulted by the impersonal treatment, or by the way "smith" apparently ignored the questions put to him. Anyway, you probably already have a user "nobody" on your computer. If not, you will want to add an entry in the password file, and give Mr. Nobody a home directory:

    nobody:*:65534:65534:Mr. Nobody:/usr/nobody:/bin/sh

My "nobody" entry, in this example, gives Mr. Nobody a home directory in */usr/nobody*. There's no password; Mr. Nobody can never log in. Accordingly, when you are configuring his directory, you will probably want to "su" to root first, and then "su" to nobody.

Mailagent needs the following files:

.forward
  The *.forward* file immediately forwards Mr. Nobody's mail to a *mailagent* for processing.

.mailagent
  This file contains general configuration parameters that *mailagent* uses when it runs.

---

* See *ftp://ftp.foretune.co.jp/pub/network/mail/mailagent/*.

./var

A *mailagent* subdirectory keeps track of queued mail, processed mail, and logfiles.

.rules

The *.rules* file tells *mailagent* how messages should be processed.

Additionally, we will want to craft some canned responses, and make them part of the collection too.

Assuming that our first project is to process mail for *info@gizniz.com*, let's place an entry in the sendmail *alias* file:

```
info: nobody
```

In Mr. Nobody's home directory (*/usr/nobody*, in this example), we will create a *forward* file that passes incoming mail to *mailagent*:

```
"| exec /usr/local/lib/mailagent/filter >> /usr/nobody/.bak 2>&1"
```

Keep the quotes; they are significant. Also, make sure the file is owned by "nobody," and readable by all.

Next, we need to set up the *.mailagent* configuration file. You will find a prototype in */usr/local/lib/mailagent/mailagent.cf* (provided you have already done a "make install"). (On the latest revisions of *mailagent*, you can just type mailagent –I to have the prototype and directories created by the program.) Most of the parameters can remain as they are. Accordingly, I have detailed just the changes we need for our mail transponder project:

```
home  : /usr/nobody      # Mr. Nobody's home directory

user  : nobody           ...
name  : Information Server
email : nobody@gizniz.com
```

Change the contents of *.mailagent* as appropriate to fit your Mr. Nobody and your organization.

Mailagent also requires a small subdirectory tree to house logging and work files. Assuming you took the default *.mailagent* settings for spool and logdir, type the following to create the necessary subdirectories under *~nobody*:

```
$ cd ~nobody
$ mkdir var
$ cd var
$ mkdir log mailagent
$ cd mailagent
$ mkdir queue
```

The directories will be populated as *mailagent* runs.

Now we get to the meat—the *.rules* file. *Mailagent* rules support PERL-style pattern matching and assignment, and a variety of operations. A match can result in mail being forwarded, archived, answered, deleted, or passed to an external command—you are limited only by your imagination. The "man" pages that come with *mailagent* explain rule creation in detail. However, for illustration, I have bundled together a very simple collection of rules for serving information to the Internet community:

```
Subject: test { MESSAGE /usr/nobody/test.txt };
To: info@zugzug.com { FORWARD smith; SAVE};
To: info@freck.com { FORWARD jfreck@ix.netcom.com; SAVE};
Subject: /WWW/, Subject: /web/ { MESSAGE /usr/nobody/web.txt };
To: /info/ { MESSAGE /home/nobody/info; FORWARD postmaster; SAVE};
To: fortune { RUN /usr/games/fortune | /usr/lib/sendmail %r;
              NOTIFY postmaster /usr/nobody/notify; SAVE};
```

The first rule says that if a message arrives with a subject of test, *mailagent* should respond with a copy of *test.txt*, from Mr. Nobody's home directory:

```
Hello, %N, and thank you for testing....
```

Right away, we see something interesting: a macro substitution within the text of the message (%N) gives us a way to customize the response to include the sender's name. Fred Smith's message would say:

```
Hello, Fred Smith, and thank you for testing....
```

Other possible substitutions include:

%R   the subject of the message

%t   time of day (hh:mm)

%d   day of the month

%m   month of the year

%l   the number of lines in the message

%L   number of bytes in the message body

%f   the sender's "from" line

And more.

Stepping forward in the *.rules* file, notice the two lines that scan the recipient's full domain name in search of "info" requests (*info@zugzug.com* and *info@freck.com*). Because the recipient rules are explicit to the domain, we are able to accommodate the situation where multiple organizations' addresses resolve to the same computer. In either case, mail is forwarded to real users, and a copy of the original message is saved in Mr. Nobody's mailbox; the person requesting "info" does not get a canned reply.

The third line of *.rules* looks for any messages with a subject containing either WWW or *web*, and returns a canned response from a file called *web.txt*. The /s around the patterns indicate that these are regular expressions in PERL syntax. Of course, in this case, both are literals (WWW, web). However, they may appear anywhere in the subject line, and still trigger a match.

The fourth line catches any "info" requests that might have slipped through. Again, we have a pattern (albeit boring) within /s; recipients product-info, informa-tion, misinformation, etc. will all match. The sender gets a canned response, the postmaster gets a copy of the original message, and Mr. Nobody gets a copy for his records.

The last rule illustrates one of a number of ways to execute a command upon receipt of a letter. Mail to fortune will be answered with a pithy saying. Notice that, in this case, the postmaster receives a kind of canned response of her own (via the NOTIFY command). The text will be taken from */usr/nobody/notify*):

```
Dear Postmaster: I got a fortune request from %f.
```

Up to this point, I haven't said anything about the order in which rules are evaluated, but by now I suspect you have guessed: evaluation proceeds from top to bottom. If nothing matches at the end, the message is simply left in Mr. Nobody's mail folder.

This may have occurred to you too: *mailagent* processing isn't limited to a single alias; one set of rules can collect mail for many different pseudo-users.

```
info: nobody
orders: nobody
marketing: nobody
```

The rules can get arbitrarily complex, too. You can look for combinations of patterns—a particular recipient, with a particular subject line, for instance. Furthermore, there's no reason why multiple *real* users can't take advantage of *mailagent*. Think about it: what permissions has Mr. Nobody got that you ain't got? The answer is none. *Mailagent* is a general purpose package for processing an individual's mail. We merely approached it from the point of view of an Internet information service.

F

USENET News

Picture the typical "bulletin board" system, and you probably think of a PC in the basement with a big hard disk and a choke-roll of phone lines. The scenario works okay for perhaps several hundred users, but how well would it scale to fifty million users, all over the world?* To create a large-scale conferencing system, the process has to be re-thought; the system has to be *distributed*.

Interestingly, the "bulletin board" of the Internet (and beyond), *USENET news*, doesn't have any centralized control; there isn't any single person or group who decides what gets through, where it goes, or who should participate. These decisions are made locally, on site-by-site bases. Newsgroups (conferences) that have broad interest are propagated to many sites. Specialized groups may remain within a small community. Anyone can create a new newsgroup, but generally ones does so only after offering the idea up for a public vote.

If there isn't any central source for news, where does the news come from? The answer is that that it comes from everywhere: articles migrate outward from their origins, spreading like drops of ink on wet paper towels. Sites offer postings to their "neighbors," not knowing whether they have may already received them from somewhere else. Each server keeps a history of the articles it has received, so duplicates are merely discarded, or never transmitted in the first place. After a while, a given article will be replicated around the world.

Eventually, articles kept on the server get old and outdated. The system administrator decides how long the messages will be kept before they are "expired"— often the decisions are dictated by available disk space. Depending on the interests of the local community, different newsgroups can be expired at different rates. Expiry is an ongoing process; new articles come in as old ones are being deleted.

---

* Not well.

Locally, news is kept on a *news hub*—a computer running some collection of USENET news software (it can be the same computer that runs everything else). Readers of news (humans) connect to the server with a client, called a *news-reader*. Information about the user's "state"—the newsgroups they subscribe to, the articles they have read—is kept back on the the humans' own computers, or in their login accounts; the news hub keeps no records of user activity.

News Software

Often, what we call 'news' is more than a single collection of programs. For our purposes, we are actually going to be discussing *two* separate packages: *c-news* and *nntp*. *c-news* is the set of tools that maintains news articles; *nntp* is the component that moves news across a network, between sites, and out to the desktop. We need both of them to form a complete picture. *

Before proceeding, I should make a couple of disclaimers. The first is that I will be describing a narrow *c-news/nntp* configuration: batched transfer over a network. News is much more flexible than my description might lead you to believe. But I have a specific purpose: to help you trade news with your Internet service provider over your Internet connection.

Second, you should be aware that there is a completely different suite of tools, called *InterNet News* (INN), that provides the same functionality as c-news/nntp. There's a little bit of religion to go along with it; proponents of one often feel it is better than the other. I'm not religious about it—just a bit more comfortable with c-news. The common wisdom is that INN is preferable if you have several news pads or feed news to several sites downstream. c-news is preferable if you're short on resources, particularly memory.

How c-news and nntp Play Together

Packages of *nntp* and *c-news* touch one another at various spots—the news spool directory, the *active* file, the history files, the areas where incoming and outgoing articles are kept. Like bootleggers, *nntp* and *c-news* drop packages for one another in pre-appointed alleyways and keep tabs on each other's business. Figure F-1 shows the process.

There's a grand cycle to it all: it starts with *nntpd* (the news transfer daemon) listening for connections from upstream news "feeds." When a connection comes in, a little conversation takes place: the sender goes through its docket of articles, saying "I Have X, do you want it?" "Yes" or "No" is the answer, depending on

---

* Watch out here: *NNTP* (Network News Transfer Protocol) is a method for moving news across a network. *nntp*, on the other hand, is a package that implements NNTP.

whether the news hub already has the article in question; *nntpd* checks *c-news'* history files to see. If the article is a new one for the collection, the transfer takes place. Eventually the conversation completes, and the sender hangs up.

Either immediately, under control of *nntpd*, or a little while later, under control of *cron*, a script called *newsrun* comes to life and discovers the incoming articles dropped in a pile by *nntpd*. One armload at a time, *newsrun* grabs the articles and feeds them through *relaynews* to decide whether they are valid, to update the history files, and to stuff the articles into the appropriate newsgroups (see Figure F-1). When finished, the articles are ready for viewing by NNTP clients (newsreaders).

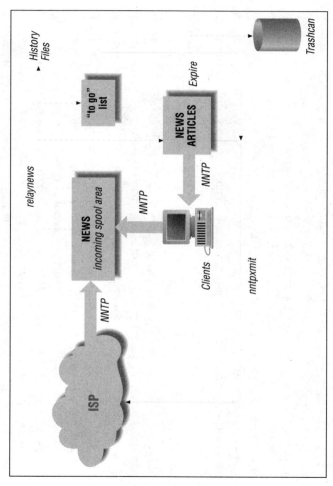

Figure F–1: News processing

nntpd does double-duty, acting both as an agent for the transfer of news articles from site to site and as a back-end server for newsreaders. At some point, a desktop user will start a newsreader (it could be *Netscape*). The newsreader will hold a meandering, interactive session with the daemon: "Give me the headers of articles in *comp.arch*," "Give me article thus-and-such," "Now I want to post an article." All the while, *nntpd* keeps its fingers in the *c-news* history records, created earlier, so that it knows what articles it can offer. When the session is over, the conversation is forgotten.*

Now say that someone decides to "post" an article. Or perhaps an article arriving from an "upstream" site has to be fed to another site, "downstream." In either case, a pointer to article X is appended to a roster (a "to go" list), kept under the remote site's name. Later, *cron* wakes up a script called *nntpsend* that "discovers" the roster. *nntpsend* hands the roster to a program called *nntpxmit*, which feeds the "downstream" site. This is the very conversation we began our example with, except that in this case we are considering it from the point of view of the sending site rather than the receiving site.

External to the business of sending and receiving articles is the business of housecleaning. Once a day, *cron* invokes a script called *doexpire*, which in turn runs a program called *expire*. *expire* consults a file named *explist* to see how long articles should live and what should become of them when they are deleted—should they be tossed out, should they be archived? As *expire* runs, it deletes articles from the spool directory and updates the history files.

Well, that's the cook's tour. In the next few sections we will cover *c-news* and *nntp* configuration in fast-moving detail. I'm going to deviate from the install notes that come with packages slightly—particularly in the case of *nntp*.

Building c-news

Unfortunately, news can be a challenge to configure and maintain. It's not that the software is defective in some fashion. The trouble is that there is a lot to think about—compiling, obtaining a feed, creating hierarchies, assigning permissions, expiring articles; it can be difficult to get your arms around it on the first date. Furthermore, news is gangly. Installation scripts broadcast pieces of news software all through the disk hierarchy. The result is that you can't shake a stick at a particular directory of the disk and say "that's news." You will, instead, find a little bit of software under every manhole cover. To be fair, part of news' girth can be attributed to its flexibility; news can be received and distributed via many media—from magnetic tape to IP networks.

My strategy is to offer you just enough information about news—particularly about *c-news* and *nntp*—for you to get it up and functioning. Luckily, once tuned, news often takes care of itself. Only occasionally, perhaps if you overflow your spool directory, do you have to go back in and mop up. Just in case, we'll talk about disaster recovery briefly too.

---

* You can have an NNTP conversation without a newsreader. Telnet into your news hub on port 119, and type help.

Before you can start, you will need a copy of the *c-news* source distribution. Sources for c-news are *ftp://ftp.cs.toronto.edu/pub/c-news/c-news.tar.Z* or *ftp://ftp.zoo.toronto.edu/pub/cnews.tar.Z*.* The instructions that come with the package are good, and the build process has become pretty clean with the latest release—particularly considering the amount of software involved. To give you a second source of help, however, I though I would go over the basic steps.

Running quiz

To begin, create a source directory, and give ownership to user bin. "**su**" to bin, go into the new directory, and un-tar the c-news code. Once unpacked, execute the script *quiz*.

```
# cd /home
# mkdir cnews
# chown bin.bin cnews
# cd cnews
# su bin
$ cp <wherever>/cnews.tar.Z .
$ uncompress cnews.tar
$ tar xf cnews.tar.Z
$ quiz
```

quiz will ask a series of questions about your site configuration, the contents of your system libraries, where you want to put configuration files, etc. It would be a good idea to open a second window so that you can research your answers (such as "do my C libraries have *stderror()*?"). Furthermore, be aware that because I am suggesting that we build news to support NNTP exchanges, and because I'm kind of old and set in my ways, I am going to try to steer you to configure c-news in a specific fasion; I will suggest answers to the questions posed by *quiz*.

Getting underway, when asked what ID should be used for news, choose *news*. This will be the administrator for news on your machine, and the owner of many news-related files. If you have no such user on your machine (check */etc/passwd*), then you should take a moment to create one. Likewise, you will want to create a group called *news*.

```
What user id should be used for news files [news]?
What group id should be used for news files [news]?
```

quiz offers default choices for homes for articles, overview files, control files, and programs. Below, I override the choices in favor of more traditional directories. You may follow my lead, or take the defaults. In either case, you should plan to have a fair amount of spare disk space—particularly within the article tree.

---

* Henry Spencer—one of the authors—requests that you avoid transferring during the afternoon peaks.

Furthermore, it might be a good idea to keep the control files and articles on separate file systems. This avoids the compound failures that can occur when one overcrowds the other. Note that even if you don't have the necessary space on a particular file system, you can always copy the directory elsewhere and make a soft link after installation is complete.

Skipping ahead a bit, *quiz* will ask you where it should mail emergency and maintenance messages about news processing. The script suggests a *newscrisis* alias—perhaps pointing to you—for emergency messages. Routine messages can go the news user itself.

```
Where should the article tree go [/var/news]? /usr/spool/news
Where should overview files go [/var/spool/news]? /usr/spool/news
Where should control files go [/etc/news]? /usr/lib/news
Where should programs go [/usr/libexec/news]? /usr/lib/newsbin

Where should C News mail urgent reports [newscrisis]?
Where should C News mail non-urgent reports [newsmaster]? news
```

quiz will ask you about a list of system library routines that may or may not be available on your computer. In your second window, you can research each one as it comes up. One way to tell if you have a given module is to look for the manual page, ala "**man fcntl**." For those routines for which you answer "no," c-news will substitue an equivalent routine into one of its libraries, *libfake.a*. If you make a mistake—if you say you do have a particular routine, when in fact you don't—you can always go back and fix it later (go into *include/config.make* and add the missing routine to the OFAKE list).

```
Does your system have    fgetline()   [yes]?
Does your system have    getopt()     [yes]?
Does your system have    gettimeofday() [yes]?
Does your system have    memcpy()     [yes]?
Does your system have    mkdir()      [yes]?
etc.
```

Though it is possible to create news spool or maintenance directories on NFS-mounted file systems, it isn't a very good idea. In most cases, you would answer "no" to the question below.

```
Will processing be done over NFS [yes]? no
```

News article histories are kept in a database. Unless you have a compelling reason not to use the *dbz* package included with c-news, then you should accept "yes" as the answer to the question below.

```
Do you want to use the "dbz" package [yes]?
```

Skipping ahead, you'll be asked if you have a few ANSI C-conforming header files, as below. Again, check for the header files' existence in your second window.

Does your system have an ANSI-C-conforming <string.h> [yes]?
Does your system have an ANSI-C-conforming <stdlib.h> [yes]?
Does your system have an ANSI-C-conforming <stddef.h> [yes]?

ranlib is a utility for maintaining object libraries. Most machines (in my experience) have a copy of *ranlib* (though it may do nothing). The best way to check is to go to your second window and type **ranlib**.

Does your system use ranlib [no]? *check*

The next batch of questions asks about *make*, the C compiler, and UUCP and linking. Answer the *make* questions as best you can. For the C compiler, a -O flag is usually sufficient. The UUCP question probably doesn't matter in your case (we are not using UUCP).

quiz will want to know which of a variety of *df* outputs your machine will produce. It needs this information in order to appropriately configure the interface for another script (called *spacefor*) that checks to see if you have sufficient disk space and i-nodes to process news.

Which one is most appropriate [statfs]?

Usually, the right answer will be **statfs**, with output like the following:

```
Filesystem    1024-blocks   Used  Available  Capacity  Mounted on
/dev/hda1         79310     66692     8512      89%      /
/dev/hda3        578817    533025    15880      97%      /usr
```

A few more questions follow; stick with the defaults. When you get to the end, you will see the following output:

```
saving defaults...

building conf/makeinc...
building conf/substitutions...
building include/config.make...
done
```

If you made a mistake partway through, or if you want to change an answer, you can go back and re-run *quiz*. For subsequent sessions, *quiz* will start by asking if you would like to re-use previous answers.

Compiling c-news

Type **make**, and hold your breath. Provided you have all the software development components you need (C compiler, make, etc.), and have chosen options appropriately, the build will proceed okay. If you *do* run into problems—particularly problems caused by missing include files, datatypes, or object modules—then you will have to be resourceful, and find your way through. Be mindful that choices you make when running *quiz* will influence compilation parameters (makefile flags, "defines," and so on). If you have difficulty with something—file handling, signal handling, etc.—it may be that you chose inappropriately. Try something else!

Once the compilation has finished, you may optionally run regression tests to see that news components are functioning okay. If you would like to run the tests, type **make r**.

Installing Files

Before proceeding, we need to make the news spool, control, and binary directories we chose above, when running *quiz*. As *root*, enter the following:

```
#  mkdir /usr/lib/news
#  chown news.news /usr/lib/news
#  mkdir /usr/lib/newsbin
#  chown bin.bin /usr/lib/newsbin
#  mkdir /usr/spool/news
#  chown news.news /usr/spool/news
```

Articles and control files will belong to *news*. Executables will (for the most part) belong to *bin*. Next, "**su**" to bin, and install the news binaries:

```
#  su bin
$  make install

   <installation proceeds>
```

Once installation is complete, exit the current shell and modify permissions on */usr/lib/newsbin/input/newsspool* (**note**: there are two *s*'s in "newsspool") as follows:

```
$  exit              <-- revert to root
#  chown news.news /usr/lib/newsbin/input/newsspool
#  chmod u+s /usr/lib/newsbin/input/newsspool
#  chmod g+s /usr/lib/newsbin/input/newsspool
```

Becoming user *news* this time, run **make setup** to copy a starter collection of news configuration files into place:

```
#  su news
$  make setup
```

Next, we'll create space (as root) for a couple of executables in the */usr/bin* directory. Following that, we will again invoke *make* to copy the executables into place.

```
$  exit              <-- revert to root
#  rm -f /usr/bin/inews
#  cp /dev/null /usr/bin/inews
#  chown bin.bin /usr/bin/inews
#  chmod a+x /usr/bin/inews
```

```
# rm -f /usr/bin/injnews
# cp /dev/null /usr/bin/injnews
# chown bin.bin /usr/bin/injnews
# chmod a+x /usr/bin/injnews

# rm -f /usr/bin/cnewsdo
# cp /dev/null /usr/bin/cnewsdo
# chown bin.bin /usr/bin/cnewsdo
# chmod a+x /usr/bin/cnewsdo

# su bin
$ make ui
```

c-news Configuration

Once you have successfully bashed your way through *c-news* compilation and installation, you can turn your attention to configuration. Again, I assume that you will have a network news feed via NNTP. Accordingly, the steps we will discuss below are specific to a co-installation of *c-news* and *nntp*. We will do it in parts; in a few spots we will make choices that we won't complete until later, when we get to *nntp* configuration.

Most of the configuration files for *c-news* live in */usr/lib/news* (assuming you followed my lead when choosing directories). I'd like to go through the important ones, in a single pass. In almost every case, the file in question will already exist; our job is to customize. *Be sure to make your changes as user* news, *so that file permissions are preserved.*

By the way, a common cause of runtime news problems is incorrect file ownerships. Be sure to "**su**" to news whenever running *c-news* maintenance scripts or programs.

whoami

You need to choose a name for your site for purposes of exchanging news. In almost all cases, your domain name (e.g *gizniz.com*) or fully qualified host name is the best bet. Other kinds of site names—such as a simple *gizniz*—will work, though they should really be registered with the UUCP Mapping Project. This is because much of the USENET traffic in the world flows over non-networked links; a non-registered site name you choose for your news hub might interfere with news delivery someplace else. Anyway, choose an appropriate site name, and enter it into the file */usr/lib/news/whoami.*

active

The next file on our tour, */usr/lib/news/active*, lists all of the newsgroups your c-news installation knows about. Newsgroups appear one per line:

```
...
news.admin.misc    0000005148 0000000114 y
news.announce      0000000000 0000000001 m
news.announce.newgroups 0000000334 0000000129 m
news.answers       0000009513 0000005756 y
news.groups        0000008643 0000000466 y
```

The leftmost field gives the newsgroup name. Above we see a few groups: *news.admin.misc*, *news.announce*, and so on. Typically, newsgroups from a single hierarchy will be grouped together within *active*, though there is no particular ordering requirement.

The second and third, numeric fields, list the highest and lowest numbered articles known to your *c-news* installation. These numbers have local significance only; they refer to the *names* of spool files containing news articles—one file per article. The snippet of an *active* file shown above, for example, indicates that *news.answers* postings can be found in files named *5756* through *9512*, in the */usr/spool/news/news/answers* directory.[*] Each file contains a single article.

The fourth field tells how postings are to be treated—should they be accepted, should they be forwarded to the group's moderator? Here's a list of possible fourth-field values, taken from the *active(5)* man page:

Value	Action
y	Local postings are allowed.
n	No local postings are allowed, only remote ones.
m	The group is moderated and all postings must be approved.
j	Articles in this group are not kept, but only passed on.
x	Articles cannot be posted to this newsgroup.
=foo.bar	Articles are locally filed into the "foo.bar" group.

One doesn't typically update *active* by hand. That's usually the work of a script (*/usr/lib/news/bin/maint/addgroup*) or a control message—a special kind of posting that, among other things, can cause groups to be created.

There is an exception to the not-updating-by-hand principal. At the outset, you are probably going to need a sample *active* file to bootstrap your server. Fortunately, these are cloned and passed around like brandied fruit. You should be able to find a prototype on your access provider's anonymous FTP server, or get one from a

---

* There may be holes; articles may have been deleted.

friend. Edit the *active* file to remove the hierarchies you don't need, and keep the ones you want. Once you have the new *active* file in place, you can create the necessary spool directories with the *adddirs* command:

```
$ /usr/lib/newsbin/maint/adddirs
```

In fact, you can re-run *adddirs* whenever you update *active* to include a new hierarchy (e.g., *misc*, *alt*, etc.).

sys

The next configuration file, *sys*, tells *c-news* three things: the hierarchies you are willing to receive from "upstream" sites, the "downstream" sites you are willing to feed, and the hierarchies you are willing to feed to them.

```
ME:comp,news,sci,rec,misc,soc,talk

foo.freck.com/frecknntp:comp/all:F:/usr/spool/news/foo.freck.com
newsfeed.provider.net:comp,news,sci,rec/all:F:/usr/spool/news/
    newsfeed.provider.net
```

In the *sys* file above, for example, we list our site ("ME") and the news hierarchies we will accept—*comp,news,sci,rec,misc,soc,talk*. Below that, we list two downstream sites and the newsgroups we will forward to them, via NNTP.

Notice that the first downstream site, foo.freck.com, is listed with an additional qualifier—frecknntp. This is an exclusion; it says that if an article has already visited site *frecknntp* it shouldn't be forwarded to *foo.freck.com*. You might use the exclusion if both names—*foo.freck.com* and *frecknntp*—actually refer to the same news hub. This would prevent your server from offering them articles that they sent to you in the first place. You might wonder how can your news server tell where an article has been: the Path: header at the top of an article lists all the intervening sites between the origin and yours.

Copy the rest of the *sys* prototype, above, keeping a similar structure; replace just those components that are specific to your feed. That should be sufficient. You can find more details in the *newssys.5* man page that comes with the *c-news* package.

explist

Bringing articles in is part of the job; you have to get rid of them too. You never want to get into the situation where you run out of disk space. Things can get so tight that you find yourself in a *Catch-22*: you can't delete old articles because you don't have enough space to run the program that deletes old articles (more about how to fix this later). On the other hand, you don't want to let space go wasted; depending on the size of your feed, a leftover 100 Mbytes might be worth two days of news. Anyway, we're looking for a happy medium, and this is what makes "expiry" a black art.

```
# note that the order of lines in this file is significant

/expired/          x    14       –
/bounds/           x    0-1-30   –

news.answers       x    14       –
junk               x    1        –

all                x    7        –
```

File *explist*, represented above, controls article expiration, and archiving. The first non-comment line, /expired/, tells *expire* how many days it should retain article records in the history files. You can keep records long after articles are expired, in case the articles reappear: an "upstream" site might offer one you have already seen and deleted, for instance. The second time around, *c-news* will just reject it. There's a practical limitation to the amount of history you can keep, however. History files containing just a few weeks of data can grow very large. Accordingly, you might prefer to keep the /expired/ parameter low—equal to the median amount of time you allow *any* articles to live—and risk receiving some of the same articles twice. If you have just a single feed, this probably isn't even an issue; it is unlikely that the same site will feed you repeats.

There is another role for the /expired/ parameter as well: *c-news* uses the value as a measure of the number of days out-of-date an arriving article can be before it is declared "ancient" and tossed immediately.

Moving along to the /bounds/ line, we see three numbers separated by hyphens. The first gives the *minimum* amount of time an article is allowed to live on the news hub before it can be considered for a target for expiration. A value of 0, as shown below, means that articles are eligible for expiration as soon as they arrive.

```
/bounds/              x    0-1-30   –

news.answers          x    14       –
```

The third number tells how long an article can live before it gets expired uncondi-tionally. We need this parameter because it is possible for articles to declare how long *they* think they should live, without regard for the expiration period you sug-gest for them. The middle number is ignored.

Below the /bounds/ and /expired/ lines we list news hierarchies, along with suggested lifespans for articles. The lifespan can be a single value, in which case it will be subject to the "bounds," set above.

The expiration specification can also be expanded to a three-valued triple:

```
news.answers          x     0-14-30     -
```

The "0" and "30" in this example have the same meanings as they do for the /bounds/ line. The "14", again, gives the suggested lifespan for articles. This can be overridden—up to the maximum lifespan specified (30)—by the article itself.

The x field says that expiration applies to both moderated and unmoderated groups.* If you want to single out either subset, you can change the x to m or u, respectively.

The last field is for archiving. The dash, as shown above, means "just expire—don't archive." Replacing the dash with a directory name tells *expire* that you want to archive articles as they are deleted.

```
news.answers          x     14     /usr/spool/archives
```

Article heaven, in this case, will be a subdirectory of */usr/spool/archives*, arranged just like the subdirectory of */usr/spool/news* where the articles lived when they walked this earth (so they'll be comfortable, I suppose). For instance, an article from *news.answers*—say 3892—will retire into */usr/spool/ archives/news/ answers/3892*.

```
news.answers          x     14     =/usr/spool/archives
```

If, on the other hand, you specify =/usr/spool/archives, the dead articles will be dumped directly into */usr/spool/archives*, without the replicated subdirectory.

Lastly, you can place an "@" in the last field. This tells *expire* to learn of the archive directory's name from the command line (specified with -a archive-dir). Note that if you choose to use the "@" construct, you will probably also need to change the script that runs *expire*, */usr/lib/newsbin/doexpire*, to include the -a flag.

By the way, it's up to you to clean out the archive directories from time to time. *expire* will take care of heaving the news articles. However, once they become archives, they are essentially forgotten by *c-news*.

Other Files

Directory */usr/lib/news* houses a number of other configuration files as well. For the most part, these will be initialized to sample values and installed by "**make setup**." As part of the installation process, you should visit each of the files, and set them appropriately for your site.

---

* Retro-note: the second whole field ("x") and last ("-") are ignored on the /bounds/ and /expire/ lines.

mailname   This file holds the mailing address for your site. Change this to something meaningful.

mailpaths   When someone attempts to post to a moderated group (as indicated by the "m" flag in *active*), *injnews* (or *relaynews*) will consult the *mailpaths* file to see who the moderator is, and forward the posting directly to them. *mailpaths* is arranged as a list of tab-separated newsgroup – moderator pairs—one per line. You will probably find, however, that your copy of *mailpaths* contains the line: `all uunet!%s`. This is sufficient; moderated postings will be forwarded to UUNET, and then on to the moderators.

organization   This file holds the name of your organization. Set it to something meaningful.

That's basically it for *c-news* configuration files in */usr/lib/news*, though we will visit the directory once more to configure *nntp*. We also have a few odds and ends to take care of: *cron* requires an update, and we need to make a change in *rc.local*. We'll come back to these later. The good news is that we are now ready to test *c-news*.

Quick c-news Tests

The installation process will have created an *active* file with a few newsgroups in it—particularly *news.newusers.answers*, *junk*, and *control*. By this point you may have replaced it—you may have snatched a full copy of *active* from somewhere else, and run *addactiv*, as suggested above. Whichever the case, I now want to add another newsgroup for testing. Begin by "*su*"-ing to user *news*. Create a newsgroup, *general*, and an associated article directory by typing:

```
$ /usr/lib/newsbin/maint/addgroup general y
```

Additionally, I want to add an imaginary site to your *sys* file (temporarily). Please edit */usr/lib/news/sys*, and include the following entry at the bottom:

```
foo.gizniz.com:general/all:F:/usr/spool/news/foo.gizniz.com
```

With this, we can check our ability to feed other, "downstream" sites.

Posting

Script */usr/bin/inews* (inject news) is one of the many programs created when you build c-news. First, doublecheck to see that *inews* is present, and that it is executable. Also, see that */usr/bin/inews* and */usr/bin/cnewsdo* have their "x" permission bits set. We'll start by testing your ability to post. Invoke *inews* like so:

```
$ inews -h
Newsgroups: general
Subject: Testing

If I had an uncle Pete, he could wash my smelly feet.

^D
$
```

The script should end silently, without complaints. Change directories to */usr/spool/news/in.coming*. You should see a file of the form *x.xxxxxxxxx.t*, where the *x*'s represent digits (the number of seconds since New Years, 1970, actually). The file is your article, ready to be posted. Take a look. You should also see a directory named *bad* (this is where broken articles and batches go). If you see a file called *stop*, type */usr/lib/newsbin/input/newsrunning on*, and continue.

Next, we will crank *c-news*' machinery once around to see if the article gets posted correctly. Type the following:

```
$ /usr/lib/newsbin/input/newsrun
```

Be patient; it will take 45 seconds to complete. If it comes back right away, then something is wrong. Check to see that you have a fair amount of space in your news spool directory; a script called */usr/lib/newsbin/spacefor* decides whether there is enough room available to proceed. You might also run prefix */usr/lib/newsbin/input/newsrun* with **sh -x** so you can watch the script execute.

When your prompt comes back, change directories to *./general*, and type **ls**. Your article should appear as a numbered file. Take a look!

There should be a few other side effects as well. Check to see that you have a file named */usr/spool/news/foo.gizniz.com*, and that it contains a line that points to the article you just posted—e.g. general/1. A similar file will be created for each remote site you are feeding, provided there are articles to be forwarded. If *foo.gizniz.com* doesn't appear, check to see that you have correctly added the entry to *sys*, as described above. The file */usr/lib/news/log* should also show that the article was received (locally), and that it is to be forwarded to *foo.gizniz.com*.

If you had trouble, you may see error messages; these will help you pinpoint the problem (hopefully). Also, check */usr/lib/news/errlog* for clues. Once things seem to be working smoothly, you should try posting under your own ID rather than posting as user *news*. This will expose any file permissions problems that might have snuck through.

c-news Miscellany

We have a couple of clean-up items for *c-news* before we can declare it "production ready." First, we have to add an entry to *rc.local* (or equivalent) to clean up any turd files that might be left behind by *c-news* or *nntp* when the computer gets rebooted or crashes. Find an appropriate "rc" file, and add the following line:

```
su news -c /usr/lib/newsbin/maint/newsboot
```

Next, we need to add some entries to *cron*'s tables to perform scheduled delivery and housekeeping tasks. Switch to the place where *cron* entries are kept (most likely */usr/spool/cron/crontabs*), and edit the file *root*.

```
0,15,30,45  *     1-31  *    0-6  su news -c '/usr/lib/newsbin/input/newsrun'
#30 8       1-31  1-5        su news -c '/usr/lib/newsbin/input/newsrunning off'
00 17       1-31  1-5        su news -c '/usr/lib/newsbin/input/newsrunning on'
#40 *       1-31  0-6        su news -c '/usr/lib/newsbin/batch/sendbatches'
59 0        1-31  0-6        su news -c '/usr/lib/newsbin/expire/doexpire'
10 8        1-31  *     0-6  su news -c '/usr/lib/newsbin/maint/newsdaily'
00 5,13,21  1-31  *    0-6   su news -c '/usr/lib/newsbin/maint/newswatch \
                             | mail news'
```

The cron entries shown above were copied from the file *conf/cron*, in the *c-news* source directory. You will notice that I have commented out a couple of lines (via "#"). The first of these is designed to shut down news processing once a day, at 8:30 AM. The subsequent line, which I left active, restarts news at 5:00 PM. You can remove the comment character, if you like, and shut down news processing during working hours. A little warning: you will probably find that some folks in your organization will think news is broken or slow if you shut it off. If I were you, I would just leave it running. The second commented line runs a program that assembles news into batches (typically, compressed groups of articles), to be forwarded "downstream." We won't need this for our *NNTP* feed.

Paste the lines as shown into the *root* crontab table. You will have to restart *cron* for the changes to take effect.

Compiling nntp

Where are we headed? In case you got lost somewhere in the middle of the last section, we are constructing a news hub, in pieces. *c-news* is the part that catalogs, stores, and deletes news articles. *nntp* has the job of moving articles across the network. The good news is that we are done configuring *c-news*. Provided your news software successfully completed the simple tests above, you should be ready to go. The bad news is that we still have to compile and configure *nntp*. Fortunately, this job shouldn't take quite as long.

First, you will need to locate a recent copy of the *nntp* server code. The latest copy (version 1.5.12.2 as of this writing) is available from the site *ftp://ftp.academ.com/pub/nntp/server*. Earlier versions (in both server-only and server plus client collections) will function. However, you will find the most support for new kinds of client requests—server-based article summaries, article threading—in the latest code.

"Untar" the *nntp* distribution in a convenient spot. We will make most of our configuration choices in one file—*conf.h*—in the top level directory. File *conf.h* comes packed as *conf.h.dist*; make a copy before beginning.

Because *nntp* runs on many flavors of UNIX, it has to be configurable. Accordingly, you will find a number of #defines in *conf.h* that will require your attention. I'm afraid I can't help you too much with these—I don't know what kind of machine you have. However, I will make a few suggestions to assure that the resulting binaries are compatible with the *c-news* installation we just built. *README-conf.h* will help walk you through the #define choices appropriate to your operating system.

For our purposes, the #defines that are of direct importance are:

DBZ
This says that we should use the *DBZ* database routines for the history files. "Undef" DBM when you "define" DBZ.

CNEWS
This tells *NNTP* that we are running *c-news*.

CNEWS-CLEARTEXT
Transferred articles will be placed in files named xxxxxxxxxxxx.t; the ".t" tells *newsrun* that these are text, and don't have to be uncompressed.

BATCHED_INPUT
This tells *NNTP* to collect incoming articles into batches, before handing them to *c-news* for processing. You should set this option, particularly if you leave news shut down during daytime hours.

ACCESS_FILE
Set this to */usr/lib/news/nntp_access*.

MSGID
This tells *nntp* whether we want a separate daemon to track late arriving articles with a daemon. I suggest that you "undef" this; it will be one less piece we have to shuttle through the compiler.

The top level *Makefile* needs a few tweaks. Because we are using the *dbz* database routines from *c-news*, we need to make the appropriate include and object modules available to *nntp*. Edit *Makefile*, and set DBLIBS as follows:

```
DBLIBS = <c-news directory>/libbz/dbz.o <c-news directory>/libbz/dbzdbm.o
```

Likewise, change CFLAGS:

```
CFLAGS = -O -I<c-news directory>/libbz
```

Depending on your computer and operating system, *nntp* server compilation could go easily, or it could be difficult. From the handful of binaries (potentially) created when you run a "make," we only really care about three: *nntpd*, *nntpxmit*, and a simple program called *sblock*. If you have problems, you might concentrate on these three, and let the rest go. To start compilation, type *make* server from the shell prompt in the top level *nntp* directory. You can also create *nntpxmit* independently (if you need to) by going into directory *xmit*, and typing *make*.

Configuring nntp

The two most important binaries have distinct roles: *nntpd* sits and waits for incoming connections—either from other sites or from individuals' newsreaders. *nntpxmit*, on the other hand, makes outbound connections with remote sites, in order to deliver news articles. They serve different purposes. Accordingly, we have to configure *nntpd* and *nntpxmit* independently.

A word of disclaimer: I am going to step around a makefile-controlled installation, and approach the job manually. We could let *make* do it. However, I don't know that you were actually able to compile everything; *make* would have a problem with us trying to install binaries that hadn't built successfully. And we have to get dirt under our fingernails anyway; we may as well perform the installation ourselves.

Begin by creating a directory for *nntp* binaries. My examples will assume that you have chosen */usr/local/etc/nntp*. Of course, you don't have to follow my lead; you could place *nntp* components into a common system directory, such as */usr/sbin*; it's up to you. Anyway, assuming that you are doing it my way, copy *server/nntpd*, *xmit/nntpxmit*, *xmit/nntpsend.csh*, and *xmit/sblock* from the *nntp* source directory into */usr/local/etc/nntp*. The files should all end up at the same level; you don't need to preserve the subdirectories.

Configuring nntpd

Installation of *nntpd* has a lot in common with installation of other daemons; we tell *inetd* to invoke *nntpd* in response to inbound connections. To start, see that you have a line like the following in */etc/services*:

```
nntp      119/tcp      usenet
```

Also, you will need a line in */etc/inetd.conf*:

```
nntp   stream  tcp  nowait  root   /usr/local/etc/nntp/nntpd   nntpd
```

Note the path in the line above: it refers back to the */usr/local/etc/nntp* subdirectory we discussed a moment ago. If you are running behind a service wrapper (see Chapter 16), then the line in *inetd.conf* will look more like this:

```
nntp   stream  tcp  nowait  root   /usr/sbin/tcpd   /usr/local/etc/nntp/nntpd
```

Once you have made your changes, send *inetd* a *HUP* signal to make it re-read */etc/inetd.conf*:

```
# ps aux | grep inetd        "ps -ae" or "ps -ef" under SYSV
  <process ID list returned>
# kill -HUP <inetd's process ID>
```

nntp_access

In */usr/lib/news/nntp_access*, we specify who can connect to the news server via NNTP, and what they are allowed to do—can they read news, are they allowed to post articles, can they transfer (feed) news? Note that the file may not exist; you may have to create it. A minimal configuration—one line—looks like:

```
default     both     post
```

In this case, anyone may access the news hub, for any purpose. You should leave your *nntp_access* this way for now, so that we can test. Once you are confident that inbound NNTP is working, you can come back and tighten access more securely.*

A more richly configured *nntp_access* might be as follows:

```
newsfeed.provider.net   xfer   no
gizniz-net              both   post
*.zugzug.com            read   post
localhost               read   post
```

---

* By the way, *nntp_access* probably isn't going to be your only protection against unwanted connections. Router access lists will be your front line of defense.

This says that host *newsfeed.provider.net* has permission to transfer (feed) news to us, but not to engage in interactive conversation—they are not allowed to read or post individual articles. By contrast, hosts **.zugzug.com* (anyone in the domain), and *localhost* (this computer), are allowed to interact; they can read and post articles—but are not allowed to transfer. Anyone on network *gizniz-net* is allowed to either transfer or post articles.

Here's the general scheme: the leftmost field contains a host specification or a network. You may list individual hosts, or a domain (via `*`). In the case of a network, the name refers back to an entry in */etc/networks*, e.g.:

```
gizniz.net    198.252.200
```

The second field can take on values {both, read, xfer, no}, where read grants the ability to browse through articles, xfer gives the ability to feed, and both and no allow or deny the complete access, respectively.

The third field can be one of {post, no}, were post grants the ability to interactively post articles to the server. A fourth field, not depicted, lists a subset of news hierarchies to which the entry applies.

Testing nntpd

It is time to run a couple of tests. First, we will try to read and post news through the daemon. Following that, we will attempt to transfer news, as though we were a remote news hub, providing a feed. Be sure that you have completed all of the steps outlined above, and have broad permissions specified in *nntp_access*. When you are ready, telnet into *nntpd* like so:

```
$ telnet localhost 119
Trying 127.0.0.1...
Connected to localhost.
Escape character is '^]'.
200 maddie NNTP[auth] server version 1.5.12.1 (1 Jan 1995) ready at
Wed May 31 12:05:33 1995 (posting ok).
```

You should be greeted with a banner, as shown above. Now let's try to read the article that we posted to newsgroup *general* several sections ago:

```
group general
211 2 1 2 general              Note: this is info from "active"
article 1
220 1 <D9735L.616@atlantic.com> Article retrieved; head and body follow.
Newsgroups: general
Path: atlantic.com!dowd
From: dowd@atlantic.com (Kevin Dowd)
Subject: Testing
Organization: Atlantic Computing Technology Corp.
Message-ID: <D9735L.616@atlantic.com>
```

```
Date: Fri, 26 May 1995 16:58:33 GMT

If I had an uncle Pete, he could wash my smelly feet.

.
quit
205 maddie closing connection.  Goodbye.
```

Success (at least on paper)! If you weren't able to retrieve an article, double-check that the newsgroup general exists, that the articles are there, and that the file permissions are reasonable. Also, make sure that */usr/lib/news/active* is in place, and that it is generally readable.

Now we will post an article:

```
$ telnet localhost 119
Trying 127.0.0.1...
Connected to localhost.
Escape character is '^]'.
200 maddie NNTP[auth] server version 1.5.12.1 (1 Jan 1995) ready at
   Wed May 31 12:15:33 1995 (posting ok).
post
340 Ok
Newsgroups: general
Subject: I have a bone in my leg.

That's why I can't go to the dance with you.
.
240 Article posted successfully.
quit
205 maddie closing connection.  Goodbye.
```

The blank line between the headers and the article text is significant. Also, be sure to end your note with a solo period (.). Now, hurry down to */usr/spool/news/in.coming* and see if you can catch the article before *newsrun* grabs it. If you arrive late, you should be able to find the article in */usr/spool/news/general*, just as we did when we ran our *c-news* tests earlier.

Finally, let's try to transfer some news:

```
$ telnet localhost 119
Trying 127.0.0.1...
Connected to localhost.
Escape character is '^]'.
200 maddie NNTP[auth] server version 1.5.12.1 (1 Jan 1995) ready at
   Wed May 31 12:15:33 1995 (posting ok).
ihave <xxxxx@gizniz.com>
335 Ok
Newsgroups: general
Subject: testing again
Path: foo
Message-ID: <xxxxx@gizniz.com>
Date: Fri, 31 May 1995 16:58:33 GMT
```

From: mr.tube@gizniz.com

A 30 foot high neon 12A×7 marks Mr. Tube's All Night Radio Tube Store, and shimmers like a beacon of hope across the evening desert floor....

.

235 Thanks.

quit

205 maddie closing connection. Goodbye.

The message has to have all the components shown above (Date:, Message-ID, etc.), in their correct forms. When you type "quit," it will take a little while for the prompt to come back; *nntpd* waits for *newsrun* to complete (remember the 45-second delay in our last *newsrun* test?). When it's all over, you should find a new article in */usr/spool/news/general.* *

Configuring *nntpxmit*

We still have to think about moving news "downstream" to other sites. Fortunately, there's not much left to do; we have already staged a dry run with *c-news*; recall that we had *relaynews* drop off a list of articles bound for *foo.freck.com* into the */usr/spool/news* directory. We pick up basically where we left off: *nntpxmit* is going to grab the list of articles and forward them off to another news hub.

nntpxmit runs under control of a script called *nntpsend.csh*. Change directories to */usr/local/etc/nntp*, and edit */nntpsend.csh*.† You will find a foreach loop, which steps through the names of remote news hubs. Change this to reflect your own "downstream" sites. The entries here must match those listed in your */usr/lib/news/sys* file. For example:

```
    ...
    foreach host ( foo.freck.com newsfeed.provder.net )
    ...
```

While we're at it, we need to change the directory referenced in the set batchdir=/usr/spool/news/batch .... line to:

```
    ...
    set batchdir=/usr/spool/news libdir=/usr/spool/news/lib
    ...
```

* As you can see, I was able to tell the daemon almost anything I wanted about the article I transferred—origin, path, responsible person, etc. *NNTP* has additional (proposed) capabilities for authenticating connections. You will find more information included with the source.

† This script runs under the C Shell. There is an analogous Bourne Shell script in *nntp* source distribution *xmit* subdirectory. If, for some reason, you don't have the C Shell on your computer, or if you prefer the Bourne Shell, feel free to substitute.

And since we are hacking this script mercilessly, we may as well change the references to a few binaries so that they include the correct path (this is ugly; I apologize). Where you see:

```
shlock -p $$ -f ${lock}
```

change it to:

```
/usr/local/etc/nntp/shlock -p $$ -f ${lock}
```

Do the same with the reference to *nntpxmit*, save the file, and get out.

nntpsend has to run periodically. The more often you run it, the quicker postings from your organization will reach the outside world; every 15 minutes is probably reasonable. Edit */usr/spool/cron/crontabs/root* as before, and append the following line:

```
15  *  1-31  *  0-6  su news -c '/usr/local/etc/nntp/nntpsend.csh'
```

Again, you will have to restart *cron* so that the new entry will take effect.

Testing nntpsend

Testing an upstream feed is a little tricky because you can't run your tests in a vacuum; someone on the other end of the wire has to let you in. If you are getting a feed from your access provider, you may be required to fill out a form, or call on the phone before they will let you connect. Once that's done, you can make sure that they have granted your computer the necessary permissions to transfer news by the same method with which we tested our own server: from your news hub, telnet into port 119 on the remote hub, and type ihave <whatever>. If everything goes well, the remote news hub will say "OK." If not, you will get a message like the following:

```
$ telnet localhost 119
Trying 127.0.0.1...
Connected to localhost.
Escape character is '^]'.
200 maddie NNTP[auth] server version 1.5.12.1 (1 Jan 1995) ready at
  Wed May 31 12:15:33 1995 (posting ok).
ihave <whatever>
400 You do not have transfer permission
```

Once you are convinced that you are able to transfer news, you can post an article, and run *nntpsend.csh* by hand to see that your message gets out. In fact, you might post to *misc.test*; if it works you will receive responses from all over the world.

```
nntpsend.csh: [3571] begin Wed May 31 19:21:54 EDT 1995
nntpsend.csh: [3571] begin newsfeed.provider.net
nntpsend.csh: [3571] begin newsfeed.provider.net
nntpxmit: newsfeed.provider.net stats 1 offered 1 accepted 0 rejected 0 failed
nntpxmit: newsfeed.provider.net xmit user 0.000 system 0.040 elapsed 7.070
nntpsend.csh: [3571] end newsfeed.provider.net
nntpsend.csh: [3571] end Wed May 31 19:22:02 EDT 1995
```

Above, we have the output from *nntpsend.csh*—the way it should look if everything goes OK. *nntpxmit* provides a few statistics about the number of articles it offered ("IHAVE . . ."), the numbers that were accepted or rejected, and the number of article failures. In the example, you can see that a single article was offered and accepted by the remote news hub.

A few things could go wrong: if you don't see any "offered, accepted . . ." statistics, that's a sign that *nntpxmit* didn't find the docket of articles behind by relaynews. If, on the other hand, you get the statistics, but it looks like your articles aren't being offered, it may be that *nntpxmit* can't find them when it runs—*nntpxmit* may be looking in the wrong place.

What to Do When News Overflows

On occasion, news will flow over the brim. It could happen for one of several reasons: perhaps you live dangerously close to the edge on disk space. Or maybe your feed is disrupted for a day or so; upon restoration, backed-up news may gush in as if from a sewer pipe explosion. Whatever the case, you will have to take a couple of steps to get news working again.

Here's where the logjam often occurs: as part of normal processing, *expire* wants to delete old records from the history files. To do that, it has to create a new, blank history file, and copy over the records that need to be preserved. That means that, for a while anyway, *expire* will need roughly twice the amount of disk space taken by the current *history.pag*, *history.dir*, and *history* files. For a normal feed, this can be many tens of megabytes.

The problems start when incoming news gobbles all the space that *expire* might have used: if there isn't enough room, *expire* won't run in its normal fashion. Instead it will punt, and leave the history files a bit out of date and just a little larger than they should be. If too much time goes by, the history files will grow huge, exacerbating the problem.* Aside from the most obvious sign of trouble— no disk space—a quick check of the mail that the news administrator receives (probably user *news*) should reveal some warning messages. A serendipitous ps aux may reveal *expire* circling overhead, looking for room to land; if you repeat-

---

* Here's one way to avoid the problem: keep the history files on a separate file system from the news spool directory.

edly see *sleep 600* in the process list, you should suspect that this is the work of *doexpire*, taking a nap, and hoping things will get better somehow.

Slash and burn is one strategy for freeing up space. You could slip into the *junk* directory (or any other place where you don't think people will care about missing news), and delete, delete, delete. When you have created sufficient room, *expire* will run normally.

A more promising strategy—especially if the history files have grown unchecked for some time—is to first shut down news, delete some articles, delete the history files, and then recreate article histories from scratch. As user *news*:

```
$ /usr/lib/newsbin/input/newsrunning off
$ <slash and burn>
$ cd /usr/lib/news
$ rm history*
$ /usr/lib/newsbin/expire/mkhistory

  <A long time passes>

$ /usr/lib/newsbin/input/newsrunning on
```

Of course, if you get into a jam like this, you might consider tuning *explist* so that news is expired sooner. Perhaps the biggest problem with news getting stuck isn't the maintenance hassle; it's the addicted users who complain when their flow of news gets cut.

G

Internet Service Providers

All providers listed support PPP, SLIP, or leased-line connections at rates of at least 56K; many support ISDN. An asterisk (*) indicates providers who also offer dedicated connections at T1 or higher levels, making good choices for LAN connections or other multi-user networks.

Table G–1: Regional and National Service Providers: U.S. and Canada

State/City/Provider	Email	Telephone
ALABAMA		
Birmingham		
Cheney Communications Company*	info@cheney.net	(800) CHENEY-1
Viper Computer Systems, Inc.*	vipersys@viper.net	(205) 978-9850
Mobile		
WSNetwork Communications Services*	info@wsnet.com	(334) 263-5505
ALASKA		
All points		
Corcom, Inc.	support@corcom.com	(907) 563-1191
Internet Alaska*	info@alaska.net	(907) 562-4638
MicroNet Communications	info@lasertone.com	(907) 333-8663
ALBERTA		
Calgary		
OA Internet Inc.*	info@oanet.com	(403) 430-0811
Edmonton		
Alberta SuperNet, Inc.	info@supernet.ab.ca	(403) 441-3663
CCINet	info@ccinet.ab.ca	(403) 450-6787

Table G-1: Regional and National Service Providers: U.S. and Canada (continued)

State/City/Provider	Email	Telephone
ARIZONA		
Phoenix/Mesa		
Crossroads Communications*	info@xroads.com	(602) 813-9040
Evergreen Internet*	evergreen@enet.net	(602) 926-4500
GetNet International, Inc.*	info@getnet.com	(602) 943-3119
Internet Access*	bang@neta.com	(602) 820-4000
Internet Direct, Inc.*	info@indirect.com	(602) 274-0100
NETWEST Communications, Inc.*	webmaster@netwest.com	(602) 948-5052
Primenet*	info@primenet.com	(602) 395-1010
Systems Solutions Inc.*	webmaster@sypac.com	(602) 955-5566
Tuscon		
ACES Research*	sales@aces.com	(520) 322-6500
Internet Direct, Inc.*	info@indirect.com	(520) 324-0100
Opus One*	info@opus1.com	(520) 324-0494
ARKANSAS		
All points		
Axess Providers*	info@axs.net	(501) 225-6901
Information Galore!*	info@elvis.infogo.com	(501) 862-0777
IntelliNet, LLC*	info@intellinet.com	(800) 290-7677
world lynx	ivars@cei.net	(501) 562-8297
BRITISH COLUMBIA		
Vancouver		
auroraNET, Inc.*	sales@aurora.net	(604) 294-4357 x101
Cyberstore Systems, Inc.*	info@cyberstore.net	(604) 482-3400
Helix Internet*	info@helix.net	(604) 689-8544
Internet Direct	sales@direct.ca	(604) 691-1600
MIND LINK! Communication Corporation*	info@mindlink.net	(604) 668-5000
All other points		
Wimsey Information Services Inc.*	info@wimsey.com	(604) 257-1111
A&W Internet Inc.*	info@awinc.com	(604) 763-1176
Island Net, AMT Solutions Group, Inc.	mark@islandnet.com	(604) 383-0096
Okanagan Internet Junction*	info@junction.net	(604) 549-1036
UNIserve Online*	info@uniserve.com	(604) 856-6281
Whistler Networks*	webmaster@whistler.net	(604) 932-0606
CALIFORNIA		
Bakersfield		
Kern Internet Services	support@kern.com	(805) 397-4513
Lightspeed Net*	hostmaster@lightspeed.net	(805) 324-4291

Table G–1: Regional and National Service Providers: U.S. and Canada (continued)

State/City/Provider	Email	Telephone
CALIFORNIA (continued)		
Fresno		
InfoNet Communications*	johnb@icinet.net	(209) 446-2360
ValleyNet Communications*	info@valleynet.com	(209) 486-VNET
Los Angeles		
Artnet Communications*	info@artnet.net	(310) 659-0122
Cogent Software, Inc.*	info@cogsoft.net	(818) 585-2788
DigiLink Network Services	info@digilink.net	(310) 542-7421
DirectNet*	sales@directnet.com	(213) 383-3144
EarthLink Network*	info@earthlink.net	(213) 644-9500
Lightside, Inc.*	info@lightside.net	(818) 858-9261
PacificNet*	info@pacificnet.net	(818) 717-9500
Oakland		
Beckemeyer Development*	info@bdt.com	(510) 530-9637
Direct Network Access (DNAI)*	info@dnai.com	(510) 649-6110
Idiom Consulting	info@idiom.com	(510) 644-0441
LanMinds, Inc.	info@lanminds.com	(510) 843-6389
Surf Communications, Inc.	info@expressway.com	(800) 499-1517
Orange County		
Delta Internet Services*	sales@delta.net	(714) 778-0370
Riverside/San Bernadino		
EmpireNet	support@empirenet.com	(909) 787-4969
Sacramento/Yolo		
CalWeb Communications*	info@calweb.com	(916) 641-WEB0
Coastal Web Online*	info@cwo.com	(916) 552-7922
mother.com, Inc.*	info@mother.com	(916) 757-8070
NSNet*	sales@ns.net	(916) 856-1530
ProMedia*	info@promedia.net	(916) 853-5520
QuikNet*	sales@quiknet.com	(916) 773-0917
Sacramento Network Access, Inc.*	ghall@sna.com	(916) 565-4500
San Diego		
American Digital Network*	info@adnc.com	(619) 576-4272
ConnectNet	sales@connectnet.com	(619) 450-0254
CTSNet*	info@cts.com	(619) 637-3637
ZNet*	info@znet.com	(619) 755-7772
San Francisco		
The Little Garden/TLGnet*	info@tlg.net	(415) 487-1902
QuakeNet Internet Services*	info@quake.net	(415) 655-6607
Sirius Connections	info@sirius.com	(415) 284-4700
SlipNET*	info@slip.net	(415) 281-3196

Table G–1: Regional and National Service Providers: U.S. and Canada (continued)

State/City/Provider	Email	Telephone
CALIFORNIA (continued)		
San Jose/Palo Alto		
Ablecom	support@ablecom.net	(408) 280-1000
Aimnet Information Services*	info@aimnet.com	(408) 257-0900
Bay Area Internet Solutions*	info@bayarea.net	(408) 447-8690
InterNex Tiara*	info@internex.net	(408) 496-5466
InterServe Communications, Inc.*	info@interserve.com	(415) 328-4333
Internet Public Access Corporation*	info@ipac.net	(408) 532-1000
ISP Networks*	info@isp.net	(408) 653-0100
NETCOM On-Line Communication Services*	info@netcom.com	(408) 983-5950
NetGate Communications*	info@netgate.net	(408) 565-9601
West Coast Online*	info@wco.com	(800) 926-4683
Ventura		
FishNet Internet Services of Ventura	daveh@fishnet.net	(805) 650-1844
Internet Access of Ventura County	info@vcnet.com	(805) 383-3500
Silicon Beach Communications*	info@silcom.com	(805) 730-7740
WestNet Communications, Inc.	info@west.net	(805) 892-2133
COLORADO		
Denver/Boulder/Greeley		
Colorado Internet Cooperative Association*	info@coop.net	(303) 443-3786
Colorado SuperNet, Inc.*	info@csn.net	(303) 296-8202
Computer Systems Design Company*	support@csd.net	(303) 443-0808
DASH*	custserv@dash.com	(303) 674-9784
@denver.net	info@denver.net	(303) 973-7757
Indra's Net, Inc.	info@indra.com	(303) 546-9151
Colorado (southeast)		
Internet Express*	service@usa.net	(800) 592-1240
OldColo Company	dave@oldcolo.com	(719) 636-2040
Rocky Mountain Internet, Inc.*	info@rmii.com	(800) 900-RMII
CONNECTICUT		
Hartford		
imagine.com*	postmaster@imagine.com	(860) 293-3900
MiraCom*	sales@miracle.net	(860) 523-5677
NETPLEX*	info@ntplx.net	(860) 233-1111
North American Internet Company*	info@nai.net	(800) 952-INET
New Haven/Meriden		
CallNet Information Services	info@callnet.com	(203) 389-7130
Connix	info@connix.net	(203) 349-7059
PCNet*	info@pcnet.com	(203) 250-7397

Table G–1: Regional and National Service Providers: U.S. and Canada (continued)

State/City/Provider	Email	Telephone
DELAWARE		
All points		
Business Data Systems, Inc.*	info@bdsnet.com	(302) 674-2840
DCANet*	info@dca.net	(302) 654-1019
iNET Communications*	info@inetcom.net	(302) 454-1780
The Magnetic Page*	info@magpage.com	(302) 651-9753
SSNet, Inc.*	info@ssnet.com	(302) 378-1386
DISTRICT OF COLUMBIA		
All points		
Capital Area Internet Service*	info@cais.com	(703) 448-4470
ClarkNet*	info@clark.net	(410) 254-3900
CrossLink*	sales@crosslink.net	(703) 642-1120 x175
Internet Access Group, Inc.	info@iagi.net	(301) 652-0484
Internet Interstate*	info@intr.net	(301) 652-4468
NetRail, Inc.*	info@netrail.net	(703) 524-4800
RadixNet*	info@radix.net	(301) 567-9831
USNet*	info@us.net	(301) 572-5926
World Web Limited*	info@worldweb.net	(703) 838-2000
FLORIDA		
Jacksonville		
Jax Gateway to the World*	sales@jax.gttw.com	(904) 730-7692
Southeast Network Services, Inc.*	sysop@jaxnet.com	(904) 260-6064
Miami/Fort Lauderdale		
Acquired Knowledge Systems, Inc.*	info@aksi.net	(954) 525-2574
BridgeNet, LC	access@bridge.net	(305) 374-3031
CyberGate*	sales@gate.net	(954) 428-4283
Icanet*	sales@icanet.net	(954) 733-2556
Internet Gateway Connections*	info@igc.net	(954) 430-3030
NetPoint Communications, Inc.*	info@netpoint.net	(305) 891-1955
Paradise Communications*	sales-info@paradise.net	(305) 598-4426
Shadow Information Services, Inc.	admin@shadow.net	(305) 594-3450
World Information Network	info@winnet.net	(305) 535-3090
Orlando		
AccNet*	info@acc.net	(407) 834-2222
Global DataLink, Inc.*	info@gdi4.gdi.net	(407) 841-3690
GS-Link Systems, Inc.	info@gslink.net	(407) 671-8682
Internet Access Group*	sales@iag.net	(407) 786-1145
MagicNet, Inc.*	info@magicnet.net	(407) 657-2202
Online Orlando Internet Services	support@oo.com	(407) 647-7559
World Ramp, Inc.*	info@worldramp.net	(407) 740-5987

Table G–1: Regional and National Service Providers: U.S. and Canada (continued)

State/City/Provider	Email	Telephone
FLORIDA (continued)		
Tampa/St. Petersburg/Clearwater		
Bay-A-Net*	info@bayanet.com	(813) 988-7772
CFInet*	info@cfinet.com	(813) 980 1317
Intelligence Network Online, Inc.*	info@intutel.net	(813) 442-0114
OpenNet*	info@opennet.com	(813) 446-6558
PacketWorks, Inc.	info@packet.net	(813) 446-8826
West Palm Beach/Boca Raton		
The EmiNet Domain*	info@emi.net	(407) 731-0222
Magg Information Services, Inc.*	help@magg.net	(407) 642-9841
GEORGIA		
Atlanta		
America Net	sales@america.net	(770) 667-7200
Digital Service Consultants	john@dsca.com	(770) 455-9022
Intergate, Inc.*	info@intergate.net	(770) 429-9599
Internet Atlanta*	info@atlanta.com	(770) 410-9000
Lyceum Internet Services	info@lyceum.com	(404) 248-1733
Mindspring*	info@mindspring.com	(800) 719-4332
Navigator Communications	sales@nav.com	(770) 441-4007
NetDepot, Inc.*	info@netdepot.com	(770) 434-5595
Random Access, Inc.*	marius@randomc.com	(770) 804-1190
Georgia (north)		
Znet*	info@znet.augusta.ga.us	(706) 722-2175
Georgia (south)		
Homenet Communications, Inc.	info@hom.net	(912) 329-8638
HAWAII		
All points		
1Source*	info@1source.com	(808) 293-0733
Data Plus Systems*	hostmaster@dps.net	(808) 678-8989
Hawaii Online (HOL)*	info@aloha.net	(800) 207-1880
Inter-Pacific Networks*	sysman@interpac.net	(808) 935-5550
LavaNet	info@lava.net	(808) 545-5282
Maui Global Communications Co.*	info@maui.net	(808) 875-2535
Pacific Information eXchange (PixiNet)*	info@pixi.com	(808) 596-7494
IDAHO		
All points		
Micron Internet Services*	info@micron.net	(208) 368-5400
SRVnet, Inc.*	nlp@srv.net	(208) 524-6237

Table G–1: Regional and National Service Providers: U.S. and Canada (continued)

State/City/Provider	Email	Telephone
ILLINOIS		
Chicago/Gary/Kenosha		
American Information Systems*	info@ais.net	(312) 255-8500
CINnet*	sales@cin.net	(708) 310-1188
Macro Computer Solutions, Inc.*	rate-request@mcs.net	(312) 248-8649
Millenia Services*	sales@miint.net	(312) 341-0192
OnRamp, Ltd.*	info@theramp.net	(708) 222-6666
StarNet, Inc.*	info@starnetinc.com	(708) 382-0099
Sun Valley SoftWare, Ltd.*	ken@svs.com	(708) 983-0889
Tezcat Communications*	info@tezcat.com	(312) 850-0181
ThoughtPort Authority of Chicago*	info@thoughtport.com	(312) 862-6870
Wink Communications*	sales@winkcomm.com	(708) 310-9465
WorldWide Access*	info@wwa.com	(708) 367-1870
XNet Information Systems*	info@xnet.com	(708) 983-6064
East St. Louis		
see St. Louis, MISSOURI		
Illinois (central)		
Cen-Com Internet*	info@cencom.net	(217) 793-2771
FGInet, Inc.	admin@fgi.net	(217) 787-2775
ICEnet*	icenet@ice.net	(309) 454-4638
Itek*	jasegler@itek.net	(309) 691-6100
Shouting Ground Technologies*	admin@shout.net	(217) 351-7921
INDIANA		
Gary		
see Chicago, ILLINOIS		
Indianapolis		
Internet Indiana*	info@in.net	(317) 876-5NET
IQuest Network Services*	info@iquest.net	(800) 844-8649
Net Direct*	kat@inetdirect.net	(317) 251-5252
IOWA		
Council Bluffs		
see Omaha, NEBRASKA		
Des Moines		
Des Moines Internet, Inc.*	brent@dsmnet.com	(515) 270-9191
Freese-Notis WeatherNet*	info@weather.net	(515) 282-9310
INS Info Services*	info@netins.net	(515) 830-0110
KANSAS		
Kansas City		
see Kansas City, MISSOURI		

Table G-1: Regional and National Service Providers: U.S. and Canada (continued)

State/City/Provider	Email	Telephone
KANSAS (continued)		
Wichita		
DTC Supernet*	info@dtc.net	(316) 683-7272
SouthWind Internet Access, Inc.*	info@southwind.net	(316) 263-7963
KENTUCKY		
Covington		
see Cincinati, OHIO		
Louisville		
BluegrassNet*	info@bluegrass.net	(502) 589-INET
The Point Internet Services*	staff@thepoint.com	(812) 246-7187
LOUISIANA		
Baton Rouge		
Premier One*	info@premier.net	(504) 751-8080
New Orleans		
AccessCom Internet Providers*	info@accesscom.net	(504) 887-0022
CommNet Information	info@comm.net	(504) 836-2844
Communique, Inc.*	info@communique.net	(504) 527-6200
MAINE		
All points		
AcadiaNet	support@acadia.net	(207) 288-5959
Agate Internet*	ais@agate.net	(207) 947-8248
Biddeford Internet*	info@biddeford.com	(207) 756-8770
Internet Maine, Inc.*	mtenney@mainelink.net	(207) 780-0416
The Maine InternetWorks, Inc.*	info@mint.net	(207) 453-4000
Midcoast Internet Solutions	info@midcoast.com	(207) 594-8277
MANITOBA		
Winnipeg		
Internet Solutions, Inc.*	info@solutions.net	(204) 982-1060
Gate West Communications	info@gatewest.net	(204) 663-2931
All other points		
MTS Internet*	registration@mts.net	(800) 280-7095
MARYLAND		
Baltimore		
ABSnet Internet Services, Inc.*	info@abs.net	(410) 361-8160
Charm Net*	info@charm.net	(410) 558-3900
Clark Internet Services, Inc.*	info@clark.net	(410) 254-3900
jaguNET	info@jagunet.com	(410) 931-3157
Maryland (west)		
ARInternet Corporation*	info@ari.net	(301) 459-7171
Digital Express Group–DIGEX*	info@digex.net	(800) 969-9090
Fred.Net*	info@fred.net	(301) 631-5300

Table G–1: *Regional and National Service Providers: U.S. and Canada (continued)*

State/City/Provider	Email	Telephone
MASSACHUSETTS		
Boston/Worcester/Laurence		
Blue Sky, Inc.*	info@bluesky.net	(617) 270-4747
CENTnet, Inc.*	info@cent.net	(617) 492-6079
CyberAccess Internet	info@cybercom.net	(617) 396-0491
Communication, Inc.*		
North Shore Access	info@shore.net	(617) 593-3110
One World Network*	sales@oneworld.net	(617) 267-2440
Pioneer Global Telecommunications*	sales@pn.com	(617) 375-0200
Software Tool & Die	support@world.std.com	(617) 739-0202
TerraNet Internet Services*	info@terra.net	(617) 450-9000
TIAC	info_ma@tiac.net	(617) 276-7200
Wilder InterNet Gateway*	info@wing.net	(617) 932-8500
The Xensei Corporation*	info@xensei.com	(617) 376-6342
Fall River		
see Providence, RHODE ISLAND		
Springfield		
MAP Internet Services*	info@map.com	(413) 732-0214
MICHIGAN		
Detroit/Ann Arbor/Flint		
Branch Internet Services, Inc.*	info@branch.com	(800) 349-1747
CICNet*	info@cic.net	(313) 998-6703
ICNet*	info@ic.net	(313) 998-0090
Isthmus Corporation	info@izzy.net	(313) 973-2100
Merit/MichNet*	info@merit.edu	(313) 764-9430
Msen*	service@msen.com	(313) 998-4562
Michigan (central)		
Sojourn Systems Ltd.*	info@sojourn.com	(800) 949-3993
Michigan (west and north)		
Alliance Network, Inc.*	info@alliance.net	(616) 774-3010
Freeway*	info@freeway.net	(616) 347-3175
Iserv*	info@iserv.net	(616) 847-5254
Novagate*	info@novagate.com	(616) 847-0910
The Portage*	fuzzy@portage1.portup.com	(906) 487-9832
MINNESOTA		
Minneapolis/St. Paul		
gofast.net	info@gofast.net	(612) 647-6109
GoldenGate Internet Services, Inc.*	timmc@goldengate.net	(612) 574-2200
InterNetwork Services*	info@proteon.inet-serv.com	(612) 391-7300
Millennium Communications, Inc.*	info@millcomm.com	(612) 338-8666
MinnNet*	info@minn.net	(612) 944-8660

Table G-1: Regional and National Service Providers: U.S. and Canada (continued)

State/City/Provider	Email	Telephone
MINNESOTA (continued)		
Minneapolis/St. Paul (continued)		
Minnesota Online*	sales@mn.state.net	(612) 225-1110
The Minnesota Regional Network*	info@mr.net	(612) 342-2570
Protocol Communications	info@protocol.com	(612) 541-9900
Sihope Communications*	info@sihope.com	(612) 829-9667
SkyPoint Communications, Inc.*	info@skypoint.com	(612) 475-2959
Vector Internet Services, Inc.*	info@visi.com	(612) 288-0880
WaveFront Communications, Inc.*	info@wavefront.com	(612) 638-9594
WebSpan	info@webspan.com	(612) 333-LINK
Winternet (Startnet Communications)*	info@winternet.com	(612) 333-1505
Minnesota (north)		
Computer Pro*	info@computerpro.com	(218) 772-4245
Minnesota (south)		
Desktop Media*	isp@dm.deskmedia.com	(507) 373-2155
Information Superhighway Limited	info@isl.net	(507) 289-5543
Internet Connections, Inc.*	info@ic.mankato.mn.us	(507) 625-7320
Millennium Communications, Inc.*	info@millcomm.com	(507) 282-1004
MISSISSIPPI		
All points		
Aris Technologies*	info@aris.com	(601) 324-7638
Datasync Internet Services	info@datasync.com	(601) 872-0001
EBI Comm, Inc.*	hostmaster@ebicom.net	(601) 243-7075
Internet Doorway, Inc.*	info@netdoor.com	(800) 952-1570
InterSys Technologies, Inc.*	info@inst.com	(601) 949-6992
Southwind Technologies, Inc.	info@southwind.com	(601) 374-6510
TecLink*	info@teclink.net	(601) 949-6992
MISSOURI		
Kansas City		
AccuNet, Inc.*	dwhitten@accunet.com	(816) 246-9094
Databank, Inc.*	info@databank.com	(913) 842-6699
Internet Direct Communications*	sales@idir.net	(913) 842-1100
Interstate Networking Corporation*	info@interstate.net	(816) 472-4949
Q-Net, Inc.*	info@qni.com	(816) 795-1000
SkyNet*	info@sky.net	(816) 421-2626
Unicom Communications, Inc.*	fyi@unicom.net	(913) 383-8466
St. Louis		
Cybergate L.L.C.	info@cybergate.org	(314) 214-1013
iCON	info@icon-stl.net	(314) 241-ICON
Inlink	support@inlink.com	(314) 432-0149

Table G–1: Regional and National Service Providers: U.S. and Canada (continued)

State/City/Provider	Email	Telephone
MONTANA		
All points		
Cyberport Montana*	skippy@cyberport.net	(406) 863-3221
Internet Montana	support@imt.net	(406) 255-9699
Internet Services Montana, Inc.*	support@ism.net	(406) 542-0838
Montana Communications Network	info@mcn.net	(406) 254-9413
Netrix Internet System Design, Inc.*	leesa@netrix.net	(406) 257-4638
NEBRASKA		
Omaha		
Nebraska On-Ramp, Inc.*	info@neonramp.com	(402) 339-6366
NFinity Systems*	info@nfinity.com	(402) 551-3036
Nebraska (west)		
KDS Internet Services	info@kdsi.net	(308) 382-5670
NEVADA		
Las Vegas		
Access Nevada, Inc.*	info@accessnv.com	(702) 294-0480
InterMind*	info@intermind.net	(702)878-6111
@wizard.com*	george@wizard.com	(702) 871-4461
All other points		
Connectus*	info@connectus.com	(702) 323-2008
Great Basin Internet Services*	info@greatbasin.com	(702) 348-7299
SourceNet*	info@source.net	(702) 832-7246
Tahoe On-Line*	info@tol.net	(702) 588-0616
NEW BRUNSWICK		
All points		
Maritime Internet Services, Inc.*	sales@mi.net	(506) 652-3624
NEWFOUNDLAND		
All points		
Data Bits, Inc.*	info@databits.com	(709) 786 5660
NEW HAMPSHIRE		
All points		
The Destek Group, Inc.*	info@destek.net	(603) 635-3857
Empire.Net, Inc.*	info@empire.Net	(603) 889-1220
MonadNet Corporation*	info@monad.net	(603) 352-7619
NEW JERSEY		
Bergen/Passaic		
Interactive Networks, Inc.*	info@interactive.net	(201) 881-1878
Internet Online Services*	info@ios.com	(201) 928-1000

Table G-1: Regional and National Service Providers: U.S. and Canada (continued)

State/City/Provider	Email	Telephone
NEW JERSEY (continued)		
Middlesex/Somerset/Hunterdon		
ECLIPSE Internet Access*	info@eclipse.net	(800) 483-1223
Internet For 'U'*	info@ifu.net	(908) 435-0600
Superlink*	info@superlink.net	(908) 828-8988
Monmouth/Ocean		
Atlantic Internet Technologies, Inc.*	info@exit109.com	(908) 758-0505
Monmouth Internet	sales@shell.monmouth.com	(908) 389-6094
NEW MEXICO		
Albuquerque		
Internet Direct, Inc.*	info@indirect.com	(505) 888-4624
New Mexico Internet Access, Inc.*	info@nmia.com	(505) 877-0617
New Mexico Technet, Inc.*	granoff@technet.nm.org	(505) 345-6555
Rt66-Engineering International, Inc.*	info@rt66.com	(505) 343-1060
All other points		
Community Internet Access*	sysadm@cia-g.com	(505) 863-2424
CyberPort Station*	info@cyberport.com	(505) 324-6400
Roadrunner Communications*	sysop@roadrunner.com	(505) 988-9200
Southwest Cyberport*	info@swcp.com	(505)293-5967
NEW YORK		
Albany/Schenectady/Troy		
AlbanyNet*	info@albany.net	(518) 465-0873
Global One*	info@globalone.net	(518) 452-1465
LogicalNet*	sales@logical.net	(518) 452-9090
Wizvax Communications*	info@wizvax.net	(518) 273-4325
Nassau/Suffolk Counties		
Long Island Internet HQ & Pointblank BBS Ltd.*	support@pb.net	(516) 549-2165
Long Island Information, Inc.*	info@liii.com	(516) 248-5381
New York City		
Angel Networks*	info@angel.net	(212) 947-6507
BrainLINK*	info@brainlink.com	(718) 805-6559
bway.net (Outernet, Inc.)*	info-bot@bway.net	(212) 982-9800
Calyx Internet Access*	info@calyx.net	(212) 475-5051
Cloud 9 Internet*	info@cloud9.net	(914) 682-0626
dx.com*	info@dx.com	(212) 929-0566
EscapeCom*	info@escape.com	(212) 888-8780
i-2000*	info@i-2000.com	(800) 464-3820
Ingress Communications, Inc.*	info@ingress.com	(212) 268-1100
Internet Channel*	info@inch.com	(212) 243-5200
Internet Exchange*	ksc@inx.net	(212) 935-3322

Table G–1: Regional and National Service Providers: U.S. and Canada (continued)

State/City/Provider	Email	Telephone
NEW YORK (continued)		
New York City (continued)		
Internet Quicklink Corp.*	info@quicklink.com	(212) 307-1669
Interport Communications Corp.*	info@interport.net	(212) 989-1128
Maestro Technologies, Inc.*	info@maestro.com	(212) 240-9600
New York Net*	info@new-york.net	(718) 776-6811
The New York Web, Inc.*	nysurf@nyweb.com	(212) 748-7600
NY WEBB, Inc.	gwg7@webb.com	(212) 242-4912
Panix*	info@panix.com	(212) 741-4400
PCW Internet Services*	sales@pcwnet.com	(718) 937-0380
PFM Communications*	marc@pfmc.net	(212) 254-5300
RealNet*	reallife@walrus.com	(212) 366-4434
ThoughtPort Authority of NYC*	info@thoughtport.com	(212) 645-7970
TunaNet/InfoHouse	info@tunanet.com	(212) 229-8224
Rochester		
E-Znet, Inc.*	info@eznet.net	(716) 262-2485
ServiceTech, Inc.*	sales@servtech.com	(716) 263-3360
Syracuse		
EMI Communications*	info@emi.com	(800) 456-2001
NORTH CAROLINA		
Charlotte/Gastonia/Rock Hill		
Cybernetx, Inc.*	info@cybernetx.net	(704) 561-7000
SunBelt.Net*	info@sunbelt.net	(800) 950-4726
Vnet Internet Access, Inc.*	info@vnet.net	(800) 377-3282
Greensboro/Winston-Salem/High Point		
Kinetics, Inc.*	info@kinetics.net	(910) 370-1985
Raleigh/Durham/Chapel Hill		
Atlantic Internet Corporation*	info@ainet.net	(919) 833-1252
Interpath*	info@interpath.net	(800) 849-6305
NC-REN Data Services*	info@ncren.net	(919) 248-1999
Network Data Link, Inc.	staff@nc.ndl.net	(919) 878-7701
NORTH DAKOTA		
All points		
Red River Net*	info@rrnet.com	(701) 232-2227
The Internet Connection, Inc.*	tic@emh1.tic.bismarck.nd.us	(701) 222-8356
NORTHWEST TERRITORIES		
All points		
Internet North	stevel@internorth.com	(403) 873-5975

Table G-1: Regional and National Service Providers: U.S. and Canada (continued)

State/City/Provider	Email	Telephone
NOVA SCOTIA		
All points		
Atlantic Connect Inc.	info@atcon.com	(902) 429-0222
internet services and	info@isisnet.com	(902) 429-4747
information systems (isis), Inc.		
North Shore Internet Services	support@north.nsis.com	(902) 928-0565
OHIO		
Cincinnati/Hamilton		
Exodus Online Services	info@eos.net	(513) 522-0011
Internet Access Cincinnati /	info@iac.net	(513) 887-8877
M&M Engineering*		
OneNet Communications*	info@one.net	(513) 326-6000
Premiere Internet Cincinnati*	pic@cinti.com	(513) 561-6245
Primax.Net	info@primax.net	(513) 772-1223
Cleveland/Akron		
APK*	info@apk.net	(216) 481-9428
CyberGate*	info@cybergate.net	(216) 247-7660
ExchangeNet (EN)*	info@en.com	(216) 261-4593
GWIS*	info@gwis.com	(216) 656-5511
Multiverse	noc@mail.multiverse.com	(216) 344-3080
New Age Consulting Services*	info@nacs.net	(216) 524-8388
Winfield Communication, Inc.	info@winc.com	(216) 867-2904
Columbus		
Infnet, Infinite Systems*	info@infnet.com	(614) 268 9941
Internet Concourse*	info@coil.com	(614) 242-3800
OARnet*	info@oar.net	(614) 728-8100
Dayton/Springfield		
Dayton Internet Services, Inc.*	info@dayton.net	(513) 643-0188
EriNet Online Communications*	support@erinet.com	(513) 291-1995
HCST-Net*	info@hcst.com	(513) 390-7486
Youngstown/Warren		
CISNet, Inc.*	todd@cisnet.com	(216) 629-2691
OKLAHOMA		
Oklahoma City		
InterConnect On-Line*	info@icon.net	(405) 949-1800
Internet Oklahoma*	info@ionet.net	(405) 721-1580
Keystone Technology*	sales@keytech.com	(405) 848-9902
Tulsa		
Galaxy Star Systems*	info@galstar.com	(918) 835-3655
OKNET*	oksales@oknet.com	(918) 481-5899

Table G–1: Regional and National Service Providers: U.S. and Canada (continued)

State/City/Provider	Email	Telephone
ONTARIO		
Ottawa		
Achilles Internet Ltd.	info@achilles.net	(613) 723-6624
Channel One Internet Services*	getwired@sonetis.com	(613) 236-8601
Cyberus Online, Inc.	info@cyberus.ca	(613) 233-1215
In@sec	info@inasec.ca	(613) 746-3200
Internet Access, Inc.*	info@ottawa.net	(613) 225-5595
Magma Communications Ltd.*	info@magmacom.com	(613) 228-3565
Toronto		
9 To 5 Communications	staff@inforamp.net	(416) 363-9100
InfoRamp, Inc.	info@inforamp.net	(416) 363-9100
Interlog Internet Services	info@interlog.com	(416) 975-2655
Internex Online	info@io.org	(416) 363-8676
ONet Networking*	info@onet.on.ca	(416) 978-4589
TerraPoint Online, Inc.	info@terraport.net	(416) 492-3050
World Wide Wave*	info@wwwave.com	(416) 499-7100
Xenon Laboratories	info@xe.net	(416) 214-5606
OREGON		
Portland/Salem		
aracnet.com	info@aracnet.com	(503) 626-7696
Europa	info@europa.com	(503) 222-9508
One World Internetworking, Inc.	info@oneworld.com	(503) 758-1112
Spire Communications*	info@spiretech.com	(503) 222-3086
Structured Network Systems*	sales@structured.net	(503) 656-3530
Transport Logic*	info@transport.net	(503) 243-1940
All other points		
BendNet	info@bendnet.com	(503) 385-3331
Data Research Group, Inc.	info@ordata.com	(503) 465-DATA
Empire Net, Inc.*	webmaster@empnet.com	(503) 317-3437
InfoStructure*	info@mind.net	(503) 488-1962
Magick Net, Inc.	peabody@magick.net	(503) 471-2542
RAINet	help@rain.net	(503) 227-5665
PENNSYLVANIA		
Allentown/Bethlehem/Easton		
Enter.Net*	info@enter.net	(610) 366-1300
You Tools Internet*	info@fast.net	(610) 954-5910
Harrisburg/Lebanon/Carlisle		
CPCNet	webmaster@news.cpcnet.com	(717) 393-2956
LebaNet*	office@leba.net	(717) 270-9790
SuperNet Interactive Services, Inc.*	info@success.net	(717) 393-7635

Table G-1: Regional and National Service Providers: U.S. and Canada (continued)

State/City/Provider	Email	Telephone
PENNSYLVANIA (continued)		
Philadelphia		
Micro Control, Inc.	info@inet.micro-ctrl.com	(215) 321-7474
Net Access*	info@netaxs.com	(215) 576-8669
RE/COM - Reliable Communications*	sales@recom.com	(609) 225-3330
Voicenet*	info@voicenet.com	(800) 835-5710
Pittsburgh		
CityNet, Inc.*	info@city-net.com	(412) 481-5406
Nauticom*	info@pgh.nauticom.net	(800) 746-6283
Pittsburgh Online, Inc.*	sales@pgh.net	(412) 681-6130
Stargate*	info@sgi.net	(412) 942-4218
Telerama Public Access Internet*	info@telerama.lm.com	(412) 481-3505
ThoughtPort Authority of Pittsburgh*	info@thoughtport.com	(412) 963-7099
USA OnRamp*	info@usaor.net	(412) 391-4382
Scranton/Wilkes-Barre/Hazelton		
The Internet Café, Scranton, PA*	info@lydian.scranton.com	(717) 344-1969
MicroServe Information Systems, Inc.*	helpdesk@admin.microserve.net	(717) 821-5964
QUEBEC		
Montreal		
Accent Internet	admin@accent.net	(514) 737-6077
CiteNet Telecom Inc.*	info@citenet.net	(514) 861-5050
Communications Accessibles	info@cam.org	(514) 288-2581
Montreal		
Connection MMIC, Inc.	michel@connectmmic.net	(514) 331-6642
Global Info Access	info@globale.net	(514) 737-2091
NetAxis Inc. of Montreal*	info@netaxis.qc.ca	(514) 482-8989
Odyssey Internet*	info@odyssee.net	(514) 861-3432
PubNIX Montreal*	info@PubNIX.net	(514) 990-5911
ZooNet	info@zoo.net	(514) 935-6225
All other points		
ClicNet Telecommunications, Inc.*	info@qbc.clic.net	(418) 686-CLIC
Valiquet Lamothe, Inc. (VLI)	info@vli.ca	(819) 776-4438
RHODE ISLAND		
Providence/Fall River/Warwick		
Log On America	info@loa.com	(401) 453-6100
All other points		
brainiac services, inc.*	info@brainiac.com	(401) 539-9050
SASKATCHEWAN		
All points		
SaskTel	info@www.sasknet.sk.ca	(800) 644-9205

Table G–1: Regional and National Service Providers: U.S. and Canada (continued)

State/City/Provider	Email	Telephone
SOUTH CAROLINA		
Charleston		
Coastal Cruiser Internet Access	htc@sccoast.net	(803) 365-2155
SIMS, Inc.*	info@sims.com	(803) 853-4333
A World of Difference*	sales@awod.com	(803) 769-4488
Rock Hill		
see Charlotte, NORTH CAROLINA		
SOUTH DAKOTA		
All points		
RapidNet LLC	gary@rapidnet.com	(605) 341-3283
TENNESSEE		
Knoxville		
Internet Communications Group	info@netgrp.net	(423) 691-1731
United States Internet, Inc.*	info@usit.net	(800) 218-USIT
Memphis		
Magibox, Inc.	info@magibox.net	(901) 452-7555
Synapse	info@syncentral.com	(901) 767-9926
World Spice	info@wsp1.wspice.com	(901) 454-5808
Nashville		
Edge Internet Services*	info@edge.net	(615) 726-8700
ISDNet*	info@isdn.net	(615) 377-7672
The Telalink Corporation*	info@telalink.net	(615) 321-9100
United States Internet, Inc.*	info@usit.net	(615) 259-2006
TEXAS		
Austin/San Marcos		
Commuter Communication Systems	info@commuter.net	(512) 257-CCSI
The Eden Matrix	info@eden.com	(512) 478-9900
Freeside Communications, Inc.	info@fc.net	(512) 339-6094
i-link	info@i-link.net	(512) 388-2393
Onramp Access, Inc.	info@onr.com	(512) 322-9200
OuterNet Connection Strategies	info@outer.net	(512) 345-3573
Real/Time Communications*	sales@bga.com	(512) 206-3124
@sig.net*	sales@sig.net	(512) 306-0700
Turning Point Information Services*	info@tpoint.net	(512) 499-8400
Zilker Internet Park	info@zilker.net	(512) 206-3850
Dallas/Fort Worth		
CompuNet*	info@computek.net	(214) 994-0190
Connect! On-Line*	info@online.com	(214) 396-0038
ConnectNet*	info@connect.net	(214) 490-7100
CyberRamp.net	admin@cyberramp.net	(214) 340-2020
Dallas Internet*	manager@dallas.net	(214) 881-9595

Table G–1: Regional and National Service Providers: U.S. and Canada (continued)

State/City/Provider	Email	Telephone
TEXAS (continued)		
Dallas/Fort Worth (continued)		
DFWNet*	info@dfw.net	(800) 2-DFW-NET
Fastlane Communications, Inc.*	info@fastlane.net	(817) 589-2400
Internet America	info@iadfw.net*	(214) 491-7134
National Knowledge Networks, Inc.*	info@nkn.net	(214) 880-0700
On-Ramp Technologies, Inc.*	info@onramp.net	(214) 746-4710
Plano Internet*	manager@plano.net	(214) 881-9595
Spindlemedia	info@spindle.net	(817) 332-5661
UniComp Technologies, Inc.	info@unicomp.net	(214) 663-3155
Houston/Galveston/Brazoria		
Access Communications*	info@accesscomm.net	(713) 896-6556
Black Box	info@blkbox.com	(713) 480-2684
Connections.Com, Inc.	info@concom.com	(713) 680-9333
Digital MainStream, Inc.*	schmidt@main.com	(713) 364-1819
GHG Corporation	info@ghgcorp.com	(713) 488-8806
InfoCom Networks	info@infocom.net	(713) 286-0399
Info-Highway International, Inc.*	info@infohwy.com	(713) 447-7025
Insync Internet Services*	jimg@insync.net	(713) 961-4242
NeoSoft, Inc.*	info@neosoft.com	(713) 968-5800
NetOne*	info@net1.net	(713) 688-9111
Phoenix DataNet*	helpdesk@mailserv.phoenix.net	(713) 486-8337
Sesquinet*	info@sesqui.net	(713) 527-6038
South Coast Computing Services, Inc.*	sales@sccsi.com	(713) 917-5000
Wantabe, Inc.	ggkelley@wantabe.com	(713) 493-0718
San Antonio		
South Texas Internet Connections	info@stic.net	(210) 828-4910
Texas Networking, Inc.	helpdesk@texas.net	(210) 272-8111
UTAH		
Salt Lake City/Ogden		
ArosNet*	info@aros.net	(801) 532-AROS
Internet Alliance*	adm@alinc.com	(801) 964-8490
KDC On-Line	support@kdcol.com	(801) 497-9931
ThoughtPort Authority of Salt Lake City*	info@thoughtport.com	(801) 596-2277
Utah Wired	pam@utw.com	(801) 532-1117
X-Mission*	support@xmission.com	(801) 539-0852

Table G–1: Regional and National Service Providers: U.S. and Canada (continued)

State/City/Provider	Email	Telephone
UTAH (continued)		
All other points		
AXXIS Internet Service*	webmaster@axxis.com	(801) 565-1443
CacheNET*	hal@cachenet.com	(801) 753-2199
DirecTell LC*	kathy@ditell.com	(801) 647-5838
Fibernet Corporation*	info@fiber.net	(801) 223-9939
InfoWest*	info@infowest.com	(801) 674-0165
VERMONT		
All points		
SoVerNet	info@sover.net	(802) 463-2111
TGF Technologies, Inc.	info@together.net	(802) 862-2030
VIRGINIA		
Norfolk/Virginia Beach/Newport News		
Exis Net, Inc.*	support@exis.net	(804) 552-1009
InfiNet*	sales@infi.net	(804) 622-4289
Richmond/Petersburg		
I 2020*	info@i2020.net	(804) 330-5555
Widomaker Communication Services	info@widomaker.com	(804) 253-7621
WASHINGTON		
Seattle/Tacoma		
Access One*	info@accessone.com	(206) 827-5344
Alternate Access, Inc.*	info@aa.net	(206) 728-9585
Blarg! Online Services*	info@blarg.com	(206) 784-9681
Compumedia, Inc.*	support@compumedia.com	(206) 623-8065
Cyberspace	info@cyberspace.com	(206) 505-5577
Eskimo North*	nanook@eskimo.com	(206) FOREVER
Interconnected Associates, Inc.*	info@ixa.com	(206) 622-7337
Northwest Link*	staff@nwlink.net	(206) 451-1151
Northwest Nexus, Inc.*	info@halcyon.com	(206) 455-3505
NWNet*	info@nwnet.net	(206) 562-3000
NWRAINET, Inc.*	info@nwrain.com	(206) 566-6800
Olympic Computing Solutions	ocs@oz.net	(206) 989-6698
Seanet*	seanet@seanet.com	(206) 343-7828
TCM Communications*	rgrothe@tcm.nbs.net	(206) 941-1474
WOLFE Internet Access, LLC*	info@wolfe.net	(206) 443-1397
Washington (east)		
AT-NET Connections, Inc.*	support@atnet.net	(509) 766-7253
Computech*	admin@iea.com	(509) 624-6798
EagleNet*	info@soar.com	(509) 466-3535
One World Telecommunications, Inc.*	info@oneworld.owt.com	(509) 735-0408
Televar Northwest*	info@televar.com	(509) 664-9004

Table G–1: Regional and National Service Providers: U.S. and Canada (continued)

State/City/Provider	Email	Telephone
WEST VIRGINIA		
All points		
CityNet Corporation*	info@citynet.net	(304) 342-5700
Intrepid Technologies, Inc.*	info@intrepid.net	(304) 876-1199
MountainNet, Inc.*	info@mountain.net	(304) 594-9075
WISCONSIN		
Kenosha		
see Chicago, ILLINOIS		
Milwaukee/Waukesha		
alpha.net*	info@alpha.net	(414) 274-7050
Internet Connect, Inc.*	info@inc.net	(414) 476-ICON
WYOMING		
All points		
NETConnect*	office@tcd.net	(307) 789-8001
Visionary Communications*	info@vcn.com	(307) 682-1884
wyoming.com LLC*	info@wyoming.com	(307) 332-3030
YUKON		
All points		
YKNet	yknet@yknet.yk.ca	(403) 668-8202
NATIONAL COVERAGE: U.S.		
Allied Access, Inc.*	sales@intrnet.net	(800) 463-8366
BBN Planet Corporation*	net-info@bbnplanet.com	(800) 472-4565
CERFnet*	infoserv@cerf.net	(800) 876-2373
CICNet*	info@cic.net	(800) 947-4754
Cogent Software, Inc.*	info@cogsoft.com	(818) 585-2788
CyberENET Network (KAPS, Inc.)*	access-sales@cyberenet.net	(609) 753-9840
Databank, Inc.*	info@databank.com	(913) 842-6699
The Destek Group, Inc.*	info@destek.net	(603) 635-3857
EMI Communications*	info@emi.com	(800) 456-2001
Global Enterprise Services, Inc.*	info@jvnc.net	(800) 358-4437 x7325
HoloNet*	info@holonet.net	(510) 704-0160
INS Info Services*	info@netins.net	(800) 546-6587
Institute for Global Communications	igc-info@igc.apc.org	(415) 442-0220
Interconnected Associates, Inc. (IXA)*	info@ixa.com	(800) IXA-8883
Internet America*	info@iadfw.net	(800) BE-A-GEEK
Internet Connect, Inc.*	info@inc.net	(414) 476-ICON
Internet Direct Communications*	sales@idir.net	(913) 842-1100
Internet Express*	service@usa.net	(800) 592-1240
Internet Online Services, Inc.*	info@ios.com	(201) 928-1000
INTERNEXT*	info@internext.com	(703) 502-1899

Table G–1: Regional and National Service Providers: U.S. and Canada (continued)

State/City/Provider	Email	Telephone
NATIONAL COVERAGE: U.S. (continued)		
Interpath*	info@interpath.net	(800) 849-6305
IONet	info@ionet.net	(405) 721-1580
Msen*	info@msen.com	(313) 998-4562
National Internet Source, Inc.*	info@nis.net	(201) 825-4600
New Mexico Technet, Inc.*	granoff@technet.nm.org	(505) 345-6555
Nothing But Net*	info@trey.com	(800) 951-7226
OARnet*	info@oar.net	(614) 728-8100
OnRamp, Ltd.*	info@theramp.net	(708) 222-6666
Opus One*	info@opus1.com	(520) 324-0494
Pacific Rim Network, Inc.*	info@pacificrim.net	(360) 650-0442
PSI (Performance Systems International)*	info@psi.com	(800) 82PSI82
The Point Internet Services, Inc.*	info@thepoint.net	(812) 246-7187
Protocol Communications, Inc.*	info@protocom.com	(612) 541-9900
Questar Microsystems, Inc.*	fbarrett@questar.com	(800) 925-2140
Random Access, Inc.*	marius@randomc.com	(800) 463-8366
Sacramento Network Access, Inc.*	ghall@sna.com	(916) 565-4500
ServiceTech, Inc.*	sales@servtech.com	(716) 263-3360
Synergy Communications*	sales@synergy.net	(402) 346-4638
Traders' Connection*	info@trader.com	(800) 753-4223
Turning Point Information Services, Inc.*	info@tpoint.net	(512) 499-8400
Viper Computer Systems, Inc.*	vipersys@viper.net	(800) VIPER-96
Voicenet*	info@voicenet.com	(800) 835-5710
The WELL	info@well.com	(415) 332-9200
WLN Internet Services*	info@wln.com	(800)-DIALWLN
Zocalo Engineering*	info@zocalo.net	(510) 540-8000
NATIONAL COVERAGE: CANADA		
Focus Technologies*	info@ftn.net	(800) FTN-INET
HoloNet	info@holonet.net	(510) 704-0160
HookUp Communications	info@hookup.net	(905) 847-8000
UUNET Canada*	info@uunet.ca	(800) 463-8123
see also NATIONAL COVERAGE: U.S.		

Table G–2. International Service Providers

Provider	E-mail	Telephone
UNITED KINGDOM		
AirTime Internet Resources Ltd UK	sales@airtime.co.uk	1254 676 921
Aladdin	info@aladdin.co.uk	1489 782 221
Atlas InterNet	info@atlas.co.uk	171 312 0400
Bournemouth Internet	sales@bournemouth-net.co.uk	1202 292 900
BTnet*	internet@bt.net	345 585 110
Celtic Internet Services Limited	enquiry@celtic.co.uk	1633 811 825
Demon Internet, Ltd.*	internet@demon.net	181 371 1234
Easynet	admin@easynet.co.uk	171 209 0990
EUnet GB Ltd	sales@Britain.EU.net	1227 266 466
Foobar Internet	sales@foobar.co.uk	116 233 0033
Frontier Internet Services	info@ftech.net	171 242 3383
NetKonect	info@netkonect.net	171 345 7777
Nildram On-Line	info@nildram.co.uk	01442 891 331
Onyx	onyx-support@octacon.co.uk	1642 210 087
Pinnacle Internet Services*	info@pncl.co.uk	1293 613 686
PIPEX (Public IP Exchange Limited)*	sales@pipex.com	500 646 566
Technocom	sales@technocom.co.uk	1753 673 200
Telecall	support@telecall.co.uk	117 941 4141
Total Connectivity Providers Ltd	sales@tcp.co.uk	1703 393 392
U-NET Limited*	hi@u-net.com	1925 633 144
Wintermute Ltd.	info@wintermute.co.uk	1224 622 477
AUSTRALIA		
Access One	info@aone.net.au	1 800 818 391
APANA	propaganda@apana.org.au	02 635 1751
AUSNet Services Pty Ltd	sales@world.net	02 241 5888
Australia On Line	sales@ozonline.com.au	1 800 621 258
connect.com.au pty ltd	connect@connect.com.au	03 528 2239
Fastlink Communications	sysop@cooee.com.au	43 696 224
Geko	info@geko.com.au	02 439 1999
iiNet Technologies Pty Ltd	iinet@iinet.net.au	09 307 1183
Kralizec Dialup Internet System	info@zeta.org.au	02 837 1397
Microplex Pty Ltd*	info@mpx.com.au	02 438 1234
Netro, Your Internet Connection	info@netro.com.au	02 876 8588
OzEmail	info@ozemail.aust.com	02 391 0480
Penrith NetCom	info@pnc.com.au	04 735 7000
Really Useful Communications Company	info@rucc.net.au.	03 9818 8711
World Reach Pty Ltd	info@wr.com.au	02 436 3588

Table G–2. International Service Providers (continued)

Provider	E-mail	Telephone
INTERNATIONAL/WORLDWIDE COVERAGE		
AGIS*	elan@net99.net	(301) 699-1840
	oliver@net99.net	
IBM Global Network*	globalnetwork@info.ibm.com	*United States:*
		(800) 933-3997
		Canada:
		(800) 463-8331
		United Kingdom:
		800 614 012
		Australia:
		1 800 811 094

Index

About the Author

Kevin Dowd lives in central Connecticut. He has a degree in Mathematics from the University of Connecticut, 1981. After graduation, Kevin worked for Combustion Engineering, developing accident monitoring systems, simulators, and miscellaneous analog and digital hardware.

In 1985, Kevin abandoned the sinking nuclear power business to join Multiflow Computer, and the then-burgeoning minisupercomputer market. Those interesting days of hard work, venture-funded hors d'oeuvres, and expensive beer lasted about four years until the money dried up. In 1990, Kevin abandoned the sinking minisupercomputer business, eventually taking a position with Computer Sciences Corporation (CSC), on-site at United Technologies Research Center. Kevin was part of the staff of the "Advanced Computing Technology Center" (ACTC), an experiment designed to facilitate advanced computing within United Technologies.

After the CSC contract ran out, Kevin and an associate formed the "Atlantic Computing Technology Corporation" (ACTC, again). Atlantic Computing provides Internet/IP firewalls, hardware, and consulting nationwide. Kevin is the company's president.

This is the second book Kevin has written for O'Reilly & Associates. His first book was *High Performance Computing*. In addition to burning the candle at both ends, Kevin enjoys playing music, practical jokes, experiments with actual physical things (electronics, chemistry), and running a company. He hopes one day to have a laboratory where he can spend the rest of his life inventing. You can reach Kevin at *dowd@atlantic.com*. If the matter is book-related, please use the address *book@atlantic.com*. You can also find Kevin and his company on the Web at *http://www.atlantic.com/*.

Colophon

Our look is the result of reader comments, our own experimentation, and distribution channels. Distinctive covers complement our distinctive approach to technical topics, breathing personality and life into potentially dry subjects. UNIX and its attendant programs can be unruly beasts. Nutshell Handbooks help you tame them.

Edie Freedman designed the cover of this book, using a 19th-century engraving from the Dover Pictorial Archive. The cover layout was produced with Quark XPress 3.3 using the ITC Garamond font.

The inside layout was designed by Edie Freedman, Jennifer Niederst, and Nancy Priest. Text was prepared by Erik Ray in SGML DocBook 2.4 DTD. The print version of this book was created by translating the SGML source into a set of gtroff macros using a filter developed at ORA by Norman Walsh. Steve Talbott designed and wrote the underlying macro set on the basis of the GNU troff -gs macros; Lenny Muellner adapted them to SGML and implemented the book design. The GNU groff text formatter version 1.09 was used to generate PostScript output. The text and heading fonts are ITC Garamond Light and Garamond Book. The illustrations that appear in the book were created in Macromedia Freehand 5.0 by Chris Reilley.

Web Server Administration

Apache: The Definitive Guide

By Ben Laurie & Peter Laurie
1st Edition Winter 1997
300 pages (est.), ISBN 1-56592-250-6

Despite all the hype about Netscape, Apache is far and away the most widely used Web server platform in the world. It runs on about half the world's existing Web sites and is rapidly increasing market share. *Apache: The Definitive Guide* is the only complete guide on the market today describing how to obtain, set up, and secure the Apache software. Officially authorized by the Apache Group, this book is the definitive documentation for the world's most popular Web server.

Contents include:

* The history of the Apache Group
* Obtaining and compiling the server
* Configuring and running Apache, including such topics as directory structures, virtual hosts, and CGI programming
* The Apache Module API
* Apache security
* The Apache manuals
* A complete list of configuration directives
* A complete demo of a sample Web site

UNIX Web Server Administration

By John Leavitt
1st Edition Winter 1997
325 pages (est.), ISBN 1-56592-217-4

With our increasing dependence on Web sites for our daily work, the Web server has emerged as one of the most crucial services a company can offer. When the server is slow, customers are frustrated. When the server or network is down, customers are turned away.

UNIX Web Server Administration tells Web administrators how to keep a server running smoothly. This book not only covers Apache, the most popular server on the Internet, but also the NCSA, CERN, and Netscape servers.

Managing Internet Information Services

By Cricket Liu, Jerry Peek, Russ Jones, Bryan Buus & Adrian Nye
1st Edition December 1994
668 pages, ISBN 1-56592-062-7

Managing Internet Information Services describes how to create services for the millions of Internet users. By setting up Internet servers for World Wide Web, Gopher, FTP, Finger, Telnet, WAIS (Wide Area Information Services), or email services, anyone with a suitable computer and Internet connection can become an "Internet Publisher."

Services on the Internet allow almost instant distribution and frequent updates of any kind of information. You can provide services to employees of your own company (solving the information distribution problems of spread-out companies), or you can serve the world. Perhaps you'd like to create an Internet service equivalent to the telephone company's directory assistance. Or maybe you're the Species Survival Commission, and you'd like your plans online; this book describes a prototype service the authors created to make SSC's endangered species Action Plans viewable worldwide. Whatever you have in mind can be done. This book tells you how.

Creating a service can be a big job, involving more than one person. This book separates the setup and maintenance of server software from data management, so that a team can divide responsibilities. Sections and chapters on data management, a role we call the Data Librarian, are marked with a special icon.

"Excellent book . . . carefully written, informative and readable . . . [well] organized. . . . I'm enjoying it considerably. I picked it up to flip through—I'm a writer of Internet books myself, and I do a lot of 'been there, done that' when I approach an Internet book—and after an hour or so, I discovered I was actually reading the book. I have even taken the step of . . . using my post-it-notes tabs to mark the good stuff."
—Jill Ellsworth, Ph.D., Author of *The Internet Business Book*, *Education on the Internet, and Marketing on the Internet*

For information: **800-998-9938**, 707-829-0515; **info@ora.com; http://www.ora.com/**
To order: **800-889-8969** (credit card orders only); **order@ora.com**

Developing Web Content

Building Your Own WebSite

By Susan B. Peck & Stephen Arrants
1st Edition July 1996
514 pages, ISBN 1-56592-232-8

This is a hands-on reference for Windows® 95 and Windows NT™ desktop users who want to host their own site on the Web or on a corporate intranet. This step-by-step guide will have you creating live Web pages in minutes. You'll also learn how to connect your web to information in other Windows applications, such as word processing documents and databases. Packed with examples and tutorials on every aspect of Web management. Includes highly acclaimed WebSite™ 1.1—all the software you need for Web publishing.

Web Client Programming with Perl

By Clinton Wong
1st Edition Fall 1996
250 pages (est.), ISBN 1-56592-214-X

Web Client Programming with Perl teaches you how to extend scripting skills to the Web. This book teaches you the basics of how browsers communicate with servers and how to write your own customized Web clients to automate common tasks. It is intended for those who are motivated to develop software that offers a more flexible and dynamic response than a standard Web browser.

JavaScript: The Definitive Guide

By David Flanagan
1st Edition Winter 1997
700 pages (est.), ISBN 1-56592-234-4

This definitive reference guide to JavaScript, the HTML extension that gives Web pages programming language capabilities, covers JavaScript as it is used in Netscape 3.0 and 2.0 and in Microsoft Internet Explorer 2.0. Learn how JavaScript really works (and when it doesn't). Use JavaScript to control Web browser behavior, add dynamically created text to Web pages, interact with users through HTML forms, and even control and interact with Java applets and Navigator plug-ins.

HTML: The Definitive Guide

By Chuck Musciano & Bill Kennedy
1st Edition April 1996
410 pages, ISBN 1-56592-175-5

A complete guide to creating documents on the World Wide Web. This book describes basic syntax and semantics and goes on to show you how to create beautiful, informative Web documents you'll be proud to display. The HTML 2.0 standard and Netscape extensions are fully explained.

Designing for the Web: Getting Started in a New Medium

By Jennifer Niederst with Edie Freedman
1st Edition April 1996
180 pages, ISBN 1-56592-165-8

Designing for the Web gives you the basics you need to hit the ground running. Although geared toward designers, it covers information and techniques useful to anyone who wants to put graphics online. It explains how to work with HTML documents from a designer's point of view, outlines special problems with presenting information online, and walks through incorporating images into Web pages, with emphasis on resolution and improving efficiency.

WebMaster in a Nutshell

By Stephen Spainhour & Valerie Quercia
1st Edition October 1996
378 pages, ISBN 1-56592-229-8

Web content providers and administrators have many sources of information, both in print and online. *WebMaster in a Nutshell* pulls it all together into one slim volume—for easy desktop access. This quick-reference covers HTML, CGI, Perl, HTTP, server configuration, and tools for Web administration.

For information: **800-998-9938**, 707-829-0515; **info@ora.com; http://www.ora.com/**

To order: **800-889-8969** *(credit card orders only);* **order@ora.com**

Business, Career, & Health

Electronic Publishing on CD-ROM

By Steve Cunningham & Judson Rosebush
1st Edition August 1996
412 pages, ISBN 1-56592-209-3

Publishers are no longer limited to paper and ink. Electronic publications can now incorporate text, images, sound, video, and interactive games and simulations. And publishing has become a more democratic activity—with the explosive growth of both the Internet and CD-ROM technology, more and more people are publishing their own titles.

This book looks at the many kinds of electronic publications being produced today. Although it focuses on CD-ROM, the discussion is also relevant to publishing on the World Wide Web. *Electronic Publishing on CD-ROM* describes examples and alternatives for the design, authoring, manufacturing, marketing, and distribution of CD-ROMs. It covers electronic document authoring systems (e.g., Adobe's Acrobat, Macromedia's Director, Apple's HyperTalk, and more). It discusses traditional and emerging document standards and formats (e.g., SGML, HTML, and Java), as well as physical disc standards (e.g., ISO 9660, HFS). It also provides detailed information on the costs of CD-ROM publishing projects—staff, manufacturing, and phases of development. In addition, it includes an extensive list of resources and a helpful glossary and bibliography, along with a CD-ROM full of information resources and software.

Building a Successful Software Business

By Dave Radin
1st Edition April 1994
394 pages, ISBN 1-56592-064-3

This handbook is for the new software entrepreneur and the old hand alike. If you're thinking of starting a company around a program you've written—and there's no better time than the present—this book will guide you toward success. If you're an old hand in the software industry, it will help you sharpen your skills or will provide a refresher course. It covers the basics of product planning, marketing, customer support, finance, and operations.

Love Your Job!

By Dr. Paul Powers & Deborah Russell
1st Edition August 1993
210 pages, ISBN 1-56592-036-8

Love Your Job! is an inspirational guide to loving your work. In addition to providing solid practical advice to anyone who is dissatisfied with work and wants to get more out of it, this book challenges readers to look inside themselves—at what really motivates them at work and at what kinds of lives they want to lead. *Love Your Job!* consists of a series of one-page reflections, anecdotes, and exercises aimed at helping readers think more deeply about what they want out of their jobs. Each can be read individually (anyplace, anytime, whenever you need to lift your spirits), or the book can be read from start to finish.

The Future Does Not Compute

By Stephen L. Talbott
1st Edition May 1995
502 pages, ISBN 1-56592-085-6

This book explores the networked computer as an expression of the darker, dimly conscious side of the human being. What we have been imparting to the Net—or what the Net has been eliciting from us—is a half-submerged, barely intended logic, contaminated by wishes and tendencies we prefer not to acknowledge. The urgent necessity is for us to wake up to what is most fully human and unmachinelike in ourselves, rather than yield to an ever more strangling embrace with our machines. The author's thesis is sure to raise a controversy among the millions of users now adapting themselves to the Net.

The Computer User's Survival Guide

By Joan Stigliani
1st Edition October 1995
296 pages, ISBN 1-56592-030-9

The bad news: You *can* be hurt by working at a computer. The good news: Many of the factors that pose a risk are within your control. This book looks squarely at all the factors that affect your health on the job, including positioning, equipment, work habits, lighting, stress, radiation, and general health.

For information: **800-998-9938**, 707-829-0515; **info@ora.com; http://www.ora.com/**
To order: **800-889-8969** (credit card orders only); **order@ora.com**

Security

Practical UNIX & Internet Security, 2nd Edition

By Simson Garfinkel & Gene Spafford
2nd Edition April 1996
1004 pages, ISBN 1-56592-148-8

This second edition of the classic *Practical UNIX Security* is a complete rewrite of the original book. It's packed with twice the pages and offers even more practical information for UNIX users and administrators. In it you'll find coverage of features of many types of UNIX systems, including SunOS, Solaris, BSDI, AIX, HP-UX, Digital UNIX, Linux, and others. Contents include UNIX and security basics, system administrator tasks, network security, and appendixes containing checklists and helpful summaries.

Building Internet Firewalls

By D. Brent Chapman & Elizabeth D. Zwicky
1st Edition September 1995
546 pages, ISBN 1-56592-124-0

More than a million systems are now connected to the Internet, and something like 15 million people in 100 countries on all seven continents use Internet services. More than 100 million email messages are exchanged each day, along with countless files, documents, and audio and video images. Although businesses are rushing headlong to get connected to the Internet, the security risks have never been greater.

Some of these risks have been around since the early days of networking—password attacks (guessing them or cracking them via password dictionaries and cracking programs), denial of service, and exploiting known security holes. Some risks are newer and even more dangerous—packet sniffers, IP (Internet Protocol) forgery, and various types of hijacking. Firewalls are a very effective way to protect your system from these Internet security threats.

Building Internet Firewalls is a practical guide to building firewalls on the Internet. If your site is connected to the Internet, or if you're considering getting connected, you need this book. It describes a variety of firewall approaches and architectures and discusses how you can build packet filtering and proxying solutions at your site. It also contains a full discussion of how to configure Internet services (e.g., FTP, SMTP, Telnet) to work with a firewall, as well as a complete list of resources, including the location of many publicly available firewall construction tools.

PGP: Pretty Good Privacy

By Simson Garfinkel
1st Edition January 1995
430 pages, ISBN 1-56592-098-8

PGP is a freely available encryption program that protects the privacy of files and electronic mail. It uses powerful public key cryptography and works on virtually every platform. This book is both a readable technical user's guide and a fascinating behind-the-scenes look at cryptography and privacy. It describes how to use PGP and provides background on cryptography, *PGP's* history, battles over public key cryptography patents and U.S. government export restrictions, and public debates about privacy and free speech.

Computer Crime

By David Icove, Karl Seger & William VonStorch (Consulting Editor Eugene H. Spafford)
1st Edition August 1995
462 pages, ISBN 1-56592-086-4

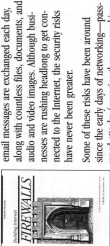

This book is for anyone who needs to know what today's computer crimes look like, how to prevent them, and how to detect, investigate, and prosecute them if they do occur. It contains basic computer security information as well as guidelines for investigators, law enforcement, and system administrators. It includes computer-related statutes and laws, a resource summary, detailed papers on computer crime, and a sample search warrant.

Computer Security Basics

By Deborah Russell & G.T. Gangemi, Sr.
1st Edition July 1991
464 pages, ISBN 0-937175-71-4

Computer Security Basics provides a broad introduction to the many areas of computer security and a detailed description of current security standards. This handbook uses simple terms to describe complicated concepts like trusted systems, encryption, and mandatory access control, and it contains a thorough, readable introduction to the "Orange Book."

For information: **800-998-9938**, 707-829-0515; **info@ora.com; http://www.ora.com/**
To order: **800-889-8969** *(credit card orders only):* **order@ora.com**

Stay in touch with O'REILLY™

Visit Our Award-Winning World Wide Web Site

http://www.ora.com/

VOTED

"Top 100 Sites on the Web" —*PC Magazine*
"Top 5% Websites" —*Point Communications*
"3-Star site" —*The McKinley Group*

Our Web site contains a library of comprehensive product information (including book excerpts and tables of contents), downloadable software, background articles, interviews with technology leaders, links to relevant sites, book cover art, and more. File us in your Bookmarks or Hotlist!

Join Our Two Email Mailing Lists

List #1 NEW PRODUCT RELEASES: To receive automatic email with brief descriptions of all new O'Reilly products as they are released, send email to: listproc@online.ora.com and put the following information in the first line of your message (NOT in the Subject: field, which is ignored): **subscribe ora-news "Your Name" of "Your Organization"** (for example: **subscribe ora-news Kris Webber of Fine Enterprises**)

List #2 O'REILLY EVENTS: If you'd also like us to send information about trade show events, special promotions, and other O'Reilly events, send email to: listproc@online.ora.com and put the following information in the first line of your message (NOT in the Subject: field, which is ignored): **subscribe ora-events "Your Name" of "Your Organization"**

Visit Our Gopher Site

- Connect your Gopher to gopher.ora.com, or
- Point your Web browser to gopher://gopher.ora.com/, or
- telnet to gopher.ora.com (login: gopher)

Get Example Files from Our Books Via FTP

There are two ways to access an archive of example files from our books:

REGULAR FTP — ftp to: ftp.ora.com (login: anonymous—use your email address as the password) or point your Web browser to: ftp://ftp.ora.com/

FTPMAIL — Send an email message to: ftpmail@online.ora.com (write "help" in the message body)

Contact Us Via Email

order@ora.com — To place a book or software order online. Good for North American and international customers.

subscriptions@ora.com — To place an order for any of our newsletters or periodicals.

software@ora.com — For general questions and product information about our software.

- Check out O'Reilly Software Online at http://software.ora.com/ for software and technical support information.
- Registered O'Reilly software users send your questions to website-support@ora.com

books@ora.com — General questions about any of our books.

cs@ora.com — For answers to problems regarding your order or our products.

booktech@ora.com — For book content technical questions or corrections.

proposals@ora.com — To submit new book or software proposals to our editors and product managers.

international@ora.com — For information about our international distributors or translation queries.

- For a list of our distributors outside of North America check out: http://www.ora.com/www/order/country.html

O'REILLY™

101 Morris Street, Sebastopol, CA 95472 USA
TEL 707-829-0515 or 800-998-9938 (6 A.M. to 5 P.M. PST)
FAX 707-829-0104

Titles from O'REILLY™

INTERNET PROGRAMMING

CGI Programming on the World Wide Web
Designing for the Web
Exploring Java
HTML: The Definitive Guide
Web Client Programming with Perl
Learning Perl
Programming Perl, 2nd. Edition (Fall '96)
JavaScript: The Definitive Guide, Beta Edition
WebMaster in a Nutshell
The World Wide Web Journal

USING THE INTERNET

Smileys
The Whole Internet User's Guide and Catalog
The Whole Internet for Windows 95
What You Need to Know:
    Using Email Effectively
Marketing on the Internet (Fall '96)
What You Need to Know: Bandits on the Information Superhighway

JAVA SERIES

Exploring Java
Java in a Nutshell
Java Language Reference (Fall '96 est.)
Java Virtual Machine

WINDOWS

Inside the Windows 95 Registry

SOFTWARE

WebSite™ 1.1
WebSite Professional™
WebBoard™
PolyForm™
Statisphere™

SONGLINE GUIDES

NetLearning
NetSuccess for Realtors
NetActivism
Gif Animation (Fall '96)
Shockwave Studio (Winter '97 est.)

SYSTEM ADMINISTRATION

Building Internet Firewalls
Computer Crime:
    A Crimefighter's Handbook
Computer Security Basics
DNS and BIND
Essential System Administration, 2nd Edition
Getting Connected:
    The Internet at 56K and Up
Linux Network Administrator's Guide
Managing Internet Information Services
Managing Usenet (Fall '96)
Managing NFS and NIS
Networking Personal Computers with TCP/IP
Practical UNIX & Internet Security
PGP: Pretty Good Privacy
sendmail
System Performance Tuning
TCP/IP Network Administration
termcap & terminfo
Using & Managing UUCP
Volume 8: X Window System Administrator's Guide

UNIX

Exploring Expect
Learning GNU Emacs, 2nd Edition (Fall '96)
Learning the bash Shell
Learning the Korn Shell
Learning the UNIX Operating System
Learning the vi Editor
Linux in a Nutshell (Fall '96 est.)
Making TeX Work
Linux Multimedia Guide (Fall '96)
Running Linux, 2nd Edition
Running Linux Companion CD-ROM, 2nd Edition
SCO UNIX in a Nutshell
sed & awk
UNIX in a Nutshell: System V Edition
UNIX Power Tools
UNIX Systems Programming
Using csh and tsch
What You Need to Know:
    When You Can't Find Your UNIX System Administrator

PROGRAMMING

Applying RCS and SCCS
C++: The Core Language
Checking C Programs with lint
DCE Security Programming
Distributing Applications Across DCE and Windows NT
Encyclopedia of Graphics File Formats, 2nd Edition
Guide to Writing DCE Applications
lex & yacc
Managing Projects with make
ORACLE Performance Tuning
ORACLE PL/SQL Programming
Porting UNIX Software
POSIX Programmer's Guide
POSIX.4: Programming for the Real World
Power Programming with RPC
Practical C Programming
Practical C++ Programming
Programming Python (Fall '96)
Programming with curses
Programming with GNU Software (Fall '96 est.)
Pthreads Programming
Software Portability with imake
Understanding DCE
Understanding Japanese Information Processing
UNIX Systems Programming for SVR4

BERKELEY 4.4 SOFTWARE DISTRIBUTION

4.4BSD System Manager's Manual
4.4BSD User's Reference Manual
4.4BSD User's Supplementary Documents
4.4BSD Programmer's Reference Manual
4.4BSD Programmer's Supplementary Documents

X PROGRAMMING

THE X WINDOW SYSTEM

Volume 0: X Protocol Reference Manual
Volume 1: Xlib Programming Manual
Volume 2: Xlib Reference Manual
Volume. 3M: X Window System User's Guide, Motif Edition
Volume 4: X Toolkit Intrinsics Programming Manual
Volume 4M: X Toolkit Intrinsics Programming Manual, Motif Edition
Volume 5: X Toolkit Intrinsics Reference Manual
Volume 6A: Motif Programming Manual
Volume 6B: Motif Reference Manual
Volume 6C: Motif Tools
Volume 8: X Window System Administrator's Guide
Programmer's Supplement for Release 6
X User Tools (with CD-ROM)
The X Window System in a Nutshell

HEALTH, CAREER, & BUSINESS

Building a Successful Software Business
The Computer User's Survival Guide
Dictionary of Computer Terms
The Future Does Not Compute
Love Your Job!
Publishing with CD-ROM

TRAVEL

Travelers' Tales: Brazil (Fall '96)
Travelers' Tales: Food (Fall '96)
Travelers' Tales: France
Travelers' Tales: Hong Kong
Travelers' Tales: India
Travelers' Tales: Mexico
Travelers' Tales: San Francisco
Travelers' Tales: Spain
Travelers' Tales: Thailand
Travelers' Tales: A Woman's World

TO ORDER: **800-889-8969** (CREDIT CARD ORDERS ONLY); **order@ora.com; http://www.ora.com/**
OUR PRODUCTS ARE AVAILABLE AT A BOOKSTORE OR SOFTWARE STORE NEAR YOU.

International Distributors

Customers outside North America can now order O'Reilly & Associates books through the following distributors. They offer our international customers faster order processing, more bookstores, increased representation at tradeshows worldwide, and the high-quality, responsive service our customers have come to expect.

EUROPE, MIDDLE EAST AND NORTHERN AFRICA (except Germany, Switzerland, and Austria)

INQUIRIES

International Thomson Publishing Europe
Berkshire House
168-173 High Holborn
London WC1V 7AA, United Kingdom
Telephone: 44-171-497-1422
Fax: 44-171-497-1426
Email: **itpint@itps.co.uk**

ORDERS

International Thomson Publishing Services, Ltd.
Cheriton House, North Way
Andover, Hampshire SP10 5BE,
United Kingdom
Telephone: 44-264-342-832 (UK orders)
Telephone: 44-264-342-806 (outside UK)
Fax: 44-264-364418 (UK orders)
Fax: 44-264-342761 (outside UK)
UK & Eire orders: **itpuk@itps.co.uk**
International orders: **itpint@itps.co.uk**

GERMANY, SWITZERLAND, AND AUSTRIA

International Thomson Publishing GmbH
O'Reilly International Thomson Verlag
Königswinterer Straße 418
53227 Bonn, Germany
Telephone: 49-228-97024 0
Fax: 49-228-441342
Email: **anfragen@oreilly.de**

AUSTRALIA

WoodsLane Pty. Ltd.
7/5 Vuko Place, Warriewood NSW 2102
P.O. Box 935, Mona Vale NSW 2103
Australia
Telephone: 61-2-9970-5111
Fax: 61-2-9970-5002
Email: **info@woodslane.com.au**

NEW ZEALAND

WoodsLane New Zealand Ltd.
21 Cooks Street (P.O. Box 575)
Wanganui, New Zealand
Telephone: 64-6-347-6543
Fax: 64-6-345-4840
Email: **info@woodslane.com.au**

ASIA (except Japan & India)

INQUIRIES

International Thomson Publishing Asia
60 Albert Street #15-01
Albert Complex
Singapore 189969
Telephone: 65-336-6411
Fax: 65-336-7411

ORDERS

Telephone: 65-336-6411
Fax: 65-334-1617

JAPAN

O'Reilly Japan, Inc.
Kiyoshige Building 2F
12-Banchi, Sanei-cho
Shinjuku-ku
Tokyo 160 Japan
Telephone: 81-3-3356-5227
Fax: 81-3-3356-5261
Email: **kenji@ora.com**

INDIA

Computer Bookshop (India) PVT. LTD.
190 Dr. D.N. Road, Fort
Bombay 400 001
India
Telephone: 91-22-207-0989
Fax: 91-22-262-3551
Email: **cbsbom@giasbm01.vsnl.net.in**

THE AMERICAS

O'Reilly & Associates, Inc.
101 Morris Street
Sebastopol, CA 95472 U.S.A.
Telephone: 707-829-0515
Telephone: 800-998-9938 (U.S. & Canada)
Fax: 707-829-0104
Email: **order@ora.com**

SOUTHERN AFRICA

International Thomson Publishing Southern Africa
Building 18, Constantia Park
240 Old Pretoria Road
P.O. Box 2459
Halfway House, 1685 South Africa
Telephone: 27-11-805-4819
Fax: 27-11-805-3648

O'REILLY™

O'REILLY™

O'Reilly & Associates, Inc.
101 Morris Street
Sebastopol, CA 95472-9902
1-800-998-9938

Visit us online at:
http://www.ora.com/
orders@ora.com

O'REILLY WOULD LIKE TO HEAR FROM YOU

Which book did this card come from?

Where did you buy this book?
- ☐ Bookstore
- ☐ Direct from O'Reilly
- ☐ Bundled with hardware/software
- ☐ Other
- ☐ Computer Store
- ☐ Class/seminar

What operating system do you use?
- ☐ UNIX
- ☐ Windows NT
- ☐ Other
- ☐ Macintosh
- ☐ PC(Windows/DOS)

What is your job description?
- ☐ System Administrator
- ☐ Network Administrator
- ☐ Web Developer
- ☐ Other
- ☐ Programmer
- ☐ Educator/Teacher

☐ Please send me O'Reilly's catalog, containing a complete listing of O'Reilly books and software.

Name _____ Company/Organization _____

Address _____

City _____ State _____ Zip/Postal Code _____ Country _____

Telephone _____ Internet or other email address (specify network) _____

POST CARD

PLACE
STAMP
HERE

BUSINESS REPLY MAIL

FIRST CLASS MAIL   PERMIT NO. 80   SEBASTOPOL, CA

Postage will be paid by addressee

O'Reilly & Associates, Inc.
101 Morris Street
Sebastopol, CA 95472-9902